Contributions to Political Science

More information about this series at http://www.springer.com/series/11829

Birgit Bujard

The British Prime Minister in the Core Executive

Political Leadership in British European Policy

Springer

Birgit Bujard
Cologne, Germany

The present work is the author's Ph.D. thesis (Dissertation). It was accepted in 2017 at the Universität der Bundeswehr München (Neubiberg, Germany) under the title "The British prime minister in the core executive. An analysis of prime ministerial political leadership in British European policy from James Callaghan to Tony Blair using the example of European monetary policy".

ISSN 2198-7289 ISSN 2198-7297 (electronic)
Contributions to Political Science
ISBN 978-3-030-07903-1 ISBN 978-3-319-89953-4 (eBook)
https://doi.org/10.1007/978-3-319-89953-4

Softcover re-print of the Hardcover 1st edition 2019

Printed on acid-free paper

This Springer imprint is published by the registered company Springer International Publishing AG part of Springer Nature.
The registered company address is: Gewerbestrasse 11, 6330 Cham, Switzerland

Preface

This book is based on my doctoral thesis, which I submitted in November 2016 at the Universität der Bundeswehr München (University of the Federal Armed Forces Munich) and defended in July 2017.

My academic interest in British politics began about 20 years ago with several seminars on Tony Blair's New Labour government which then had just come into office in the United Kingdom.

What particularly interested (and still interests) me was the United Kingdom's relationship with the European Union as well as the country's view of the European integration process. Britain's long-standing scepticism about the European project and its reluctance to fully engage with its European partners in the EEC and EU have always puzzled me. Therefore, the attempt to understand this approach to European integration better as well as the role of the prime minister in it has led me to select this topic for my doctoral dissertation.

What I hope this book shows is that the roots for the British public's vote in 2016 to leave the European Union lie not merely in the (European) policies of various UK governments as well as the political discourse in Britain of the past few years but run deeper than that. To understand the outcome of the 2016 referendum, a look further back in the UK's history of European integration has to be taken as well, which the study at hand does. Moreover, this book illustrates that a prime minister's political leadership in this policy field is more constrained than public, media and academic debate sometimes suggests.

Cologne, Germany
March 2018

Birgit Bujard

Preface

Acknowledgements

In researching this subject and completing my doctoral dissertation I owe a considerable debt of gratitude to a number of people and organisations.

First and foremost, I would like to thank my doctoral supervisor Prof. Dr. Ursula Münch for her intellectual input, guidance as well as encouragement and patience throughout the research and writing process. I am very grateful for her kind and valuable advice and for the time she took to discuss my research project over the years. I am, moreover, thankful to Prof. Dr. Carlo Masala for having been the second supervisor as well as for his initial suggestion to write my doctoral thesis at the Universität der Bundeswehr and for encouraging me to return to university to pursue my doctoral degree.

I would also like to thank my interview partners Sir Brian Bender, Sir Michael Butler (†), Lord Bernard Donoughue, Lord David Hannay, Lord John Kerr, Lord Tom McNally, Lord Roger Liddle, Sir Stephen Wall, Sir Nigel Wicks and Lord David Williamson (†) for taking time to speak to me and for sharing their perspectives on British European policy and the UK prime minister's political leadership.

Furthermore, I am indebted to the help I received from my fellow PhD students at the Universität der Bundeswehr, who provided valuable comments and feedback on my research during our meetings in Neubiberg and Tutzing. In particular I would like to thank Nora Sánchez Gassen for her support throughout the years, for her hugely helpful feedback on so many issues covered in this study and for spending many hours discussing them with me.

Moreover, I am thankful to Nigel Bennett and Tina Kastenbein for their comments on the English language in the various drafts of my dissertation.

For the permission to reproduce copyright material, I am grateful to Cambridge University Press (R. Putnam: Diplomacy and domestic politics: The logic of two-level games, *International Organization*), John Wiley & Sons (J. B. Christoph: The effects of Britons in Brussels: The European Community and the culture of Whitehall, *Governance*; P. Dunleavy & R. A. W. Rhodes: Core executive studies in Britain, *Public Administration*; S. James: Taming the 'awkward state'? The changing face of European policy-making under Blair, *Public Administration*; C. Seymour-

Ure: *Prime ministers and the media: Issues of power and control*; M. J. Smith: The core executive and the resignation of Mrs Thatcher, *Public Administration*, M. J. Smith: Reconceptualizing the British state: Theoretical and empirical challenges to central government, *Public Administration*), Pan Macmillan (J. Bruce-Gardyne, *Ministers and mandarins: Inside the Whitehall village*; P. Stephens, *Politics and the pound: The Tories, the economy and Europe;* H. Young: *This blessed plot: Britain and Europe from Churchill to Blair*), The Financial Times, Oxford University Press (S. Bulmer & C. Lequesne (Eds.): *The member states of the European Union*; M. Bennister: Blair and Howard: Predominant prime ministers compared, *Parliamentary Affairs*; S. George: *An awkward partner: Britain in the European Community*; S. Wall: *A stranger in Europe: Britain and the EU from Thatcher to Blair*), SAGE Publishing (R. Heffernan: Prime ministerial predominance? Core executive politics in the UK, *British Journal of Politics and International Relations*; R. Heffernan: Exploring (and explaining) the British prime minister, *British Journal of Politics and International Relations*); St. John's College, Cambridge (P. Cradock: *In pursuit of British interests: Reflections on foreign policy under Margaret Thatcher and John Major*) and Taylor & Francis (T. Bale & K. Sanders: 'Playing by the book': Success and failure in John Major's approach to prime ministerial media management, *Contemporary British History*; P. Daniels: From hostility to 'constructive engagement': the Europeanisation of the Labour Party, *West European Politics*; E. Dell & Lord Hunt of Tanworth: The failings of cabinet government in mid to late 1970s, *Contemporary British History*; B. Donoughue: The prime minister's day, *Contemporary British History*; B. Jones, D. Kavanagh, M. Moran & P. Norton (Eds.): *Politics UK*; D. Shell & R. Hodder-Williams (Eds.): *Churchill to Major: The British prime ministership since 1945*).

I would like to thank HarperCollins Publishers for the permission to reproduce copyright material from the following books:

Kavanagh, D. & Seldon, A., *The Powers behind the Prime Minister, The Hidden Influence of Number Ten*, 2000, 2nd edition, London: HarperCollins. Reprinted by permission of HarperCollins Publishers Ltd © Dennis Kavanagh & Anthony Seldon 2000

Major, J., *The Autobiography*, 2nd edition, 2000, London: HarperCollins. Reprinted by permission of HarperCollins Publishers Ltd © John Major 1999, 2000

Mandelson, P., *The Third Man, Life at the Heart of New Labour*, 2010, London: Harper Press. Reprinted by permission of HarperCollins Publishers Ltd © Peter Mandelson 2010

Thatcher, M., *The Downing Street Years*, 2011, London: Harper Press. Reprinted by permission of HarperCollins Publishers Ltd © Margaret Thatcher 1993

To Palgrave Macmillan I am grateful for the permission to reproduce copyright material from these publications:

Elgie, R., *Political Leadership in Liberal Democracies*, 1995, Basingstoke/London: Macmillan Press, reproduced with permission of Palgrave Macmillan.

Smith, M. J., *The Core Executive in Britain*, 1999, Basingstoke/London: Macmillan Press, reproduced with permission of Palgrave Macmillan.

The quotations from the House of Commons Debates, the UK Parliament Website and the House of Commons Library used in this book contain Parliamentary information licensed under the Open Parliament Licence v3.0 (http://www.parliament.uk/site-information/copyright-parliament/open-parliament-licence/).

The quotations from The National Archives used in this book contain public sector information licensed under the Open Government Licence v3.0 (http://www.nationalarchives.gov.uk/doc/open-government-licence/version/3/).

Last but not least, I would like to thank my parents, family and Tobias Grimm as well as my friends for their support and their patience when having to listen to my lectures on UK European policy and the political leadership of the British prime minister.

Contents

List of Abbreviations

BDOHP	British Diplomatic Oral History Project
BSE	Bovine Spongiform Encephalopathy (mad cow disease)
COES	Cabinet Office European Secretariat
COREPER	Committee of Permanent Representatives
CPRS	Central Policy Review Staff
DOP	Cabinet Committee on Defence and Overseas Policy
DSC	Departmental Select Committee
DTI	Department of Trade and Industry
EC	European Community/ies
ECU	European Currency Unit
EDM	Early Day Motion
(E)DOP	Cabinet Sub-Committee on European Affairs
EEC	European Economic Community
EM	Explanatory Memorandum
EMS	European Monetary System
EMU	Economic and Monetary Union
EP	Cabinet Committee on European Policy
EQ(O)	European Questions (Official Committee)
ERM	Exchange Rate Mechanism
ESC	European Scrutiny Committee
EU	European Union
EUS	Cabinet Committee on European Strategy
FCO	Foreign and Commonwealth Office
FT	Financial Times
IGC	Intergovernmental Conference
JMC[E]	Joint Ministerial Committee (Europe)
MP	Member of Parliament
NATO	North Atlantic Treaty Organization
NEC	National Executive Committee
OMD	Open Method of Coordination
PCP	Parliamentary Conservative Party

PLP	Parliamentary Labour Party
PM	Prime Minister
PMB	Private Members' Bill
PMO	Prime Minister's Office
PMQ	Prime Minister's Question Time
PPS	Parliamentary Private Secretary
SDP	Social Democratic Party
SEA	Single European Act
TEU	Treaty on European Union
TUC	Trades Union Congress
UK	United Kingdom
UKIP	United Kingdom Independence Party
UKREP	United Kingdom Permanent Representation to the EC/EU
USA	United States of America

List of Figures

List of Tables

Chapter 1
Prime Ministerial Political Leadership and British European Policy: An Introduction

1.1 The British Prime Minister and European Policy

The role of the prime minister in British politics has for long been a much debated issue in political science (e.g. Crossmann 1963; Shell and Hodder-Williams 1995; Hennessy 2001; Blick and Jones 2010). Assessments of the premierships of Margaret Thatcher and Tony Blair, who have been considered to exhibit a dominant leadership style (e.g. Seldon 2008; Young 1989), corresponded with research in the past years which has argued that contemporary politics in liberal democracies has become increasingly personalised and that heads of government today have more power resources and autonomy than their predecessors, which gives them a larger capacity to act (e.g. Foley 1993, 2000; Mughan 2000; Poguntke and Webb 2005; Peters et al. 2000: 7). But have a premier's options to shape his government's policies actually increased and made his leadership in the core executive more dominant? What about prime ministers such as James Callaghan or John Major, who have rather been seen as exercising a form of collective leadership? To make a contribution to this debate the study at hand analyses the political leadership of the UK prime minister (PM) in European policy. The PM appears to be well placed to exert dominant political leadership in this subject area. Compared to other heads of government such as the German chancellor, for example, he has to deal with fewer constraints when trying to influence the government's decision-making process in general. This is, for instance, the case if one considers single party governments[1] in contrast to coalition governments or a centralised state instead of a federal one.[2] Moreover, national leaders have a special role to play in the European context as they

[1]Despite a Conservative-Liberal Democrat coalition from 2010 to 2015, the British first-past-the-post-electoral system has since 1945 tended to facilitate single party governments.

[2]Particularly under the Blair government there were changes in this respect as it furthered a process of devolution giving more political autonomy to the regions Northern Ireland, Scotland and Wales. But the British political system remains less federally structured than, for instance, the German one.

B. Bujard, *The British Prime Minister in the Core Executive*, Contributions to Political Science, https://doi.org/10.1007/978-3-319-89953-4_1

take decisions with EU-wide relevance in the European Council. In the past years the euro crisis has contributed to the institution becoming even more of a key arena of European politics with heads of state and government taking decisions with considerable long term impact on member states (Brincker and Wessels 2012: 65). In addition, despite strengthening the roles of the European Commission, the European Parliament as well as the Court of Justice of the European Union in the Lisbon Treaty, the heads of government and state have at the same time included the European Council in a rising number of treaty articles and allowed it to take binding decisions (Wessels 2016: 87).

Defining Britain's role in Europe[3] and the resulting European policy have been difficult issues which every British government has had to confront since the end of World War II. At the beginning of the European integration process in the 1950s, the United Kingdom could not make up its mind to join, still seeing herself as one of the great international powers and believing there was no need to become part of some form of regional project. Lord Carrington (1988), Margaret Thatcher's first foreign secretary, characterised the British position at that time as: "We wished the club well but it wasn't for us" (312). It took many years before Britain became a member of the European Community (EC). Yet even after joining in 1973, the country remained to be viewed as somewhat of an "awkward partner" (George 1998: 1). Differences between Britain and the other member states have concerned many policy fields but have been particularly pronounced with respect to the ultimate concept of European integration with the UK having strong reservations about establishing a federal Europe and pooling sovereignty with other states (Rose 2001: 213).

The currently (2018) governing Conservative Party (Tories) has been divided over Europe since the late 1980s. In light of the rising electoral success of the United Kingdom Independence Party (UKIP) a number of strongly Eurosceptic Conservative party members continuously put pressure on then Prime Minister David Cameron to change his European policy by demanding a referendum to determine whether Britain should remain part of the European Union. In January 2013 Cameron conceded this. However, the referendum was to be preceded by a renegotiation of Britain's relationship with the European Union (EU) (Cameron 2013). In February 2016 Cameron announced that he had achieved a renegotiation of Britain's EU membership in terms of financial protection, economic competitiveness, migration, safeguards for national parliaments as well as an exclusion from the goal to reach an ever closer union of the peoples of Europe. An in/out-referendum on Britain's EU membership would be held on 23 June 2016 (Cameron 2016). Due to intraparty pressure the PM had previously agreed to free ministers from the obligation of collective responsibility during the referendum campaign (Quinn 2016). This led to him campaigning for Britain to remain a member of the European Union, while high-profile members of his party campaigned to leave. A divisive campaign over Britain's place in Europe was initiated and either side tried to persuade an

[3]'Europe' is, of course, strictly speaking not synonymous with 'the EU' or 'the EC'. But in common jargon, and in this study as well, they are treated as if they were interchangeable.

electorate, which for long has been less than enthusiastic about Britain's European integration and in parts Eurosceptic, of its arguments for or against Britain's EU membership (Bujard 2016: 595–596; on the public's Euroscepticism, see Curtice and Evans 2015). The campaign was accompanied by a print media coverage which was strongly Eurosceptic on the part of the largest selling press titles and showed a pro Leave bias (Levy et al. 2016). It ended on 23 June 2016 with the British public's decision to leave the European Union after 43 years of membership. With a turnout of 72.2%, 51.9% of voters voted to leave while 48.1% voted to remain. As a result of the vote David Cameron announced his resignation as prime minister. He was succeeded by the long-term home secretary Theresa May (Bujard 2016: 596–597, 599). Her task now was to unite her party as well as a deeply divided country. Moreover, apart from organising the exit itself the government had to develop a plan as to what Britain's future relationship with the European Union should look like. It became clear that the vote had not ended the divisions in the Tory Party over Europe. After the referendum three factions emerged in the party: those who preferred a hard Brexit (leaving the single market and ending freedom of movement), those who favoured a soft Brexit (remaining in the single market, even if it meant fewer options to curb freedom of movement) and those in the middle who thought access but not membership of the single market was the right way forward for the UK (Helm 2016). Despite these divisions, the government in March 2017 formally triggered Article 50 of the Lisbon Treaty in order to begin the exit negotiations with the European Union later that year (Bujard 2017: 586). Yet, regardless of the decision to leave the European Union, Britain's relationship with the other EU members and the European Union itself is likely to remain a key part of policy-making for any British prime minister and government, at least for the foreseeable future.

This episode of contemporary British politics illustrates the difficulties European integration poses for a UK government even though the country has been a member of the EC/EU for more than 40 years. At the same time it demonstrates that the prime minister is not wholly unconstrained in shaping his government's European policy even if he leads a single party government. Factors remain that might inhibit his options to set policy. In addition to the parliamentary party the premier's political leadership may be influenced by the behaviour of other actors in the executive as well as by British media and public opinion. These are all factors which can offset the PM's chances to exert dominant political leadership.

1.2 Purpose of this Book

To answer the question whether a prime minister's options to shape his government's policies have increased and made his leadership of the executive more dominant or not, a systematic comparison of the political leadership of several office holders is useful. Political leadership is here understood as "the extent to which heads of state and heads of government, that is, the individuals who occupy the most prominent positions of authority in the state structure, are able to determine the outcome of the decision-making process" (Elgie 1995: 4). The definition indicates that political leadership is influenced by the individual in office—that is his preferences and agency. The British political system has shown to be flexible in accommodating various leadership styles over the years, ranging from premiers taking a predominant role in their government to those focusing on a collective form of leadership in collaboration with fellow ministers. A longitudinal analysis of several office holders avoids presenting a static snapshot of prime ministerial political leadership and provides the possibility to acquire more solid findings. Given that the premier's role is likely to differ between policy fields, a wide-ranging assessment of prime ministerial political leadership covering several policy fields is necessary. To take a first step to enable such a broad evaluation, the analysis at hand focuses on European policy. Taken together with studies analysing other policy fields it can contribute to a more comprehensive picture of prime ministerial leadership in Britain in the future.

When studying political leadership, a decision has to be made on which political level to focus. This study examines the prime minister's role in the British executive. It does not address the question of leadership of the executive as a whole in the political system. Nor does it focus on the PM's political leadership at the European level, although his activities here are considered as far as they are relevant to his leadership of the domestic executive.

The present study analyses how the prime minister can shape European policy. The questions to be answered are:

(a) Can the political leadership of the British prime minister in European policy be characterised as prime ministerial predominance or as collective leadership?
(b) Has there been a trend towards more prime ministerial predominance between 1976 and 2007?

In the analysis at hand the political leadership of Prime Ministers James Callaghan (1976–1979), Margaret Thatcher (1979–1990), John Major (1990–1997) and Tony Blair (1997–2007) in European policy is studied. As European policy is a wide-ranging subject area, in which the prime minister's role is likely to vary as well, the study has to limit its focus. It does so by centring on European monetary policy, which is a fitting subject area for such an analysis as the head of government here plays a key role in the domestic decision-making process. Moreover, it is a subject area which has gained prominence in the European integration process over the years—at first with plans to achieve closer cooperation, then with a single currency. Between 1976 and 2007 significant developments in European monetary integration took place. Key decisions had to be taken, most notably on the establishment of the Exchange Rate Mechanism (ERM), the centre piece of the European Monetary System (EMS), and Economic and Monetary Union (EMU). They comprise the cases for this analysis.

There are several reasons to select these four office holders for comparison: firstly, the ways in which they have led their governments appear to have varied significantly. Blair and Thatcher have often been characterised as having exhibited a particularly dominant leadership in office. In contrast, Major and Callaghan have frequently been described as having shown a more conciliatory and collective leadership (e.g. Hennessy 2001; Rose 2001). Their party affiliation does not appear to have affected their leadership style: Blair and Callaghan were Labour prime ministers whereas Thatcher and Major were Conservative party leaders. Their stances on European integration have varied, ranging from pragmatic pro-European to more Eurosceptic. Yet there have not only been variations between the prime ministers' views of European integration. Sometimes they have also changed their attitude to Europe within a premiership.

Apart from their varying leadership styles and political orientation, the comparison allows for a longitudinal study covering 31 years (1976–2007). Yet one caveat has to be mentioned on the comparability of the four premierships. As with any longitudinal comparison the temporal context needs to be considered. It has to be taken into account that the process and the mechanisms of European integration have changed over the years and that European policy has received a more prominent place in British politics. During James Callaghan's premiership European integration did not play such an important role for the British government as it did during the premierships of his successors (for a similar assessment by an early 1990s study, see Christoph 1993: 529). This is because the member states have widened and deepened European integration by transferring competences in more and more policy fields to the European level. Moreover, in the European context "the PM's role has grown, partly out of choice and partly because the EU itself is increasingly driven by the European Council" (Allen 2013: 120). This has implications for the comparison of the four prime ministers' political leadership, as they have become more directly involved in European policy-making due to their membership of the European Council. But, while changes to the political context have to be considered when drawing conclusions from the analysis, it makes the comparison of Callaghan, Major, Thatcher and Blair with view to their political leadership and their role in European policy no less significant and the analysis of the factors shaping prime ministerial political leadership in a specific policy field remains of value.

1.3 Current Research, Methodology and Structure

In the second half of the twentieth century the executive was primarily analysed with two opposing concepts in British political science. Depending on which was seen as the dominant institution in the executive, there was either cabinet or prime ministerial government (see Rhodes 1995: 11–26 for an overview of the debate). Various works from a historical or political science perspective have dealt particularly with the UK premiership (e.g. Hennessy 2001; Blick and Jones 2010). Margaret Thatcher's and Tony Blair's premierships in particular have been popular objects of research due to their apparently predominant political leadership styles (e.g. Seldon 2008; Young 1989). John Major's political leadership has been studied, too—but often to portray it as an example of what was considered ineffective leadership (e.g. Kavanagh and Seldon 1994 for a general assessment; Clark 1999 as an example for a critique of Major's political leadership as insufficient). Few studies have analysed James Callaghan's political leadership in detail (e.g. Donoughue 1987).

Almost all studies covering these issues do not concentrate on a specific policy field. It is often ignored that a prime minister's political leadership may differ between policy fields as well as within a policy field over time. Several studies tend to suggest—especially with view to the political leadership of Blair and Thatcher—that over the past 20–30 or more years a process of presidentialization has taken place in the British political system. A prominent representative of this thesis is Michael Foley with his study 'The British Presidency' (Foley 1993, 2000, 2004). Such approaches are problematic for a number of reasons, but in this case particularly because they do not analyse a prime minister's political leadership in a specific policy field.[4] As other studies tend to do, they characterise it as identical across all policy fields (in this case as presidential). Research such as this tends to remain sketchy. Exceptions are, for instance, Robert Dover's liberal-intergovernmentalist analysis of Tony Blair's role in shaping UK defence policy between 1997 and 2000 (Dover 2005) and the author's own comparison of Tony Blair's and Margaret Thatcher's political leadership in European monetary policy (Bujard 2003). The latter study used Martin J. Smith's model of prime ministerial power (Smith 1999) to analyse prime ministerial leadership in European policy. This model is applied here too, but the theoretical basis is broadened and its framework revised to make it an even more useful tool for comparison. The present analysis also extends the scope to include four prime ministers.[5] Therefore, a key result of the four-fold comparison conducted here is to make a contribution to reduce this deficiency in political leadership studies on the British political system.

To answer the research questions posed here, primarily qualitative research methods are used. They centre on a review of political science and historical literature, political memoirs and diaries as well as media coverage and official documents. It is taken into account that political memoirs and diaries pose difficulties as sources as political actors might use them to justify political decisions in hindsight (Gamble 2002: 145). Also, an individual writing about an event might (sub-) consciously depict his part in it differently—for instance as more influential than he actually was. Someone might also claim a political decision was long planned when in fact it was merely a reaction to circumstances or events. Yet these problems can be minimised to an extent by trying to compare various accounts of an event, decision or relationship. Where considered beneficial to the analysis diverging interpretations by actors involved are discussed.

For the premierships of the four prime ministers memoirs or diaries by all ministers involved in European monetary policy-making have been published—with the

[4]Heffernan (2005) compares the offices of British prime minister and US-President and concludes that the latter has to govern with more institutional constraints than the former.

[5]Moreover, when the thesis was submitted in 2003 the British government's decision on joining the Eurozone was still pending so the case study for Blair could not be completed at the time.

exception of Tony Blair's Chancellor Gordon Brown.[6] The memoirs display differences in the extent and detail to which they report about developments in government. The recollections of Douglas Hurd and Nigel Lawson, for example, provide valuable information on decision-making processes in the British political system in general and also contain detailed accounts of the Thatcher administration (and in Hurd's case of the Major government, too) (Hurd 2009; Lawson 1992). On the other hand, some memoirs do not say much about the political process in British government and seem to be geared primarily towards the interests of the tabloid media as the memoir of John Prescott, Blair's deputy prime minister (Prescott 2008).

For the Callaghan and the Thatcher period cabinet memoranda (official material distributed to cabinet members for their sessions) and cabinet conclusions (official protocols of the meetings) from 1976 to 1988 could be used. They were closed to the public but have recently been made available by the British National Archives.

Furthermore, semi-structured expert interviews were used. In 2010 the author interviewed ten former officials or members of prime ministerial political staff. The interviewees were selected as their accounts can function as a corrective to those given by politicians in their memoirs and provide a different perspective on the issues in question. Most interviewees worked for successive governments and prime ministers and were closely involved with European policy decision-making. Sir Michael Butler (1979–1985), Lord David Hannay (1985–1990), Lord John Kerr (1990–1995) and Sir Stephen Wall (1995–2000) were British Ambassadors to the EC/EU. In this post they worked with several prime ministers. Lord David Williamson (1983–1987) and Sir Brian Bender (1994–1998) were like Sir Stephen Wall (2000–2004) in charge of the Cabinet Office European Secretariat (COES), responsible for the coordination of European policy in the British executive and also advisory body to cabinet and prime minister. Sir Nigel Wicks was not only head of Margaret Thatcher's Private Office in the mid-1980s, but as Treasury official also closely involved in the negotiations of the British opt-out from the third stage of EMU at Maastricht in December 1991. Lord Bernard Donoughue was a member of James Callaghan's Policy Unit and Lord Roger Liddle of Tony Blair's Policy Unit—the prime minister's think-tank in No. 10 Downing Street. Lord Tom McNally was Callaghan's political secretary. The three were political appointees in contrast to the others who were career civil servants. Interviews with former British diplomats from the 'British Diplomatic Oral History Programme' (BDOHP)[7] were used, too. These cover various aspects of UK foreign policy, including information about processes in the domestic core executive and about the European policy of successive governments.

A substantial number of publications are available on British European policy in general (e.g. George 1998; Gowland et al. 2010) and European monetary policy in particular (e.g. Stephens 1997; Thompson 1996). Yet few studies cover the role of

[6]His memoirs were published after this study was completed.

[7]The BDOHP was initiated in 1995 and is available to the public through the Churchill Archives Centre at Churchill College, Cambridge (https://www.chu.cam.ac.uk/archives/collections/bdohp/, accessed 8 March 2018).

individual actors such as the premier in the policy field (for a journalistic perspective on this see Young 1999). The position of the major political parties on Europe is dealt with in some detail (e.g. Gowland and Turner 2000; Baker and Seawright 1998). In addition, there is research on the voting behaviour of government MPs since the 1970s which includes European policy decisions and gives an overview of the unity of the parliamentary parties in their attitude to this policy field (e.g. Norton 1980; Cowley 2005).

Accounts of UK European policy frequently address Euroscepticism in the British media. However, such case studies tend to cover short time periods (e.g. Carey and Burton 2004; De Vreese 2001). Longitudinal studies on the British media's position on European integration are rare. An exception is a study by George Wilkes and Dominic Wring, in which the authors analysed the media coverage on Europe between 1948 and 1996 (Wilkes and Wring 1998). Due to the lack of longitudinal research on this topic the author decided to conduct her own media analysis. This analysis focuses on specific case studies, as the scope of this study (1976–2007) is too large to be covered completely. These case studies comprise key decisions in European monetary policy the UK government had to take. The aim was to evaluate in how far the premier can influence media coverage and the media's evaluation of his European monetary policy. To test whether a prime minister could influence the media coverage in the relevant case, his parliamentary statement on it, which includes his arguments for the decision, was analysed. The newspaper coverage by selected papers 2 weeks before and 2 weeks after the event was studied to analyse whether it changed, which could then be attributed to the prime minister's influence. For a comprehensive look five national newspapers were chosen: the *Financial Times*, the *Guardian*, the *Independent*,[8] the *Daily Mail* and the *Sun*. This selection includes papers with diverse readerships, pro-European and Eurosceptic outlooks and various party political agendas. The examination was done by a summarising qualitative content analysis using inductively developed categories (for an overview of qualitative content analysis, see Mayring 2000).[9] The categories were sourced from either PM's parliamentary statement. They were then used to structure the content of the media coverage and analyse whether it changed over the course of the 4 week period due to the premier's framing of the issue in question in parliament.[10]

In Chap. 2 the theoretical basis for the analysis and the policy field is introduced. The main approaches to the study of political leadership are reviewed. Approaches focusing on personal or structural aspects are contrasted with those combining both. Moreover, concepts of the British political system are identified. They include the classical Westminster approach as well as a contrasting model: Patrick Dunleavy's

---

[8]The *Independent* was founded in the 1980s and therefore not used in the Callaghan case study.

[9]For more on the summarising qualitative content analysis ('zusammenfassende qualitative Inhaltsanalyse') see Mayring (2010: 67–85); for more on inductive category development ('induktive Kategorienbildung') see Mayring (2010: 83–85).

[10]For more on structuring with regard to content ('inhaltliche Strukturierung') see Mayring (2010: 98).

and Roderick Rhodes' core executive concept. In addition, concepts for the assessment of the UK prime minister's political leadership in government decision-making are considered. These include Martin J. Smith's model of prime ministerial power and Richard Heffernan's thesis of prime ministerial predominance. On the basis of these, a modified model of prime ministerial power is developed. It is used to study the four PMs and their political leadership in European monetary policy. The aim is to identify whether their leadership in this particular area showed a form of prime ministerial predominance or collective leadership.

Chapter 3 provides an overview of European monetary policy and the British response to it between 1976 and 2007 with a particular focus on the two case studies: the Exchange Rate Mechanism (ERM), the centre piece of the European Monetary System (EMS), and Economic and Monetary Union (EMU).

Chapters 4–6 introduce the leadership environment, in which the premier conducts his political leadership, and his resources. In Chap. 4 the main features of British European policy-making and coordination are introduced. An overview of the institutional organisation of the executive and legislature in the subject area is given. In Chap. 5 the attitude to European integration of the actors covered in this study is looked at: the four prime ministers, their parliamentary parties, the media and the public. In Chap. 6 an overview is given of the resources a premier has at his disposal to lead his government. These can be of an institutional nature, meaning they are available to an incumbent due to the office he holds. This includes, for example, the prime minister's option to use two-level politics to influence policy-making at the domestic level due to his position in the European Council (Sect. 6.1). The resources can also be of an individual nature, thus are based on his personal preferences and agency (Sect. 6.2).

Chapters 7–10 comprise the case study analysis. The prime minister's political leadership in European policy analysis covers four key aspects:

First of all, their institutional resources, already introduced in the previous chapter, are specifically defined with regard to European (monetary) policy decision-making (Chap. 7).

Secondly, the agency and activities of other actors in the European policy core executive apart from the PM are looked at more closely. Actors dealing with European monetary policy decisions such as the chancellor or the foreign secretary and their departments are considered. Sometimes these also include ministers who influence the decision-making process though they have no departmental responsibility to do so. Additionally, the prime minister's options in handling these actors who potentially constrain his room for action are analysed and how he can attempt to broaden his leeway in that respect (Chap. 8).

Thirdly, the position of the governing party in parliament and its voting behaviour on European policy is analysed to understand in how far it affects the prime minister's room for manoeuvre in the policy field. A premier's resources to influence his parliamentary party concerning European policy-making are taken into account as well (Chap. 9).

Fourthly, an analysis of parliamentary statements on particular European monetary policy decisions by the four prime ministers and their adoption by the national press is conducted. The aim is to evaluate in how far the premier can influence media coverage and the media's evaluation of his European monetary policy (Chap. 10).

Lastly, the different aspects which potentially influence a premier's political leadership in European (monetary) policy set out before are brought together and evaluated (Chap. 11).

References

Allen, D. (2013). The United Kingdom. In S. Bulmer & C. Lequesne (Eds.), *The member states of the European Union* (2nd ed., pp. 108–133). Oxford: Oxford University Press.

Baker, D., & Seawright, D. (Eds.). (1998). *Britain for and against Europe: British politics and the question of European integration*. Oxford: Clarendon.

Blick, A., & Jones, G. (2010). *Premiership: The development, nature and power of the British prime minister*. Exeter: Imprint Academic.

Brincker, G.-S., & Wessels, W. (2012). Europäischer Rat. In W. Weidenfeld & W. Wessels (Eds.), *Jahrbuch der Europäischen Integration 2012* (pp. 65–80). Baden-Baden: Nomos Verlagsgesellschaft.

Bujard, B. (2003). *Die politische Führung des britischen Premierminister: Das "Model of Prime Ministerial Power" am Beispiel der Europapolitik Margaret Thatchers und Tony Blairs* (unpublished M.A. thesis), University of Cologne, Cologne.

Bujard, B. (2016). Vereinigtes Königreich. In W. Weidenfeld & W. Wessels (Eds.), *Jahrbuch der Europäischen Integration 2016* (pp. 591–600). Baden-Baden: Nomos Verlagsgesellschaft.

Bujard, B. (2017). Vereinigtes Königreich. In W. Weidenfeld & W. Wessels (Eds.), *Jahrbuch der Europäischen Integration 2017* (pp. 583–592). Baden-Baden: Nomos Verlagsgesellschaft.

Cameron, D. (2013, January 23). *EU speech at Bloomberg*. https://www.gov.uk/government/speeches/eu-speech-at-bloomberg. Accessed May 29, 2013.

Cameron, D. (2016, February 22). *PM Commons statement on EU reform and referendum*. https://www.gov.uk/government/speeches/pm-commons-statement-on-eu-reform-and-referendum-22-february-2016. Accessed April 8, 2016.

Carey, S., & Burton, J. (2004). The influence of the press in shaping public opinion towards the European Union in Britain. *Political Studies, 52*(3), 623–640.

Carrington, P. A. (1988). *Reflect on things past: The memoirs of Lord Carrington*. London: Collins.

Christoph, J. B. (1993). The effects of Britons in Brussels: The European Community and the culture of Whitehall. *Governance, 6*(4), 518–537.

Clark, A. (1999). *The Tories: Conservatives and the nation state 1922–1997* (2nd ed.). London: Phoenix.

Cowley, P. (2005). *The rebels: How Blair mislaid his majority*. London: Politico's.

Crossmann, R. H. S. (1963). Introduction. In W. Bagehot (Ed.), *The English constitution* (2nd ed., pp. 1–57). London: Collins/Fontana Library.

Curtice, J., & Evans, G. (2015). Britain and Europe: Are we all Eurosceptics now? In J. Curtice & R. Ormston (Eds.), *British social attitudes: The 32nd report*. London: NatCen Social Research. http://www.bsa.natcen.ac.uk/media/38975/bsa32_eu.pdf. Accessed September 1, 2016.

De Vreese, C. H. (2001). 'Europe' in the news: A cross-national comparative study of the news coverage of key EU events. *European Union Politics, 2*(3), 283–307.

Donoughue, B. (1987). *Prime minister: The conduct of policy under Harold Wilson & James Callaghan*. London: Jonathan Cape.

Dover, R. (2005). The prime minister and the core executive: A liberal intergovernmentalist reading of UK defence policy formulation 1997–2000. *British Journal of Politics and International Relations, 7*(4), 508–525.

Elgie, R. (1995). *Political leadership in liberal democracies*. Basingstoke: Macmillan.

Foley, M. (1993). *The rise of the British presidency*. Manchester: Manchester University Press.

Foley, M. (2000). *The British presidency: Tony Blair and the politics of public leadership*. Manchester: Manchester University Press.

Foley, M. (2004). Presidential attribution as an agency of prime ministerial critique in a parliamentary democracy: The case of Tony Blair. *British Journal of Politics and International Relations, 6*(3), 292–311.

Gamble, A. (2002). Political memoirs. *British Journal of Politics and International Relations, 4*(1), 141–151.

George, S. (1998). *An awkward partner: Britain in the European Community* (3rd ed.). Oxford: Oxford University Press.

Gowland, D., & Turner, A. (2000). *Reluctant Europeans: Britain and European integration 1945–1998*. Harlow: Longman.

Gowland, D., Turner, A., & Wright, A. (2010). *Britain and European integration since 1945: On the sidelines*. London: Routledge.

Heffernan, R. (2005). Why the prime minister cannot be a president: Comparing institutional imperatives in Britain and America. *Parliamentary Affairs, 58*(1), 53–70.

Helm, T. (2016, October 1). Bitter Tory fight over Brexit set to overshadow conservative conference. *The Observer*.

Hennessy, P. (2001). *The prime minister: The office and its holders since 1945* (2nd ed.). London: Penguin.

Hurd, D. (2009). *Memoirs*. London: Abacus.

Kavanagh, D., & Seldon, A. (Eds.). (1994). *The Major effect*. London: Macmillan.

Lawson, N. (1992). *A view from No. 11: Memoirs of a Tory radical*. London: Bantam.

Levy, D. A. L., Aslan, B., & Bironzo, D. (2016). *UK press coverage of the EU referendum*. Oxford: Reuters Institute for the Study of Journalism. http://reutersinstitute.politics.ox.ac.uk/sites/default/files/UK%20Press%20Coverage%20of%20the%20EU%20Referendum_0.pdf. Accessed October 11, 2016.

Mayring, P. (2000). Qualitative content analysis. *Forum Qualitative Sozialforschung/Forum: Qualitative Social Research, 1*(2), Art. 20.

Mayring, P. (2010). *Qualitative Inhaltsanalyse* (11th ed.). Weinheim: Beltz Verlag.

Mughan, A. (2000). *Media and the presidentialization of parliamentary elections*. Basingstoke: Palgrave.

Norton, P. (1980). *Dissension in the House of Commons 1974–1979*. Oxford: Clarendon.

Peters, B. G., Rhodes, R. A. W., & Wright, V. (2000). Staffing the summit – the administration of the core executive: Convergent trends and national specificities. In B. G. Peters, R. A. W. Rhodes, & V. Wright (Eds.), *Administering the summit: Administration of the core executive in developed countries* (pp. 3–22). Basingstoke: Macmillan.

Poguntke, T., & Webb, P. (Eds.). (2005). *The presidentialization of politics: A comparative study of modern democracies*. Oxford: Oxford University Press.

Prescott, J. (with Davies, H.) (2008). *Prezza: My story: Pulling no punches*. London: Headline Review.

Quinn, B. (2016, January 14). EU membership terms 'disastrous' for UK, says cabinet minister Chris Grayling. *The Guardian*.

Rhodes, R. A. W. (1995). From prime ministerial power to core executive. In R. A. W. Rhodes & P. Dunleavy (Eds.), *Prime minister, cabinet and core executive* (pp. 11–37). Basingstoke: Macmillan.

Rose, R. (2001). *The prime minister in a shrinking world*. Cambridge: Polity.

Seldon, A. (with Snowdon, P., & Collings, D.) (2008). *Blair unbound* (2nd ed.). London: Pocket Books.

Shell, D., & Hodder-Williams, R. (Eds.). (1995). *Churchill to Major: The British prime ministership since 1945*. Armonk: M.E. Sharpe.

Smith, M. J. (1999). *The core executive in Britain*. Basingstoke: Macmillan.

Stephens, P. (1997). *Politics and the pound: The Tories, the economy and Europe* (2nd ed.). London: Papermac.

Thompson, H. (1996). *The British Conservative government and the European Exchange Rate Mechanism, 1979–1994*. London: Pinter.

Wessels, W. (2016). *The European Council*. London: Palgrave.

Wilkes, G., & Wring, D. (1998). The British press and European integration: 1948 to 1996. In D. Baker & D. Seawright (Eds.), *Britain for and against Europe: British politics and the question of European integration* (pp. 185–205). Oxford: Clarendon.

Young, H. (1989). *One of us: A biography of Margaret Thatcher* (2nd ed.). London: Macmillan.

Young, H. (1999). *This blessed plot: Britain and Europe from Churchill to Blair* (2nd ed.). London: Papermac.

Chapter 2
Theoretical Framework: Prime Ministerial Political Leadership in the British Political System

2.1 Approaches to the Study of Political Leadership

Political leadership is possible in practically all political and social contexts and not linked to a particular office (Helms 2005a: 737). Being a socially constructed concept there are competing definitions of political leadership (Elgie 1995: 2; for various definitions, see Elgie 1995: 3). Here it is understood as "the process by which governments exercise control over public policy decisions... Political leadership deals with the question of who controls the outcome of public policy decisions within a state and how they do so" (Elgie 1995: 4). To be more precise, this study analyses the prime minister's political leadership within the British executive. There are different normative and empirical approaches to analyse how and to what extent a head of government can influence political decision-making through political leadership (Helms 2005c: Sect. 2.2) Normative concepts focusing on what constitutes 'good governance' and 'good government' can be dated back to Platonic philosophy. Today, approaches to the study of political leadership using normative aspects still exist and are often found in research on individual political leaders such as a normative preference for the leadership style of Franklin D. Roosevelt in the USA (Helms 2005b: 17). As the research questions posed here ask what the premiers' political leadership in European policy actually looked like and not what it should have, an empirically-oriented approach to analyse political leadership is used. The following chapter provides an overview of empirical approaches. They can be divided depending on which factor(s) are seen to shape the political process most strongly: (a) personal attributes, (b) structural aspects, or (c) the interaction of both (Helms 2005c: 34).

Leader-centred approaches to the study of political leadership focus on personal attributes. They concentrate on the leader, his work and his influence on the political decision-making process (Helms 2005b: 17). The nineteenth century 'Great Man' school of political leadership argued that the leader's personality was the most important factor to explain political processes (Elgie 1995: 5). Today such a view

B. Bujard, *The British Prime Minister in the Core Executive*, Contributions to Political Science, https://doi.org/10.1007/978-3-319-89953-4_2

is seen as reductionist, particularly as in contemporary liberal democracies political leadership cannot be analysed without considering structural and institutional factors, which, at least to an extent, constrain a leader's scope of action (Elgie 1995: 5, 6; Helms 2000: 416). However, there are still studies drawing strongly on a leader's personality such as case studies on leadership in undemocratic or totalitarian political systems (Helms 2005c: 34–35). Moreover, they can be found in US leadership research due to the specific institutional conditions for political leadership in the US presidential democracy.[1] These distinctive institutional features also help explain why sophisticated studies on the link between a leader's personal attributes and political leadership have tended to remain restricted to US-American presidential studies (Helms 2000: 416).

Despite such leader-centred approaches, for much of the nineteenth and the early twentieth century leadership concepts focusing on structural aspects were dominant (Helms 2005b: 18). They make up the second group of approaches to study political leadership mentioned above. According to a radically structural perspective there is none or only little room for political leadership by individuals in the political decision-making process (Helms 2000: 419). Like classical approaches focusing entirely on a leader's personality such views are seen as reductionist today (Elgie 1995: 6). Nonetheless, structure-centred perspectives have remained influential in contemporary political science in the form of (neo-) institutionalism (Helms 2005c: 38). Today, leadership research approaches focusing on personality and those that focus on structural aspects acknowledge that other factors impact on a leader's political leadership, too. Thus interactionist approaches have gained more attention (Helms 2000: 420).

Interactionist approaches, which make up the third group of approaches to the study of political leadership mentioned above, take personal as well as systemic factors into account. They attempt to show the interdependence and dynamic relationship between the two (Helms 2005b: 19–20). A political leader's influence on the decision-making process is assumed to depend on the interaction between him and his environment—the "leadership environment" (Elgie 1995: 7). Political leaders with individual ambitions and idiosyncratic behaviour act in an environment which shapes their behaviour and constrains them (Elgie 1995: 7–8). The leadership environment is composed of "relatively fixed institutional structures, long-term historical and social conditions and short-term social, economic and political demands" (Elgie 1995: 8). Thus it does not just cover a political system's institutional aspects. Political culture, which consists of the values, beliefs and attitudes of a society towards the political system, matters as well. Due to a political system's political culture there are certain expectations as to how political actors interact and how political leaders behave (Helms 2005b: 20). Moreover, historical experiences shape norms and expectations concerning a political system. Thus they shape the

[1]According to Helms (2000: 416) the de facto direct elections of the head of state and a monocratic structure of the executive grant the president larger room for manoeuvre than heads of government/state in other political systems.

leadership environment. Margaret Thatcher's political leadership for example influenced the view of what effective governance entailed and so affected succeeding prime ministers' leadership environments (Helms 2005c: 40). But political leaders are not just agents of their environment. They can shape it, too. Yet their influence on the decision-making process depends on the extent and form in which the leadership environment allows them to do so (Elgie 1995: 8). Also short-term political circumstances can lead to unforeseen "windows of opportunity" (Helms 2000: 421) which might even permanently affect the scope for political leadership in a political system. Difficult economic circumstances, for instance, can give a leader the opportunity to realise political reforms he would have liked to do but would not have been able to implement under less difficult conditions. Thatcher's economic and social policy reforms in the 1980s come to mind as examples.

With regard to the question which factors shape political leadership most strongly, Robert Elgie (1995: 191) concludes from his study of political leadership in six liberal democracies that these are institutional factors. The 'actor-centred institutionalism' approach developed by Fritz Scharpf and Renate Mayntz takes a similar view (Mayntz and Scharpf 1995; Scharpf 2000). Similar to interactionist approaches it views social phenomena as a product of interactions between intentionally operating actors. These interactions are structured by the institutional context in which they take place. The institutional context influences the results of these interactions (Scharpf 2000: 17). Here, too, institutions are seen as the most important factors influencing actors and their interactions. This is because individuals depend on socially constructed rules[2] to cope with their environment. These rules are part of a common knowledge system shared by all actors in a political system. Institutions help to explain political processes as they specify the scope of possible action by defining which behaviour is called for, allowed or prohibited. Moreover, they define how actors interpret the results of decisions they have taken and therefore also influence actors' preferences regarding the options they can choose from (Scharpf 2000: 78, 79). Once the institutional context of the interactions between actors is known, researchers can more easily draw conclusions about actors' preferences, options and perceptions (Scharpf 2000: 81). In the study at hand as well institutional factors are seen as the ones shaping political leadership the most. Here the term institutions is understood according to neo-institutional thinking as including formal institutions but also formal and informal rules and norms which structure the political decision-making process (Kaiser 2001: 256). Yet in line with interactionist approaches to the study of political leadership the analysis does not exclude personal preferences of the actors involved. It refers to them where necessary to help understand how actors have handled particular situations.

The next chapter gives an overview of research approaches on the institutions in the British political system with specific reference to the executive and prime ministerial leadership. Like the interactionist approach for the study of political

[2]According to this approach institutions are not only formal constitutional rules but also social norms, which are accepted by actors in a political system (Scharpf 2000: 77).

leadership these add to the theoretical basis for the following analysis of prime ministerial political leadership in the UK executive.

2.2 Approaches to the Study of the British Political System

2.2.1 The Westminster Model: Cabinet Versus Prime Ministerial Government/Presidentialization

Traditional approaches to conceptualise the British political system can be subsumed under the term 'Westminster model'. This concept has dominated the study of British central government explicitly and implicitly for much of the twentieth century (Smith 1998: 46). It is based on the assumption that there is no higher authority than parliament in the UK political system: there is parliamentary sovereignty (Smith 1999: 10). According to Arend Lijphart, the Westminster model has ten central elements: executive power is concentrated in one-party majority cabinets, cabinet dominance, a two-party system, a majoritarian and disproportional election system, interest group pluralism, a unitary and centralised government, a concentration of legislative power in a unicameral legislature, a flexible constitution, an absence of judicial review and a central bank controlled by the executive (Lijphart 2012: 10–20).[3]

While the model has been a tool for analysis and comparison of political systems, it has also been a normative ideal. With regard to British politics it has been used to portray a specific image of the political system (Marsh et al. 2003: 306). It was seen as an ideal of what government should be like (Smith 1999: 10). The model's normative aspects affected the way in which political scientists analysed the centre of the UK political system. It even influenced which research questions were posed and answered: "The normative presumptions of the Westminster model underpinned empirical analysis of central government" (Smith 1998: 46–47).

During the latter part of the twentieth century alternative approaches to study the British political system were developed such as the core executive approach, outlined in the next chapter. This was mainly because British political science became less insular and opened itself to research from American and European political science. Also, the political crises of the 1970s and the Thatcher premiership in the 1980s became catalysts to question the traditional model's adequacy to explain current developments in British politics and political institutions (Gamble 1990: 414).

According to the Westminster model power relations are zero-sum-games (Smith 1999: 13). While the principle of defining power as an object attached to an institution or an office as described in the model was not contested, a discussion

[3]Despite changes to its political system in the past years, Lijphart (2012: 20) argues that the UK can still be seen as a very fitting example of a majoritarian democratic system.

ensued in the 1960s and 1970s about where power in the executive was located. The different positions in the debate can be subsumed under the terms 'cabinet government' and 'prime ministerial government', depending on which institution was seen to dominate the political decision-making process (Smith 1998: 47; for more on both concepts, see Rhodes 1995: 13–15; Hennessy 2001: 55–57). An early representative of the prime ministerial government thesis was Richard Crossman (1963: 51–53), who thought the cabinet government concept no longer adequately explained what he perceived as an extreme power shift in the executive towards the prime minister. Particularly during the Thatcher premiership the debate focused on prime ministerial government. To consider executive leadership as prime ministerial government became almost "conventional wisdom" (Dunleavy and Rhodes 1990: 8) supported by media and political scientists alike. John Major's premiership tended to be seen as a return to cabinet government (e.g. Seldon 1994), while Tony Blair's incumbency again as a sign of power flowing from cabinet to premier (e.g. Foley 2000).

A variation to the prime ministerial government concept was developed with the presidentialization thesis (e.g. Foley 1993, 2000; Mughan 2000; Poguntke and Webb 2005).[4] For instance, Richard Foley (2000: 25) argued that the type of political leadership by the UK prime minister has significantly changed because of the profound shifts his leadership has gone through. These changes are not just due to the circumstances or the personality of an office-holder but are more substantial. They, for instance, are related to aspects such as what the public expects of political leadership and the conventions that define it.

In the early 1990s Roderick Rhodes and Patrick Dunleavy criticised that British executive studies remained focused on long-running debates such as that over prime ministerial versus cabinet government. However, the evidence cited in support of each case by proponents of either side was thin and mostly anecdotal. At the same time there was a lack of large-scale or systematic research. Hence, the political science debate remained limited and static (Dunleavy and Rhodes 1990: 4, 5). Moreover, it was largely overlooked that a prime minister's role in the political decision-making process fluctuates and varies, and the impact of a shifting context was not considered (Rhodes 1995: 14). They therefore came up with a different approach to study the executive, which is considered next.

2.2.2 *The Core Executive Approach*

As a result of their critique and as an alternative to the Westminster model Roderick Rhodes and Patrick Dunleavy developed the core executive approach in the early 1990s. In contrast to the view that power in the executive is either located with the

[4]The concept is contested, e.g. Heffernan (2005b) compares the offices of UK prime minister and US president and concludes that the latter has to govern with more institutional constraints than the former.

prime minister or the cabinet, they took the view that the centre of UK government is more complex. Dunleavy and Rhodes (1990) define it as

> a complex web of institutions, networks and practices surrounding the PM, Cabinet, cabinet committees and their official counterparts, less formalized ministerial 'clubs' or meetings, bilateral negotiations, and interdepartmental committees. It also includes some major coordinating departments—chiefly, the Cabinet Office, the Treasury, the Foreign Office, the law officers, and the security and intelligence services. (3)

Traditionally (at least some of) these institutions and processes have been subsumed under the term 'cabinet government'. But the authors find this label problematic, as it implies a cabinet dominance over the other institutions which are part of the executive's centre. Moreover, the concept is not only a description of a specific form of government but also has a normative connotation. To use a neutral term the authors propose to call the central part of the executive 'core executive' instead. They define it as consisting of a wide range of institutions including those mentioned above "which primarily serve to pull together and integrate central government policies, or act as final arbiters within the executive of conflicts between different elements of the government machine" (Dunleavy and Rhodes 1990: 4). So, key to the concept is the proposition that the complex network of formal and informal rules and institutions at the centre of government has to be analysed to understand how political decisions are taken. Not just formal institutions such as cabinet or prime minister but also less formalised structures such as informal meetings or bilateral negotiations have to be considered. Another key assumption of the approach is that the core executive's composition changes over time and depends on the policy field (Rhodes 1995: 26).

2.2.3 Martin J. Smith's Model of Prime Ministerial Power

Based on the core executive approach, Martin J. Smith developed a framework similar to interactionist approaches to analyse prime ministerial political leadership (Smith 1994, 1995, 1999). Like Rhodes and Dunleavy he considered the Westminster model as too simplistic to adequately describe the UK centre of government. In his opinion particularly the assumption that executive power is either located with the premier or the cabinet is overly simplistic (Smith 1999: 36). He, too, suggested that the UK government's centre is much more complex than the Westminster model suggests. To conceptualise this complexity Smith based his analytical framework on five elements: resources, power, agency, structure and context (Smith 1998: 68, 1999: 29). The analysis of prime ministerial political leadership in this study is based on these aspects.

Every actor in the core executive has *resources*, for example, the prime minister's right to control the cabinet agenda or the Prime Minister's Office (Smith 1999: 76). These resources are partly structurally defined, that is they are related to the role an actor has. But they can also be of an individual nature. Thus all actors have something to bargain with when interacting with others in the core executive. The strength of their negotiating position depends on (a) which resources they have and (b) how much other actors need these to achieve their goals (Smith 1999: 31).

Resources are not the equivalent of *power* (Smith 1994: 347, 1998: 66). Power in Smith' approach is based on resource dependency. While all core executive actors have resources, none has a monopoly. Hence, none can set policy alone. Even actors with many resources (e.g. the PM) do not automatically have more power. For power to be exerted an actor has to exchange resources with others in the core executive. Thus to reach their goals actors have to cut deals, make concessions and negotiate (Smith 1998: 67–68, 1999: 35). Power according to this definition is not static. It does not belong with prime minister or cabinet as the Westminster model suggests. Various actors across the core executive can influence political decisions. Also power varies depending on the policy field, context, available resources and the tactics actors use (Smith 1999: 36).

The tactics and strategies which actors in the core executive use form the third part of Smith's framework: *agency*. Actors operate intentionally to use their resources and to transform them into power. Hence the exercise of power by actors depends on their intentions, on how they use their resources to achieve goals (Smith 1998: 66, 1999: 32). They have a range of strategies available to influence the policy-making process, which they have developed by taking their environment into account. Hence they have been shaped in the context of certain situations, values and existing cultural and social norms (Smith 1999: 33). Smith (1999: 33) defines strategies as the general style with which actors attempt to achieve goals and tactics as measures used in specific situations. Which strategy or tactic is applied and whether it is successful depends on the situation and the structural circumstances. Agency also has implications for the understanding of power: it helps to explain why an actor with fewer resources can assert himself over another with more (Smith 1998: 66, 1999: 33–34).

Another aspect of Smith's approach is *structure*. All core executive actors operate in some form of structural environment (Smith 1999: 31). This structure is a result of agency, therefore it can change. It influences the actors' behaviour as it marks out the boundaries in which they can realise their aims. It is "the limit of action" (Smith 1998: 65). It defines several potential strategies actors can employ to accomplish their goals. Yet structure does not only constrain actors. It also enables them by providing them with a range of choices (Hay 1995: 199, 205).

Actors operate within a *context*. According to Smith it is partly structural but also coincidental and made up of at least three aspects: the political, the historic and the institutional. Power relationships between core executive actors in a policy field are based on how institutions in that area developed historically and the institutionalisation of past decisions. Overlying the historical and institutional aspects of the context are the political as well as economic circumstances a government faces (Smith 1998: 67, 1999: 35). These affect the issues the government has to handle and the constraints and options it has to deal with them (Smith 1994: 343).

Using these five aspects, Martin J. Smith developed a 'model of prime ministerial power' to analyse political leadership. It is outlined in the remainder of this chapter.

The British prime minister as any other core executive actor has *resources*. These are either formal or structural (derived from his office) or informal or personal (based on his personal style) (Smith 1999: 74). Formal resources include, for instance, his right (a) to appoint and dismiss the members of his government, (b) to control the cabinet agenda and (c) to influence the executive's structure by determining the number and composition of cabinet committees and other core executive bodies. Another formal or institutional resource is the Prime Minister's Office, which supplies him with administrative support (Smith 1999: 75–76). The PM is located at the centre of all networks pervading the core executive. He has access to every policy area the government handles and can select those in which he wants to involve himself directly. Smith (1999: 76, 77) considers this an informal resource. Moreover, the premier can gain an overview over his government's activities—a resource ministers with departmental interests to consider lack (Smith 1999: 76). Another informal resource is the premier's authority. It is a relational resource and is derived from others such as the cabinet (Smith 1994: 346). It also depends on the premier's position. He has, for instance, more authority after a decisive election victory than after having barely succeeded (Smith 1999: 77). One caveat has to be mentioned with regard to the classification in institutional and personal resources. While it is helpful for the analysis, a look at political science literature shows that the classification of resources into these categories varies (e.g. Bennister 2007; Heffernan 2003; Smith 1999). Thus it has to be taken into consideration that this division is not always as clear-cut as one might hope. For instance, the application of an actor's institutional resources is influenced by his personal preferences.

As with any core executive actor, the basis for a prime minister's *power* lies in his capacity to exchange resources with others—mostly ministers, but civil servants or Members of Parliament (MPs) as well (Smith 1999: 74). If he wants to exercise power, he depends on his ministers (Smith 1999: 85). They have resources as well such as expert knowledge and administrative means to make policy in the area they are responsible for. They can also have their own authority (Smith 1995: 110). At the same time they need prime ministerial support to be able to realise a policy. They will have more chances to do so, if the premier backs them (Smith 1999: 85). The prime minister, in turn, needs political support and support on policy, as most policies are developed by ministers (Smith 1998: 67). Moreover, a premier's authority depends on the cabinet as authority needs to be recognised by others (Smith 1999: 79).

Agency is an important part of the analysis of prime ministerial political leadership. How successful a PM is in achieving his political aims depends on his strategies and tactics. There are a range of strategies and tactics a prime minister can employ. He can, for instance, be interventionist, working with a small group of ministers, or he can be collectivist using the cabinet to establish a consensus around policy decisions (Smith 1999: 88). He can also delegate and let his ministers do the work in their departments (Burch 1995: 111). Yet even prime ministers who prefer a dominant leadership style need to build coalitions with ministers because they cannot force them to implement a policy they do not support (Smith 1999: 90). A premier is not likely to use the same strategy across policy fields or time. For instance, Margaret Thatcher used a collective strategy when dealing with the

Falkland crisis in the early 1980s, but an interventionist one in health policy in the late 1980s (Smith 1994: 347). Which tactic a premier applies in a situation depends on (a) how dependent he is on the support of others, (b) how he perceives his situation and (c) the resources others control (Smith 1999: 97, 74). As tactics are a form of agency this explains why heads of government can take decisions which turn out to be unsuccessful (Smith 1999: 97). Overall, it is important to note that "personal strategy is not a result of prime ministerial personality but derives from strategic choices made by the Prime Minister" (Smith 1994: 347).

The prime minister's resources and their application are also influenced by *structure*. In the core executive, he as well as his relationships with other actors are shaped by the rules and institutions of the British executive. Yet these structures are not independent from the actors operating in them. The way in which they use their resources also influence the core executive's structure. A PM can, for example, decide against a policy-making process centred on the cabinet system, if he and the other members of the core executive consider this alternative form of decision-making as legitimate (Smith 1999: 79). External structures affecting the PM's scope of action can, for instance, be the public perception of what constitutes acceptable prime ministerial behaviour (Smith 1999: 80). Although premiers can affect and reinterpret the structure they are in, there is a limit to possible changes to it (Smith 1999: 80). Yet they sometimes can change the structure for their successors (Smith 1999: 105). An example is Tony Blair's change of Prime Minister's Question Time in parliament from a bi-weekly to a weekly session which his successors maintained.

The premier's options to achieve his political aims depend on the *context* in which he operates. If it is positive such as in terms of the economic situation or electoral success, he is less dependent on his colleagues (Smith 1999: 88). His position depends on contextual factors such as the economic situation, the success of policies already implemented, the amount of public support and further external factors such as activities at EU level (Smith 1994: 348).

Key to Smith's model is the idea that prime ministerial power does not automatically come with the office. There are variations to it depending on the context and the distribution of resources (those of the premier and those of other actors' in the core executive). Moreover, it depends on the strategies employed, the relationships in the core executive and the policy field itself (Smith 1995: 110, 112, 124).

2.2.4 The Prime Ministerial Predominance Thesis

Richard Heffernan (2003, 2005a) proposes a variation to the analysis of prime ministerial political leadership with his prime ministerial predominance thesis. His approach is based on the works of Rhodes, Dunleavy and Smith on the core executive combined with elements of Foley's presidentialization thesis.[5]

[5]Marc Bennister applies and further develops the approach (Bennister 2007, 2008).

According to Heffernan (2003: 348) the argument that power is relational in the networks traversing the core executive is only partly correct. Power has not just a relational but also a locational dimension. It depends on where actors are located in the core executive, especially whether at the centre or the periphery. The closer an actor is to the centre the more chances he has to influence the political decision-making process (Heffernan 2005a: 610). Depending on the actors involved and the network in question, dominance of actors over others can be as important as dependency between them. As resources are not evenly distributed among core executive actors, the core executive is not fully pluralistic (Heffernan 2003: 348).

Heffernan (2003: 349) argues that the presidentialization approach can be helpful as it illustrates the changes that have occurred to political leadership in the UK in recent years which, together with a favourable political context, can give a prime minister the opportunity for dominant political leadership. According to Foley (2000: 4) these changes are an increased focus on the individual aspects of leadership as well as on the office-holder's communication and style of presentation. However, Heffernan (2003: 349; 2005a: 608–609) criticises presidentialization approaches for not sufficiently taking into account the amount of collegiality which exists in parliamentary systems. While rejecting them as adequate approaches to explain the governing process in the UK, he believes the explanatory power of the core executive approach can be improved by not just defining power relations in the core executive as pluralistic but also by considering the dominant intra-executive role of the prime minister as presidentialization approaches do. According to this perspective it is possible for the premier to develop a predominant core executive position:

> Being predominant provides the prime minister with more authority and power than other actors. It enables him or her to be a 'stronger or main element' within the core executive, providing them with considerable, but never overwhelming intra-executive influence. Such influence makes the prime minister 'resource rich' within the executive, providing easy access to the resources of other actors and institutions, all of whom may therefore be 'resource poorer', thus empowering the prime minister within all sorts of executive networks. Predominance enables the prime minister to lead, but not command, the executive, to direct, not control, its policy development, and to manage, but not wholly dominate, the legislature. (Heffernan 2003: 349–350)

However, a premier's political leadership is only sometimes predominant. It depends on a number of factors: "Predominance grants the prime minister the 'potential' for leadership within government, but only when personal power resources are married with institutional power resources, and when the prime minister is able to use both wisely and well." (Heffernan 2003: 350). Also dominant political leaders are "not dictators and interaction with colleagues, followers and the public is the key to gain authority and trust" (Bennister 2008: 351).

According to the approach a prime minister can possess a number of institutional and personal resources. Personal resources include "reputation, skill and ability; association with actual or anticipated political success; public popularity; and high standing in his or her party" (Heffernan 2003: 351). These individual resources can strengthen a premier's use of institutional resources (Heffernan 2003: 350).

Heffernan (2003) identifies four key institutional resources. Firstly, the premier is legally the head of the government. Because of this he has certain rights to lead the government such as "appointing and dismissing ministers, allocating and reallocating ministerial portfolios, overseeing government business, managing the cabinet system, and generally supervising the machinery of government" (357). Secondly, he has the ability to set the government's policy agenda with his control of the cabinet system and his influence in Whitehall. Thirdly, he can establish a Prime Minister's Department in all but name using No. 10 Downing Street and the Cabinet Office. Moreover, he can practise political agenda-setting through effective media management (Heffernan 2003: 357). These resources, when possessed, can result in the premier having much authority and impact in the core executive (Heffernan 2003: 347).

With modern parties increasingly led from the centre, the premier's position in the core executive is affected by his position in the party. If a head of government is seen as authoritative this can strengthen his position as party leader and vice versa: "his leadership predominance within the party *facilitates* [emphasis in the original] his prime ministerial predominance within the executive; at the same time prime ministerial predominance *reinforces* [emphasis in the original] his leadership predominance within the party" (Heffernan 2003: 356; see also Heffernan 2005a: 610–611).

The prime ministerial predominance approach does not claim that the premier completely dominates and is independent from other core executive actors. Neither does it argue that every prime minister is predominant. None can lead his government merely according to his own wishes and interests and always has to work with other actors:

> The core executive model, despite stressing the collective nature of UK government, does not simply reassert the notion of cabinet government. The personalisation of the political process and the key role that falls to individual actors within leading institutions makes the prime minister always *a* [emphasis in the original], and sometimes *the* [emphasis in the original] key figure within the key networks comprising UK government. Here the possibility of prime ministerial predominance, and the factors that encourage or impede it, help us understand that the prime minister can only possess considerable, but not overwhelming intra-executive authority and influence. (Heffernan 2003: 364)

There is a valid point in stressing that there is some hierarchy in the core executive focused on the prime minister, resulting in an uneven dependency between actors. Thus, while the PM's capacity for political leadership depends on his ability to exchange resources with others, it does not mean he might never be predominant, if he uses his personal and institutional resources effectively and his leadership environment is favourable to such a leadership. This aspect is again considered in the next chapter in which a modified model of prime ministerial power is developed using Smith's model and the prime ministerial predominance thesis.

2.2.5 A Modified Model of Prime Ministerial Power

Studies on prime ministerial leadership have, as mentioned in Chap. 1, the tendency to remain too broad in their assessment of the distribution of power in the core executive. There is a lack of research analysing changes in the allocation of power in the long term, for instance, by systematic comparison of prime ministers in a specific policy field. The core executive approach assumes that the composition of the core executive differs depending on the policy field and that actors have to operate within an ever changing context. Therefore it can be expected that a prime minister's leadership also varies across time and in each policy field. To close this gap in research a study of prime ministerial political leadership which is (a) long term (covering 31 years), (b) comparative (analysing four office holders) and (c) covering a specific policy field (European policy) is conducted here.

The theoretical tools introduced in this chapter have to be modified to help answer the research questions posed in the introduction. Particularly Smith's model has the disadvantage of introducing many variables which potentially influence a premier's political leadership, but are not sufficiently prioritised. This impedes the development of hypotheses and their operationalisation. To apply the model in its original form risks not to explain much in the end—as everything might have an impact in some way. Such criticism has been made of interactionist leadership approaches in general (Fliegauf et al. 2008: 415). To minimise this problem the present study focuses on three dimensions: (a) the actors in the core executive apart from the premier, (b) the parliamentary party and (c) public opinion. Despite this focus it is not argued that factors such as economic or political context are irrelevant to a PM's political leadership. Yet one can expect these three to potentially have a particularly large influence for several reasons:

For one, by focusing on actors in the core executive such as ministers handling a policy area, the basic assumption of the core executive approach is taken into account that power is based on interdependence. It can only be exerted by exchanging resources with others. This also applies to the premier who never has all resources necessary to make policy on his own. The prime ministerial predominance thesis shares this view and argues that no matter how predominant a head of government might be, he needs the support of the other core executive actors to exert power. Therefore, these actors in the European policy core executive need to be identified and their resources, strategies and tactics analysed as they constrain or enable the prime minister in his political leadership. Moreover, the PM's behaviour towards these potential constraints is studied, including his management of cabinet and other core executive actors, for instance, through his rights of appointment and dismissal and of setting the cabinet agenda.

It is also possible for the premier to conduct two-level politics in European policy. According to the two-level-game approach international and domestic politics cannot be analysed separately as they are linked and influence each other (Putnam 1988: 459). Partly due to media attention

> participation on the world stage normally gives a head of government a special advantage vis-à-vis his or her domestic opposition. Thus, although international policy coordination is hampered by high transaction costs, heads of government may also reap what we might term 'transaction benefits'. (Putnam 1988: 452)

Negotiators with higher status (e.g. heads of government) tend to have more bargaining power in the negotiations due to their status. As a result other negotiators tend to prefer to negotiate directly with them than with lower ranked ones (e.g. ministers) (Putnam 1988: 452). It is also important to note that a national player negotiating at the international—here the European—level does not just act as agent of his domestic constituents but has his own preferences and policy interests (Putnam 1988: 456). Also, the head of government can use decisions taken in international negotiations as leverage to facilitate domestic policy change he would otherwise not have been able to enforce: "International negotiations sometimes enable government leaders to do what they privately wish to do, but are powerless to do domestically" (Putnam 1988: 457). This has implications for the prime minister's relationship with the other actors in the core executive, because his membership in the European Council potentially enhances his leeway in relation to his ministers as he speaks for the UK at these meetings (Kavanagh and Seldon 2000: 320). Therefore, when studying the relationships in the core executive, the premier's options for two-level politics are analysed as well.

Interactionist approaches to the study of political leaders are criticised for ignoring the aspect of the follower. While the leader and his behaviour are analysed in detail, his relationship to his followers, for instance the members of his party in parliament, is not taken into account (Fliegauf et al. 2008: 399; for their argument see Fliegauf et al. 2008: 407–410). This criticism is valid. If the premier wants to implement policies, he depends on the parliamentary party's support. Without it he will not be successful in the long term and will not be able to exert power: "the leader's power (in majoritarian systems) is contingent on tolerance of the party. Parties will tend to [be] tolerant as long as the leader appears an electoral asset" (Bennister 2008: 347). Also, by specifically considering the relationship between parliamentary party and premier in this study, Heffernan's argument that prime ministerial predominance in the party and in the core executive reinforce each other, is taken into account (Heffernan 2003: 356). By choosing the parliamentary party in government and not the opposition as focal point of analysis it is taken into consideration that the government controls the legislature in the British political system (Norton 2003: 16). The parliamentary opposition therefore does not have the possibility to influence the legislative process as much as in other political systems such as, for instance, the German one (Hübner and Münch 1999: 136). Thus it is less of a potential constraint on the prime minister's political leadership than his own parliamentary party.[6] The premier can manage his parliamentary party, for example, with his right of appointment and dismissal. In the present study his party management is analysed and the parliamentary party's behaviour in European policy. In this context the size of the government's parliamentary majority needs to be considered, too. For a head of government with a decisive majority it tends to be easier to enact his legislative programme even if not all MPs support it, than for one with a slim or non-existent majority (Riddell 2004: 826–827).

Beside the prime ministerial followers in the parliamentary arena there are also the voters. Smith's model does consider the public as an influencing factor on a prime minister's political leadership, but only very generally in form of popular support as part of the context a prime minister operates in (Smith 1999: 75). Yet followers are an important part of analysing a democratic head of government's political leadership: "Leadership is relational, a process of interaction with followers. Without supporters, followers and indeed voters, a leader's tenure will not survive" (Bennister 2008: 347). A PM can try to lead public opinion in a certain direction to be able to implement a policy. But he might also try to avoid discussing an issue publicly, if he thinks he might not be able to persuade the public of his policy. Moreover, as with any other democratic politician the premier's mandate depends on the support of the electorate. To remain electable, he needs to consider the public's view (as these are his potential supporters at the next election) and cannot discount it completely. Situational and societal change can also be covered by considering public opinion. Such contextual changes are important for a prime minister's political leadership, if they result in a change in the public's preferences (Fliegauf et al. 2008: 416).

With regard to this third key aspect impacting on prime ministerial political leadership, a caveat needs to be mentioned. Public opinion is a diffuse phenomenon. It is not a collective actor such as the parliamentary party or cabinet, both of which a premier can try to influence directly. Instead a PM can only exert influence on public opinion in a constrained and mediated way by using his resources of media management and political communication. As mass media has become a crucial part of the political system today, political leadership cannot be studied without explicit reference to it (Helms 2000: 426). From the perspective of the prime minister this is because he attempts to use the media to project a positive image and to strengthen his position as leader (Heffernan 2006: 597). Moreover, his media management can contribute to him becoming an "opinion leader" (Seymour-Ure 2003: 57), allowing him to influence or even change the public's attitude on an issue or policy or to give priority to particular policy aims. In this context it can also be analysed whether the personalisation of politics and centralisation of the political decision-making process in the executive in recent years as mentioned by presidentialization concepts (e.g. Mughan 2000; Foley 2000; Poguntke and Webb 2005) have enhanced a

[6]This analysis will focus on the parliamentary party in the House of Commons. The House of Lords is part of the legislative process, but its powers are limited. It can delay a bill's passage for a year. Yet with few exceptions, the Commons can then reintroduce and pass it in the next session without the Lords' consent (Kelly and Maer 2016).

prime minister's leadership role. The study at hand analyses public opinion on European policy between 1976 and 2007 and how it changed during this time period. In a second step prime ministerial media management is analysed to understand how the four prime ministers tried to influence these trends in public opinion on Europe through it.

Based on the theoretical background outlined in this chapter, two hypotheses on prime ministerial political leadership can be developed. One suggests a form of collective leadership, the other a prime minister-centred approach.

With regard to the relevant core executive actors, it can on the one hand be expected that the PM can retain a predominant position in the core executive due to his central position in it and despite his need to exchange resources with other core executive actors. He is, moreover, assumed to be successful in two-level-politics. In the context of his political leadership in European policy the prime minister is potentially more powerful than his domestic colleagues as it is he who speaks for the UK in the European Council, which for long has been an influential force shaping European political decision-making. If the heads of government and state reach agreement on an issue, it is expected to be difficult for ministers to oppose it even if they would have preferred another outcome. Yet for a prime minister in a collective leadership setting this can be assumed to be different. For him the other core executive actors such as ministers with their own authority and autonomy constrain his scope of action. He has to involve them in the policy-making process and to consider their interests.

On the second dimension—the parliamentary party—the premier in the constellation of a prime minister-centred political leadership is expected to be only marginally constrained by his parliamentary party. A premier with a solid majority is able to enact his legislative programme even if not all MPs support it. In this case, his predominant position in the core executive enhances his predominance in his parliamentary party and vice versa. But for a premier bound in a form of collective leadership this is expected to be different. He has to consider his parliamentary party's interests much more. If his policies split the party, he risks losing his power base. Premiers in such constellations often lack decisive parliamentary majorities. To be able to enact their legislative programme they are expected to have to compromise with the various factions within their parliamentary party.

With regard to the third aspect—public opinion—again two different hypotheses can be drawn up: from a prime minister-centred view the personalisation of politics in recent years and a centralisation of the political decision-making process in the executive as noted in presidentialization concepts have enhanced the PM's leadership role. Through media management he is expected to be capable of influencing and partly dominating public debate and to become an opinion leader. Yet, if the prime minister is seen as part of a form of collective political leadership, his options to become an opinion leader are expected to be more limited, as he is only one of several government actors who use media management to try to shape public debate and influence public and media opinion. Therefore, he is unable to influence the public debate, cannot be an opinion leader and has to consider public and media opinion as constraining factors.

In the following the two theses on prime ministerial political leadership in European policy are summarised:

Thesis 1: Prime Ministerial Predominance-Thesis
The political leadership of the British prime minister in European policy is dominant and has become more dominant over the years. One can expect that he can retain a predominant position in the core executive due to his position at its centre and if he uses his resources of which he has a wide range at his disposal effectively. If this is the case, he can successfully achieve his preferred policies despite the need to exchange resources with other core executive actors.

If one assumes that the prime minister is a predominant leader, in particular the following can be expected:

- He is able to conduct two-level-politics and through his European Council membership to build up pressure to overcome domestic resistance to his policies.
- He is only marginally constrained by his parliamentary party and therefore able to enact his legislative programme in this policy area.
- He is strengthened as a leading figure who becomes an opinion leader dominating the public debate. This is due to the increasing personalisation of political debate and the centralisation of political decision-making.

Thesis 2: Collective Leadership-Thesis
The prime minister is embedded in the European policy core executive and one of several actors who all have resources they need to exchange to exert power. While he has more resources than others one can assume that he is constrained in his freedom to take political decisions in European policy by the need to exchange resources with other actors in the core executive. Therefore, political leadership of government is a collective endeavour requiring the prime minister to consider potential constraints.

If one assumes that the prime minister is a collective leader, in particular the following can be expected:

- He depends on the other actors in the core executive, who potentially constrain his leeway, and needs to consider their positions when taking political decisions.
- He has to take into account the interests of his parliamentary party when trying to enact his legislative programme in this policy area and has to avoid intraparty splits as they might endanger his own power base.
- His options to become an opinion leader are more limited, as he is only one of several core executive actors using media management to try to shape public debate and influence public and media opinion.

In the following analysis it is studied which of the two hypotheses is more fitting to explain prime ministerial political leadership in UK European policy and to what extent the prime minister's leadership changed over the course of the time period covered in the study. The analysis takes place on two levels. The first is temporal: by analysing the Prime Ministers James Callaghan, Margaret Thatcher, John Major and Tony Blair a systematic comparison over 31 years can be made. Secondly, the analysis focuses on European policy. Due to the long period covered in this study a limitation of scope is necessary. Therefore, it deals with European monetary policy focusing on the Exchange Rate Mechanism (ERM), the core of the European Monetary System (EMS), as well as Economic and Monetary Union (EMU) and the euro. As European monetary policy is a sensitive issue with significant domestic implications, any prime minister is expected to show much interest in it. To what extent he can influence the decision-making process on it is analysed from Chap. 7. But first a short overview is given of European monetary policy between 1976 and 2007 and the UK's role in it.

References

Bennister, M. (2007). Tony Blair and John Howard: Comparative predominance and 'institution stretch' in the UK and Australia. *The British Journal of Politics and International Relations, 9*(3), 327–345.

Bennister, M. (2008). Blair and Howard: Predominant prime ministers compared. *Parliamentary Affairs, 61*(2), 334–355.

Burch, M. (1995). Prime minister and Whitehall. In D. Shell & R. Hodder-Williams (Eds.), *Churchill to Major: The British prime ministership since 1945* (pp. 104–136). Armonk: M. E. Sharpe.

Crossmann, R. H. S. (1963). Introduction. In W. Bagehot (Ed.), *The English constitution* (2nd ed., pp. 1–57). London: Collins/Fontana Library.

Dunleavy, P., & Rhodes, R. A. W. (1990). Core executive studies in Britain. *Public Administration, 68*(1), 3–28.

Elgie, R. (1995). *Political leadership in liberal democracies*. Basingstoke: Macmillan.

Fliegauf, M. T., Kießling, A., & Novy, L. (2008). Leader und Follower – Grundzüge eines interpersonalen Ansatzes zur Analyse politischer Führungsleistung. *Zeitschrift für Politikwissenschaft, 18*(4), 399–421.

Foley, M. (1993). *The rise of the British presidency*. Manchester: Manchester University Press.

Foley, M. (2000). *The British presidency: Tony Blair and the politics of public leadership*. Manchester: Manchester University Press.

Gamble, A. (1990). Theories of British politics. *Political Studies, 38*(3), 404–420.

Hay, C. (1995). Structure and agency. In D. Marsh & G. Stoker (Eds.), *Theory and methods in political science* (pp. 189–206). Basingstoke: Macmillan.

Heffernan, R. (2003). Prime ministerial predominance? Core executive politics in the UK. *British Journal of Politics and International Relations, 5*(3), 347–372.

Heffernan, R. (2005a). Exploring (and explaining) the British prime minister. *British Journal of Politics and International Relations, 7*(4), 605–620.

Heffernan, R. (2005b). Why the prime minister cannot be a president: Comparing institutional imperatives in Britain and America. *Parliamentary Affairs, 58*(1), 53–70.

Heffernan, R. (2006). The prime minister and the news media: Political communication as a leadership resource. *Parliamentary Affairs, 59*(4), 582–598.

Helms, L. (2000). "Politische Führung" als politikwissenschaftliches Problem. *Politische Vierteljahresschrift, 41*(3), 411–434.

Helms, L. (2005a). Politische Führung. In D. Nohlen & R.-O. Schultze (Eds.), *Lexikon der Politikwissenschaft, Part 2* (3rd ed., pp. 737–738). Munich: Verlag C.H. Beck.

Helms, L. (2005b). *Presidents, prime ministers and chancellors: Executive leadership in western democracies*. Basingstoke: Palgrave.

Helms, L. (2005c). *Regierungsorganisation und politische Führung in Deutschland*. Wiesbaden: VS Verlag für Sozialwissenschaften.

Hennessy, P. (2001). *The prime minister: The office and its holders since 1945* (2nd ed.). London: Penguin.
Hübner, E., & Münch, U. (1999). *Das Politische System Großbritanniens: Eine Einführung* (2nd ed.). Munich: Verlag C.H. Beck.
Kaiser, A. (2001). Die politische Theorie des Neo-Institutionalismus: James March und Johan Olsen. In A. Brodocz & G. S. Schaal (Eds.), *Politische Theorien der Gegenwart II: Eine Einführung* (pp. 253–282). Opladen: Leske + Budrich.
Kavanagh, D., & Seldon, A. (2000). *The powers behind the prime minister: The hidden influence of Number Ten* (2nd ed.). London: HarperCollins.
Kelly, R., & Maer, L. (2016, February 25). *The Parliament Acts,* House of Commons Library Briefing Paper No. 00675.
Lijphart, A. (2012). *Patterns of democracy: Government forms and performance in thirty-six countries* (2nd ed.). New Haven: Yale University Press.
Marsh, D., Richards, D., & Smith, M. J. (2003). Unequal plurality: Towards an asymmetric model of British politics. *Government and Opposition, 38*(3), 306–332.
Mayntz, R., & Scharpf, F. W. (1995). Der Ansatz des akteurszentrierten Institutionalismus. In R. Mayntz & F. W. Scharpf (Eds.), *Gesellschaftliche Selbstregulierung und politische Steuerung*. Campus: Frankfurt.
Mughan, A. (2000). *Media and the presidentialization of parliamentary elections*. Basingstoke: Palgrave.
Norton, P. (2003). National parliaments and the European Union. *Managerial Law, 45*(5/6), 5–25.
Poguntke, T., & Webb, P. (Eds.). (2005). *The presidentialization of politics: A comparative study of modern democracies*. Oxford: Oxford University Press.
Putnam, R. D. (1988). Diplomacy and domestic politics: The logic of two-level games. *International Organization, 42*(3), 427–460.
Rhodes, R. A. W. (1995). From prime ministerial power to core executive. In R. A. W. Rhodes & P. Dunleavy (Eds.), *Prime minister, cabinet and core executive* (pp. 11–37). Basingstoke: Macmillan.
Riddell, P. (2004). Prime ministers and parliament. *Parliamentary Affairs, 57*(4), 814–829.
Scharpf, F. W. (2000). *Interaktionsformen: Akteurszentrierter Institutionalismus in der Politikforschung*. Opladen: Leske + Budrich.
Seldon, A. (1994). Policy making and cabinet. In D. Kavanagh & A. Seldon (Eds.), *The Major effect* (pp. 154–166). London: Macmillan.
Seymour-Ure, C. (2003). *Prime ministers and the media: Issues of power and control*. Oxford: Blackwell.
Smith, M. J. (1994). The core executive and the resignation of Mrs Thatcher. *Public Administration, 72*(3), 341–363.
Smith, M. J. (1995). Interpreting the rise and fall of Margaret Thatcher: Power dependence and the core executive. In R. A. W. Rhodes & P. Dunleavy (Eds.), *Prime minister, cabinet and core executive* (pp. 108–124). Basingstoke: Macmillan.
Smith, M. J. (1998). Reconceptualizing the British state: Theoretical and empirical challenges to central government. *Public Administration, 76*(1), 45–72.
Smith, M. J. (1999). *The core executive in Britain*. Basingstoke: Macmillan.

Chapter 3
The United Kingdom and European Monetary Policy 1976–2007: Exchange Rate Mechanism and Economic and Monetary Union

When the EC members in the late 1980s began planning for an economic and monetary union, it was not a novel idea. Once before, in December 1969, the leaders of the six founding members had decided to establish an economic and monetary union (Knipping 2004: 156, 167). In the late 1960s, the Bretton Woods system of fixed but adjustable exchange rates, based on the Dollar's gold parity and with the US-currency as anchor, had run into problems. The EC members had to battle growing inflation due to hurried capital movements and unrealistic exchange rates. Already then about 50% of their trade was conducted within the group, so that some kind of closer European level monetary cooperation became necessary. The Werner Plan from October 1970 argued for a three-step process to establish a common economic policy, a common central bank system and to fix the exchange rates of the EC member states among each other by 1980 (Hillenbrand 2008: 403, 404). The first step to closer monetary integration was taken in the early 1970s with the creation of the 'snake in the tunnel', a mechanism to limit exchange rate fluctuations between the member states' currencies. Although Britain was not yet a European Community member when the project started, Edward Heath's government committed it to join. However, when it did in May 1972, the mechanism had already come under strain as a result of turbulences on the international financial markets. Due to strong pressure from speculators, sterling had to leave the system already in July 1972 (Gowland et al. 2010: 79). When the world economic crisis deepened during the 1970s, the EC members eventually gave up the Werner Plan and the goal of EMU (Hillenbrand 2008: 405).[1]

Interest in actively achieving more exchange rate stability at the European level resurfaced at the end of the 1970s. Based on a French-German proposal, the European Council on 5 December 1978 agreed to establish the European Monetary System (EMS). The system's core was the Exchange Rate Mechanism (ERM), which was to regulate exchange rate fluctuations between participating currencies

[1]For details on the crisis' impact on the EC members' economies, see Ludlow (1982: 7–12).

B. Bujard, *The British Prime Minister in the Core Executive*, Contributions to Political Science, https://doi.org/10.1007/978-3-319-89953-4_3

(Stephens 1997: 5). James Callaghan and his government had reacted reluctantly to the proposal for several reasons. One was the devastating experience of having been forced out of the 'snake' in 1972 (Gowland et al. 2010: 79). While the government welcomed the goal of greater monetary stability in Europe, it voiced doubts as to whether the planned EMS could prove durable unless measures to create a greater degree of convergence between the EC economies were introduced as well (Financial Times 1978). Moreover, it preferred the establishment of a wider monetary regime which would include the USA and Japan (De Jonquieres 1978). It also expected that sterling would have to devalue, if it joined the ERM, which would result in a rise of prices. With a general election coming up, the PM was not willing to jeopardise his chances of re-election (Jenkins 1978). Therefore, Callaghan announced that the UK at this time would not join the ERM. It would, however, take part in the development of the wider monetary system (HC Deb 6 December 1978, cc1421–1424). By way of this "halfway house solution" (The Guardian 1978) the government intended to ensure its inclusion in the decision-making process on the EMS and to appease its parliamentary party of which a large section opposed the EMS. After this, the question of ERM membership was off the political agenda for the remainder of Labour's time in office. In May 1979 the Conservatives won the general election.

The European Monetary System established in 1979 consisted of four parts: a currency unit, an exchange rate and intervention system, various credit mechanisms and a coordinated exchange rate policy towards third countries. The European Currency Unit (ECU) functioned as a basket of the EC members' currencies and was related to their economic performance. The currencies in the ERM were allowed to fluctuate by 2.25% on either side of an agreed central parity against the ECU. If the other members agreed, the central parity could be adjusted in line with the economic development through realignment. The central banks were responsible for balancing the currency fluctuations in the ERM through buying and selling currency reserves. There were several credit mechanisms central banks could use to stabilise their currencies (Hillenbrand 2008: 405–406).

With the Conservatives in office the UK government's reluctant position on the ERM appeared to change. The Tories were viewed as a pro-European party in the late 1970s (Geddes 2013: 67). Moreover, Margaret Thatcher had criticised the decision to stay out of the ERM when Callaghan had announced it in parliament on 6 December 1978 (HC Deb 6 December 1978, c1424). At her first European Council in June 1979 the new prime minister declared that the country would deposit its quota of foreign currency and gold reserves with the European Monetary Co-operation Fund, which had been set up to manage the EMS. Thus, from now on the pound would be part of the basket of currencies which formed the basis on which the ECU's value was decided. This was taken as a sign that Britain would soon join the ERM (George 1998: 148). Yet before coming into office the Tories had at no time promised to revise the previous government's decision, if they were to take over the government and their election manifesto had not included any reference to the ERM (Thompson 1996: 14).

Meanwhile, the ERM in the 1980s was an increasingly successful system of fixed but adjustable exchange rates. It could not eliminate exchange rate risks but managed to avoid stark short term fluctuations and made the assessment of currency developments easier and more reliable. With the effective operation, trust in the ERM grew (Hillenbrand 2008: 406–407).

The completion of the Single European Act (SEA) in the mid-1980s and the establishment of the internal market led some EC members to reconsider further European monetary policy integration. Many supporters thought that earlier attempts like the Werner Plan had failed because they had lacked political integration, which was now to be changed (Gowland et al. 2010: 118). In June 1988 the European Council agreed to set up an expert group consisting of the presidents of the national central banks, which was to make suggestions for a European economic and monetary union (Hillenbrand 2008: 407). The Delors group, named after its chairman Jacques Delors, the President of the European Commission, published its final report on 12 April 1989. It envisaged a three-step process to establish economic and monetary union. During the first stage, planned to begin on 1 July 1990, the coordination of monetary policy between the EC members was to be intensified. Additionally, all were to join the ERM and the necessary treaty changes for the further integrative steps were to be initiated. During the second stage a European central bank with initially limited competences was to be created. In the third stage the exchange rates of member currencies were to be fixed and a single currency introduced. Moreover, member states would transfer economic and monetary policy competences onto the European level (Hillenbrand 2008: 408).

Despite British reservations the European Council in June 1989 decided to start the first stage on 1 July 1990. An intergovernmental conference (IGC) was to be set up to develop the necessary institutional requirements for the Delors Plan's further stages. In autumn 1990 the European Council agreed that stage two was to begin on 1 January 1994 (Hillenbrand 2008: 408).

Margaret Thatcher, though vehemently opposed to a single currency, did not take much interest in the Delors Groups' activities. She trusted assurances by German Chancellor Helmut Kohl that he opposed monetary and economic union as well. Moreover, her government at the time focused on another issue related to European monetary policy: the possibility of joining the ERM (Gowland et al. 2010: 109). Like Callaghan, Thatcher was sceptical about the ERM. She favoured flexible exchange rates, believing fixed ones would not work because there was "no way in which one can buck the market" (Thatcher 2011: 703). Yet the Conservative Party's official position on European monetary cooperation since 1979 had been that Britain should join the ERM "when the time is right" (Thatcher 2011: 692). In the early 1980s Thatcher's scepticism was shared by most of her cabinet. The government discussed the issue several times between 1979 and 1983, yet did not alter the policy. But there was a shift in the mid-1980s. Throughout 1985 ERM membership was discussed at several core executive meetings. At one meeting in November most ministers including Chancellor Nigel Lawson and Foreign Secretary Geoffrey Howe argued for entry. Thatcher vetoed it (Burch and Holliday 1996: 220–223). This remained the status quo until June 1989, when before the Madrid European Council Lawson and

Howe pressed her to tone down her opposition to entry. She relented and in Madrid named more precise conditions for joining. But she managed to keep up her veto on entry until 1990 (Gowland et al. 2010: 113, 114).

As Thatcher did not allow her chancellor to put sterling into the ERM, he decided to pursue a policy close to that. From February 1987 sterling shadowed the Deutschmark as if it was part of the ERM. In spring 1988 Thatcher publicly made Lawson's exchange rate policy responsible for the growing inflation. From then on the divisions between the two became increasingly public. In October 1989 Lawson resigned (Gowland et al. 2010: 114).

Thatcher remained sceptical about ERM entry. But after Lawson's resignation and her dismissal of Geoffrey Howe from the Foreign Office,[2] she had two new supporters of ERM membership in her government: Chancellor John Major and Foreign Secretary Douglas Hurd (Burch and Holliday 1996: 224). They eventually persuaded her to agree to entry. This had several reasons. Firstly, Major's and Hurd's relationship with Thatcher was better than that of Howe and Lawson had been (at least in the second half of the 1980s). Secondly, she could not afford to lose another two cabinet members over the ERM. Thirdly, in July 1990 Thatcher lost a loyal and outspoken supporter in her quest to prevent ERM membership when Trade and Industry Secretary Nicolas Ridley had to resign.[3] Fourthly, the government's anti-inflation policy had been shattered by the economic boom of the late 1980s. Interest rates were higher than ever since 1981 and sterling was vulnerable to speculative pressure (Gowland et al. 2010: 114–115).

At a meeting with her chancellor on 13 June 1990 Thatcher finally agreed that the UK would join the ERM, although Major failed to persuade her to assent to immediate entry. She insisted to wait until autumn. After further pressure from Major, Thatcher at last backed down at a meeting on 4 October. To forestall any possible further doubts on Thatcher's part, the chancellor pushed for the announcement of the decision on the next day and the UK joined the ERM on the following Monday, 8 October 1990 (Stephens 1997: 157, 171–172).

Despite ERM membership, Thatcher remained unconvinced about further European monetary integration in form of a single currency (Thatcher 2011: 724–726). Yet at the Madrid European Council she had also announced that Britain would propose an alternative to the Delors Plan. The government subsequently came up with two proposals. Firstly, John Major in November 1989 introduced a concept for a system of competing currencies, drawn up by Lawson before his resignation. The basic idea was that currencies would compete with each other. The weaker ones would be driven out of the market and this might eventually lead to a single currency. The plan did not gain much support with the European partners, who soon considered it a device to delay further monetary integration (Stephens 1997: 160–161). In July 1990 the government then presented the 'hard ECU' plan which consisted of

[2]Thatcher had moved Howe after the Madrid summit to be leader of the House of Commons.

[3]This was due to an interview in which he had made anti-German remarks. For the interview, see Lawson (1990).

developing the existing European Currency Unit (ECU) into a common currency. The plan proposed an evolutionary process which could eventually result in a single currency but did not have to. It also proved unsuccessful, in part because it was introduced too late into the European level discussions (Stephens 1997: 161–162; Wall 2008: 102, 103). Moreover, Thatcher sabotaged the plan when she said in parliament in October that she did not believe the 'hard ECU' would become much used. Furthermore, being a member of the British parliament and agreeing to join a European single currency were mutually exclusive, she commented, and with it effectively destroyed her government's current European policy (Stephens 1997: 181–182). Her comments also prompted Geoffrey Howe to resign as deputy prime minister. In his resignation speech he criticised her European policy: "The tragedy is... that the Prime Minister's perceived attitude towards Europe is running increasingly serious risks for the future of our nation. It risks minimizing our influence and maximising our chances of being once again shut out" (HC Deb 13 November 1990, c466). His resignation helped trigger a leadership contest which on 22 November 1990 saw Thatcher's resignation (Gowland et al. 2010: 116).

Her successor John Major had to continue to deal with the plans for EMU. He supported ERM but not EMU membership. Nonetheless, he wanted to keep all options open for Britain on the single currency (Major 2000: 142, 585). When a new European treaty was negotiated at Maastricht in December 1991, he achieved an opt-out for Britain from the third stage of EMU (Stephens 1997: 188).

The ratification of the Treaty on European Union (TEU) or Maastricht Treaty proved difficult and exposed the divisions in the Conservative Party over European integration. The main point of contention concerned the concept of a future European Union. Many Conservatives believed the treaty would lead to a European entity that would constrain Britain's freedom of action and diminish its national sovereignty (Heath et al. 2001: 69). In May 1992 the Conservatives unexpectedly won the general election.[4] The election outcome had severe consequences for the treaty ratification, which only began after the election. The government's majority shrunk from 88 to 21 mandates and several strongly Eurosceptic Conservative politicians became new MPs. Shortly after the election 22 Conservative MPs voted against the treaty bill—the *European Communities (Amendment) Bill*—in its second reading (Gowland et al. 2010: 120). When in early summer the Danes voted against the Maastricht Treaty in a referendum, 70 Conservative MPs signed an Early Day Motion requesting the government to change its European policy (Stephens 1997: 204–205). Cabinet ministers such as Michael Portillo, Peter Lilley and Michael Howard argued for the UK to step back from the treaty. Major refused, but agreed to temporarily suspend the ratification process (Stephens 1997: 205; Wallace 1994: 294).

[4]It had been unexpected among other things because the election had taken place in the middle of the longest recession since the 1930s and went against the trend in Europe, which in other countries saw government parties being voted out of office (Butler and Kavanagh 1992: 269).

Meanwhile, Britain's ERM membership led to major problems. The exchange rate at which sterling had joined in 1990 could not be maintained. In the early 1990s the British economy was declining. Like the other ERM members the UK aligned its interest rates to those of Germany. Due to reunification there was a higher inflation risk in Germany, which the Bundesbank tried to contain by setting high interest rates. This weakened the other members' currencies and their exchange rates came closer to the bottom of their bands in the mechanism. A solution to the problem would have been to devalue these currencies. But France refused to contemplate this (Gowland et al. 2010: 121). On 16 September 1992 the UK government announced the suspension of ERM membership as sterling's exchange rate had fallen beneath its allowed lower limit in the mechanism due to speculative pressure (Gowland et al. 2010: 122). The exit destroyed the Conservative government's reputation for competent economic policy-making (Geddes 2013: 175). Moreover, ERM membership had not only been the central pillar of the government's European policy but also the basis for its economic policy (Jay 1994: 186).

Meanwhile, the Major government still had to ratify the Maastricht Treaty. On 4 November 1992 it narrowly won a paving motion, a vote to revive the ratification process of the Maastricht Bill, with 319 to 316 votes (Cowley and Stuart 2012). But the treaty still had hurdles to take. On 22 July 1993 the government lost a vote on an amendment to the Social Charter with 316 to 324 votes. Major called a vote of confidence, which the government won the next day. This cleared the way for the UK to finally ratify the treaty on 2 August 1993 (Baker et al. 1994: 60).

After the ERM exit European monetary integration remained much debated in British politics as the establishment of the single currency progressed. In 1994 the second stage of EMU began with the formation of the European Monetary Institute. From 1997 to 1999 the EU members taking part in EMU would be in the third stage, which meant the establishment of the single currency under the charge of a European Central Bank. John Major further intended to keep all options open on Britain's position towards the single currency. Due to the opt-out negotiated at Maastricht the UK did not have to inform the other members of its position on EMU until December 1997. The premier tried to ignore the issue as much as possible, hoping the single currency might not come into existence after all. His avoidance strategy, however, proved unfeasible as the Eurosceptics in his party demanded that the 1997 general election manifesto included a refusal to join EMU (Gowland et al. 2010: 124). Moreover, an increasing number of cabinet ministers saw the promise of a referendum on membership in the single currency as eventually inevitable, though Ken Clarke, chancellor since May 1993, was opposed. Major favoured a referendum as well (Stephens 1997: 337–339). In April 1996 a compromise was reached: the Conservative election manifesto would pledge a referendum. But it would only be called after government and parliament had taken the decision to join the euro. This meant that during the 1997 election campaign the Conservatives would keep the option to join the single currency open (Stephens 1997: 342–344).

When the Labour Party took over the government on 1 May 1997 it was expected at home and in the EU member states that Britain's relation with Europe would improve. This was partly due to the Conservatives' performance as well as to promises Labour had made with regard to Britain's role in Europe (Bache and Nugent 2007: 529). During the election campaign Labour had also pledged to hold a referendum on the single currency, if the government should decide to join it. Through this move the party managed to neutralise the euro as an election issue (Geddes 2013: 89).

On 6 May 1997, 5 days after coming into office, the new Chancellor Gordon Brown announced the operational independence of the Bank of England. From now on interest rates would be set by the Bank, not the government. This could be interpreted as a step to fulfil the Maastricht convergence criteria to prepare entry to the Eurozone, but Brown argued that the decision had been taken for reasons of domestic financial policy (Gowland et al. 2010: 144–145).

On EMU the government faced logistical problems. Although the euro was only to be launched on 1 January 1999, the Maastricht Treaty stipulated that every EU member wanting to join in the first wave had to inform the others of its intention by the end of 1997. This meant that the government would have had less than 7 months to conclude the practical and legislative preparations for entry, including conducting the referendum it had promised, if it wanted to adopt the euro (Gowland and Turner 2000: 332). Yet the new government was reluctant to take a decision on the single currency. This was among other things because views on whether Britain should join in 1999 (or at all) tended to be sceptical in various places: the Treasury was against joining in 1999 because of the lack of convergence between the British economy and those of the other member states. Industry and business were sending out mixed signals. While most industry representatives in principle supported joining the euro, they did not necessarily back a starting date of January 1999. Opinion polls and focus groups pointed to strong public opposition to membership. The British press, too, was predominantly against entry. The PM worried that their hostility might have a negative impact on his government's popularity as well as on a yes-vote in a referendum (Gowland et al. 2010: 156–158). Blair's chief press secretary Alastair Campbell wanted to avoid a dispute with the mostly Eurosceptic (and conservative) media he had for so long wooed to support New Labour (Rawnsley 2001: 75). Also, senior Labour politicians were divided on the euro. While Blair wanted to keep all options open—including entry before the next general election—to demonstrate to the other EU members the UK's commitment to European integration, Brown thought it wrong to see the issue as a political one. To him it was only an economic question. He believed there was not enough convergence between the economies of the UK and the other EU members and thought the Treasury had not sufficiently prepared entry (Rawnsley 2001: 79–80).

On 27 October 1997 the chancellor gave a statement in the House of Commons on the euro. While he said that the government principally supported entry to a successful euro, he also announced that a final decision would be taken in the next parliament. To be able to come to an informed verdict five economic tests were to be conducted. Based on their outcome the government would decide whether Britain should join the Eurozone (HC Deb 27 October 1997, cc583–588). Despite Brown's announcement the government's position on the euro appeared ambiguous in subsequent years. One of the reasons for this was infighting in the core executive over the government's euro policy. Cabinet members such as Peter Mandelson and Foreign Secretary Robin Cook repeatedly made the case for joining the euro in public. Such statements often led to conflicts with the chancellor, who wished to stifle the debate about the single currency and thought the other ministers infringed on his area of responsibility (Rawnsley 2001: 386–389). Moreover, the prime minister did not appear to want to conduct an early referendum. Instead he preferred a step-by-step approach hoping to create an environment in which joining the euro was eventually seen as a positive development. His strategy was two-fold: at the political level the government tried to establish a non-party alliance in support of membership together with the Liberal Democrats and several Conservatives. But the chances of success for 'Britain in Europe', the cross-party organisation launched on 14 October 1999, were limited as its leading members were divided on the strategy the organisation should pursue. At the economic level Blair's strategy concerned the collaboration between Whitehall and industry to jointly prepare for the practical questions arising from entry. This process was to be supported by the national changeover plan which included several government measures to prepare for the euro such as making computer systems of departments euro-compatible (Gowland et al. 2010: 164–166). But the premier's announcement of the plan painted once more an ambiguous picture as Blair omitted to name a possible entry date to the euro. This was surprising as the plan included a detailed timetable by which the euro could be introduced once government, parliament and the public in a referendum had voted for entry. The PM also did not indicate when such a referendum could be held (HC Deb 23 February 1999, cc179–183). His announcement was extensively discussed in the British press (see Sect. 10.4), but the government did not follow up the momentum Blair had generated with his speech in the British debate on euro membership and it eventually faded (Rawnsley 2001: 236).

The government also had to address the question of re-entry to the ERM. According to the Maastricht Treaty one of the criteria for being allowed to join the Eurozone was for the applicant country to be part of the ERM 2 years prior to entry. Members of the Blair administration well remembered the disastrous experience of the exit in 1992. The government attempted to persuade the other EU members that it would suffice to achieve exchange rate stability for 2 years without re-entering the ERM, but was overruled (Gowland et al. 2010: 163). In any case, Britain did not re-join the ERM during Blair's premiership.

On 9 June 2003 Brown presented his assessment of the five tests on euro compatibility. The parliamentary announcement had been preceded by many discussions about how the results were to be presented, as No. 10 Downing Street and the Treasury had different views on this (Seldon 2008: 208–213). In his statement the chancellor said that only one test had been fully met. On the other four the government still had work to do (HC Deb 9 June 2003, cc407–415). But his announcement was composed in a way that membership supporters and opponents in the Labour Party alike could support it. Moreover, the government managed to persuade Brussels and the other EU members that Britain actually wanted to join the Eurozone (Gowland et al. 2010: 170). At a subsequent press conference Blair and Brown announced the plan to conduct a series of public events to make the case for membership (Seldon 2008: 213). But this road show never took place (Wall 2008: 171). Blair and Brown continued to support entry in public. Yet the Treasury division responsible to rate the UK's capacity to join the Eurozone was reduced from a staff of about 100 to 10 shortly after Brown's statement, showing that the government did not expect to conduct a referendum soon (Gowland et al. 2010: 171).

In subsequent years the political context changed and the government's chances to put euro entry into effect declined ever more. For one, domestic policy reforms became a prime focus of New Labour after re-election in 2001. Yet the most important reason for the issue's marginalisation was the UK's involvement in the Iraq war, which had begun in March 2003. Iraq became one of the most important issues on Blair's political agenda at the expense of the euro (Gowland et al. 2010: 171). Moreover, his decision to side with the United States on Iraq resulted in a conflict with European partners such as Germany and France, who took another view (Baker and Sherrington 2004: 347). This also made Blair's attempts to persuade the public as to the merits of joining the euro more difficult. At the same time, Iraq and the overstated allegations on weapons of mass destruction intensified existing doubts among the public whether the prime minister was trustworthy (Kavanagh 2005: 18).

Until Tony Blair's resignation in June 2007 euro membership was effectively a dead issue. His successor Gordon Brown chose not to revive it during his premiership.

References

Bache, I., & Nugent, N. (2007). Europe. In A. Seldon (Ed.), *Blair's Britain, 1997–2007* (pp. 529–550). Cambridge: Cambridge University Press.

Baker, D., Gamble, A., & Ludlam, S. (1994). The parliamentary siege of Maastricht 1993: Conservative divisions and British ratification. *Parliamentary Affairs, 47*(1), 37–60.

Baker, D., & Sherrington, P. (2004). Britain and Europe: Europe and/or America? *Parliamentary Affairs, 57*(2), 347–365.

Burch, M., & Holliday, I. (1996). *British cabinet system*. Hemel Hempstead: Prentice Hall Harvester Wheatsheaf.

Butler, D., & Kavanagh, D. (Eds.). (1992). *The British general election of 1992*. Basingstoke/London: St. Martin's Press/Macmillan.

Cowley, P., & Stuart, M. (2012, October 30). *Europe: The gift that keeps giving misery to Conservative whips*. http://nottspolitics.org/2012/10/30/europe-the-gift-that-keeps-on-giving-misery-to-conservative-whips/. Accessed June 4, 2016.

De Jonquieres, G. (1978, December 4). Shaky path to monetary union. *Financial Times*.

Financial Times. (1978, November 25). *Government not ready to decide whether it is in Britain's best interest to join*.

Geddes, A. (2013). *Britain and the European Union*. Basingstoke: Palgrave Macmillan.

George, S. (1998). *An awkward partner: Britain in the European Community* (3rd ed.). Oxford: Oxford University Press.

Gowland, D., & Turner, A. (2000). *Reluctant Europeans: Britain and European integration 1945–1998*. Harlow: Longman.

Gowland, D., Turner, A., & Wright, A. (2010). *Britain and European integration since 1945: On the sidelines*. London: Routledge.

Heath, A. F., Jowell, R. M., & Curtice, J. K. (2001). *The rise of New Labour: Party policies and voter choices*. Oxford: Oxford University Press.

HC Deb. (1978, December 6), Vol 959, cc1421–1424.

HC Deb. (1990, November 13), Vol 180, cc461–465.

HC Deb. (1997, October 27), Vol 299, cc583–588.

HC Deb. (1999, February 23), Vol 326, cc179–183.

HC Deb. (2003, June 9), Vol 406, cc407–415.

Hillenbrand, O. (2008). Die Wirtschafts- und Währungsunion. In W. Weidenfeld (Ed.), *Die Europäische Union: Politisches System und Politikbereiche* (pp. 402–433). Bonn: Bundeszentrale für Politische Bildung.

Jay, P. (1994). The economy 1990–94. In D. Kavanagh & A. Seldon (Eds.), *The Major effect* (pp. 169–205). London: Macmillan.

Jenkins, P. (1978, December 1). PM given a blank cheque. *The Guardian*.

Kavanagh, D. (2005). The Blair premiership. In A. Seldon & D. Kavanagh (Eds.), *The Blair effect 2001–5* (pp. 3–19). Cambridge: Cambridge University Press.

Knipping, F. (2004). *Rom, 25. März 1957: Die Einigung Europas*. Munich: Deutscher Taschenbuch Verlag.

Lawson, D. (1990, July 14). Saying the unsayable about the Germans. *The Spectator*.

Ludlow, P. (1982). *The making of the European Monetary System*. London: Butterworth.

Major, J. (2000). *The autobiography* (2nd ed.). London: HarperCollins.

Rawnsley, A. (2001). *Servants of the people: The inside story of New Labour* (2nd ed.). London: Penguin.

Seldon A. (with Snowdon, P. & Collings, D.) (2008). *Blair unbound* (2nd ed.). London: Pocket Books.

Stephens, P. (1997). *Politics and the pound: The Tories, the economy and Europe* (2nd ed.). London: Papermac.

Thatcher, M. (2011). *The Downing Street years*. London: Harper Press.

The Guardian. (1978, November 29). *Half-way to a better Europe*.

Thompson, H. (1996). *The British Conservative government and the European Exchange Rate Mechanism, 1979–1994*. London: Pinter.

Wall, S. (2008). *A stranger in Europe: Britain and the EU from Thatcher to Blair*. Oxford: Oxford University Press.

Wallace, W. (1994). Foreign policy. In D. Kavanagh & A. Seldon (Eds.), *The Major effect* (pp. 283–300). London: Macmillan.

Chapter 4
European Policy-Making and Coordination in Executive and Legislature 1976–2007

This chapter outlines the institutional framework in the UK core executive and legislature on European policy coordination. It focuses on the institutional organisation in the analysed time period 1976–2007.[1] Together with the attitudes to Europe integration held by the four prime ministers, their parliamentary parties, the media and the public, which are traced in Chap. 5, these are necessary preliminaries for the subsequent case study analysis. The institutional arrangements in European policy-making and the attitudes to European integration taken by actors in and outside the core executive are part of the leadership environment in which a premier's political leadership unfolds.

4.1 The Ministerial Level

Ministerial departments have a key function in European policy coordination (Kassim 2000: 27). When Britain joined the EC in the early 1970s, departments handling relevant policy fields were given responsibility to deal with the corresponding European aspects. By spreading responsibility for European policy development across Whitehall, it was hoped that politicians and officials would consider the European dimension when making policy (Stack 1983: 127, 130).

With the evolvement of European integration an increasing number of departments were affected by and participated in European policy-making (Forster and Blair 2002: 56). By the late 1990s all had created divisions which coordinated European policy (Bulmer and Burch 1998: 616). While there were variations

[1]This is not to say that the institutional framework described here no longer exists, but this chapter does not refer to changes related the UK's decision to leave the EU. Theresa May's government in autumn 2016 began reorganising its institutional framework of European policy coordination, e.g. by establishing Departments for Exiting the European Union and for International Trade (Mance and Neville 2016).

B. Bujard, *The British Prime Minister in the Core Executive*, Contributions to Political Science, https://doi.org/10.1007/978-3-319-89953-4_4

between departments concerning their way of working and responsibilities, in most of them technical experts took a leading role. Their staff kept in touch with colleagues from other member states, the UK Permanent Representation in Brussels (see Sect. 4.2) and EU institutions. Organisational differences between departments reflected particularly three factors: (a) a department's history of European integration, (b) how much its work was affected by it and (c) the options the European level provided for it to pursue its own institutional interests (Kassim 2000: 27–28). For some, such as the Department of Industry, engagement with Europe meant new opportunities. For others, such as the Treasury, it was a constraining factor (Buller and Smith 1998: 166; Marsh et al. 2001: 213). Individual ministers and the departmental culture could also affect the department's coordination of European policy-making (Kassim 2000: 28).

Some departments were involved in European policy-making from the start of Britain's membership, such as the Foreign and Commonwealth Office (FCO), the Treasury, the Department of Trade and Industry (DTI)[2] and the Department of Agriculture[3] (Forster and Blair 2002: 56). Apart from the last one they are covered here, as they were concerned with European monetary policy. Treasury and FCO were involved in the negotiations on EMS and EMU. As monetary policy directly affects the policy areas covered by the DTI, it had an interest in it, too.

Formally, the *Foreign and Commonwealth Office (FCO)*[4] was the lead department on European policy (Forster and Blair 2002: 60). However, when the UK joined the EC, it was decided that it would not be entrusted with the task of coordinating European policy-making in the core executive. It was seen as a challenge for the FCO to pursue its own institutional interests separate from a neutral coordinating role (Kassim 2000: 34). Furthermore, it was already then clear that European negotiations often concerned issues on which the FCO had little expertise such as agricultural policy. There was also the worry that other departments might see the FCO as preferring consensus with the European partners over safeguarding the national interest. Therefore, a non-departmental institution was to do the coordination: the European Secretariat in the Cabinet Office (see Sect. 4.2) (Forster and Blair 2002: 60, 61). But the FCO was not fully excluded from taking a role in coordination process as it coordinated written communication between Brussels and London (Stack 1983: 127). Moreover, Britain's Permanent Representation in Brussels is part of the FCO (Bender 1991: 16).

Responsibility for the definition of Britain's European policy lay with the foreign secretary. But his leeway to do so, much depended on the prime minister's interests and in how far their views aligned (Kassim 2000: 37–38). At the domestic level the

[2]In 2018: Department for International Trade and Department for Business, Energy and Industrial Strategy; from 1976 to 2007 it was mostly called Department of Trade and Industry; therefore this name is used here.

[3]In 2018: Department for Environment, Food and Rural Affairs (DEFRA).

[4]For details on the FCO's institutional organisation of EU policy coordination, see Bulmer and Burch (2009: 97–100).

foreign secretary presented European policy in the full cabinet and chaired the cabinet committee on it ((E)DOP). At the European level he attended the General Affairs Council and the European Council,[5] accompanied the premier to Intergovernmental Conferences (IGCs) and had a key role in the diplomatic relationship with the European partners (Forster and Blair 2002: 60; Kassim 2000: 38). There was also a Minister for Europe, a junior minister, who handled managerial tasks, such as during Britain's EU presidency, and who was the foreign secretary's deputy on European affairs (Kassim 2000: 38; Forster and Blair 2002: 60).

While the FCO remains a key actor in UK European policy, it has lost influence since the 1970s. With more issues handled at the European level, the other departments developed their own contacts and expertise in European policy-making. Furthermore, technical innovations (e.g. the Internet) weakened the FCO's role as communication gateway between the national and the European level. Moreover, the General Affairs Council lost its crucial role in the European decision-making process (Kassim 2000: 39). However, this loss of influence by the foreign ministry happened across member states and was no British particularity.[6]

The *Treasury*[7] had no formal coordination role in European policy, but strongly influenced it (Kassim 2000: 31). It has been the leading department on European finances and expenditure and tax policy. It later added the liberalisation of financial services as an area of activity. Sometimes it also intervened in areas other departments were in charge of such as trade policy in the 1990s (Pickering 2002: 587).

The chancellor has the general responsibility for policy in the Treasury and was (and still is) a central actor in EU policy. Successive chancellors showed significant interest in monetary policy and tried to keep control of the issue in the core executive (Bulmer and Burch 2009: 137).

The Treasury was inclined to have an ambivalent view on European integration, because it meant that economic policy was no longer a domestic issue. Moreover, the department lost parts of its autonomy in economic policy-making to the EU (Buller and Smith 1998: 177; Marsh et al. 2001: 224). It tended to object to new legislation out of principle, if it could contribute to rising public expenditure. Thus even when headed by a pro-European chancellor such as Ken Clarke in the 1990s it attempted to slow down integrative measures, if it feared they would lead to a rise in costs (Buller and Smith 1998: 178; Marsh et al. 2001: 225). In the 1970s and 1980s the department pursued a more or less defensive policy on Europe, which might have partly been due to the problems with Britain's contribution to the European budget.[8] The short but disastrous experience of membership in the European currency mechanism,

[5]This changed with the Lisbon treaty, when the European Council's membership was restricted (Treaty on European Union (TEU), entered into force on 1.12.2009, Art. 15).

[6]Interview with S. Wall, 8 January 2010.

[7]For details on the Treasury's institutional organisation of European policy coordination, see Bulmer and Burch (2009: 135–136).

[8]The UK's budget contribution in the early 1980s was disproportionally high. By 1979 the UK was paying twice as much as France, despite a lower GDP. It was the only other net contributor to the budget beside Germany (Gowland et al. 2010: 90–91).

the 'snake in the tunnel', in the early 1970s (see Chap. 3) might have contributed to it, too (Bulmer and Burch 2009: 133–134). Since the late 1980s the Treasury supported more European initiatives, such as a common market in financial services or further economic liberalisation. Yet, where it gave pro-integration impulses, it favoured intergovernmental methods such as the Open Method of Coordination (OMC)[9] or negative integration (the abolishment of constraints in a policy field) (Bulmer and Burch 2009: 134).

The *Department of Trade and Industry (DTI),*[10] since its establishment in 1970, was strongly affected by Britain's EC/EU-membership. Due to its responsibility for trade policy it managed to set itself up as a key actor in European policy coordination (Bulmer and Burch 2009: 145).

The department was subject to repeated reorganisation and reallocation of responsibilities and was headed by pro-European and Eurosceptic ministers (Kassim 2000: 30). During James Callaghan's premiership and Margaret Thatcher's first term separate departments handled trade and industry policy. After the 1983 general election they were merged into the Department of Trade and Industry which remained the case under John Major and Tony Blair (Department for Business, Innovation and Skills 2010). Ministerial turnover was high as ministers' tenures tended to be short (Bulmer and Burch 2009: 145–146).[11]

The DTI tended to view European integration favourably. Thatcherite policies such as privatisation and the abolishment of subsidies to industry threatened the DTI because they meant a loss of responsibilities for it. European integration and particularly the establishment of the internal market provided the DTI with new responsibilities and it was able to compensate the loss of influence at the domestic level (Buller and Smith 1998: 173–174).

In the British political system many decisions are taken at cabinet committee level. Until the 1990s, the Defence and Overseas Policy committee (DOP), chaired by the PM, and its sub-committee on Europe ((E)DOP) held the main responsibility for European policy. As the DOP addressed a wide-range of issues, most European policy was handled in the sub-committee (Forster and Blair 2002: 62). Under Tony Blair there were changes to the system. The sub-committee on Europe (then known as EP) was no longer so important for the discussion of European policy at the ministerial level. The Joint Ministerial Committee (Europe) (JMC[E]) (founded in 1998, remodelled in 2003), chaired by the foreign secretary and including representatives of the devolved administrations, became the main forum to do so. Blair also

[9]"Under this intergovernmental method, the EU countries are evaluated by one another (peer pressure), with the Commission's role being limited to surveillance. The European Parliament and the Court of Justice play virtually no part in the OMC process." Definition available at http://europa.eu/legislation_summaries/glossary/open_method_coordination_en.htm, accessed 7.5.2016.

[10]For details on the DTI's institutional organisation of European policy coordination, see Bulmer and Burch (2009: 145–148).

[11]In this study only the activities of ministers of whom it is documented that they dealt with European monetary policy in detail are analysed.

set up a European Union strategy committee (EUS) in 2003 to promote strategic thinking and the coordination between departments on key issues such as the euro. Yet by 2006 it had only met three times (James 2009: 611–612).

In the subsequent case study analysis particularly individual ministers and their behaviour in the context of European monetary policy projects are considered. This does not mean that departments are irrelevant, but it is the ministers who are in direct contact with the premier in the core executive such as in cabinet. Moreover, departmental officials accept that ministerial preferences restrict their options in European negotiations. This is particularly important if a minister's view differs from that of his department. In the 1990s, for instance, Treasury officials had to balance Ken Clarke's pro-Europeanism with the institution's cautious stance on European integration. In addition, ministers do not define their policy position detached from that of the institution they lead and are also influenced by it (Marsh et al. 2001: 229, 230).

4.2 The Official Level

The *Cabinet Office* in general coordinates the policy-making process and ensures that the interests of all departments are considered. Individual secretariats do this for different policy fields (Forster and Blair 2002: 68). A European Unit was established in the Cabinet Office in 1967 to coordinate Britain's second EC application. It was later re-named *European Secretariat (COES)* (Bulmer and Burch 1998: 609, 614).[12] The COES was pro-active in coordinating policy. For instance, it set up meetings to discuss issues, if it considered them necessary (Bender 1991: 16). While the leading department decided how an issue was handled, the COES ensured that all departments affected by it were consulted and contributed to the policy-making process. To do so, COES staff kept close contacts with departmental officials responsible for Europe and to the UK representation in Brussels (Kassim 2000: 34–35).

From its establishment to the year 2000, the COES' organisational structure remained largely unchanged. Since the late 1970s it consisted of about 20 to 24 officials seconded from other departments and was headed by a Deputy Secretary (until 1977 a Second Permanent Secretary post) (Bender 1991: 16; Bulmer and Burch 1998: 614; Kassim 2000: 34). Traditionally, officials with long-standing experience in European policy were appointed as Deputy Secretary from one of the home departments much concerned with Europe (e.g. Trade and Industry or Agriculture). This changed with the appointment of Stephen Wall from the Foreign

[12]The Cabinet Office Secretariats' responsibilities have been subject to change, e.g. in 2016 the European Secretariat also covered international economic policy, thus the name European and Global Issues Secretariat (EGIS) (GOV.UK 2016). Moreover, shortly before he left the government David Cameron announced the establishment of a Europe unit in the Cabinet Office (Mance and Neville 2016).

Office in 2000 as head of the COES (Stack 1983: 128; Forster and Blair 2002: 69). At the time Tony Blair began to reorganise foreign policy decision-making processes in the core executive which also affected the European Secretariat's composition and size (outlined in Sect. 7.4.2).

In addition to leading the secretariat, the head of the COES attended cabinet meetings and advised the prime minister on European affairs. At EU level he was involved in negotiations such as in the context of European Councils and Intergovernmental Conferences. In later years he and his deputy also increasingly coordinated contacts between the Prime Minister's Office and the offices of other EU heads of government and state (Kassim 2000: 37).

Apart from the traditional Cabinet Office duties of preparing and servicing ministerial meetings and conducting discussions on EC/EU issues, the COES also ensured that the UK had a policy on every European issue on which it needed one. It assured that this position was realistic, in line with Britain's overall European policy and implemented (Bender 1991: 16–17).

Until the 1990s official level coordination was done in several standing committees, but their use gradually declined as they proved too inflexible to adequately address the increasing complexity of the European policy-making process. During Tony Blair's premiership there was a greater reliance on ad hoc meetings which could be convened at short notice and which no longer included all departments with an interest in an issue, but only the key ministries (James 2009: 611; Bulmer and Burch 1998: 616). A further key coordination forum was the weekly Friday meeting also chaired by the head of the COES. Attended by Britain's ambassador to the EC/EU—the Permanent Representative—and senior officials from FCO, Treasury and other relevant departments, upcoming EC/EU business was discussed and the UK's negotiating line developed (Marsh et al. 2001: 215; Bulmer and Burch 2005: 872).

The COES also published 'Guidance Notes' for departments on how the EU was organised and functioned, how certain procedures work and how European policy was handled properly at the domestic and the European level. Moreover, ministries had to clear document drafts such as correspondence with the European Commission which affected other departments or major policy documents which included European policy issues with the Secretariat (Bulmer and Burch 1998: 620).

Besides coordinating core executive European policy-making, the COES ensured that parliament was informed about EC/EU developments and the government's policy on them. It made sure that the leading department transmitted the necessary documents in time to the relevant parliamentary committees (see Sect. 4.3) (Bender 1991: 19; Kassim 2000: 36–37).

Although small, the COES was an integral part of British European policy coordination. Through its proximity to the prime minister—the Cabinet Office is located close to No. 10 Downing Street—it was also important with respect to his role in European policy. It worked closely with the Permanent Representation in Brussels which is introduced next.

As any other EU member Britain has an embassy in Brussels called *United Kingdom Permanent Representation (UKREP)*. It is headed by the Permanent Representative, who was usually a diplomat, while his deputy often came from

Treasury or DTI (Kassim 2000: 40). UKREP belongs to the FCO, but does not work like a regular embassy. With EU policy often being technical, expert knowledge is important. Therefore a large number of staff was and is seconded from the home departments (Bulmer and Burch 1998: 615).

UKREP functioned as the government's "eyes and ears" (Nugent 2000: 211) at the European level. It was the UK's representation in Brussels and its formal communication channel with the European Commission (Bulmer and Burch 2009: 100). The Permanent Representative and his deputy met regularly with the other members' representatives in the Committee of Permanent Representatives (COREPER) which prepared sittings of the Council of the European Union and discussed policy proposals (Forster and Blair 2002: 75).

Yet UKREP did not just negotiate on the basis of instructions from London. It also shaped them and thereby contributed to the development of British European policy. It did so by advising Whitehall which policy initiatives were feasible at the European level (Forster and Blair 2002: 75). An important element linking UKREP and Whitehall was the above-mentioned Friday meeting, in which the Permanent Representative took part regularly.

In Whitehall a European affairs policy network centring on Cabinet Office, FCO, UKREP and No. 10 developed over the years, which became more and more institutionalised and consolidated (Marsh et al. 2001: 214; Bulmer and Burch 1998: 626). But as departments increasingly administered their own EU level contacts the COES and the FCO lost their monopolist position in the European policy coordination process (Marsh et al. 2001: 216). No. 10's role in this network and its relationship to the COES is considered in Chap. 7 with regard to the four leaders analysed here in the period of 1976 to 2007.

4.3 The Parliamentary Level

In the British political system the legislature is dominated by the government which controls the parliamentary timetable (Norton 2003: 16). Most bills submitted by the government become law. Between 1987 and 1992, for example, the government introduced 213 bills in parliament. Only 11 failed to be passed into law. Meanwhile, individual MPs submitted 584 Private Members' Bills (PMB).[13] Few were debated, only 65 became law (Norton 1993: 54).

A key duty of parliament is to scrutinise the government. It can do so with parliamentary debates and questions, select committees, Early Day Motions

[13]PMBs are "Public Bills introduced by MPs and Lords who are not government ministers… A minority of Private Members' Bills become law but, by creating publicity around an issue, they may affect legislation indirectly." Definition available at http://www.parliament.uk/about/how/laws/bills/private-members, accessed 7.5.2016.

(EDMs),[14] correspondence with government representatives and party committees in parliament (Norton 1994: 272, 276–286). With regard to Britain's engagement in the European Union there were the European Scrutiny Committee (ESC) in the House of Commons and the European Union Committee (EU Select Committee) in the House of Lords. The ESC reviewed all European Union documents submitted by the government on their legal and/or political significance (Norton 2003: 16, 17). Either committee reviewed propositions before they were decided at the Council of the EU level (Riddell 2000: 29). They complemented each other as the Lords committee covered selected issues in more detail, while the one in the Commons handled a larger case load (Bulmer and Burch 1998: 617; Norton 2003: 19). All EU documents had to be forwarded to the relevant parliamentary committee within 48 hours after the government received them together with an 'Explanatory Memorandum' (EM) provided by the leading department on the issue. As mentioned, the European Secretariat oversaw this process (Bulmer and Burch 1998: 618). The memorandum provided information such as the government's view on the issue, whether the process concurred with the principles of proportionality and subsidiarity and its implications for UK law. They could also include details on financial implications and the expected EU level decision-making timetable (Norton 2003: 16).

The House of Lords EU committee published about 20 detailed reviews per year on specific legislative proposals or subject areas such as EMU (Riddell 2000: 31; Miller 2005: 16).

By 2003 the ESC examined about 1300 documents per year and classified around 500 as legally or politically significant and of those about 30 for further debate. This tended to be done in one of the European Standing Committees which were organised according to subject areas. Debates on the floor of the house tended to be avoided as these were limited to a length of 90 min. A thorough questioning of ministers was therefore not possible. Moreover, due to the government's control of the parliamentary timetable there was no guarantee it would schedule a debate on the floor of the house (Norton 2003: 16). An ESC recommendation for debate in one of the standing committees was binding; one for a debate on the floor of the house was not (Miller 2005: 14).

Departmental Select Committees (DSCs)—Commons committees dealing with the work, organisation and expenditure of departments—could also cover Europe. Every week the ESC informed them about upcoming EU legislation relevant to their subject areas/departments (Norton 1996: 99). But according to a study from 2000, DSCs only occasionally examined European policy in detail. Exceptions were the Foreign Affairs Committee which did so every 6 months before the European Council or the Treasury Committee on issues such as EMU (Riddell 2000: 37).

[14]EDMs "are formal motions submitted for debate in the House of Commons. However, very few are actually debated. EDMs allow MPs to draw attention to an event or cause. MPs register their support by signing individual motions." Definition available at http://www.parliament.uk/edm, accessed 7.5.2016.

This system of parliamentary scrutiny established in the 1970s was adjusted over the years but never fully revised. An important modification was the introduction of the 'Scrutiny Reserve' in 1980. It meant that no member of government was to agree to a legislative proposal in the Council of Ministers, if it had not yet completed the parliamentary scrutiny process. If a minister could or did not fulfil this requirement, he had to explain it to parliament (Bulmer and Burch 1998: 617).

Parliament can further hold the government to account with debates and questions. A regular debate on European affairs was conducted in the Commons every 6 months before the last European Council of each EU presidency. The premier also gave a statement on every European Council he attended, followed by questions from MPs. Moreover, EU decisions requiring legislation, for instance treaty changes, were debated and subject to a parliamentary vote like any other legislation (Miller 2005: 16, 17). Decisions on the UK's contribution to the European budget were debated in parliament, too, as they required legislation to be incorporated into British law (Edmonds 2001: 19).

Private Members' Bills can also be used to gather information about the government's plans and activities. They are often Early Day Motions. There tends to be little time to debate them, but they can give the government a good indication of prevailing views on their backbenches on an issue (Norton 1993: 58, 67).

Despite these measures parliament only had an advisory role in European law making (Norton 2003: 18). It was only engaged when legislation was introduced to implement EC directives in the UK or when it had to give assent to treaty changes (Norton 1993: 117). On European policy (as on other policy fields) "the fount of public policy in the United Kingdom ... [was] not Parliament, but Her Majesty's Government" (Norton 1993: 71). But the legislature's role on Europe should not be fully discounted for two reasons: firstly, when negotiating treaty changes the government needed to anticipate its position and could not ignore it. Secondly, there is the scrutiny function with which parliament could constrain the executive (Norton 1996: 106, 107). Yet effective scrutiny of the government's European policy was weakened by the executive's control of the parliamentary timetable. For instance, the legislature might have recommended a more detailed review of an issue, but the government might not have complied (Norton 2003: 19).

The opposition can set the parliamentary agenda on a number of "opposition days"[15] and can, for instance, set out its political stance following the Queen's Speech in which the government presents its legislative plans at the start of a parliamentary year. But compared, for example, to the German political system the opposition's institutionalised participatory rights are more limited. Moreover, it has less ambition to modify governmental policy than to win the next election. Therefore it rather focuses on the electorate than on the government party in parliament

[15]"Opposition days are allocated in the House of Commons for the discussion of subjects chosen by the opposition (non-government) parties. There are 20 days allocated for this purpose per session." Definition available at http://www.parliament.uk/site-information/glossary/opposition-days, accessed 7.5.2016.

(Hübner and Münch 1999: 136–137). Hence, it is particularly the government's own backbenchers who can affect the prime minister's role in the policy-making process. This is especially to be expected on European policy as Labour as well as the Conservative Party faced strong internal divisions over Britain's role in Europe at different points in time (see Sect. 5.2). Therefore, the analysis here focuses on the governmental parliamentary party, not on the opposition.

The institutional arrangements in European policy-making in the British political system as outlined in this chapter form part of the leadership environment in which a prime minister's political leadership unfolds. To what extent particular institutions or institutional arrangements enable or constrain a premier's political leadership in European monetary policy-making is analysed in Chap. 7. Before the attitudes to Europe integration held by the four prime ministers, their parliamentary parties, the media and the public need to be identified as they also constitute elements of this leadership environment.

References

Bender, B. G. (1991). Whitehall, central government and 1992. *Public Policy and Administration, 6* (1), 13–20.

Buller, J., & Smith, M. J. (1998). Civil service attitudes towards the European Union. In D. Baker & D. Seawright (Eds.), *Britain for and against Europe: British politics and the question of European integration* (pp. 165–184). Oxford: Clarendon.

Bulmer, S., & Burch, M. (1998). Organizing for Europe: Whitehall, the British state and European Union. *Public Administration, 76*(4), 601–628.

Bulmer, S., & Burch, M. (2005). The Europeanization of UK government: From quiet revolution to explicit step-change? *Public Administration, 83*(4), 861–890.

Bulmer, S., & Burch, M. (2009). *The Europeanisation of Whitehall: UK central government and the European Union*. Manchester: Manchester University Press.

Department for Business, Innovation & Skills. (2010). *Introduction to history of BERR*, archived on February 22, 2010. http://webarchive.nationalarchives.gov.uk/20100216092443/http://www.berr.gov.uk/aboutus/corporate/history/outlines/page19795.html. Accessed September 11, 2016.

Edmonds, T. (2001, July 2). *The European Communities (Finance) Bill, Bill 1 2001–02*, House of Commons Library Research Paper No. 01/62.

Forster, A., & Blair, A. (2002). *The making of Britain's European foreign policy*. Harlow: Longman.

GOV.UK (2016). *European and Global Issues Secretariat (EGIS)*. https://www.gov.uk/government/groups/european-global-issues-secretariat. Accessed September 11, 2016.

Gowland, D., Turner, A., & Wright, A. (2010). *Britain and European integration since 1945: On the sidelines*. London: Routledge.

Hübner, E., & Münch, U. (1999). *Das Politische System Großbritanniens: Eine Einführung* (2nd ed.). Munich: Verlag C.H. Beck.

James, S. (2009). Taming the 'awkward state'? The changing face of European policy-making under Blair. *Public Administration, 87*(3), 604–620.

Kassim, H. (2000). The United Kingdom. In H. Kassim, B. G. Peters, & V. Wright (Eds.), *The national coordination of EU policy: The domestic level* (pp. 22–53). Oxford: Oxford University Press.

Mance, H., & Neville, S. (2016, July 15). Strategic intends drives reform of ministries. *Financial Times*.

Marsh, D., Richards, D., & Smith, M. J. (2001). *Changing patterns of governance in the United Kingdom: Reinventing Whitehall?* Basingstoke: Palgrave.

Miller, V. (2005, December 2). *The UK parliament and European business*, House of Commons Library Research Paper No. 05/85.

Norton, P. (1993). *Does parliament matter?* Hemel Hempstead: Harvester Wheatsheaf.

Norton, P. (1994). *The British polity* (3rd ed.). New York: Longman.

Norton, P. (1996). The United Kingdom: Political conflict, parliamentary scrutiny. In P. Norton (Ed.), *National parliaments and the European Union* (pp. 92–109). London: Frank Cass.

Norton, P. (2003). National parliaments and the European Union. *Managerial Law, 45*(5/6), 5–25.

Nugent, N. (2000). The European Union and UK governance. In R. Pyper & L. Robins (Eds.), *United Kingdom governance* (pp. 194–218). Basingstoke: Macmillan.

Pickering, C. (2002). 'Sir Douglas in Euroland': Treasury officials and the European Union, 1977–2001. *Public Administration, 80*(3), 583–599.

Riddell, P. (2000). *Parliament under Blair* (2nd ed.). London: Politico's.

Stack, F. (1983). The imperatives of coordination. In F. E. C. Gregory (Ed.), *Dilemmas of government: Britain and the European Community* (pp. 124–152). Oxford: Martin Robertson.

Chapter 5
Attitudes to European Integration

To assess how far the parliamentary party, the media and the public affect the prime minister's leeway in European policy-making, it is necessary to consider their attitudes to European integration, which is done in this chapter. But first the four prime ministers' attitudes to European integration are outlined to understand to what extend their views concurred with or diverged from those of the parliamentary party, the media and the public.

5.1 Prime Ministerial Attitudes to European Integration

In 1971/1972 during the debate whether Britain should join the EC **James Callaghan** was one of the sceptics and publicly opposed membership (Young 1999: 273). On becoming foreign secretary in 1974, he—now in charge of the renegotiation of EC membership which Labour had promised during the 1974 election campaign—remained sceptical about EC involvement and then said to one of Britain's ambassadors that "all this European enthusiasm is not what we're in business for"[1] (Callaghan quoted in Young 1999: 278). But in the same year discussions about political cooperation in foreign policy began in the EC. Callaghan backed this, seeing it as a chance to enhance UK influence in the world and it contributed to his move to a position supportive of EC membership (Callaghan 2006: 317; Young 1999: 285).

While he slowly developed into a pragmatist on Europe, he never became an enthusiast. He wanted to make Britain's European integration work but did not want any new grand EC initiatives.[2] To Roy Denman, head of the European Secretariat

[1]Young, H. (1999), *This Blessed Plot, Britain and Europe from Churchill to Blair*, 2nd edition, London/Basingstoke/Oxford: Papermac. © Hugo Young 1998, 1999. Reproduced with permission of the Licensor through PLSclear.

[2]Interview with T. McNally, 22 March 2010.

B. Bujard, *The British Prime Minister in the Core Executive*, Contributions to Political Science, https://doi.org/10.1007/978-3-319-89953-4_5

from 1975 to 1977, Callaghan exhibited a "truculent insularity; that made things very difficult" (Denman 1999). Yet, Michael Butler, who at the time handled European policy in the Foreign Office, qualified this assessment: "I think he was more convinced of the need for us to be playing a central role in Europe than he wished to say."[3] Callaghan was an Atlanticist and on becoming foreign secretary was determined to strengthen the alliance with the US. He argued that the previous premier Edward Heath's "deep and lasting commitment to Europe had weakened our relations with the United States" (Callaghan 2006: 295). His Atlanticism was also apparent in his view on economic cooperation: he wanted to include the United States in any plans to solve the economic problems of the second half of the 1970s instead of focusing solely on Europe. With regard to plans for a European Monetary System (EMS), for instance, Callaghan demanded at a meeting with German Chancellor Helmut Schmidt in April 1978 that a mechanism was developed which was not directed against the US, but supportive of the dollar (Donoughue 2009: 318). At the same time, he thought the strength of the British economy depended only on the country itself and regarded EC membership not as significant in this context (Callaghan 2006: 305, 326).

Once re-negotiation was completed in 1975, Callaghan did not place Europe, an issue which still divided his party (see Sect. 5.2.1), high up on his political agenda. The difficult political situation he faced contributed to this. He lacked a parliamentary majority and among other things had to look to the International Monetary Fund in 1976 for help to keep the British economy afloat. Thus a more positive engagement in Europe would not only have spelled trouble for his relationship with the anti-Europeans in his party and cabinet, but would also have distracted from handling other problems he faced such as the state of the economy (Young 1999: 299–300).[4]

While it is clear that Callaghan eventually opposed joining the ERM, there are different assessments as to when he decided this. According to his cabinet colleague Edmund Dell (1994: 32) he did so early on, but chose to keep up the impression during the negotiations that UK membership was possible, because he feared a sterling crisis. But Michael Franklin (2013: 763), head of the COES from 1977 to 1981, suggested there were indications that Callaghan might initially have been open to the idea of joining and became doubtful about it during the negotiations. Peter Ludlow (1982: 217), on the other hand, argued that, whatever Callaghan's personal view on the ERM, the prime minister concluded already in October 1978 that membership was not feasible due to the extensive opposition to it in large sections of his party. Moreover, Callaghan did not think that he could gain sufficient support in his cabinet or in parliament to override it, Ludlow suggested.

[3]Interview with M. Butler, 22 March 2010.

[4]His political secretary Tom McNally came to a similar conclusion, see interview with T. McNally, 22 March 2010.

Margaret Thatcher was considered neither a European enthusiast nor a Eurosceptic when she became prime minister in 1979. Douglas Hurd (2009: 263), her last foreign secretary, noted that during the 1975 referendum Thatcher did not have strong views on the issue. While she wanted a Remain vote, she saw the issue primarily as a party political one.

Her world view was shaped by the conditions of the cold war rather than any European ideal (Young 1999: 309–310). She viewed European integration primarily in a defence and security policy context as she saw the EC's main task in supporting NATO in the fight against Communism (Gilmour 1992: 233). Christopher Soames, a member of her first cabinet, compared her stance on Europe to that of an agnostic who still went to church while being neither strong believer nor atheist (Young 1999: 311). But Thatcher did believe in one thing which much affected her view of European integration: the "primacy of the nation state" (Wall 2008: 38).

Yet Thatcher wanted the Conservatives to be seen as pro-European. When she became party leader she demanded her predecessor's European policy to be continued (Hurd 2009: 266). At the start of her premiership she sought to emphasise the impression that her government was more pro-European than the Labour predecessor had been (Thatcher 2011: 63).

In the mid-1980s she supported integration in those areas in which it corresponded with her view of the EC as a free trade area and where she thought it possible to advance her own political aims such as economic liberalisation across Europe. Therefore, she supported the establishment of a European Common Market (Campbell 2011: 288). To achieve it, she was willing to compromise. During the negotiations of the Single European Act (SEA), for instance, she agreed to a limitation of national sovereignty with the introduction of majority voting at the European level (Smith 2012: 1281–1282). But after the treaty was in place she increasingly began to criticise the EC. Her shift in attitude was related to the fact that she had never taken seriously the other members' views on the Community, which differed markedly from hers (Campbell 2011: 286). By her account the EC changed during her second term "from being a Community of open trade, light regulation and freely co-operating sovereign nation-states towards statism and centralism" (Thatcher 2011: 536).

The dispute over Britain's European budget contribution from 1979, which was settled in 1984 with the agreement of a long-term rebate for the UK, had led Thatcher to conclude that the other Europeans were not trustworthy (Wall 2008: 38). According to her foreign policy adviser Percy Cradock (1997) "her private attitude to Europe ranged from suspicion to undisguised hostility. She did not like the Europeans; she did not speak their languages; and she had little time for their traditions. She recoiled from the Eurojargon" (125).

Thatcher was an Atlanticist. Particularly during the Reagan presidency (1981–1989) there was a close rapport between the two leaders, who shared a very conservative view of the Cold War and saw the Soviet Union as a threat to the West (Ward 1994: 94). According to her long-time chancellor Nigel Lawson (1992: 900) the relationship to the US always had primacy for Thatcher.

On the ERM Thatcher was a sceptic as she preferred flexible exchange rates and thought a system of fixed exchange rates would not work (Gowland et al. 2010: 113). Moreover, she believed, if the UK joined, its monetary policy would be mainly determined by the German Bundesbank, not the Treasury (Thatcher 2011: 696). Yet for political reasons she criticised the Callaghan government's decision to rule out membership in December 1978 (HC Deb 6 December 1978, c1424). Although, in the 1990s, she reluctantly agreed to put the pound into the ERM, she was said to have privately rejoiced when the UK had to leave the mechanism in 1992 (Campbell 2011: 486–487).

Her opposition to EMU was even stronger. She found the project threatening (Thatcher 2011: 763) and dismissed it for reasons of sovereignty and economic policy (Wall 2008: 114). However, she did not believe the plans would be realised and underestimated the other member states' commitment to it (Major 2000: 151; Wall 2008: 84).

When **John Major** became prime minister in 1990 he was neither closely associated with the pro-Europeans nor the Eurosceptics in his party, which had contributed to his election as new party leader (Wallace 1994: 283). On Europe he considered himself to be pragmatic and cautious (Major 2000: 581). As early as November 1982 he addressed his view on European integration in parliament:

> Emotionally, I am an agnostic on the subject of a united Europe. I have taken that position ever since I first considered the matter deeply. I have no long-term vision of a federal Europe and I do not wish to diminish the languages and cultures of the member States… I am an unrepentant nationalist, in the sense that my first instinct is for the British interest in Europe and beyond. I would not willingly shed one particle of our unique traditions and habits to be part of a united Europe. Therefore, I am not by instinct a European, but I am a committed European by logic, because I believe that it is in the interests of the United Kingdom for us to remain a member of the EEC. (HC Deb 12 November 1982, c782)

Therefore, he wanted EC membership to be a success for Britain (Wall 2008: 109). Major (2000: 581) did not see much difference between his and Thatcher's policy on Europe. But he tried to present Britain's view less confrontationally and to establish good personal relations with his European counterparts. Cradock (1997), who stayed on as foreign policy adviser, confirms:

> His vision of Europe remained one of co-operating nation states, with strong Atlantic ties and a recognition that NATO would continue to provide basic European security. Development had to be by evolution, not rushed or forced. On monetary union, Britain reserved judgement. In substance the message was not so remote from Mrs Thatcher's at Bruges.[5] But the tone was very different. (136)

Yet there were differences amounting to more than a mere change of tone: Major neither shared Thatcher's antipathy towards Germany nor her fondness of the US. Nonetheless, he worked well with George Bush, Reagan's successor as

[5]In 1988 Thatcher gave a speech at the College of Europe in Bruges calling for co-operation between EC member states instead of European federalism (Thatcher 1988).

US-President (Wallace 1994: 284, 299). Major supported ERM membership early on. He did so for economic reasons as he said in parliament in 1981: "the sooner we enter the European monetary system to improve exchange rate stability the better it will be for our exports and our interests generally" (HC Deb 4 November 1981, c68).

But he took a different view on EMU. He doubted it was the right choice for Europe or Britain (Hogg and Hill 1996: 75). Yet unlike Thatcher he was aware of the other members' determination on it and that the UK would not be able to keep them from pursuing it, if they wanted to. He intended to keep all options open for Britain on EMU knowing that, if realised, it would affect the country's economy (Wall 2008: 114–115). Hence, he did not want to take a decision about membership until the consequences of participation or non-participation for the economy could be estimated (Major 2000: 603–604).

There are differing assessments on whether Major's attitude to European integration changed in the aftermath of Britain's exit from the ERM in 1992 (see Chap. 3) and in the context of having to govern with a small but increasingly vocal group of Eurosceptic rebels in his party (see Sect. 5.2.2). Hugo Young (1999), for instance, argued that Major's attitude to Europe changed in autumn 1993, though it remained a point of contention whether conviction or strategy was "converting him from a genuine sceptic—quizzical, calculating, negotiating—into something more like what 'sceptic' had become as a term of art, which is to say an enemy of 'Europe' and a disbeliever in its driving purposes"[6] (447–448). Steve Ludlam (1998: 52–53), on the other hand, argued that Major's scepticism was not a result of pressure from the Eurosceptic rebels, but reflected the majority view of his party. Moreover, his stance on European integration was consistent throughout his premiership and did not change in the years leading up to the 1997 general election, Ludlam suggested. In any case, Major refused to rule out EMU participation for the remainder of his premiership (Seldon 1998: 663).

When he became prime minister in 1997, **Tony Blair** was considered a pro-European but not an enthusiast (Rentoul 2001: 473; see also Seldon 2005: 316). By his own account his interest in integrating the UK into Europe was not based on idealism but on national interest. To him Britain was too small to exercise significant influence in world politics. To do so, it had to take action together with the other European states (Blair 2010: 502). Blair saw no contradiction between European integration and a close relationship with the US. He thought Britain could exercise more influence with the US, if it was an influential member of the EU (Blair 2010: 534). He wanted the country to function as a bridge between the US and Europe, but underrated the differences of interest between the two sides, which increased during George W. Bush's presidency. In the context of the Iraq war, which

[6]Young, H. (1999), *This Blessed Plot, Britain and Europe from Churchill to Blair*, 2nd edition, London/Basingstoke/Oxford: Papermac. © Hugo Young 1998, 1999. Reproduced with permission of the Licensor through PLSclear.

caused deep splits between the EU members, a mediator role for Britain was not possible (Riddell 2005: 367; Gowland et al. 2010: 185).

Blair's pro-Europeanism had an opportunistic streak which showed for example during the 1997 general election campaign, when he scaled down his pro-European rhetoric and even made some sceptical remarks about the EU—presumably not to alarm the widely Eurosceptic press (Seldon 2005: 317). His European adviser Roger Liddle suggested that Blair might have thought a successful European policy would be the key achievement of his premiership, but that after 9/11 he shifted his focus to Iraq and the task of fighting international terror.[7]

In private, Blair was positive on the question of joining EMU before he became prime minister, but in public he remained cautious (Seldon 2005: 316). There were suggestions that he eventually became an enthusiastic supporter of membership. It is unclear when this shift exactly might have happened, if it did at all. There are suggestions that it happened in autumn 1997, though only became public knowledge in 1999 (Gowland et al. 2010: 169). Yet Stephen Wall, head of the European Secretariat from 2000, questioned the idea that joining the euro was a goal Blair seriously considered for his first term (1997–2001) and suggested he had intended to pursue it in his second (2001–2005).[8] In any case, the suggestion that Blair was enthusiastically seeking EMU entry indicates that he succeeded in giving ambiguous signals as to what his ambitions actually were. According to his chief of staff Jonathan Powell, Blair was an expert at expressing himself in deliberately ambivalent ways (Powell 2010: 54).

Blair's motive for joining the euro was political. He saw it as a key element of making Britain a leading power in the EU (Seldon 2005: 317). But he accepted that the question of entry would be decided on an economic basis with the five tests the Treasury conducted to evaluate the advantages and disadvantages of the UK joining the single currency (see Chap. 3). Yet his first economic adviser Derek Scott (2004: 3) suggested that Blair only wanted to present the sceptical public with an economic reason for what in his mind essentially was a political case for joining. Blair later acknowledged his support for joining the euro for political reasons, but claimed that the economic case had not shown decisively that membership would be good for the country. Therefore, he could not take the decision to take the UK into the Eurozone (Blair 2010: 537).

All the prime ministers considered here at some point during their premierships took a pragmatic view on European integration—even Margaret Thatcher. Of the four, James Callaghan appears to have been the one with the least interest in the issue. But it has to be taken into account that during his premiership only few larger European projects were realised apart from the European Monetary System. Moreover, unlike his successors, he did not have to deal with treaty negotiations. As a result, it was relatively easy for him to give scant attention to European affairs. In

[7]Interview with R. Liddle, 28 October 2010.

[8]Interview with S. Wall, 8 January 2010.

any case, the difficulties of the economy in the late 1970s and the conflicts with the trade unions meant that domestic policy dominated the Callaghan government's political agenda.[9] Over 10 years later, John Major was no longer able to give Europe only fleeting attention. By then European integration had a much bigger impact on the country, its government and the Conservative Party. Tony Blair was, at least early in his premiership, considered to be the most pro-European prime minister since Edward Heath—a view which, for instance, his European policy adviser Roger Liddle (2014: 55) has somewhat qualified. However, pooling national sovereignty with other countries to enhance Britain's influence appears to have been less of a problem for him than for his predecessors. But Blair's position on UK-US relations particularly after 9/11 illustrates that he did not attach less importance to the relationship with the US than his predecessors.

Next, Labour's and the Conservative Party's attitudes to Europe are outlined to see whether they were united or divided on the issue and whether the attitude to Europe of the four PMs in question was in line with the predominant party view. Both aspects affect his leeway in policy-making.

5.2 Parliamentary Party Attitudes to European Integration

5.2.1 The Labour Party

Since the early 1960s Britain's role in Europe had been a problematic issue for the Labour Party. Although the official party line in the 1960s and 1970s was in favour of EC membership, the issue was a source of intraparty division (Daniels 1998: 72). During James Callaghan's premiership the previous renegotiation process and the referendum on EC membership in 1975 had only papered over these divisions. Due to the public's decisive vote in the referendum to remain a member,[10] the split in the Labour Party was not so obvious.[11] The party had three main blocks with differing views on European integration. There were the left-wing Anti-Europeans, who opposed EC membership. They saw the Community as a capitalist club, which they did not want to belong to and which they thought would only hinder the establishment of socialism in the UK. The second group were the pro-Europeans mainly from the party's social democratic wing. They made up about a fifth of all Labour MPs between 1964 and 1979, but had little support among the unions and the rest of the party. Thirdly, there were the pragmatists who accepted Britain's

[9]For details of the government's dispute with the trade unions over pay which culminated in extensive strikes by the unions during the 'Winter of Discontent' 1978/1979, see Hay (2009).

[10]67% voted for the UK to remain in the EC, 33% against it (Butler 1979: 151).

[11]In Parliament the government only succeeded with support of the opposition: 248 Conservatives, 138 Labour MPs and 12 Liberal MPs voted for Britain to remain in the EC; 145 Labour MPs voted against it, while others abstained (Norton 1980: 60).

European integration but were not enthusiastic about it. Most of the parliamentary party's centre-left and the party leadership belonged to this group (Ashford 1992: 143–145). Overall, Labour's period in office in the 1970s was characterised by a "lack of enthusiasm for European integration" (Daniels 1998: 73).

After the defeat at the 1979 general election the left wing managed to achieve a dominant position in the party and enforced an anti-European policy. At the 1980 Labour party conference the aim to leave the EC became official party line. This contributed to the decision of leading pro-Europeans such as Roy Jenkins, David Owen and Shirley Williams to leave the party and found the Social Democratic Party (SDP) in 1981 (Ashford 1992: 128; Daniels 1998: 73).

Under Neil Kinnock, party leader after the 1983 general election defeat, Labour gradually gave up its anti-European position. By the 1987 general election the demand for an EC exit had been abandoned (Ashford 1992: 128–129). But it took a policy review after Labour's third successive election defeat in 1987 until the party formulated an explicitly pro-European policy approach. This showed that the left had lost its dominant role in the party. Also, Labour was now able to criticise the Conservative government's policy on Europe and depict itself as representative of a "constructive Europeanism" (Daniels 1998: 76–77) previously embodied by the Conservatives, who had moved away from this stance since the late 1980s (see Sect. 5.2.2). Developments in the European Community were conducive to the party's policy change. Plans to establish a 'social' Europe correlated with Labour thinking and the party achieved positive results at European elections. Thus it was able to exert political influence at the European level which it could not do at home. This made a positive engagement with Europe attractive (Smith 2012: 1282–1283).

During the 1990s Labour remained pro-European. Under John Smith, party leader from 1992, it supported ERM membership and the ratification of the Maastricht Treaty. His successor from 1994, Tony Blair, continued the pro-European policy (Daniels 1998: 77–78). In government from 1997, Labour wanted to present a positive attitude to European integration. It did so by joining the Social Chapter on which the Major government had negotiated an opt-out in Maastricht. But on EMU it remained cautious, much as it had been in opposition. Then it had said that there was no constitutional reason to rule out joining the euro, while suggesting that it was not likely Britain would join in the first wave in 1999 and not without a referendum on membership (Gamble and Kelly 2000: 1–2). Divisions in the party over Europe in general and EMU in particular remained. A small number of Labour MPs still opposed European integration, but the largest section of the Parliamentary Labour Party (PLP) was pragmatic about it (Gamble and Kelly 2000: 11, 14).

5.2.2 The Conservative Party

Similar to Labour the Conservatives had to deal with party splits during the ratification of the *European Communities Act* in 1972, which gave legal effect in UK law to membership of the EC (Norton 2011). Yet by the late 1970s/early 1980s they presented themselves as the party of Europe (Ashford 1992: 123; Ludlam 1998: 31).

As prime minister from 1979 Margaret Thatcher robustly defended British interests at the European level such as on Britain's contribution to the European budget. The party supported her course (Baker et al. 1993: 420). Despite the robust defence of British interests, the Conservative Party (1983) advocated European integration and in its 1983 general election manifesto referred to the disastrous impact an exit from the Community would have:

> The European Community is the world's largest trading group. It is by far our most important export market. Withdrawal would be a catastrophe for this country... It would be a fateful step towards isolation, at which only the Soviet Union and her allies would rejoice. (44)

Yet from the mid-1980s intraparty tensions over Europe grew. They related to the Single European Act and the question of ERM membership (Baker et al. 1993: 420). The party strongly supported the abolishment of trade barriers to complete the Common Market in the negotiations leading to the Single European Act in 1985–1986. The treaty was seen as a reflection of Thatcherite economic policy, thus as part of a British success story. At the same time, it included the transfer of significant national sovereignty rights to the EC. Moreover, the treaty cleared the way for two projects unacceptable to a number of Conservatives including Thatcher: Economic and Monetary Union (EMU) and Europe-wide social standards (Smith 2012: 1281–1282).

The intraparty tensions became real conflicts during the ratification of the Maastricht Treaty in the early 1990s (Baker et al. 1993: 420). The main point of contention was the concept of a future European Union. Many Conservatives believed the treaty would lead to a European entity that would constrain Britain's freedom of action and diminish national sovereignty (Heath et al. 2001: 69). The ratification process was only begun after the 1992 general election, which saw a number of new more Eurosceptic Conservatives join parliament. Despite the opt-outs from the Social Chapter and EMU, several new MPs rejected the treaty. The government secured ratification only after fierce disputes and repeated backbench rebellions (see Sect. 9.3) (Smith 2012: 1283).

The Eurosceptic right wing became larger after the 1997 general election, yet the party remained divided over Europe under the leadership of the Eurosceptic William Hague. When the shadow cabinet in October 1997, for example, decided to rule out joining the Eurozone for the current and the following parliament, two members of the frontbench resigned and former ministers such as Michael Heseltine and Douglas Hurd publicly criticised the decision (Norton 2002: 70–71, 81–82).

Over the following years the Conservative Party became ever more Eurosceptic. By the time Michael Howard was party leader (2003–2005) the Conservative Party was mainly Eurosceptic (Kavanagh and Butler 2005: 41). This remained the case after David Cameron became party leader in 2005 (Grant 2009: 2).

This short overview illustrates that both parties significantly shifted their positions on European integration in the time period covered in this study. When comparing the four prime ministers' attitudes on European integration with the prevailing views in their respective parties, James Callaghan and John Major faced the most difficulties. Both led parties divided over Europe. Therefore their attitude to European integration was bound to diverge from the view of at least one section of their party. Margaret Thatcher and Tony Blair, by contrast, led parties largely united on the issue. Either PM's view was in line with the prevailing party view. In Thatcher's case the Conservatives began to divide over Europe later in her premiership, but she did not yet have to address the split much. John Major in turn had to do so, for instance, during the Maastricht Treaty ratification.

The next chapter outlines the British media's attitudes to Europe, particularly those of the newspapers. They, too, are part of the prime minister's leadership environment.

5.3 Media Attitudes to European Integration

In the British media there is a difference between political news coverage by the press and by television. While broadcasters are to be impartial in their reports, which is also ensured by regulation, the print media can explicitly voice political attitudes and be biased (McNair 1999: 50, 51). Therefore, this overview of media attitudes to European integration between 1976 and 2007 focuses on the press, as it is newspapers that voice a political stance on it. Moreover, as a study from 2001 found, television coverage of European affairs tends to rise in the context of special events such as the introduction of the euro or European Council meetings. But before and after these events it tends to be hardly visible on the television news agenda (De Vreese 2001).

By the 1970s massive changes had taken place on the British newspaper market. The number of papers supporting the political left had declined after the end of the Second World War. The market was now dominated by conservative papers which supported the corresponding party (Temple 2008: 64). This became particularly obvious, when the tabloid *Sun*, now owned by Rupert Murdoch, moved to the right. While claiming in the run up to the 1979 general election that it was not a Tory newspaper, it nevertheless recommended to its traditional Labour readership to vote for the Conservatives (Greenslade 2003: 362). Despite events such as the first election to the European Parliament in 1979, the media in the late 1970s did not take much interest in European affairs. Newspapers such as *The Times* and magazines like *The Economist* informed regularly about developments in Europe, but many other national newspapers and broadcasters did not (Butler and Marquand 1981: 148). When it was discussed in autumn 1978 whether Britain should join the European Monetary System, apart from *The Times* all the quality newspapers—the *Guardian*, the *Financial Times*, the *Daily Telegraph*, the *Sunday Telegraph*, the *Observer* and the *Sunday Times*—supported entry. So did *The Economist* (Ludlow 1982: 222).

In the early 1980s British public debate on Europe focused on the question whether the country should leave the EC, with Labour arguing for exit. The press, however, was inclined to support Prime Minister Thatcher's view that membership brought economic advantages. While they criticised issues such as the British budget contribution and the Community's agriculture and fishery policies, an intensive debate on European integration had no priority for them. This was among other things because it was a complex issue, in which the public appeared to show little interest. Also, other topics such as trade union power or the threat from the Soviet Union were seen as more important and received more coverage (Wilkes and Wring 1998: 196–197).

The decline in support by the press for European integration was a gradual development over the course of the 1980s. It first affected the conservative tabloids and later the broadsheets (Wilkes and Wring 1998: 204). It was facilitated by several factors. Changes in the ownership of several newspapers had an effect. Proprietors such as Rupert Murdoch or Conrad Black were no longer private owners of these papers as their predecessors had been. They depended on their international companies to fund these ventures. Hence, they needed to be financially viable (Greenslade 2003: 375). This also meant more competition on the newspaper market. The publication of sensational stories and the use of Eurosceptic populism were viewed by many papers as an important tool to succeed in the competition for readers (Wilkes and Wring 1998: 205). Euromyth stories, reports about the EC/EU's apparent regulation spleen, particularly published by the tabloids, were part of it (Bates 1999: 36). Also, the tabloids now covered Europe differently. For instance, treaty changes were increasingly depicted as threats to Britain's identity and sovereignty. Their coverage exhibited ever more chauvinistic tendencies, regularly attacked the other EC members and used military analogies and language to do so (Daddow 2012: 1232). When Thatcher spoke at the College of Europe in Bruges in 1988 attacking European federalism and demanding the EC to be a partnership based on trade, the conservative print media (as well as the Labour-supporting *Daily Mirror*) backed her (Wilkes and Wring 1998: 197).

While the press in general moved into a more Eurosceptic direction, there were attempts to counter this process. In 1990, for example, Robert Maxwell founded the pro-European weekly *European*. But by 1992 he had sold it already. The new owners hired Andrew Neil, a staunch critic of European integration, as editor of the media group to which the *European* now belonged. He used the paper to voice his opposition to the EU and the single currency. As the paper continued to do badly financially—not least because Neil's political line was unpopular in a paper formerly committed to advancing European integration—it was closed in 1998 (Greenslade 2003: 516, 671–672).

After Thatcher's resignation in November 1990 the print media's attitude towards European integration appeared to become ever more unpredictable. Initially most national newspapers unenthusiastically accepted the results of the Maastricht Treaty. But after the ERM exit in autumn 1992 they in part adjusted their position and became much more critical of European integration (Wilkes and Wring 1998: 198). From then on Prime Minister Major was continually exposed to massive press criticism which was much related to his government's European policy. Despite the fact that the press was predominately conservative they much criticised Major's failed economic policy signified by the ERM exit and what they saw as a flawed European policy (Temple 2008: 71; Greenslade 2003: 613–614). Proprietors such as Rupert Murdoch, Conrad Black and Lord Rothermere were opposed to European integration and influenced their papers' approach to Europe accordingly (Greenslade 2003: 613; Daddow 2012: 1231). Newspapers like *The Times* and the *Daily Mail* had for a long time followed a Eurosceptic line and the *Daily Telegraph* did so from the mid-1990s (Scammell and Harrop 1997: 159).

Shortly before the 1997 general election the *Sun* switched its political allegiance from the Tories to Labour. Its Sunday sister *The News of the World* followed shortly after (Jones 2001: 179). But it soon showed that the *Sun*'s support for Labour was not all-encompassing. While it praised Blair as leader it remained suspicious of his party's European policy (including on EMU). As a result, its coverage was ambivalent because it attempted to combine its animosity to the euro and European integration with support for the less Eurosceptic of the two main parties (Scammell and Harrop 1997: 160).

During Blair's premiership the *Guardian*, the *Independent* and the *Daily Mirror* were in general positive about European integration and the EU, while papers such as the *Daily Telegraph*, the *Daily Mail* and *The Times* were Eurosceptic (Morgan 2003: 38). On EMU some journalists and proprietors joined forces with anti-euro lobby groups. For instance, Murdoch supported 'Business for Sterling', an industry lobby group opposing the euro. Senior staff of *The Times* joined the 'New Europe Group', which backed EU but not Eurozone membership (Seymour-Ure 2002: 122).

By the time of the 2001 general election the Eurosceptic dominance in the print media was less strong than it had been in 1997, though only because the *Daily Express* and *Daily Star* had a new owner sympathetic to European integration. Various newspapers remained suspicious of the government's European policy and the *Sun*, for instance, continued to oppose joining the euro vehemently (Seymour-Ure 2002: 136–137).

The press became increasingly Eurosceptic between 1976 and 2007. But the papers' views of European integration were not necessarily in line with their partisan support. An example is the *Sun* during Blair's premiership as it continuously criticised the government's European policy while declaring its support for New Labour.

The media analysis in Chap. 10 focuses on press coverage of governmental European policy during the four prime ministers' terms in office. Due to the Eurosceptic dominance in the British press, the readership exposed to Eurosceptic coverage of European affairs is by far larger than the group which regularly consumes a positive or at least neutral coverage of it (Daddow 2012: 1227). This development is relevant to a prime minister and might affect his political leadership in European policy, if he attempts through media management to use the print media as a communication channel between him and the public.

5.4 Public Attitudes to European Integration

Opinion poll data of the time period covered in this study illustrates that British public opinion has tended to be fairly unenthusiastic about Britain's European integration. Eurobarometer surveys from 1976 to 2007 in which a representative section of the public was asked what they thought of Britain's EC/EU membership (see Figs. 5.1, 5.2 and 5.3)[12] show the public's limited support for membership in the late 1970s and first half of the 1980s. Even shortly after Britain's accession to the European Community and the subsequent referendum vote on membership in 1975, the public exhibited fairly low support for European integration. In spring 1980, for instance, only 22% of the respondents thought it was a good thing, while 48% saw membership as a bad thing (see Fig. 5.1). This low support had a number of reasons. For one, the UK had joined at a time when the European economies were in recession and had to battle domestic problems such as inflation and rising unemployment. The public appears to have blamed the country's economic problems on the EC (Nugent 1992: 191). Secondly, several politicians voiced hostility towards European integration in general or specific aspects of it in the late 1970s and early 1980s. As seen in Sect. 5.2.1, already during Callaghan's premiership the Labour left agitated against the EC (so did a small part of the Conservative right) and in the early 1980s Labour demanded an exit from the Community. The drawn-out dispute with the other member states over Britain's contribution to the European budget between 1979 and 1984 as well did not contribute to the public putting European integration in a positive light. This was similar with Thatcher's rallying against plans to give the Community a social dimension in the late 1980s. Voters who were largely uninformed about and not much interested in the EC tended to follow the lead of the parties they supported and reflected their views. Voters of Labour, therefore, were much more hostile to European integration until the late 1980s than their Conservative counterparts. Yet also the Conservative voters did not favour the EC as much as might have been expected (Nugent 1992: 191).

However, from the mid-1980s support for membership grew and peaked in 1991. In both 1991 surveys 57% of respondents thought membership to be a good thing, while only 13% (in spring) and 15% (in autumn) saw it as a bad thing. It is interesting to note that the proportion of the public, who viewed European integration positively, grew at the end of Thatcher's premiership and continued to do so

[12]Since 1973 the European Commission twice a year does a survey of member states citizens' views on European integration. Part of the Eurobarometer survey series is the question: "Generally speaking, do you think that (your country's) membership of the European Union/European Community (Common Market) is...?" Possible answers are: a good thing, a bad thing, neither good nor bad, DK—don't know.

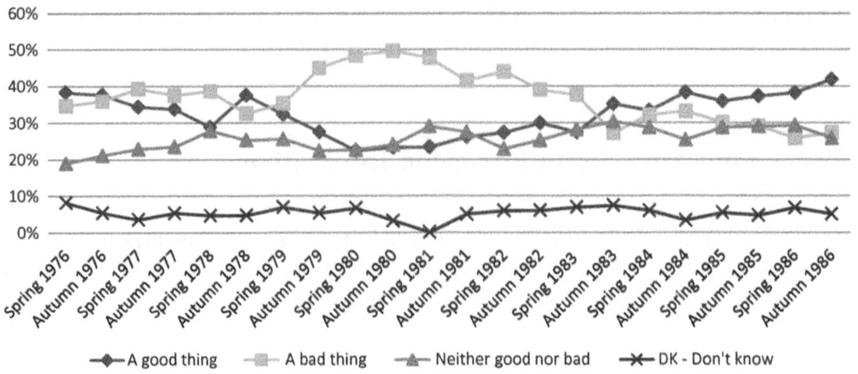

Fig. 5.1 Support for British EC membership 1976–1986 (Own illustration based on data from European Commission 2016)

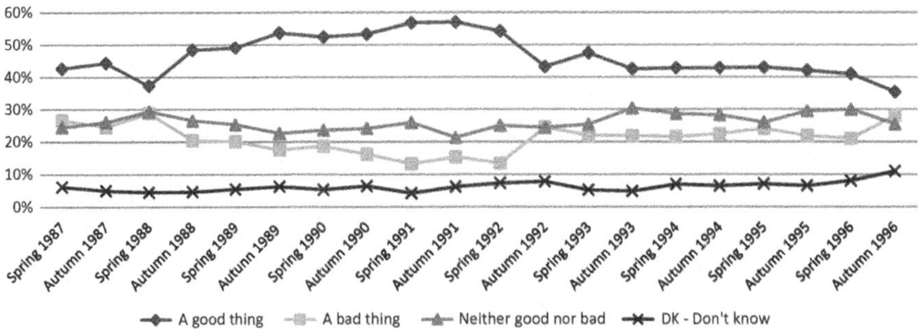

Fig. 5.2 Support for British EC/EU membership 1987–1996 (Own illustration based on data from European Commission 1995, 1996, 2016)

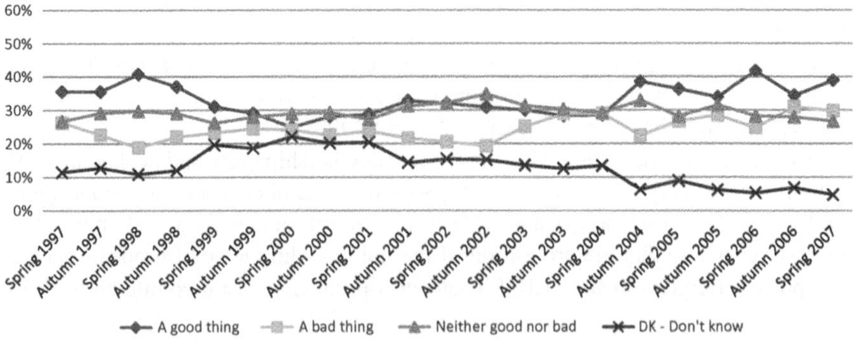

Fig. 5.3 Support for British EU membership 1997–2007 (Own illustration based on data from European Commission 1999, 2016)

after her resignation (see Fig. 5.2). As Jorgen Rasmussen (1997) noted, despite the fact that Thatcher held a more sceptical position on the EC and particularly on EMU in the late 1980s, there was no transmission of her views to the British public on these issues at the time. Meanwhile the Labour Party as well as the trade unions changed their attitude from rejection of European integration to support (Nugent 1992: 192, 193). Public support, however, already declined after the end of the Maastricht Treaty negotiations (December 1991). Then the Conservative government exhibited severe divisions over the ratification of the treaty. The reason for a further decline in public support of membership in the following year is probably related to Britain's ERM exit in autumn 1992 (see Chap. 3). Yet the surveys for the subsequent years up to the 1997 general election also show that disagreements in the Conservative Party between pro-Europeans and Eurosceptics did not much affect public opinion, which remained fairly stable. The dip in public support for membership by 6% between spring and autumn 1996 (see Fig. 5.2) probably relates to the BSE crisis, when the Major administration in spring/summer 1996 responded to the EU's decision to ban all imports of British beef products with a policy of non-cooperation at EU level (Seldon 1998: 641, 650).

During Tony Blair's premiership (1997–2007) public support for European integration appeared to decline (see Fig. 5.3). In parallel the Conservatives became increasingly Eurosceptic (see Sect. 5.2.2). Nonetheless, the Tories could not profit from this alignment with public opinion. A study by Geoffrey Evans (1998) indicates that the Conservative's stance on Europe at the 1997 general election was a handicap. This was because the public, although by then also more Eurosceptic, saw the party—due to its remaining divisions—either as too Eurosceptic or too pro-European. This discouraged pro-European as well as Eurosceptic voters to vote for them.

In subsequent years, supporters of membership remained in a majority, yet by autumn 2003/spring 2004 their share was almost even with those considering it a bad thing. In autumn 2003 28% of respondents thought EU membership was good, while 29% rated it as a bad thing. In spring 2004 both were at 29%.

Overall, it has to be taken into account with regard to British public opinion on EC/EU membership that there have been significant shifts in the proportion of respondents who saw EC/EU membership as a good or a bad thing. In comparison, the proportion of those stating they did not know or thought EC/EU membership was neither good nor bad fluctuated less (at least until 1997). This supports Simon Usherwood's suggestion that the public's preferences on this issue have tended not to run very deep, but to have been highly receptive to leadership from parties or other groups (Usherwood 2002: 217). Moreover, Europe has tended to be no particularly salient issue for British voters in the analysed time period. Between 1976 and 2000, for instance, voters when asked what they considered the most important issues in their country repeatedly placed topics such as unemployment and costs of living, not Britain's relationship with the EC/EU at the top of the list (King 2001: 263–273). Europe also did not tend to be a prominent issue at general elections, because the main parties tended to keep it out of the campaign, fearing they might have to defend their position on it and appeared to show no interest in leading on it

Table 5.1 British turnout at European elections between 1976 and 2007 (European Parliament 2016)

Date	Election turnout in % (UK)	Election turnout in EC/EU-average in %	Election turnout in % (Denmark)
7 June 1979	32.35	61.99	47.82
7 June 1984	32.57	58.98	52.38
15 June 1989	36.37	58.41	46.17
9 June 1994	36.43	56.67	52.92
10 June 1999	24.00	49.51	50.46
10 June 2004	38.52	45.47	47.89

(Smith 2012: 1286). Further indication for the public's somewhat marginal interest in European integration is the fairly stable data over longer time periods in the Eurobarometer surveys of the group of people who viewed EC/EU membership as neither good nor bad. It was hardly ever below 20% and peaked at 35% in 2002. This suggests that one fifth to one third of the public did not necessarily oppose Britain's European integration, but seemed to be largely indifferent to it.

The public's lack of interest in European affairs during the time period analysed here is also discernible when looking at the turnout for European Parliament elections. UK turnout rates have over the years come closer to EU average (which has declined) but even in 2004 with a peak of 38.52% remained well below average (see Table 5.1).[13] When comparing Britain's election turnout with Denmark's, which also joined in 1973 and whose public has also not been enthusiastic about Europe, there are also differences (see Table 5.1).

Overall, the UK public in the 31 years covered in this study appears to have broadly accepted or resigned itself to EC/EU membership, albeit without enthusiasm about European integration. At the same time, the data does not suggest that EC/EU membership then was a salient issue for the public. In contrast, membership appears to have been important to the political elites resulting in massive intraparty divisions over time (see Sect. 5.2). Moreover, it seems to have been an issue on which the press (particularly the tabloids) took an increasing interest (see Sect. 5.3). The following case study analysis looks at how far these attitudes by press and party posed constraints on the prime minister's political leadership in European policy and how the PM dealt with them. Before, however, the premier's resources for political leadership in European policy need to be outlined. This is done in the next chapter.

[13]European elections are considered second-order elections: If voters, not much interested in the EU, choose to vote at all in them, they tend to do this on the basis of domestic not European issues and to use their vote to send a message to their national government (Curtice and Steed 2000: 240).

References

Ashford, N. (1992). The political parties. In S. George (Ed.), *Britain and the European Community: The politics of semi-detachment* (pp. 119–148). Oxford: Clarendon.

Baker, D., Gamble, A., & Ludlam, S. (1993). 1846... 1906... 1996? Conservative splits and European integration. *The Political Quarterly, 64*(4), 420–434.

Bates, S. (1999). Brussels with the blinkers on. *British Journalism Review, 10*(1), 35–40.

Blair, T. (2010). *A journey*. London: Hutchinson.

Butler, D. (1979). Public opinion and Community membership. *The Political Quarterly, 50*(2), 151–156.

Butler, D., & Marquand, D. (1981). *European elections and British politics*. London: Longman.

Callaghan, J. (2006). *Time and chance*. London: Politico's.

Campbell, J. (2011). *The Iron Lady: Margaret Thatcher: From Grocer's daughter to prime minister* (2nd ed.). London: Penguin Books.

Conservative Party. (1983). *The Conservative manifesto 1983*. https://www.margaretthatcher.org/document/131063. Accessed March 8, 2018.

Cradock, P. (1997). *In pursuit of British interests: Reflections on foreign policy under Margaret Thatcher and John Major*. London: John Murray.

Curtice, J., & Steed, M. (2000). Appendix: An analysis of the result. In D. Butler & M. Westlake (Eds.), *British politics and European elections 1999* (pp. 240–256). Basingstoke: Macmillan.

Daddow, O. (2012). The UK media and 'Europe': From permissive consensus to destructive dissent. *International Affairs, 88*(6), 1219–1236.

Daniels, P. (1998). From hostility to 'constructive engagement': The Europeanisation of the Labour Party. *West European Politics, 21*(1), 72–96.

De Vreese, C. H. (2001). 'Europe' in the news: A cross-national comparative study of the news coverage of key EU events. *European Union Politics, 2*(3), 283–307.

Dell, E. (1994). Britain and the origins of the European Monetary System. *Contemporary European History, 3*(1), 1–60.

Denman, R. (1999, May 4). *British Diplomatic Oral History Programme (BDOHP) interview*. Cambridge: Churchill Archives Centre, Churchill College.

Donoughue, B. (2009). *Downing Street diary: With James Callaghan in No. 10* (2nd ed.). London: Pimlico.

European Commission. (1995, Autumn). *Eurobarometer: Public opinion in the European Union*, Report No. 43.

European Commission. (1996, December). *Eurobarometer: Public opinion in the European Union*, Report No. 45.

European Commission. (1999, March). *Eurobarometer: Public opinion in the European Union*, Report No. 50.

European Commission. (2016). *Public opinion: Eurobarometer interactive search 1976–2007*. http://ec.europa.eu/COMMFrontOffice/publicopinion/index.cfm/Chart/getChart/chartType/gridChart/themeKy/3/groupKy/3/savFile/10000. Accessed September 10, 2016.

European Parliament. (2016). *Turnout by country (in %)*. http://www.europarl.europa.eu/elections2014-results/en/turnout.html. Accessed September 12, 2016.

Evans, G. (1998). Euroscepticism and Conservative electoral support: How an asset became liability. *British Journal of Political Science, 28*(4), 573–590.

Franklin, M. (2013). Could and should Britain have joined the European Exchange Rate Mechanism in 1979? A personal memoir. *Journal of Contemporary European Research, 9*(5), 759–766.

Gamble, A., & Kelly, G. (2000). The British Labour Party and monetary union. *West European Politics, 23*(1), 1–25.

Gilmour, I. (1992). *Dancing with dogma: Britain under Thatcherism*. London: Simon & Schuster.

Gowland, D., Turner, A., & Wright, A. (2010). *Britain and European integration since 1945: On the sidelines*. London: Routledge.

Grant, C. (2009). *Cameron's Europe: Can the Conservatives achieve their EU objectives?* London: Centre for European Reform.
Greenslade, R. (2003). *The press gang: How newspapers make profits from propaganda*. London: Macmillan.
Hay, C. (2009). The Winter of Discontent thirty years on. *The Political Quarterly, 80*(4), 545–552.
HC Deb. (1978, December 6), Vol 959, c1424.
HC Deb. (1981, November 4), Vol 12, c68.
HC Deb. (1982, November 12), Vol 31, c782.
Heath, A. F., Jowell, R. M., & Curtice, J. K. (2001). *The rise of New Labour: Party policies and voter choices*. Oxford: Oxford University Press.
Hogg, S., & Hill, J. (1996). *Too close to call: Power and politics - John Major in No. 10* (2nd ed.). London: Warner Books.
Hurd, D. (2009). *Memoirs*. London: Abacus.
Jones, B. (2001). The mass media and political communication. In B. Jones, D. Kavanagh, M. Moran, & P. Norton (Eds.), *Politics UK* (4th ed., pp. 177–204). Harlow: Longman.
Kavanagh, D., & Butler, D. (Eds.). (2005). *The British general election of 2005*. Basingstoke: Palgrave Macmillan.
King, A. (Ed.). (2001). *British political opinion 1937–2000: The Gallup polls*. London: Politico's.
Lawson, N. (1992). *A view from No. 11: Memoirs of a Tory radical*. London: Bantam.
Liddle, R. (2014). *The Europe dilemma: Britain and the drama of EU integration*. London: I.B. Tauris.
Ludlam, S. (1998). The Cauldron: Conservative parliamentarians and European integration. In D. Baker & D. Seawright (Eds.), *Britain for and against Europe: British politics and the question of European integration* (pp. 31–56). Oxford: Clarendon.
Ludlow, P. (1982). *The making of the European Monetary System*. London: Butterworth.
Major, J. (2000). *The autobiography* (2nd ed.). London: HarperCollins.
McNair, B. (1999). *An introduction to political communication* (2nd ed.). London: Routledge.
Morgan, D. (2003). Media coverage of the European Union. In M. Bond (Ed.), *Europe, parliament and the media* (pp. 35–54). London: The Federal Trust.
Norton, P. (1980). *Dissension in the House of Commons 1974–1979*. Oxford: Clarendon.
Norton, P. (2002). The Conservative party: Is there anyone out there? In A. King (Ed.), *Britain at the polls, 2001* (pp. 68–94). New York: Chatham House.
Norton, P. (2011). Divided loyalties: The European Communities Act 1972. *Parliamentary History, 30*(1), 53–64.
Nugent, N. (1992). British public opinion and the European Community. In S. George (Ed.), *Britain and the European Community: The politics of semi-detachment* (pp. 172–201). Oxford: Clarendon.
Powell, J. (2010). *The new Machiavelli: How to wield power in the modern world*. London: The Bodley Head.
Rasmussen, J. (1997). 'What kind of vision is that?' British public attitudes towards the European community during the Thatcher era. *British Journal of Political Sciences, 27*(1), 111–118.
Rentoul, J. (2001). *Tony Blair: Prime minister*. London: Warner Books.
Riddell, P. (2005). Europe. In A. Seldon & D. Kavanagh (Eds.), *The Blair effect 2001–5* (pp. 362–383). Cambridge: Cambridge University Press.
Scammell, M., & Harrop, M. (1997). The press. In D. Butler & D. Kavanagh (Eds.), *The British general election of 1997* (pp. 156–185). Basingstoke: Macmillan.
Scott, D. (2004). *Off Whitehall: A view from Downing Street by Tony Blair's adviser*. London: I.B. Tauris.
Seldon, A. (with Baston, L.) (1998). *Major: A political life* (2nd ed.). London: Phoenix.
Seldon, A. (with Ballinger, C., Collings, D., & Snowdon, P.) (2005). *Blair* (2nd ed.). London: Free Press.

Seymour-Ure, C. (2002). New Labour and the media. In A. King (Ed.), *Britain at the polls, 2001* (pp. 177–142). New York: Chatham House.

Smith, J. (2012). The European dividing line in party politics. *International Affairs, 88*(6), 1277–1295.

Temple, M. (2008). *The British press*. Maidenhead: Open University Press.

Thatcher, M. (1988, September 20). *Speech to the College of Europe ("The Bruges Speech")*. http://www.margaretthatcher.org/document/107332. Accessed August 31, 2016.

Thatcher, M. (2011). *The Downing Street years*. London: Harper Press.

Usherwood, S. (2002). Opposition to the European Union in the UK: The dilemma of public opinion and party management. *Government and Opposition, 37*(2), 211–230.

Wall, S. (2008). *A stranger in Europe: Britain and the EU from Thatcher to Blair*. Oxford: Oxford University Press.

Wallace, W. (1994). Foreign policy. In D. Kavanagh & A. Seldon (Eds.), *The Major effect* (pp. 283–300). London: Macmillan.

Ward, A. J. (1994). Margaret Thatcher and foreign policy. In J. S. Thompson & W. C. Thompson (Eds.), *Prime minister indomitable* (pp. 73–98). Boulder: Westview.

Wilkes, G., & Wring, D. (1998). The British press and European integration: 1948 to 1996. In D. Baker & D. Seawright (Eds.), *Britain for and against Europe: British politics and the question of European integration* (pp. 185–205). Oxford: Clarendon.

Young, H. (1999). *This blessed plot: Britain and Europe from Churchill to Blair* (2nd ed.). London: Papermac.

Chapter 6
Prime Ministerial Resources

This chapter outlines the British prime minister's institutional and individual resources. As explained in Chap. 2, he has resources at his disposal to influence decision-making in the core executive. These can broadly be divided into institutional and individual resources. Such a classification is helpful to analyse an actor's political leadership and is used here. But as mentioned in Sect. 2.2.3, a look at political science literature shows that the classification of resources into these categories varies (e.g. Bennister 2007; Heffernan 2003; Smith 1999). Thus it has to be taken into account that this division is not always as clear-cut as one might hope.

6.1 Institutional Resources

Institutional resources derive from an actor's role (Smith 1999: 31). In the prime minister's case they include the right to appoint and dismiss the members of government and the management of the cabinet system with his right to set the cabinet's agenda and to set up cabinet committees. In addition, the Prime Minister's Office provides administrative support and helps the PM develop strategic oversight across his government. He regulates the Civil Service and determines the core executive's organisational structure by defining departmental areas of responsibility. Further institutional resources include, for instance, the right to award honours, negotiate treaties, declare war and send troops into armed conflict (Smith 1999: 75–76; Bennister 2007: 330). Until the introduction of the Fixed-term Parliaments Act in 2011 he was also able to decide about the dissolution of parliament (Kelly and White 2016).[1] Without formal constitutional restrictions of his capacity to exercise

[1]The Fixed-term Parliaments Act in 2011 removed the PM's power to dissolve parliament and set out that general elections had to be held every 5 years. For details on the act see Kelly and White (2016).

B. Bujard, *The British Prime Minister in the Core Executive*, Contributions to Political Science, https://doi.org/10.1007/978-3-319-89953-4_6

these rights, he can do so in the context of comparably weak parliamentary control (Bennister 2007: 330). His option to conduct two-level politics at the European and the national level can also be considered an institutional resource which can affect his role in the core executive particularly in European policy-making. It results from his membership in the European Council in his function as head of government.

In this chapter the right of appointment and dismissal, cabinet management and the Prime Minister's Office as well as the PM's options for two-level politics are reviewed more closely as the premier can influence European policy-making particularly with these resources. The prime ministers reviewed in this study could also draw on the Cabinet Office for advice and information (Clifford 2000: 26). Its European Secretariat (COES) (see Sect. 4.2) and Central Policy Review Staff (CPRS)[2] advised them on European policy. Therefore in Chap. 7 the COES and the CPRS are considered as part of the premier's resource structure, too. However, they are not included in this chapter, because as part of the Cabinet Office they were not tasked to work exclusively for the premier but for the whole of the cabinet.

6.1.1 Right of Appointment

The PM has the right to appoint and dismiss the members of his government. He can do so to reward or penalise party colleagues and sometimes to promote particular policies (Kavanagh 2001: 428). However, his right of patronage is not unencumbered and he needs to take several constraining factors into account when forming his government. For instance, he needs to ensure that the various strands in his party are represented. He has to consider colleagues with their own followership in the party (Burch 1995: 108). Due to this, up to two-thirds of cabinet posts are already allocated before a government comes into office, independently of the premier's preferences (Donoughue 1987: 14). Moreover, the candidate in question ought to be a Member of Parliament (MP). The premier can appoint a non-parliamentarian to the House of Lords and then to the government. But this can foster discontent among parliamentary party MPs (Kavanagh 2001: 429). Overall the personnel pool from which a PM can select the members of his government is limited. On average, post-war governments have consisted of about a quarter of the governing party (70–80 MPs) from the House of Commons. But there are always MPs who will not be selected for a government post because they are too old, too young or not interested. Personal expertise and ability have to be taken into account as well when choosing a candidate (Giddings 1995: 39–40).

Cabinet reshuffles are tools to demonstrate authority and give the impression of "purposeful activity" (Shell 1995: 20) on the part of the prime minster. There can be other motives, too. For example, a premier may be unhappy with a minister's work

[2]It only existed under Callaghan and Thatcher. Thatcher abolished it after the 1983 general election (Kavanagh and Seldon 2000:153).

or want to change a government's image, for instance, by promoting young, new talents (Alderman and Cross 1985: 389). The timing of a reshuffle is crucial. A PM is least inhibited if he has just won an election (Donoughue 1987: 14). Yet reshuffles are not without problems. A new minister's appointment can temporarily disrupt the existing ministerial team's work. Moreover, dismissed ministers can become a force of intraparty dissidence and provide backbencher campaigns against the government with particular authority (Alderman and Cross 1985: 389, 396).

While there are limits to a premier's freedom of appointment, he can try to counteract it by allocating key portfolios to colleagues with similar views (Burch 1995: 109). Or he can attempt to constrain an intraparty rival by promoting others as well into government—hoping they compete with each other for his succession and not with him (Alderman and Cross 1985: 391). Nevertheless, the resource of appointment and dismissal is at best a limited one as the premier most of the time has to engage in some form of intraparty coalition building when putting together his government team (Burch 1995: 108).

6.1.2 Cabinet Management

In the British political system the term 'cabinet' generally refers to the full cabinet of the cabinet ministers under chairmanship of the prime minister. But, as noted in Sect. 4.1, there is further a system of cabinet committees, in which political decisions are taken and whose set-up depends on the issue under discussion. There are permanent (standing) and temporary (ad hoc) committees. At official level there are committees as well which consist of civil servants and which are set up to complement the ministerial committees (Hennessy 1986: 5, 30–31).

The prime minister is "chairman of the cabinet" (Giddings 1995: 31). He has two key resources to manage this system. The first is his right of appointment and dismissal. As he determines the set up and chair of a cabinet committee he can influence the balance of power in it. He can constrain the leeway of colleagues with political goals different to his, for instance, by excluding them from a particular committee. He can also choose which committees to chair himself. This can provide him with further opportunity to influence political decision-making as he can veto proposals in these settings (Kavanagh 2001: 425; Smith 1999: 169). Yet there are limits to his room for manoeuvre on the composition of committees. For example he will not be able to keep the minister responsible for the subject area out of a committee—even if that minister pursues a different policy than he does (Giddings 1995: 44).

A second resource to manage the cabinet system is the premier's right to determine the agenda, date and frequency of meetings (Shell 1995: 20). His leeway is greater on temporary cabinet committees as he is less constrained in determining their scope of responsibility (Kavanagh 2001: 425). But there are limits to his ability to determine the cabinet agenda as it can seldom be based solely on the premier's preferences and is often much influenced by the external context.

A long term trend in British politics has been the full cabinet's loss of power as main decision-making body of the executive. Many political decisions are not even taken in cabinet committees any longer, but are pre-decided in small ministerial groups outside the cabinet system. Informal rules of governance have developed such as ad hoc-meetings of ministers or bilaterals of the premier with the minister handling the policy. The relevant cabinet committee then only decides on the implementation of decisions taken elsewhere (Heffernan 2003: 358, 359, 2005: 612). At the same time, such a decision-making process focused on small groups is often in the interest of ministers who may be disinclined to voice their views on policy matters as Nigel Lawson (1992) confirmed:

> Ministers too often see themselves first and foremost as departmental chiefs with their own departmental battles to fight. When an issue arises... where the Prime Minister of the day and the responsible Minister... are wholly and indeed enthusiastically at one, their colleagues—who have causes of their own over which they are either seeking Prime Ministerial support or resisting Prime Ministerial pressure—are disinclined to raise objections. (562)

Such departmentalism strengthens the PM's position in the core executive as "he or she reaggregates the disaggregated government, something that locates the prime ministership at the centre of the loop, making him or her the principal node of key core executive networks" (Heffernan 2005: 613). Moreover, as ministers need to focus on the policy field they handle, they often depend on information from No. 10, if they want to know what is happening in other parts of the government (Thomas 1998: 161). This gives the premier considerable power to interpret political events.

However, the full cabinet can still have a key function in executive decision-making, because if it is no longer a place for discussion and debate, political conflicts will be carried out somewhere else, possibly in the public arena (Bennister 2007: 334). If a prime minister wants to avoid this, he has to ensure that the full cabinet remains a place in which political decisions are discussed. This gives the full cabinet a limited potential to constrain a premier—even if it is no longer the place where political decisions are taken.

6.1.3 The Prime Minister's Office (PMO)

The premier receives administrative support from his office in No. 10 Downing Street. Officials at No. 10 such as private secretaries are delegated from departments and stay on average for 3 years. This form of delegation is to ensure that Downing Street does not lose the link to the departments (Lee et al. 1998: 52). Staff size increased between 1976 and 2007. In 1978 Callaghan's office had a staff of about 70 (HC Deb 7 February 1978, cc463–464W). Thatcher's office had 63 members of staff in 1986 (Hennessy 1990: 383). In 1993 John Major's office had a staff of 107 (Burch and Holliday 1996: 28). Already in 1998 Tony Blair had a staff of almost 200 (Kavanagh and Seldon 2000: 306). However, these are modest numbers compared to other heads of government's administrative support. The German chancellery, for instance, had a staff of about 620 in 2016 (Presse- und Informationsamt der Bundesregierung 2016).

In the following paragraphs the main sections of the Prime Minister's Office are outlined.

The *Private Office* links the premier with the cabinet system and departments (Burch and Holliday 1996: 28). It briefs ministries about the prime minister's views and decisions and him on departmental activities and thinking (Lee et al. 1998: 66). Under the Principal Private Secretary's leadership private secretaries cover different policy fields and governmental duties. For European policy this is the Private Secretary for Foreign or Overseas Affairs. He is in close contact with the relevant departments, particularly the Foreign Office (FCO). He reviews all foreign policy related documents sent to the premier and determines which he needs to see. He comments on FCO papers, drafts prime ministerial speeches and statements on foreign policy and prepares prime ministerial trips such as to international summits to which he accompanies him (Lee et al. 1998: 41, 44). He sits in on cabinet and cabinet committee meetings when foreign policy is discussed (Cartledge 2007).

All secretaries have to be able to anticipate what the premier thinks in the subject area they handle. Yet as civil servants they are not to identify too closely with the incumbent of the day and his political interests (Kavanagh and Seldon 2000: 9–10, 15). But they must be loyal to him (Cartledge 2007; Powell 2000). To ensure administrative continuity, Private Office staff stay in place if prime minister or government change (Lee et al. 1998: 52).

The *Political Office* supports the premier as party leader and handles the communication with the party (Kavanagh 2001: 412). Among other personal staff of the PM such as a constituency secretary, who handles constituency issues, it includes a political secretary and a parliamentary private secretary (Lee et al. 1998: 85, 96).

Particularly the political secretary is responsible for linking prime minister and party. He ensures that the premier does not neglect his duties as party leader. The political secretary is in close contact with the party headquarter and the party in the country (Hogg and Hill 1996: 23). With the headquarter he organises the premier's party appointments. He relays party-relevant information and handles party correspondence. He comments on papers discussed in No. 10 and drafts papers for the premier analysing political ideas and proposals from a party perspective. At the PM's request, he attends meetings with ministers and officials. In addition, he drafts prime ministerial speeches on party issues and reviews drafts written by others (Lee et al. 1998: 86). When the governing party is united the political secretary's role is less demanding than when it is divided (Kavanagh and Seldon 2000: 314).

The parliamentary private secretary (PPS) handles the party in parliament. He attends meetings of party committees and of backbenchers, keeps in touch with MPs and functions as a communication channel between premier and parliamentary party (Kavanagh and Seldon 2000: 27–28). He is "the Prime Minister's eyes and ears in the House of Commons and the House of Lords" (Hogg and Hill 1996: 23).

The Political Office, whose members are political appointees and therefore do not have the same obligation to political neutrality as civil servants, is newly set up with each change of premier or government. As a result the prime minister of the day here has more influence on structure and staff selection than in other parts of No. 10 (Lee et al. 1998: 84, 99).

The No. 10 *Press Office* handles the relationship between prime minister and media. Head is the Chief Press Secretary who is supported by a team of press officers (Burch and Holliday 1996: 28). He can, but is not required to, be a civil servant. He is seen as the premier's spokesman and for several years now holds the title 'Prime Minister's Official Spokesman' (Seymour-Ure 2003: 129, 137). One of his key tasks is to inform the lobby of political journalists of selected UK media outlets about prime ministerial and governmental activities and thinking (Kavanagh and Seldon 2000: 21). He is also "*adviser on media relations*, *agent* (or intermediary) with news media, and *coordinator* of government information [emphasis in the original]" (Seymour-Ure 2003: 125). He has to know how the premier would respond to an issue should it arise. Thus, a relationship based on confidence between prime minister and press secretary is crucial (Lee et al. 1998: 75). At the same time, he has to have a good relationship with the media (Seymour-Ure 1995: 195).[3]

The *Policy Unit* was founded by Harold Wilson in 1974 (Kavanagh and Seldon 2000: 24). It functions as a think-tank and advises the prime minister on policy (Willetts 1987: 450). It does not only react to departmental proposals but also develops policy initiatives (Clifford 2000: 32). The Unit has to be on good terms with the Private Office and departments to be effective. Its members need to be informed about important papers and invited to key meetings (Kavanagh and Seldon 2000: 25). Individual members of staff handle specific subject areas (Willetts 1987: 443). They can be career civil servants, but more often are temporary civil servants or special advisers (Lee et al. 1998: 101). How the Unit works and on which issues it focuses, depends much on the premier's interests and the style of the Head of the Unit (Lee et al. 1998: 117).

Apart from this institutionalised form of advice there are other *advisers* in No. 10. Prime ministers have increasingly turned to individual external advisers and sometimes to think-tanks (Burch and Holliday 1996: 29; Smith 1999: 173, 174).

[3]As he transmits the view of his boss who is a politician, he is sometimes criticised for being partisan. This can be difficult, if he is a career civil servant, for more see Seymour-Ure (2003: 144–150).

6.1.4 Two-Level Politics

At the European level the prime minister has particularly been active in the European Council where he interacts with his fellow heads of state and government. Since its creation in 1974 it has become "the most authoritative decision-making centre in the Community" (Dyson 1994: 95). With decisions on treaty revisions and enlargements the European Council has significantly shaped the EC/EU's constitutional system over the years. Moreover, in situations of crisis it regularly takes a leading role (Wessels and Schäfer 2014: 233, 234). Through his European Council membership the premier can exert pressure on his government in European policy. When he negotiates there he often has to take decisions on the spot without being able to draw on advice from the cabinet and to consult his government colleagues (Wall 2008: 198). This gives him some leeway to take decisions at the European level independently, which is tolerated by his cabinet colleagues as Edmund Dell, Callaghan's trade minister, observed: "The Prime Minister has to go to the European Council and he has to make decisions. His cabinet colleagues back home are not going to overthrow him because he had made a decision. He has to do that. It is part of the nature of the European Community" (Dell and Hunt 1994: 471). The European Council meets at least twice a year to decide key European policy aspects including financial, monetary, economic and foreign policy and home affairs (Wessels and Schäfer 2014: 235, 236–237). Moreover, it often functions as a court of appeal for problems for which no solution was found at lower decision-making levels (Wall 2008: 195). The negotiating style in the European Council is more direct and personal than, for instance, in the Council of the European Union (Wessels and Schäfer 2014: 238). Due to their political importance for its members and as the issues dealt with are often highly sensitive, decisions are generally taken by consensus (Hayes-Renshaw and Wallace 1997: 162). Package deals are an important element of decision-making (Wessels and Schäfer 2014: 238). Nonetheless, there are provisions for decisions which can be taken by qualified or simple majority (Wessels and Schäfer 2014: 235). This was firstly used in June 1985, when Thatcher among others was outvoted on the set up of an IGC for a treaty revision (Hayes-Renshaw and Wallace 1997: 162). Overall, the prime minister's membership in the European Council and his ability to take independent decisions there have enhanced his position in the European policy decision-making process at home.

6.2 Individual Resources

A prime minister's individual or informal resources are not derived from his post but from his personal preferences and capabilities. For instance, some PM have more political support or authority than other incumbents of the post (Smith 1999: 31). Authority is here understood as "an acceptance of power without needing to exercise any formal capabilities" (Smith 1999: 77). The post itself generates authority as Bernard Donoughue (1987), part of James Callaghan's No. 10 staff, noted:

> All Prime Ministers have a degree of authority independent of personal stature. Some authority is intrinsic to the position of Prime Minister: it comes naturally and automatically with the office. It was very striking to observe how, from the moment Mr Callaghan became Prime Minister, other politicians who had been friends and life-long colleagues began to behave differently towards him. (13)

But authority is foremost an informal resource and varies between prime ministers. Further personal resources include "reputation, skill and ability; association with actual or anticipated political success; public popularity; and high standing in his or her party" (Heffernan 2003: 351). Another personal resource is that the prime minister can decide to intervene directly in specific policy fields (Smith 1999: 76). He might do so to ensure that a wider dimension is considered, for instance, if he thinks a minister is taking too partisan or too departmental a perspective (Donoughue 1987: 6).

The PM can use his personal resources such as authority and personal popularity to lead his parliamentary party and to influence the news agenda. Therefore, his effective leadership of the party can be seen as an expression of his personal resources. At the same time, he needs to retain his party's support to remain prime minister (Heffernan 2003: 351, 354, 2005: 611). His ability to influence the news agenda through political communication can also be considered an expression of his individual resources, as the prime minister "can use his resources of public communication ... to turn authority into power, over events, people and policies" (Seymour-Ure 2003: 61).

This study focuses on the prime minister's leadership and management of his parliamentary party and his political communication and media management. These are particularly significant with regard to two of the three dimensions the subsequent analysis focuses on: the parliamentary party and public opinion.[4]

6.2.1 Parliamentary Party Management

Prime ministerial participation in parliamentary debates has declined in the post-war years. The premier still speaks at the debate of the 'Queen's Speech', the government's announcement of its legislative plans at the start of a parliamentary year. It is also common practice that he takes part in no-confidence debates and makes parliamentary statements, for instance, on international summits he attended

---

[4]Unlike the parliamentary party the premier cannot manage public opinion directly. Therefore this analysis considers media management and political communication as his tools to indirectly influence public opinion. The third dimension, the core executive actors apart from the PM, is addressed when looking at the prime ministerial institutional resources cabinet management, two-level politics and patronage.

(Thomas 1998: 101). He also takes part in Prime Minister's Question Time (PMQ) which used to be biweekly until Tony Blair changed it to once a week (Rose 2001: 137, 138–139). PMQs have added to the impression that the premier is answerable for every part of government policy. Also, his political standing has increasingly become judged by his performance at PMQs (Borthwick 1995: 72).

The premier has several tools to manage his parliamentary party. There is the right of appointment: by supplying MPs with posts, titles or functions, he can try to secure their loyalty (Thomas 1998: 126). Members of government (junior and senior ministers and increasingly parliamentary private secretaries) are bound by the convention of collective responsibility. This requires them to support government policy in parliament once it has been agreed. In the 1992 parliament, for instance, more than a third of Conservative MPs belonged to this group known as the 'payroll vote' (Norton 1993: 46). They are joined by MPs who vote with the government in the hope of eventually receiving a post in it (Thomas 1998: 126).

The PM maintains formal and informal links with his backbenchers which he can use to try to influence them. The most important link is the Whips' Office. The whips are not only responsible for enforcing party discipline in parliament, they also inform the premier about backbencher attitudes and mood, much like his parliamentary private secretary, introduced in Sect. 6.1.3 (Borthwick 1995: 84). Another link between premier and parliamentary party are backbencher organisations such as the Conservative '1922 Committee'. There are also backbench committees on specific subject areas, which can influence government policy (Kavanagh 2001: 241; Norton 1993: 62). The premier can use parliamentary party meetings to try to rally support for his government's decisions (Rose 2001: 142).

An important factor influencing the premier's parliamentary party management is, of course, the distribution of power in the legislature. He can more easily lead his parliamentary party if his government has a decisive majority. Chances of realising legislative bills without needing to modify them due to backbench pressure are better. Rebellions by government MPs need to be large to have an impact (Thomas 1998: 127). But a significant parliamentary majority can also have a paradoxical effect as it can enlarge MPs freedom and limit the whips' ability to put pressure on them to support the government. Backbenchers can decide to vote against government bills—knowing that due to the parliamentary arithmetic their behaviour does not lead to a defeat of the government (Cowley 2005: 40). On the other hand, a slim parliamentary majority does not inevitably result in existential problems for the government. The prospect of a government defeat, a snap election and the loss of one's own parliamentary seat in an election can have a disciplining effect on MPs (Borthwick 1995: 81). But if there is extensive backbench discontent and intraparty rebellions, the premier and the wider party leadership are limited in their control of MPs. With increasing voter volatility, premiers grew wary of threatening to dissolve parliament (Thomas 1998: 128).[5] Withdrawing the whip from MPs (thus excluding

[5]In addition, the 2011 Fixed-term Parliaments Act removed the PM's power to dissolve parliament and set out that general elections had to be held every 5 years; for more on the act see Kelly and White (2016).

them from the parliamentary party) because they voted against the government is problematic when a government majority is slim. It diminishes chances to calculate reliable voting results and the party leadership's remaining options to control the whipless MPs (Alderman 1996: 18). In any case, prime ministers since the 1970s have had to deal with an increase in dissenting votes and independence on the part of their own MPs (Norton 1994: 288).

But a premier's options for effective parliamentary party management do not only depend on parliamentary arithmetic. His popularity with the electorate can play a role, too: if he is seen as an electoral liability, it will be more difficult for him to gain support among MPs (Borthwick 1995: 84). Party management is also influenced by the subject area and the party's attitude to it. If it is divided on it, the premier has to manage the party differently than if it is united.

Overall, it has to be considered that while prime ministers spend less time in parliament and are less involved in parliamentary processes today, maintaining the support of their party in parliament remains crucial to ensure their stay in office (Heffernan 2003: 354). Hence, the governmental party's impact on the premier's leeway in policy-making should not be underestimated.

6.2.2 Political Communication and Media Management

With television becoming ever more popular in the second half of the twentieth century, prime ministers have devoted increasing time and resources to media management (Seymour-Ure 1995: 170). Presentation has become ever more important. How the media might perceive a policy has become a significant aspect when determining which to adopt (Thomas 1998: 143).

Prime ministerial media management can also be a helpful tool to manage the cabinet and the parliamentary party (Seymour-Ure 1995: 196). A PM can, for instance, use the media to discredit another minister's policy initiative to ensure it is not implemented or, if he is unhappy about a colleague's actions, he can make it public through the media.[6] Yet the premier is not the only member of government pursuing media management. Ministers, for instance, do it, too. If there are divisions in government, these can be publicly debated via the media. This form of infighting through media channels is more obvious if a government is unpopular and led by a weak prime minister than if it is popular and the leader strong (Heffernan 2006: 593–594, 595).

The political, economic and societal context influences whether media management is a prime ministerial resource he can use (Heffernan 2006: 598). For instance,

[6]E.g. Theresa May's spokeswoman in 2016 publicly called Brexit minister David Davis's words on the improbability of Britain remaining in the single market after Brexit not government policy but a personal opinion. Davis had said this when he made a parliamentary statement to update MPs about the government's progress on Brexit planning (Asthana 2016).

if the country faces a difficult economic situation, the premier will have greater difficulty to project a positive and assertive image of himself and his government through media management than when the country prospers.

In any case, the PM will be in a stronger position in the core executive if the media portray him as an asset to government. Thus, he can have an individual resource at hand, if he manages to generate positive and supportive media coverage. If the coverage is critical and negative, he is likely to be constrained (Heffernan 2006: 592).

In this chapter the prime minister's key institutional and individual resources on European policy were outlined. It was shown that he is not wholly unconstrained in using them. As noted in Chap. 2, he has more resources than other core executive actors, but not enough to make policy only based on his preferences. He has to exchange resources with others.

In this and the previous chapters the leadership environment, in which the prime minister's political leadership unfolds, as well as the resources available to him have been set out. Next the PM's political leadership with respect to the European monetary policy case studies is analysed. It explores to what extent James Callaghan, Margaret Thatcher, John Major and Tony Blair were able to use their institutional as well as their personal resources identified above to shape policy-making in this area. The analysis is structured according to the three key dimensions identified in Chap. 2: Firstly, the core executive actors apart from the prime minister and, secondly, the parliamentary party in government are considered. It is also of interest to see how the PM can try to influence public opinion. As he cannot manage it directly like the parliamentary party or the cabinet, this analysis considers media management and political communication as prime ministerial tools to indirectly influence public opinion. Questions addressed in the analysis are:

(a) Can the political leadership of the British prime minister in European policy be characterised as prime ministerial predominance or as collective leadership?
(b) Has there been a trend towards more prime ministerial predominance between 1976 and 2007?

References

Alderman, K. (1996). The passage of the European Communities (finance) Act (1995) and its aftermath. *Contemporary British History, 10*(3), 1–20.

Alderman, R. K., & Cross, J. A. (1985). The reluctant knife: Reflections on the prime minister's power of dismissal. *Parliamentary Affairs, 38*(4), 387–408.

Asthana, A. (2016, September 6). David Davis's single market stance 'not government policy'. *The Guardian*.

Bennister, M. (2007). Tony Blair and John Howard: Comparative predominance and 'institution stretch' in the UK and Australia. *The British Journal of Politics and International Relations, 9* (3), 327–345.

Borthwick, R. L. (1995). Prime minister and parliament. In D. Shell & R. Hodder-Williams (Eds.), *Churchill to Major: The British prime ministership since 1945* (pp. 71–103). Armonk: M. E. Sharpe.

Burch, M. (1995). Prime minister and Whitehall. In D. Shell & R. Hodder-Williams (Eds.), *Churchill to Major: The British prime ministership since 1945* (pp. 104–136). Armonk: M. E. Sharpe.

Burch, M., & Holliday, I. (1996). *British cabinet system*. Hemel Hempstead: Prentice Hall Harvester Wheatsheaf.

Cartledge, B. (2007, November 14). *British Diplomatic Oral History Programme (BDOHP) interview*. Cambridge: Churchill Archives Centre, Churchill College.

Clifford, C. (2000). Administering the summit: The British prime minister's office. In B. G. Peters, R. A. W. Rhodes, & V. Wright (Eds.), *Administering the summit: Administration of the core executive in developed countries* (pp. 25–42). Basingstoke: Macmillan.

Cowley, P. (2005). *The rebels: How Blair mislaid his majority*. London: Politico's.

Dell, E., & Lord Hunt of Tanworth (= J. Hunt). (1994). The failings of cabinet government in mid to late 1970s. *Contemporary Records, 8*(3), 453–472.

Donoughue, B. (1987). *Prime minister: The conduct of policy under Harold Wilson & James Callaghan*. London: Jonathan Cape.

Dyson, K. (1994). *Elusive union: The process of economic and monetary union in Europe*. London: Longman.

Giddings, P. (1995). Prime Minister and Cabinet. In D. Shell & R. Hodder-Williams (Eds.), *Churchill to Major: The British prime ministership since 1945* (pp. 30–70). Armonk: M. E. Sharpe.

Hayes-Renshaw, F., & Wallace, H. (1997). *The Council of Ministers*. New York: St. Martin's Press.

HC Deb. (1978, February 7), Vol 943, cc463–464W.

Heffernan, R. (2003). Prime ministerial predominance? Core executive politics in the UK. *British Journal of Politics and International Relations, 5*(3), 347–372.

Heffernan, R. (2005). Exploring (and explaining) the British prime minister. *British Journal of Politics and International Relations, 7*(4), 605–620.

Heffernan, R. (2006). The prime minister and the news media: Political communication as a leadership resource. *Parliamentary Affairs, 59*(4), 582–598.

Hennessy, P. (1986). *Cabinet*. Oxford: Basil Blackwell.

Hennessy, P. (1990). *Whitehall* (2nd ed.). London: Fontana.

Hogg, S., & Hill, J. (1996). *Too close to call: Power and politics - John Major in No. 10* (2nd ed.). London: Warner Books.

Kavanagh, D. (2001). The cabinet and prime minister. In B. Jones, D. Kavanagh, M. Moran, & P. Norton (Eds.), *Politics UK* (4th ed., pp. 409–436). Harlow: Longman.

Kavanagh, D., & Seldon, A. (2000). *The powers behind the prime minister: The hidden influence of Number Ten* (2nd ed.). London: HarperCollins.

Kelly, R., & White, I. (2016, June 24). *Fixed-term Parliaments Act 2011*. House of Commons Library Briefing Paper No. 6111.

Lawson, N. (1992). *A view from No. 11: Memoirs of a Tory radical*. London: Bantam.

Lee, J. M., Jones, G. W., & Burnham, J. (1998). *At the centre of Whitehall*. Basingstoke: Macmillan.

Norton, P. (1993). *Does parliament matter?* Hemel Hempstead: Harvester Wheatsheaf.

Norton, P. (1994). *The British polity* (3rd ed.). New York: Longman.

Powell, C. (2000, July 18). *British Diplomatic Oral History Programme (BDOHP) interview*. Cambridge: Churchill Archives Centre, Churchill College.

Presse- und Informationsamt der Bundesregierung. (2016). *Dienstsitze des Bundeskanzleramts*. http://www.bundesregierung.de/ContentArchiv/DE/Archiv17/Artikel/2009/10/2009-09-22-bk-dienstsitze.html?nn=391346. Accessed May 17, 2016.

Rose, R. (2001). *The prime minister in a shrinking world*. Cambridge: Polity Press.

Seymour-Ure, C. (1995). Prime minister and the public: Managing media relations. In D. Shell & R. Hodder-Williams (Eds.), *Churchill to Major: The British prime ministership since 1945* (pp. 169–199). Armonk: M. E. Sharpe.

Seymour-Ure, C. (2003). *Prime ministers and the media: Issues of power and control*. Oxford: Blackwell.

Shell, D. (1995). The office of prime minister. In D. Shell & R. Hodder-Williams (Eds.), *Churchill to Major: The British prime ministership since 1945* (pp. 1–29). Armonk: M. E. Sharpe.

Smith, M. J. (1999). *The core executive in Britain*. Basingstoke: Macmillan.

Thomas, G. P. (1998). *The prime minister and cabinet today*. Manchester: Manchester University Press.

Wall, S. (2008). *A stranger in Europe: Britain and the EU from Thatcher to Blair*. Oxford: Oxford University Press.

Wessels, W., & Schäfer, M. (2014). Europäischer Rat. In W. Weidenfeld & W. Wessels (Eds.), *Europa von A bis Z: Taschenbuch der Europäischen Integration* (pp. 233–240). Bonn: Bundeszentrale für Politische Bildung.

Willetts, D. (1987). The role of the prime minister's Policy Unit. *Public Administration, 65*(4), 443–454.

Chapter 7
Prime Minister's Office and Cabinet Office as Institutional Resources of the Prime Minister in the European (Monetary) Policy Core Executive

In this chapter two of the prime minister's institutional resources outlined in Chap. 6—the Prime Minister's Office (PMO) and the Cabinet Office—are considered with respect to the four incumbents studied here and European policy. It is reviewed how the premiers used these resources and whether any managed to increase their influence on European policy-making by expanding them, for instance, by hiring more staff. The study of the Prime Minister's Office and the Cabinet Office focuses on those sections of either institution which provide administrative support particularly on European policy with a specific focus on European monetary policy.[1]

7.1 James Callaghan

7.1.1 Prime Minister's Office

On European policy James Callaghan worked in his *Private Office* particularly with his Foreign Affairs Private Secretary. He had a close working relationship with his first secretary, Patrick Wright, whom he knew from the Foreign Office (FCO) when he had been foreign secretary. When Wright became Ambassador to Luxembourg in 1977, he was succeeded by Bryan Cartledge. Callaghan worked well with him, too, but their relationship was not as easy as the one with Wright had been (Kavanagh and Seldon 2000: 140). Cartledge saw his duties particularly in supporting the premier by linking him with the FCO and the other departments he covered and

[1]The heads of the Prime Minister's Office and the Cabinet Office, the Principal Private Secretary and the Cabinet Secretary, were concerned with European policy as well due to their responsibility for the general management of either institution (and in the case of the Cabinet Secretary of Cabinet). But as they were not necessarily involved in the day-to-day handling European policy, they are not considered in greater detail here.

B. Bujard, *The British Prime Minister in the Core Executive*, Contributions to Political Science, https://doi.org/10.1007/978-3-319-89953-4_7

by organising his foreign travel. According to his own recollection he made few suggestions on policy, only about two proposals in 2 years (Cartledge 2007).

Tom McNally was Political Secretary in the *Political Office*. He had previously worked with Callaghan when the latter had been shadow foreign secretary. When Callaghan moved to the Foreign Office in 1974, McNally became his political adviser, which was then still a rare post (Ballinger and Seldon 2004: 177). Callaghan gave him a comparably free reign and McNally made contributions in various policy areas (Morgan 2007). By his own account he was much involved in European policy partly because he had a long-standing personal interest in it and supported European integration.[2] However, there appears to have been some sensitivity on Callaghan's part with regard to McNally's status. On 1 July 1977, for example, Principal Private Secretary Kenneth Stowe informed him that for a planned cabinet meeting on EC policy Bernard Donoughue (head of Callaghan's Policy Unit) had suggested that McNally put forward a paper for discussion. This could then be presented as a paper by the Policy Unit. Yet Callaghan commented that he did not want this because McNally was his adviser. He instead asked for papers from the European Secretariat and the Central Policy Review Staff (CPRS) (TNA, PREM 16/1492, 1 July 1977).

McNally often joined Policy Unit discussions and according to Bernard Donoughue (1987: 26) held good relations with other colleagues in the PMO as well. For the first 2 years of Callaghan's premiership McNally was one of the most influential members of staff in No. 10. This changed due to his decision to stand for parliament in the 1979 general election, which meant that he was often away from Downing Street on campaign duties (Kavanagh and Seldon 2000: 135).

The civil servant Tom McCaffrey, whom the prime minister appointed as Chief Press Secretary in his *Press Office*, had also worked with Callaghan for a long time. Before joining the PMO, he had worked in similar posts for Callaghan at the Home and the Foreign Office (Ballinger and Seldon 2004: 178). He was familiar with No. 10, having been deputy press secretary there in the early 1970s (Kavanagh and Seldon 2000: 137). Callaghan considered him a friend and placed trust in his judgement (Callaghan 2006: 406; see also Financial Times 1976; Kavanagh and Seldon 2000: 137). McCaffrey wanted to have good relations with the media and the relationship with the press to be "as frank and honest as possible providing [sic] we are not let down"[3] (McCaffrey quoted in Financial Times 1976). He saw no reason to distrust journalists he worked with and they did not distrust him either. On moving to No. 10 he reinstated lobby briefings, which his predecessor Joe Haines (Harold Wilson's press secretary) had suspended (Price 2011: 223). Having worked with Callaghan for so long, McCaffrey felt he knew what and how the premier wanted decisions to be communicated to the media without needing to talk it over with him

[2]Interview with T. McNally, 22 March 2010.

[3]*Financial Times* (1976), Men and Matters, McCaffrey's day too, 6 April 1976. Used under licence from the Financial Times. All Rights Reserved.

before. To ensure his political neutrality at lobby briefings McCaffrey tried to refrain from attacking political rivals of the Labour Party (McCaffrey quoted in Kavanagh and Seldon 2000: 137, 138). His media briefings focused on providing information without political spin, which was how Callaghan liked his government's media management to be (Ballinger and Seldon 2004: 178).

He kept a lower profile than his predecessor Haines. He did not advise Callaghan on policy, which he left to Tom McNally (Donoughue 1987: 25; Price 2011: 223). Like McNally and Donoughue he was sometimes kept out of the loop on sensitive information concerning policy decisions by other No. 10 staff such as Callaghan's Principal Private Secretary Kenneth Stowe. This made his job more difficult (Price 2011: 223; Donoughue 2009: 113–114). Despite having no policy role McCaffrey was involved in core executive discussions on European policy and attended meetings such as on the EMS (TNA, PREM 16/1634, 3 July 1978). He also advised Callaghan on the presentation of the EMS/ERM decision from a media perspective (TNA, PREM 16/1638, 29 November 1978).

When James Callaghan came into office as prime minister it was unclear what would happen to the *Policy Unit,* which had been established only 2 years earlier. The head of the Unit, Bernard Donoughue, then noted in his diary that Callaghan wanted to keep it, but did not know how to integrate it into the structure he envisioned for his office (Donoughue 2009: 15). In the end Callaghan used it to develop initiatives for policy areas in which he had a personal interest such as education policy. It was also to oversee the work of departments—particularly those which he thought did not perform adequately. Thirdly, the Unit did background research, which the PM could use when discussing long-term political issues with ministers. It also briefed him when he met with industry or trade union representatives (Kavanagh and Seldon 2000: 133–134). Callaghan (2006) noted the Unit "provided me with systematic policy analysis distinct from that of the Departments, and thus supported by facts and figures, I was in a stronger position to challenge Departmental proposals" (404). He further welcomed that the Unit helped him gain an overview of developments in his government and its activities as a whole. If there were incongruities or gaps, the Unit would point it out to him (Callaghan 2006: 404–405).

This section of No. 10 was small, consisting of a staff of eight to nine (Burch 1995: 117). It covered European policy, but no member of staff did so exclusively. Instead the Unit collectively discussed, for instance, the government's negotiating strategy for the Bremen European Council in July 1978 at which the planned European Monetary System was debated (Donoughue 2009: 344). It also prepared a paper for the final meeting in October 1978 of the cabinet committee GEN 136, which Callaghan had set up to assess the pros and cons of joining EMS and ERM (see Sect. 8.2.1). According to Donoughue (2009), who attended the October meeting of GEN 136, the Unit then was "marginally incline[d] to go in [to the EMS] in December, for the short-run political and financial advantages, but [could] see no long-term advantages" (372).

James Callaghan showed no particular interest in recruiting further *external advisers* to his office. He appears to have worked well with the civil servants in No. 10. For political advice he turned to the Policy Unit and its head Bernard Donoughue, whom he called his "Senior Policy Adviser" (Callaghan 2006: 404), as well as his Political Office (particularly Tom McNally). He had no special adviser on European policy.

7.1.2 Cabinet Office

In the late 1970s the Cabinet Office European Secretariat (COES) had a staff of about 20. Since 1977 it was headed by a Deputy Secretary. The Secretariat's composition and its distribution of tasks had not changed since it had been set up. The three highest-ranking officials handled the Secretariat's management and coordinated European policy across Whitehall. Five desk officers were responsible for specific aspects of European policy and the rest had administrative duties (Bulmer and Burch 1998: 614). Fulfilling its duties effectively appears to have been somewhat difficult for the COES during the Callaghan premiership. The verdict on the government's European policy passed by Roy Denman (1997), head of the Secretariat from 1975 to 1977, suggests they did not see eye to eye on much:

> There seemed no understanding in London, among both ministers and many senior officials, of the simple point that the process of European unification could not be stopped. If we wanted to remain part of it then, short of leaving the Community, the British interest could best be served by our fighting our corner among partners convinced that Britain, in her heart, words and actions, was at one with them in moving to the 'ever closer union' proclaimed as the European goal by the Treaty of Rome. (259)

According to Michael Franklin, Denman's successor, the Secretariat was not deeply involved in the discussions on EMS and ERM. At a first meeting Callaghan convened on the issue on 4 April 1978 Franklin was not present. The meeting was restricted to the prime minister, foreign secretary as well as the governor and the deputy governor of the Bank of England. While Franklin did not attend, his boss, Cabinet Secretary John Hunt, did, although Franklin did not know this at the time. Another attendant was Kenneth Couzens, a Treasury official who had conducted secret talks with representatives from Germany and France on the project. The chancellor and the Treasury's permanent secretary Sir Douglas Wass were only involved later (Franklin 2013: 761). Franklin and the COES became involved in the discussions from July 1978 onwards. But in contrast to common practice, further discussions at official level on the EMS were not coordinated by the European Secretariat. According to Franklin this was the only time during his 4 years at the COES that this was the case and highly unusual. The meetings, of which there were at least two, took place at the Treasury under the chairmanship of Ken Couzens, who refused to attend meetings in the Cabinet Office. As Couzens was higher ranked than Franklin, the latter had no authority to challenge him on this. He could have drawn in the Cabinet Secretary, who would have had the necessary authority, but he did not do so. The procedure not only frustrated Franklin and the COES but also the Foreign Office, which, as leading department on European policy, had a strong interest in the EMS issue and, moreover, its own economic expertise. Thus a feeling developed that open interdepartmental discussion at official level was not possible as the Treasury kept other ministries at a distance. Much of the technical discussion was done between the Treasury and the Bank of England (Franklin 2013: 761).

James Callaghan also used the *Central Policy Review Staff* for advice. It was based in the Cabinet Office, too, and handled more long-term policy questions than the Policy Unit (Donoughue 1987: 21). Its head, Kenneth Berrill, also concerned himself with the EMS. For example, on 28 September 1978 he argued in a note to Cabinet Secretary John Hunt that it was important "to alert the Prime Minister to the dangers of being too explicitly anti-EMS before he and his colleagues had a chance to argue and think through the best course for the UK" (TNA, CAB 193/212/3, 28 September 1978). Ahead of a cabinet committee meeting of GEN 136 to which he had been invited, although he was no regular member, Berrill laid out his view on EMS and ERM in a note to Callaghan. He concluded that

> events have not moved as we would wish and we are likely to be asked if we wish to join an EMS which has been designed on lines not of our choosing. There are medium term economic arguments against our joining (though the strength of those arguments is impossible to measure). But the political and economic shorter term considerations point the other way. So the choice is far from clear cut. (TNA, PREM 16/1635, 29 September 1978)

Overall, James Callaghan did not much change the institutional structure which he found in the Prime Minister's Office and the European Secretariat upon becoming prime minister. He did not proactively try to expand his institutional resources, for instance, by developing new advisory structures such as Harold Wilson had done with the Policy Unit. He did not much extend the group of special advisers. The fact that political appointees like Bernard Donoughue or Tom McNally complained about their lack of access to government papers and that officials withheld information from them (Donoughue 2009: 50–51), makes the assumption more likely that the PM had no interest in establishing advisory structures alternative to the Civil Service. This might also have been due to personal preferences as, for example, the *Financial Times* in 1976 suggested that Callaghan was "temperamentally difficult to advise. His trust takes many years to mature and there is a streak of insecurity in his character which makes his reaction to any suggestion unpredictable"[4] (Watt 1976).

Callaghan also showed no particular ambition to extend his influence on European policy by expanding his Office's expertise on it, for instance, by closer integrating the COES with No. 10 or by looking for alternative advice in this policy field from outside Whitehall. His lack of attempts to expand his capacities to influence European policy-making in the core executive might partly be due to personal inclination because of his lack of enthusiasm over Europe (Denman

[4]Watt, D. (1976), 'Steady as we go'—at least for now, *Financial Times*, 6 April 1976. Used under licence from the Financial Times. All Rights Reserved.

1997: 252). But it also needs to be considered that, for a government in the late 1970s, EC membership was not yet as important as it would become for its successors. During the successive premierships more and more policy areas were shaped by decision-making at the European level due to further European integration. In the late 1970s this process was not yet as far developed.

On the EMS/ERM issue the European Secretariat was not closely involved and administrative support and advice came mainly from the Treasury and the Bank of England. Michael Franklin's argument that this meant that the debate at the official level failed to address the wider political implications of the issue (Franklin 2013: 761) was echoed by the *Financial Times* at the time, which noted that "the British approach to the talks has been widely criticised for quibbeling too much about details at the cost of missing the major political questions"[5] (Riddell 1978). Callaghan did receive advice on the EMS/ERM from Bernard Donoughue (Policy Unit) and Kenneth Berrill (CPRS). The European Secretariat, however, did not provide him with an extensive assessment of those wider political implications for Britain, should it decide to join this part of European integration from its start. At any rate, Franklin (2013: 764) doubts that this would have changed the outcome on EMS and ERM.

Therefore in the case of James Callaghan it does not look as if the PM tried much to strategically extend his institutional resources in Prime Minister's and Cabinet Office to take a stronger lead in European (monetary) policy making in the core executive.

7.2 Margaret Thatcher

7.2.1 Prime Minister's Office

For Margaret Thatcher the Foreign Policy Private Secretary in her *Private Office* was also important in supporting her on European policy. Michael Alexander, who held the post between 1979 and 1981, was much involved in the negotiations on the British contribution to the European budget.[6] Yet it was not until Charles Powell's appointment in 1984 that the foreign policy private secretary took up a particularly dominant role among Thatcher's staff. That Powell was able to become a leading adviser to the prime minister was facilitated by the fact that Thatcher concerned herself more with foreign policy from the mid-1980s. Mistrusting the Foreign Office, she increasingly turned to Powell for advice. He quickly understood how she thought and worked closely with her (Kavanagh and Seldon 2000: 181). Traditionally, the

[5]Riddell, P. (1978), Getting deeply involved with the technicalities, *Financial Times*, 1 December 1978. Used under licence from the Financial Times. All Rights Reserved.

[6]Thatcher had also inherited Bryan Cartledge from Callaghan. Between Alexander and Powell John Coles was foreign policy private secretary (Kavanagh and Seldon 2000: 151).

post of foreign policy private secretary was not that of an adviser. However, Powell's close rapport with Thatcher made his position more influential than it was normal (Dyson and Featherstone 1999: 569). According to Thatcher's Chancellor Nigel Lawson (1992: 680) Powell did not see it as his duty to challenge Thatcher's prejudices and views. European policy was one of the subject areas in which he strengthened her view against that of the FCO (Kavanagh and Seldon 2000: 182). Like her he considered himself an Atlanticist rather than a European. To him the so-called special relationship between the US and the UK was the central feature of British foreign policy (Powell 2000). He increasingly took over duties which were traditionally in the responsibility of the Foreign Office such as sitting in on Thatcher's meetings with foreign diplomats in No. 10. A Foreign Office representative was seldom present, though this was common practice according to Patrick Wright (2000), FCO Permanent Under-Secretary of State and Head of the Diplomatic Service from 1986 to 1991. John Kerr, FCO official working on Europe at the time, also noted the difficulty of discussing policy with Thatcher as Powell, particularly at the end of her premiership, tended to keep the Civil Service at a distance from her.[7]

When the head of the Private Office Robin Butler returned to the Treasury in 1985, the balance between the private secretaries in the Private Office changed. While Butler had been able to take the lead over Powell this was not as easily possible for his successor, Treasury official Nigel Wicks. Powell managed to further expand his position in the Private Office at the expense of the new Principal Private Secretary. This was facilitated by the fact that Thatcher was wary of Wicks whom she saw as too pro-European. She also blamed him for organising a ministerial meeting in 1985 on the ERM (see Sect. 8.2.2). To her this meeting, at which she had been in a minority with her rejection of entry, had been a Treasury ploy to force her to agree to membership. Between 1985 and 1986 Powell consolidated his status as dominant figure in the Private Office (Kavanagh and Seldon 2000: 182–183). Until Thatcher left No. 10 he remained one of the key individuals on her staff.

Bernard Ingham's appointment as Chief Press Secretary in the *Press Office* in late 1979[8] was a decision with much impact on the balance of power inside the Prime Minister's Office. Ingham was a civil servant and former Labour supporter.[9] He established a good working relationship with Thatcher, which became particularly close from 1984. Until Alastair Campbell became Tony Blair's Chief Press Secretary, Ingham was considered the most controversial individual in this post (Kavanagh and Seldon 2000: 161). Ingham was the first No. 10 press secretary

[7]Interview with J. Kerr, 23 March 2010.

[8]Between May and November 1979 Henry James, who had worked for Alec Douglas-Home, Harold Wilson and Edward Heath, held the post (Price 2011: 241).

[9]He had previously worked for Tony Benn in the energy department (Kavanagh and Seldon 2000: 160).

who became the subject of continued discussion and criticism by the media, the opposition and parts of the cabinet. According to his critics Ingham overstepped the limits of his job and was too biased (Price 2011: 242; Cockerell et al. 1985: 72). Next to Charles Powell he became one of Thatcher's most important members of staff. Like him he was extremely loyal to her (Price 2011: 272). His views were close to hers and at lobby briefings it was sometimes difficult for journalists to detect which were his views and which he relayed as Thatcher's. Yet as they mostly aligned, a distinction tended to be unnecessary (Stephens 1997: 102). Lawson (1992) saw Ingham's position on her staff not as an advantage for Thatcher as "he reinforced all her worst characteristics and, unwittingly, did her a profound disservice" (468). Due to Ingham's extraordinary long stay in No. 10 (1979–1990) and his strong identification with Thatcher, it was clear that when she resigned he would not stay in No. 10. He resigned a week later (Price 2011: 279).

On Europe Ingham appears to have taken on Thatcher's views if he had not already held them before. In his memoirs he argued that "she had done more to reform the European Community and set it on course for development than any other single individual among a Euro-population of some 320 million" (Ingham 2003: 384). On the Exchange Rate Mechanism he wrote: "For me, the ERM came to occupy the same ludicrously overrated status of a quick fix as all the earlier economic mumbo-jumbo, although there were no doubt good political reasons for entry" (Ingham 2003: 385). Nigel Lawson (1992: 467), however, questioned Ingham's knowledge of economics. While Ingham's influence on policy was limited, he accompanied Thatcher to each European Council and was present at many of her bilaterals and helped foster her increasing scepticism towards the EC (Dyson and Featherstone 1999: 569).

At the beginning of her premiership Margaret Thatcher (like Callaghan) had no plan concerning the duties which the *Policy Unit* was to take over in her administration. Under the leadership of its first head, John Hoskyns, its area of competence was limited. During Callaghan's premiership it had covered every issue the Labour government had dealt with, including Europe. Now, it was only concerned with one: the turnaround of Britain's economic decline (Kavanagh and Seldon 2000: 154, 155). Hoskyns had good relations with Alan Walters, whom the prime minister brought in as her economic adviser (see below). On economics they had a similar view. Walters, however, was not a member of the Policy Unit (Hennessy 1990: 647). Under Ferdinand Mount, Hoskyns successor from 1982, the Policy Unit's remit was again broadened. As it had done for Callaghan it covered subject areas of particular interest to the prime minister (Kavanagh and Seldon 2000: 159, 160). After Thatcher disbanded the Central Policy Review Staff (CPRS) (see Sect. 7.2.2), the Policy Unit which had been downsized before to a staff of about four went back to eight to nine full-time members. This was about the same size as during Callaghan's premiership (Burch 1995: 117–118). The Unit dealt mostly with domestic but not foreign and security policy (Willetts 1987: 443, 447). When Alan Walters cut down his workload in 1983, the Unit again began to work on economic policy. Particularly Mount's successors, John Redwood and later Brian Griffiths, both economists, advised

Thatcher on this subject area (Willetts 1987: 446; Lee et al. 1998: 118; Kavanagh and Seldon 2000: 192). In the late 1980s there were attempts to include European policy in the Policy Unit's brief as well. This was blocked by Charles Powell, who ensured that he remained her main adviser on this issue until her resignation in 1990 (Kavanagh and Seldon 2000: 192). But Griffiths was important insofar as he strengthened Thatcher's resolve to reject ERM entry (Stephens 1997: 67, 115). Overall, however, during his leadership the Unit's influence inside No. 10 declined. Thatcher increasingly turned to her Private Office for advice. Moreover, on economic and foreign policy she listened to Alan Walters (who had returned in 1989) and Charles Powell (Kavanagh and Seldon 2000: 194).

Margaret Thatcher appointed the academic Alan Walters as *external adviser* for economics in 1981. His appointment did not seem controversial at the time and his relationship with Chancellor Geoffrey Howe appeared to be good. His views on government policy were not widely discussed in the press in the early 1980s (Lee et al. 1998: 124, 127). In January 1983 Walters returned to academic life, but continued to work part-time for Thatcher. In October 1984 he left his post completely (Kavanagh and Seldon 2000: 166). It was only his official return as the PM's economic adviser in May 1989 which caused problems inside the core executive. This was because by then Walters had become a person of public interest and his return to No. 10 provoked much attention from the media (The Independent 1989). Like Thatcher, Walters opposed making the Bank of England independent—a policy championed by Chancellor Lawson. Moreover, Walters (again like Thatcher) did not share Lawson's view that joining the ERM was in Britain's economic interest. Like her he rejected Lawson's policy of shadowing the Deutschmark as well as the chancellor's conviction that inflation could be pressed out of the economy by setting high interest rates (Kavanagh and Seldon 2000: 194–195). Already in January 1982 Walters had sent a note to Thatcher in which he argued against joining the ERM, which had much influence on her thinking (Dyson and Featherstone 1999: 548). He publicly stated his opposition to membership in an article published by the *Financial Times* on 6 April 1988 which carried the headline "Britain does best outside the EMS" [10] (Walters 1988). Even after his return to No. 10 he remained openly hostile to ERM entry. This meant that he opposed official government policy which stated Britain would join the mechanism as soon as the conditions were right (Kavanagh and Seldon 2000: 195). In October 1989 the *Financial Times* quoted Walters calling the EMS "half-baked"[11] (Walters quoted in Holberton 1989). Lawson requested Thatcher to dismiss Walters. His position as her economic adviser, who opposed key aspects of government policy, made Lawson's job impossible, the chancellor argued (Lawson 1992: 960–961). She refused. Lawson resigned. So did Walters shortly after (Stephens 1997: 135, 136). Thatcher did not

[10]Walters, A. (1988), Britain does best outside the EMS, *Financial Times*, 6 April 1988. Used under licence from the Financial Times. All Rights Reserved.

[11]Holberton, S. (1989), PM's economist adds his guarded support, *Financial Times*, 18 October 1989. Used under licence from the Financial Times. All Rights Reserved.

appoint another economic adviser (Lee et al. 1998: 127). Walters continued to send her notes urging her to oppose ERM and EMU after his resignation, encouraging her anti-European stance (Dyson and Featherstone 1999: 569).

Apart from Walters on economics, Thatcher in 1982 appointed former UN Ambassador Anthony Parsons as foreign policy adviser. This was because she had not been happy with the advice she had received from the Foreign Office during the Falklands War (Cradock 1997: 8; Lee et al. 1998: 127). Initially she had been thinking of establishing a full unit separate from the Policy Unit which would give independent advice on foreign and security policy. But she then settled just for Parsons (Moore 2015: 29–30). He was also not part of the Policy Unit. At first the Foreign Office and Thatcher's Principal Private Secretary Robin Butler were sceptical of this appointment (Kavanagh and Seldon 2000: 167). Francis Pym, then foreign secretary, opposed it. He saw it as prime ministerial interference with the responsibilities of the FCO (Hennessy 1990: 652). But Parsons did more to explain the workings of the Foreign Office to Thatcher than imposing her wishes on the department (Young 1989: 381). This form of advice appears to have been helpful to her, because when Parsons left, she appointed Sir Percy Cradock—also a former diplomat—to the post in December 1983 (Kavanagh and Seldon 2000: 167). According to Cradock (1997: 9) his relationship with the FCO was without problems. Foreign Secretary Howe received no information on the advice Cradock gave Thatcher. But their foreign policy views were similar and they regularly met (Kavanagh and Seldon 2000: 185). Cradock, an expert on Chinese politics, particularly dealt with Hong Kong and security policy (Lee et al. 1998: 127). He worked closely with Charles Powell, the foreign policy private secretary. By Cradock's account they more or less divided the issues at hand: "In some areas, such as Europe, he was more active. In others, the Far East and to some extent the Soviet Union, I took the lead" (Cradock 1997: 16). Yet the pro-European Cradock (1997) tried to advise Thatcher on European policy. But he noted particularly with regard to the later years of her premiership: "In the Prime Minister's household it was easier in such times to be the executant or spokesman for her line [on Europe], like Charles Powell or Bernard Ingham, than to be her adviser, particularly when the adviser did not see entirely eye to eye with her. But at this time and on this issue dissenting advice was wasted" (130).

7.2.2 Cabinet Office

The Cabinet Office European Secretariat remained an important advisory body to Thatcher on European policy (Cradock 1997: 16). It was still comparably small. By 1982 it consisted of an administrative staff of eight including a Deputy Secretary and an Under Secretary plus support staff (Stack 1983: 128). Particularly David Williamson, head of the Secretariat from 1983 to 1987, had a key role as prime ministerial adviser on Europe. He had a good standing in Whitehall, aided by the fact that he held this post for more than 4 years, as had his predecessor Michael Franklin.

For a posting as Deputy Secretary this was extraordinarily long. Between 1979 and 1987 both belonged to a small number of officials in the Cabinet Office, who had a strong personal impact on the results of policy decisions (Seldon 1990: 108–109; 120). Williamson like his predecessors Michael Franklin and David Hancock had in-depth experience of European policy. Franklin came from the Department of Agriculture, which he had represented at the accession negotiations of the UK to the European Communities. From 1973 to 1977 he had been Director General for Agriculture in the European Commission. David Hancock, his successor at the COES from 1981 to 1983, had worked at the UK's permanent representation in Brussels between 1972 und 1974 and had later handled European policy in the Treasury. Williamson had also previously worked at the Department of Agriculture. Like Franklin he had been Director General for Agriculture in the European Commission from 1977 to 1983 (Stack 1983: 128).

Foreign Secretary Howe as well as Thatcher held Williamson in high regard. Howe thought that Williamson was able to soften Thatcher's worst prejudices on European integration. She appears to have paid more attention to his advice than to that of his successors (Dyson and Featherstone 1999: 586). Williamson had a special way of supporting her in European policy-making, as "he was adept at delivering what Mrs Thatcher knew she needed, which was not invariably the same as what she said she wanted" (Wall 2008: 66). According to Williamson his working relationship with Thatcher was good. While at times she would not agree with his advice she never out of principle resisted him advising her.[12] His role in the prime ministerial advisory structure was as follows: "As Margaret Thatcher's closest European adviser, he had never misled her but had often led her to solutions that her instincts might have rejected. He was often the oil on the troubled waters of Britain's relations with her partners" (Wall 2008: 49). Additionally, Williamson as head of the COES "was the de facto senior partner in a triumvirate of officials, also comprising the Permanent Representative to the European Communities and the Foreign Office Assistant Under Secretary, who sought to orchestrate the management of EC business in Whitehall" (Wall 2008: 60). When Williamson moved to the European Commission as general secretary in 1987, Roger Lavelle from the Treasury succeeded him at the COES (1987–1989) (Bulmer and Burch 2009: 112). With the personnel change the coordination of European policy changed, too. According to John Kerr, then Assistant Under Secretary of State (European Communities) at the FCO, Lavelle "was rather quiet" and kept a "low profile",[13] which resulted in Kerr de facto taking over the lead among the officials in London dealing with European policy. Lavelle also did not engage himself directly in European level negotiations as Williamson had done. By Kerr's account, Lavelle viewed the duties of heading the

[12] Interview with D. Williamson, 23 March 2010.

[13] Interview with J. Kerr, 23 March 2010.

COES differently from his predecessor: "He gave very wise advice, but saw his role as London-based, co-ordinating behind the scenes. Not as a roving negotiator, the way Williamson had been."[14]

In 1983 Thatcher disbanded the *Central Policy Review Staff*, which had advised Callaghan, for instance, on the European Monetary System. Ahead of the 1983 election Thatcher had been thinking about expanding her Policy Unit, which only advised her. By the election she had not decided on the details, but chose to abolish the CPRS. In her view extending her own staff meant that somewhere else savings in staff had to be made (Hennessy 1990: 655). Also, as the CPRS advised the whole cabinet, its papers had a wide circulation making leaks more likely, as happened in the last years of its existence (Willetts 1987: 445).

While Margaret Thatcher appointed external advisers and thus established new posts and structures in her office, she did not question the institutional set up she had at her disposal per se and did not attempt much to extend her capabilities in that regard (with the exception of expanding her Policy Unit, yet she did so at the cost of the CPRS). This was similar to Callaghan. Despite No. 10 increasingly engaging in foreign policy-making from the second half of the 1980s, Thatcher did not establish new institutional structures to do so. While Charles Powell's influence as foreign policy private secretary was important and his activities at least partly diminished the influence of the Foreign Office, this arrangement appears to have been based rather on Thatcher's individual preferences than on a strategic development of the post.[15] When she resigned she did not leave a structurally much changed Prime Minister's Office which could have provided her successor Major with greater institutional resources to proactively set European policy from No. 10. But the Cabinet Office gained a more central role in European policy-making during her premiership, making the European Secretariat occasionally an "untitled prime-minister's office-cum-ministry for Europe" (Christoph 1993: 529–530), which might partly have been related to Thatcher's negative view of the Foreign Office.

Overall, Thatcher also does not appear to have strategically extended her institutional resources in European policy-making. Instead she used those she already had differently (e.g. the foreign policy private secretary). Moreover, later in her premiership she seems to have listened to advice on European policy only if it reinforced her view, not if it challenged it. Thus she did not fully use the institutional resources at her disposal in that area anymore.

[14]Interview with J. Kerr, 23 March 2010.

[15]This can also be seen in the fact that Powell's successor Stephen Wall took a more traditional view of the duties of the foreign affairs private secretary than Powell had done, see Sect. 7.3.1.

7.3 John Major

7.3.1 Prime Minister's Office

Charles Powell, Thatcher's Foreign Policy Private Secretary, continued to work in this position in the *Private Office* when Major became prime minister. He left a few months after Major came into office and was succeeded by Stephen Wall, who had already been Major's private secretary at the Foreign Office (Hogg and Hill 1996: 25). While Powell had become one of Thatcher's key advisers on European and foreign policy during her premiership (see Sect. 7.2.1), Wall did the job more in the way Powell's predecessors had done it and described it as follows:

> You are not there to be an independent policy adviser. You are there to represent the prime minister's wishes and views to the rest of Whitehall, ensure that he gets the advice from ministers that he needs and provide briefing for him, take the records, to some extent engage with other governments on his behalf, although that is something else that has grown much more in recent times, otherwise going back to the departments for them to execute the prime minister's wishes.[16]

The *Independent* in 1991 called him "low-key" (Helm 1991). To Major (2000) he was "indispensable" (276) on the Maastricht Treaty negotiations. Major trusted Wall and, for instance, after Britain left the ERM in autumn 1992 discussed with him whether he should resign as prime minister (Major 2000: 335). When Wall became ambassador to Portugal in 1993, at first Roderic Lyne, then John Holmes took over as Foreign Affairs Private Secretary (Kavanagh and Seldon 2000: 211). Major valued the work of all of them (Major 2000: 515). Due to the expansion of subject areas that the foreign affairs private secretary covered, which included the Northern Ireland peace process, the treaty of Maastricht and the war in Yugoslavia among others in the 1990s, a second foreign policy private secretary post was introduced in 1994. Major had initially been against this. His foreign policy adviser Sir Rodric Braithwaite's (see below) retirement provided the possibility for him to strengthen this section of the Private Office by introducing the new post (Kavanagh and Seldon 2000: 212). The Private Office was strongly involved in European policy-making and here worked closely with the Cabinet Office (Kavanagh and Seldon 2000: 212). But according to Stephen Wall it was not so much that the foreign affairs private secretary had a decisive policy role. Instead he ensured that the PM received the best advice available and supplemented it if he thought the advice he got was not complete.[17] Particularly early in his premiership Major drew strongly on the support of Wall and his Principal Private Secretary Andrew Turnbull (Kavanagh and Seldon 2000: 211). Yet unlike Thatcher he did not have one key figure in his Private Office.

---

[16]Interview with S. Wall, 29 March 2010, see also Cradock 1997: 32.

[17]Interview with S. Wall, 29 March 2010.

John Major appointed Gus O'Donnell as his Chief Press Secretary in the No. 10 *Press Office*. O'Donnell was a career civil servant like McCaffrey and Ingham and had already worked for Major at the Treasury as press secretary (Price 2011: 285). He had been at the Treasury when Britain had joined the ERM in 1990 (Seldon 1998: 113). Major and O'Donnell were friends and Major trusted O'Donnell, who advised him not only on presentation but also on policy. Moreover, ahead of the Maastricht negotiations, at which the EMU opt-out for Britain was agreed, O'Donnell sat in on some of the PM's bilaterals with European counterparts (Stephens 1991). He "was an economist, primarily, who became a press secretary only by accident... He never entirely settled into the press mould" (Seldon 1998: 144). But journalists initially appreciated his fairness and frankness (Lee et al. 1998: 71). Though, when the relationship between No. 10 and the media soured from autumn 1992, these qualities were less successful (Kavanagh and Seldon 2000: 215). Studies assessing Major's media management suggested that for a premier in a difficult position such as he found himself in[18] a "more overtly political-cum-professional press secretary" (Bale and Sanders 2001: 100, for a similar assessment, see Seymour-Ure 1994: 413) might have had more opportunity to be effective. Also, several ministers briefed the media off-the-record, which breached the principle of collective cabinet responsibility. As a civil servant but not political appointee, O'Donnell lacked the political authority to end these alternative forms of government communication (Price 2011: 306). Upon his return to the Treasury in 1994 O'Donnell was succeeded by Christopher Meyer. Meyer was a diplomat and soon realised that he was neither much interested in the power politics of No. 10 nor in media management. He and Jonathan Haslam, his successor from 1996, were not as close to Major as O'Donnell had been. They were also not as influential on tactics as he had been (Kavanagh and Seldon 2000: 215).

John Major appointed Sarah Hogg as head of his *Policy Unit*. The former economic journalist soon became one of his most important advisers. Since she started in her post when he went to No. 10, she was able to strongly shape the role she and the Unit were going to take. Hogg appointed people from the private sector as well as officials to the Unit. She had a close relationship with Major and was at the height of her authority until the end of 1992 (Kavanagh and Seldon 2000: 219, 220). Due to her proximity to him, Major (2000: 211) argued that she was often the target of attacks which were actually meant for him. Taking over responsibility for economic policy in the Unit, she regularly attended Major's bilaterals with Chancellor Lamont to ensure her key role in economic policy-making. This apparently annoyed Lamont (Seldon 1998: 140).[19] She also went to meetings of the two men on EMU during the negotiations in the run up to Maastricht (Dyson and Featherstone

[18]Among other things the UK's exit from the ERM in autumn 1992 was seen as a massive political defeat of the government, particularly as it had been Major who had persuaded Thatcher to join in the first place.

[19]Lamont does not refer to this in his memoirs, when he mentions the bilaterals (Lamont 1999: 35).

1999: 596). In addition, she attended key cabinet committees and met the premier more regularly than previous Unit heads had done (Kavanagh and Seldon 2000: 220).

In contrast to Thatcher's office in which, at least in the second part of her premiership, European policy had been dominated by Charles Powell, Major's Policy Unit handled it as well. Although its influence here was less significant than that of Private or Cabinet Office (Kavanagh and Seldon 2000: 220). The Unit helped to prepare the Maastricht Treaty negotiations with Hogg acting as an intermediary between Major and ministers and being involved in the coordination of the presentation of the results afterwards (Seldon 1994: 158).[20] In the run up to the Maastricht summit Hogg attended the interdepartmental Wicks committee, which had been set up to follow progress on EMU and was chaired by Nigel Wicks, the Treasury's leading official on EMU. Hogg's task here was to keep Major up to date on the discussions, but not to interfere in the committee's work (Dyson and Featherstone 1999: 582, 587). After the completion of the treaty negotiations the Unit continued to show a keen interest in the European dimension of British politics (Burch and Holliday 1996: 29). Hogg was also much involved in the government's crisis meetings on sterling's future in the ERM in autumn 1992 (Major 2000: 328, 331).

Major was the first prime minister to appoint a member of the Policy Unit who specifically covered Europe. It was a post held by a career civil servant (Jonathan Rees) (Bulmer and Burch 2009: 111). From 1993 to 1996 Dominic Morris, previously in Major's Private Office as parliamentary secretary, handled European policy in the Unit (Seldon 1998: 143).

After the 1992 election and particularly the ERM exit, the Policy Unit increasingly handled day-to-day problems and crisis management. Hogg played a key role in setting up the government's new economic policy after the ERM exit (Kavanagh and Seldon 2000: 221). Norman Blackwell succeeded her when she left the Unit in 1995 (Seldon 1998: 542). He had influence but was not as close to Major as Hogg had been. During his time as head, the Unit also had to engage in crisis management such as in the BSE crisis of 1996, when the European Commission banned the import of British beef (Kavanagh and Seldon 2000: 222–223).

John Major did not show a keen interest in setting up *external advice* structures in addition to the established institutions of No. 10. From Thatcher he inherited Percy Cradock as foreign policy adviser. When Cradock left in early 1992, Major appointed former diplomat Rodric Braithwaite as successor. But when Braithwaite retired in 1994, the post was abolished. Thatcher had established it, because she had been looking for advice from outside the FCO. But Major did not share her distrust of the institution, where he had himself worked for a few months. Moreover, the FCO now was headed by Douglas Hurd, whom Major considered a friend (Kavanagh and Seldon 2000: 214). He wanted Cradock and Braithwaite to

[20]Interview with S. Wall, 29 March 2010.

complement the work of the FCO (Major 2000: 515). According to Braithwaite Major had no interest in receiving conflicting advice as he did not like a "confrontation of ideas" (Braithwaite 1998). As mentioned, from the mid-1990s Major instead extended the role of the Private Office by appointing an assistant foreign policy private secretary.

Major did not have a personal adviser for economic policy. For advice on this area he turned to the chief economic adviser, a Treasury civil servant who advised the whole government (Lee et al. 1998: 256).

7.3.2 Cabinet Office

Since 1989 the European Secretariat was headed by David Hadley, an official from the Department of Agriculture (Bulmer and Burch 2009: 112). The COES had limited influence as advisory body to the prime minister early in John Major's premiership. Michael Jay, then Assistant Under Secretary of State in the FCO responsible for the EC, characterised its status at the time as "uncharacteristically weak" (Jay 2007). According to Stephen Wall, even a year after Major had become prime minister the head of the European Secretariat had not made much of an impression on the new PM. This was not because Hadley's advice was of lesser quality than for example David Williamson's had been for Thatcher. Major's low resonance to the advice given by the head of the COES had more to do with the form in which it was presented to him.[21] Thus by Wall's assessment, while the Secretariat played an important part in coordinating European policy, for policy advice the prime minister listened more to foreign secretary and chancellor than to the European Secretariat.[22] Interestingly, John Kerr, at the time the UK's Permanent Representative in Brussels who negotiated at the Intergovernmental Conferences (IGCs) on Political Union and EMU, considered the European Secretariat under Major to be quite influential, given that the prime minister was open to the Civil Service. Moreover, there was a close working relationship between UKREP in Brussels and the Cabinet Office. According to Kerr Major was very open to Civil Servants in general and liked to see them. Although, as Kerr acknowledged, it became more difficult in the later years of his premiership when Major became weaker and the Conservatives increasingly split over Europe.[23] On EMU, as it tends to be the case with monetary policy in general, the COES played a minor role. This policy field was always dominated by the Treasury and the Bank of England. Thus, while David Hadley was much involved in coordinating British policy on political union during the Maastricht Treaty negotiations, this was not so much on EMU (Dyson and Featherstone 1999: 586). It appears that Major did not turn to the COES

[21] Interview with S. Wall, 29 March 2010.

[22] Interview with S. Wall, 29 March 2010.

[23] Interview with J. Kerr, 23 March 2010.

so much for advice on EMU in the run up to Maastricht, but to John Kerr and Nigel Wicks, who negotiated for the UK at the EMU IGC. Major knew Wicks from his time at the Treasury and trusted him. Wicks also prepared the part on EMU in the main brief that Michael Jay coordinated for Major to take to the Maastricht negotiations (Dyson and Featherstone 1999: 597, 593–594).

From 1994 the COES was headed by Brian Bender (from the DTI), who stayed in the post until 1998.[24] Like David Williamson (1983–87) and Stephen Wall (2000–04) he was one of heads of the European Secretariat, who had a noticeable impact on the making of European policy. Like the other two he was highly regarded in Whitehall, the European institutions and by the prime minister and his No. 10 staff (Bulmer and Burch 2009: 122). Bender recalls that Major's European policy was mainly concerned with "damage limitation"[25] after the ERM exit, rather than promotive proposals. The European Secretariat was constantly having to factor in domestic political risks. Thus the main question the COES had to address then was how European policy outcomes could be achieved that could be sold domestically. However, when it came to taking advice on European policy Major did look to the head of the European Secretariat for it.[26]

Similar to his two predecessors John Major did not undertake major institutional changes to extend the Prime Minister's Office's and Cabinet Office's capabilities on European (monetary) policy. His expansion in staff was modest, such as the establishment of a second foreign affairs private secretary post and a civil servant in the Policy Unit specifically tasked to cover European policy.

Under Major there was not much of a strategic expansion and reform of his institutional resources in PMO and Cabinet Office aimed at taking a stronger lead in European policy-making in the core executive. It was not until Tony Blair entered No. 10 Downing Street for this to happen. Moreover, as European policy-making became increasingly difficult due to the split in the Conservative Party over the issue, it appears that damage limitation became more important to Major than actively shaping and leading on European policy.

7.4 Tony Blair

7.4.1 Prime Minister's Office

Immediately upon entering office Tony Blair made changes to the institutional structure of the PMO as he, for instance, appointed Jonathan Powell as his Chief

[24]Between Hadley and Bender the COES was headed by Geoffrey Fitchew (Treasury) (Bulmer and Burch 2009: 112).

[25]Interview with B. Bender, 25 March 2010.

[26]Interview with B. Bender, 25 March 2010.

of Staff and placed him in the *Private Office*. The idea was to have an individual able to coordinate the liaison between political staff and civil service and between the various segments of No. 10 (Powell 2010: 86). Powell was a pro-European and supported joining EMU (Liddle 2014: 60). As contacts of the PM with his European counterparts intensified, Powell as Blair's chief of staff was like the Principal Private Secretary, drawn into the European policy process (Bulmer and Burch 2009: 111). Blair inherited John Holmes as foreign affairs private secretary (1996–1999), with whom he worked well. Holmes was succeeded by John Sawers (1999–2001) whom Blair initially did not get on with well.[27] In any case the new prime minister did not like the private secretary system

> because, as he saw it, you had a Private Secretary who, instead of being able to give advice, had to go to somewhere else to get the advice and then relay it. And he said, 'Why can't I have my own person who is expert on Europe?'[28]

At the end of his first term he ended the tradition of relying on a private secretary to act as intermediary for advice on issues of foreign and European policy. He established two new posts by appointing an adviser on European policy, who was also the head of the European Secretariat (see Sects. 4.2 and 7.4.2) and one on all other aspects of foreign policy, who headed the Overseas and Defence Secretariat in the Cabinet Office (James 2011: 63). There was still a foreign policy private secretary, but he effectively worked under the direction of the head of the COES and the head of the Overseas and Defence Secretariat. He took the records on European policy discussions and meetings in No.10. When Stephen Wall was head of the European Secretariat the post was held by Matthew Rycroft.[29]

The post of economic affairs private secretary,[30] held at first by Moira Wallace, tended to be less important as Blair and Brown continued to meet up bilaterally as they had done in opposition. Brown insisted on speaking to Blair without any civil servants present, which also applied to Treasury officials. This only changed when Jeremy Heywood from the Treasury succeeded Wallace in November 1997. Blair insisted that Heywood should be present at and document meetings and telephone conversations with Brown, which the chancellor eventually accepted. In February 1999 Heywood became Blair's Principal Private Secretary, but continued to handle economic and European issues such as EMU (Kavanagh and Seldon 2000: 263–265). When the relationship between Blair and Brown increasingly soured over the years, he acted as a go-between for Blair and liaised with Brown's economic adviser Ed Balls in order to keep the unity of government. At first Jonathan Powell had acted in this capacity for the PM but by 1999 had grown tired of it. Heywood and Balls met almost daily for a number of years (Beckett 2016).

---

[27]Interview with S. Wall, 29 March 2010.

[28]Interview with S. Wall, 29 March 2010.

[29]Interview with S. Wall, 29 March 2010.

[30]This post was not newly founded under Blair. It already existed under his three predecessors.

Tony Blair made the former tabloid journalist Alastair Campbell his Chief Press Secretary in the *Press Office*. Campbell had already been his press secretary since 1994 (Seldon 2005: 293). It was important to Blair to appoint someone who particularly understood the tabloid media (Blair 2010: 75). According to Roger Liddle (2014: 58), Blair's political adviser on Europe, Campbell was the dominant actor in No. 10 until 2003. Apart from traditional Press Office tasks such as briefing the lobby and for a time the coordination of activities of all press divisions of the departments, Campbell continued to write speeches for Blair and to give political advice (Kavanagh and Seldon 2000: 254). Thus, unlike Bernard Ingham he was not only personally close to the premier but also had a policy role.

Already in opposition Campbell had professionalised the Labour Party's media management, for example by setting up a rebuttal unit to identify false statements about the party and refute them as soon as possible (Powell 2010: 192–193). In November 1997 a Strategic Communications Unit was added to the PMO (Burch and Holliday 1999: 36). It was to work on long-term strategic planning to decide when and how governmental policy initiatives were to be communicated and what material the media should be provided with to facilitate the explanation of such initiatives to the public (Powell 2010: 199). It was to ensure that government policy was presented coherently. It reported to Campbell and closely worked with departmental press and private offices (Burch and Holliday 1999: 34).

Campbell also directly influenced the government's European policy. He had been crucial in designing the reconciliation between the Murdoch papers and the Labour Party. Due to the papers' Euroscepticism, Europe tended to be a problem in this context. Hence, Campbell's dominant role in No. 10 contributed to treating the question of joining the euro primarily as a media management issue instead of a policy decision in its own right. No other actor in No. 10 at the time matched Campbell's influence and could therefore have been a counterforce to turn the focus on the policy implications of the euro decision instead of the presentational ones (Liddle 2014: 59).[31]

Campbell was a Eurosceptic by instinct (Rawnsley 2001: 75). He did not support euro membership. On Gordon Brown's interview with *The Times* in autumn 1997 (see Sect. 8.2.4), for example, Campbell (2007: 253), who revised the Treasury draft to make it sound less pro-European, noted in his diary that he was eager to give voice to his natural anti-EMU tendencies so as to avoid Blair being outmanoeuvred by an image of Brown being more pro-EMU.

Campbell's role in No. 10 changed in 2000. From then on he spoke less often at lobby meetings and left this to his deputy. Blair wanted his press secretary to be less involved in day-to-day media management and more in establishing a long-term media strategy and the preparation of the next election (Kavanagh and Seldon 2000: 258). According to Blair (2010: 302) Campbell developed an increasing dislike of the media over the years in No. 10, which somewhat impaired his judgement as to

[31]Seldon (2005: 310–311) questions Campbell's influence on the euro arguing that the policy was Blair's and that Campbell did not see it as his job to change Blair's mind on policies.

what was the best way to deal with them. Campbell wanted to leave in 2000. Blair (2010: 302) later admitted that his desire to retain him as one of his most trusted aides resulted in him urging Campbell to stay longer than was sensible. In 2004 Campbell finally left. He was succeeded by David Hill, whose appointment was meant to signal a more toned down and stable relationship with the media (Mandelson 2010: 370).

The *Policy Unit* was headed by David Miliband, whose political views were to the left of the prime minister's (Rawnsley 2010: 370). Blair initially thought he was too young, too inflexible and in his political attitude not sufficiently New Labour. Therefore it took until May 1998 for Miliband to be officially appointed as head of the Unit though he had acted as head since Labour had come into office (Mandelson 2010: 223; Powell 2010: 96; Kavanagh and Seldon 2000: 265). Miliband was a pro-European but did not express his views explicitly, at least early on in the Policy Unit. Hence, he was not able to function as a counterforce to Alastair Campbell and his view that the euro question was an issue of media management rather than a policy decision in its own right (Liddle 2014: 59). Miliband joined parliament in 2001 and was succeeded by Andrew Adonis who, for some in the parliamentary party and in No. 10, held political views that were too much New Labour. When Adonis became education minister his Policy Unit post was taken over by David Bennett, a scientist who had previously been with McKinsey (Powell 2010: 96).

All other unit members belonged to the party's New Labour wing and Blair knew them before they were appointed. He established the largest Policy Unit of the four prime ministers analysed here (Kavanagh and Seldon 2000: 265). In 1999 it had about 18 members of staff (Burch and Holliday 1999: 35). The Unit functioned, on the one hand, as a think-tank developing policy initiatives and looking for external policy experts for new ideas. On the other hand, it worked to strengthen the prime minister's "political direction" (Kavanagh and Seldon 2000: 266). Each member of the Unit covered one or more departments and sometimes trans-departmental issues (Kavanagh and Seldon 2000: 267). Roger Liddle handled defence and Europe, Derek Scott economic policy (Mandelson 2010: 223; Kavanagh and Seldon 2000: 267). On the euro Blair received conflicting advice: Liddle supported entry, Scott opposed it (Seldon 2005: 318). Liddle, who was the first non-civil servant prime ministerial adviser on European policy, saw his brief not in competing with the civil service over the handling of EU policy but in networking with other political forces inside the country and across the EU and advising from that perspective (Liddle 2014: XVI–XVII).[32] By Liddle's account the communication between the Unit and the prime minister was not hierarchical and Blair liked receiving differing advice:

> I would often put in a note to Tony and David [Miliband] would write a note saying why he disagreed with it. But I think Blair quite liked that. He liked a diversity of view amongst his political team... he liked having different voices. And he was not very into formal processes,

[32]Interview with R. Liddle, 28 October 2010.

you know, with all the sofa government and all of that sort of stuff. So, it was a very flat, rather than hierarchical structure.[33]

Yet Liddle felt the rest of the Unit did not see the European issue to be as important as he did. He recalled that at their first meeting after the 1997 election, at which the Blair government's priorities for the first term were to be discussed, he argued that European policy was a key objective and that the focus should be to establish support for the UK adopting the euro. According to him the other members of the Unit, many of whom had a close working relationship with the new prime minister, were dismissive of this and took a cynical view of the Labour party's commitment to European integration (Liddle 2014: 55).

When Roger Liddle left the Policy Unit in 2004, his post was not reappointed. But during Blair's premiership more desk officers than before handled European issues which affected their areas of responsibility. Thus up to six or seven members of the Unit dealt with European policy issues either substantially or occasionally (Bulmer and Burch 2009: 111–112).

One of Blair's key *external advisers* was David Gould. Blair was the first prime minister who regularly met with a pollster. Based on his polling and focus group research Gould wrote memoranda for the PM and discussed with members of his office such as the head of the Policy Unit potential difficulties and possibilities the governmental party faced (Kavanagh and Seldon 2000: 271). Gould was a pro-European but reluctant to advise Blair to take any risks on European policy (Trewin 2009: 604).

7.4.2 Cabinet Office

Upon becoming prime minister, Tony Blair, as reported, questioned the traditional private secretary system and why he had to have a private secretary who would relay to him foreign policy advice instead of having his own advisers. Initially he decided to task the European Secretariat with advising him (James 2011: 62). He chose to lean heavily on the Secretariat's head Brian Bender for policy advice and to support Peter Mandelson, whom Blair had placed in the Cabinet Office to act as a "roving European ambassador" (James 2009: 609). Yet senior FCO officials were worried that this meant that the Secretariat was infringing on the department's area of responsibility, which led to an informal agreement between COES and FCO to limit Bender's role (James and Oppermann 2009: 293; James 2009: 609).

In 2000 Blair concluded that a reform of the foreign policy-advice structure inside No. 10 was necessary. On Europe he did so because relations between him and Bender's successor from 1998 David Bostock had not been as effective. Moreover, with a potential referendum on the euro, the PM felt in need of an adviser whom he

[33]Interview with R. Liddle, 28 October 2010.

could trust and who would organise the process from No. 10. Additionally, he wanted to strengthen his office's capacity on the whole to provide advice on foreign affairs (James 2009: 609, 2011: 62–63). In summer 2000 Blair appointed Stephen Wall, who until then had been the UK's Permanent Representative to the EU, as head of the COES. Staff was also added to the Secretariat. Instead of a senior staff of three there were now four and the number of desk officers rose from eight to twelve (Burch and Holliday 2004: 7). The head of the Secretariat now had the status of a Permanent Secretary, one grade above a Director General. This was the same rank as the most senior official in a government department (Bulmer and Burch 2005: 877). With the appointment of the diplomat Wall Blair changed the previous practice that only civil servants from one of the home departments were appointed to this post.[34]

After the 2001 general election Blair decided to move the heads of the European and of the Foreign Policy and Defence Secretariat from the Cabinet Office to No. 10. They were also now officially made the prime minister's advisers (Powell 2010: 80). They in effect incorporated the private secretary role with heading either secretariat in the Cabinet Office (see above) (James 2011: 63). Wall shared an office with Roger Liddle, Blair's political adviser on Europe.[35] Wall and Liddle worked closely together. At European policy meetings in the core executive Liddle was able to do the "'I think the Prime Minister would be very disappointed if'- kind of thing",[36] while Wall had to be seen more or less as an independent arbitrator. However, according to Wall these reforms of the European Secretariat were not as fundamental as they appeared

> because, although I was working inside No. 10 as opposed to inside the Cabinet Office, the basic structure was the same. I had no more influence on Tony Blair's policy than David Williamson had had on Margaret Thatcher's—probably less. So, I think, whereas on Foreign and Defence policy there was a change in kind, on Europe it was a change in degree rather than kind. The basic structure was fundamentally the same. Indeed, actually, my being inside No. 10, if anything, made it less efficient rather than more, because I was not physically located with the people who were working for me.[37]

Moreover, much of the COES's work depended on what the prime minister wanted and whether he was willing to put his authority behind it. If he did not, the Secretariat's influence on departments to change their policies was limited.[38] These reforms of the European Secretariat remained in place when in 2004 Wall was succeeded by Kim Darroch (2004–2007) (James 2009: 618; Bulmer and Burch 2009: 112).

The official task description of the COES also changed between 1998 and 2007: supporting the head of government was not explicitly mentioned in the Secretariat's list of objectives the Cabinet Office published in 1998 (Bulmer and Burch 2009:

---

[34]Interview with S. Wall, 8 January 2010.

[35]Interview with S. Wall, 29 March 2010.

[36]Interview with S. Wall, 29 March 2010.

[37]Interview with S. Wall, 8 January 2010.

[38]Interview with S. Wall, 8 January 2010.

109). Yet by 2007 the Cabinet Office website listed as one of two tasks of the Secretariat: "To support the Prime Minister in driving forward his European Union (EU) policy priorities" (Cabinet Office 2007).

On EMU specifically, the COES in late 2002 and early 2003 developed a number of scenarios setting out the necessary steps to joining the euro. These included legislating for a referendum and holding it. The planning took into account different timelines (Wall 2008: 170).

As prime minister, Tony Blair proactively sought to expand his institutional resources in the Prime Minister's Office and the Cabinet Office. Blair's institutional reforms in the area of European policy made the process more centralised and more centred on the prime minister. Moreover, staff from No. 10 and the COES became much more closely linked (Bulmer and Burch 2009: 112).

More than his three predecessors Blair attempted to strategically extend his institutional resources in Prime Minister's and Cabinet Office to facilitate stronger prime ministerial leadership in European policy-making. Yet these changes were also partly influenced by his personal preferences due to his dislike of the traditional private secretary system.

7.5 The Prime Minister's Institutional Resources in European (Monetary) Policy

This chapter took the institutional resources of the four prime ministers analysed here in Prime Minister's Office and Cabinet Office into view. It asked to what extent the PMs in question could use these resources to shape European policy-making and whether any extended them over time.

On the whole, the prime ministers extended the institutional resources available to them in European policy-making between 1976 and 2007—albeit to different degrees. There were hardly any changes during the premiership of James Callaghan and modest changes during the premierships of Margaret Thatcher and John Major. A leap came with Tony Blair, who undertook significant reforms. These can be seen as an active attempt to exert a more direct influence on his government's European policy-making through institutional reform. Yet the integration at the centre of the core executive—interweaving Prime Minister's Office and Cabinet Office—was not a process Blair initiated. The Cabinet Office secretariats already during Thatcher's and Major's premierships developed closer links with the Policy Unit (Burch and Holliday 1999: 40). Yet under Blair the COES became officially tasked with supporting the prime minister.

Thatcher and Blair also tried to use their institutional resources to gain more influence on European monetary policy. The European Secretariat under Blair was specifically entrusted with planning on EMU. Its head was also involved in the discussions with the Treasury on the outcome of the five tests in 2003 (see Sect.

8.2.4). This suggests that Blair did not want to leave this issue to the Treasury but to have his own expertise, independent of the department. Margaret Thatcher received advice independent of her chancellor and the Treasury from her economic adviser Alan Walters. As he (like her) opposed the chancellor's position on the ERM he provided her with arguments she could use against Lawson (and Howe) in the debate over ERM entry. In the cases of Major and Callaghan there was no indication of a development of similar independent advice structures. Instead Major, for example, in the run up to the Maastricht negotiations turned for advice on EMU specifically to Nigel Wicks, who was the leading Treasury official on this.

The four prime ministers' use and development of these institutional resources were influenced by several factors. There were the prime minister's personal preferences. Tony Blair's reform of his institutional resources in European policy-making, for instance, was influenced by his dislike of the traditional private secretary system. Margaret Thatcher's strong focus on her foreign affairs private secretary from the mid-1980s was influenced by her mistrust of the Foreign Office, to name another example. Yet prime ministerial agency also meant that it was possible that available resources were not used effectively. Thatcher, for instance, employed a personal foreign policy adviser, yet in the later years of her premiership chose not to take his advice on Europe because he held a different view on it from hers.

But the different use of the institutional resources was not just shaped by prime ministerial agency. It was also influenced by the context. There was the European integration process itself: between 1976 and 2007 more and more issues and policy fields gained a European dimension due to the progress of European integration. The increase in staff in the European Secretariat, for example, from Callaghan's to Blair's period in office was a consequence. Yet this did not necessarily mean that a growth in staff would result in a larger potential for leadership in European policy-making in the core executive on the part of the prime minister. It was just that more issues had to be handled, thus more staff were needed. Moreover, the institutional arrangements at the European level changed between 1976 and 2007. The process of centralisation in the UK core executive in European policy-making corresponded with a development at the European level, which saw greater participation of national leaders in European policy-making with regular European Council meetings and bilateral summits (Bulmer and Burch 2005: 877; Barber 1998).

Yet, while these factors have to be taken into account when looking at the institutional resources in Prime Minister's and Cabinet Office, at least some tentative assessment can be made with regard to their role in prime ministerial political leadership. Margaret Thatcher as well as Tony Blair modified their institutional resources in the area of European policy so that they were more focused on the prime minister. Thatcher did so, for instance, by making her foreign affairs private secretary one of her prime advisers on European policy and Blair by making the head of the European Secretariat his official European policy adviser. This suggests that both prime ministers intended to adjust their institutional resources to have more capabilities to exert a leadership role in this policy field. James Callaghan and John Major did not introduce similar changes to the institutional set-up in their Prime Minister's Office or the Cabinet Office. Thus it seems that they were either on the whole satisfied with the available institutional resources on European policy-making or even if they were not at times, there appears to have not been enough interest or means on their part to make institutional reforms similar to those of Thatcher or Blair.

Yet whether an office holder was in fact able to exert predominant political leadership in the core executive in European policy-making not only depended on his institutional resources in PMO and Cabinet Office and how he used them. It was also affected by other factors such as the government's support in the parliamentary party, the view of the media and the public as well as the other actors in the core executive. These aspects are considered in the following chapters.

References

Bale, T., & Sanders, K. (2001). 'Playing by the book': Success and failure in John Major's approach to prime ministerial media management. *Contemporary British History, 15*(4), 93–110.

Ballinger, C., & Seldon, A. (2004). Prime ministers and cabinet. In A. Seldon & K. Hickson (Eds.), *New Labour, Old Labour: The Wilson and Callaghan governments, 1974–79* (pp. 173–189). London: Routledge.

Barber, L. (1998, July 16). Move over Metternich. *Financial Times.*

Beckett, A. (2016, January 27). The most potent, permanent and elusive figure in British politics. *The Guardian.*

Blair, T. (2010). *A journey.* London: Hutchinson.

Braithwaite, R. (1998, January 28). *British Diplomatic Oral History Programme (BDOHP) interview.* Cambridge: Churchill Archives Centre, Churchill College.

Bulmer, S., & Burch, M. (1998). Organizing for Europe: Whitehall, the British state and European Union. *Public Administration, 76*(4), 601–628.

Bulmer, S., & Burch, M. (2005). The Europeanization of UK government: From quiet revolution to explicit step-change? *Public Administration, 83*(4), 861–890.

Bulmer, S., & Burch, M. (2009). *The Europeanisation of Whitehall: UK central government and the European Union.* Manchester: Manchester University Press.

Burch, M. (1995). Prime minister and Whitehall. In D. Shell & R. Hodder-Williams (Eds.), *Churchill to Major: The British prime ministership since 1945* (pp. 104–136). Armonk: M. E. Sharpe.

Burch, M., & Holliday, I. (1996). *British cabinet system.* Hemel Hempstead: Prentice Hall Harvester Wheatsheaf.

Burch, M., & Holliday, I. (1999). The prime minister's and cabinet offices: An executive office in all but name. *Parliamentary Affairs, 52*(1), 32–45.

Burch, M., & Holliday, I. (2004). The Blair government and the core executive. *Government and Opposition, 39*(1), 1–21.

Cabinet Office. (2007). *European Secretariat.* Archived on July 1, 2007. http://webarchive.nationalarchives.gov.uk/20070701080507/cabinetoffice.gov.uk/about_the_cabinet_office/units.asp. Accessed September 11, 2016.

Callaghan, J. (2006). *Time and chance.* London: Politico's.

Campbell, A. (2007). *The Blair years: Extracts from the Alastair Campbell diaries.* London: Hutchinson.

Cartledge, B. (2007, November 14). *British Diplomatic Oral History Programme (BDOHP) interview.* Cambridge: Churchill Archives Centre, Churchill College.

Christoph, J. B. (1993). The effects of Britons in Brussels: The European Community and the culture of Whitehall. *Governance, 6*(4), 518–537.

Cockerell, M., Hennessy, P., & Walker, D. (1985). *Sources close to the prime minister: Inside the hidden world of the news manipulators* (2nd ed.). London: Macmillan.

Cradock, P. (1997). *In pursuit of British interests: Reflections on foreign policy under Margaret Thatcher and John Major*. London: John Murray.

Denman, R. (1997). *Missed chances: Britain and Europe in the twentieth century* (2nd ed.). London: Indigo.

Donoughue, B. (1987). *Prime minister: The conduct of policy under Harold Wilson & James Callaghan*. London: Jonathan Cape.

Donoughue, B. (2009). *Downing Street diary: With James Callaghan in No. 10* (2nd ed.). London: Pimlico.

Dyson, K., & Featherstone, K. (1999). *The road to Maastricht: Negotiating economic and monetary union*. Oxford: Oxford University Press.

Financial Times. (1976, April 6). *Men and matters, McCaffrey's day too*.

Franklin, M. (2013). Could and should Britain have joined the European Exchange Rate Mechanism in 1979? A personal memoir. *Journal of Contemporary European Research, 9*(5), 759–766.

Helm, S. (1991, December 13). Whitehall's battle for Europe. *The Independent*.

Hennessy, P. (1990). *Whitehall* (2nd ed.). London: Fontana.

Hogg, S., & Hill, J. (1996). *Too close to call: Power and politics - John Major in No. 10* (2nd ed.). London: Warner Books.

Holberton, S. (1989, October 18). PM's economist adds his guarded support. *Financial Times*.

Ingham, B. (2003). *Kill the messenger... again* (2nd ed.). London: Politico's.

James, S. (2009). Taming the 'awkward state'? The changing face of European policy-making under Blair. *Public Administration, 87*(3), 604–620.

James, S. (2011). *Managing Europe from home: The changing face of European policy-making under Blair and Ahern*. Manchester: Manchester University Press.

James, S., & Oppermann, K. (2009). Blair and the European Union. In T. Casey (Ed.), *The Blair legacy: Politics, policy, governance and foreign affairs* (pp. 285–298). Basingstoke: Palgrave Macmillan.

Jay, M. (2007, January 4). *British Diplomatic Oral History Programme (BDOHP) interview*. Cambridge: Churchill Archives Centre, Churchill College.

Kavanagh, D., & Seldon, A. (2000). *The powers behind the prime minister: The hidden influence of Number Ten* (2nd ed.). London: HarperCollins.

Lamont, N. (1999). *In office*. London: Little, Brown.

Lawson, N. (1992). *A view from No. 11: Memoirs of a Tory radical*. London: Bantam.

Lee, J. M., Jones, G. W., & Burnham, J. (1998). *At the centre of Whitehall*. Basingstoke: Macmillan.

Liddle, R. (2014). *The Europe dilemma: Britain and the drama of EU integration*. London: I. B. Tauris.

Major, J. (2000). *The autobiography* (2nd ed.). London: HarperCollins.

Mandelson, P. (2010). *The third man: Life at the heart of New Labour*. London: Harper Press.

Moore, C. (2015). *Margaret Thatcher: The authorized biography, Volume two: Everything she wants*. London: Allen Lane.

Morgan, K. (2007, July 5). *Leadership and change: Prime ministers in the post-war-world: James Callaghan*. Lecture at Gresham College. http://www.gresham.ac.uk/lectures-and-events/leadership-and-change-prime-ministers-in-the-post-war-world-james-callaghan. Accessed May 19, 2016.

Powell, C. (2000, July 18). *British Diplomatic Oral History Programme (BDOHP) interview*. Cambridge: Churchill Archives Centre, Churchill College.

Powell, J. (2010). *The new Machiavelli: How to wield power in the modern world*. London: The Bodley Head.

Price, L. (2011). *Where power lies: prime ministers v. the media* (2nd ed.). London: Simon & Schuster.

Rawnsley, A. (2001). *Servants of the people: The inside story of New Labour* (2nd ed.). London: Penguin.

Rawnsley, A. (2010). *The end of the party* (2nd ed.). London: Penguin.

Riddell, P. (1978, December 1). Getting deeply involved with the technicalities. *Financial Times*.

Seldon, A. (1990). The Cabinet Office and coordination 1979–87. *Public Administration, 68*(1), 103–121.

Seldon, A. (1994). Policy making and cabinet. In D. Kavanagh & A. Seldon (Eds.), *The Major effect* (pp. 154–166). London: Macmillan.

Seldon, A. (with Baston, L.) (1998), *Major: A political life* (2nd ed.). London: Phoenix.

Seldon, A. (with Ballinger, C., Collings, D., & Snowdon, P.) (2005). *Blair* (2nd ed.). London: Free Press.

Seymour-Ure, C. (1994). Mass media. In D. Kavanagh & A. Seldon (Eds.), *The Major effect* (pp. 399–417). London: Macmillan.

Stack, F. (1983). The imperatives of coordination. In F. E. C. Gregory (Ed.), *Dilemmas of government: Britain and the European Community* (pp. 124–152). Oxford: Martin Robertson.

Stephens, P. (1991, December 9). Spokesman who wields unsung influence. *Financial Times*.

Stephens, P. (1997). *Politics and the pound: The Tories, the economy and Europe* (2nd ed.). London: Papermac.

The Independent. (1989, June 17). *Outsider at the heart of Thatcherism: Sir Alan Walters, No. 10's economic adviser*.

The National Archives [hereafter TNA]. (1977, July 1). *Records of the Prime Minister's Office [hereafter PREM] 16/1492*, Kenneth Stowe to the prime minister.

TNA. (1978, September 28). *Records of the Cabinet Office [hereafter CAB] 193/212/3,* Kenneth Berrill to John Hunt. The United Kingdom and the European Monetary System.

TNA. (1978, July 3). *PREM 16/1634,* Note of a meeting held at 10 Downing Street at 0930 on 3 July 1978.

TNA. (1978, September 29). *PREM 16/1635,* Kenneth Berrill to the prime minister. European Monetary System.

TNA. (1978, November 29). *PREM 16/1638,* Tom McCaffrey to the prime minister. E.M.S. Decision: Presentation.

Trewin, I. (Ed.). (2009). *The Hugo Young papers: A journalist's notes from the heart of politics* (2nd ed.). London: Penguin Books.

Wall, S. (2008). *A stranger in Europe: Britain and the EU from Thatcher to Blair*. Oxford: Oxford University Press.

Walters, A. (1988, April 6). Britain does best outside the EMS. *Financial Times*.

Watt, D. (1976, April 6). 'Steady as we go' – at least for now. *Financial Times*.

Willetts, D. (1987). The role of the prime minister's Policy Unit. *Public Administration, 65*(4), 443–454.

Wright, P. (2000, October 16). *British Diplomatic Oral History Programme (BDOHP) interview*. Cambridge: Churchill Archives Centre, Churchill College.

Young, H. (1989). *One of us: A biography of Margaret Thatcher* (2nd ed.). London: Macmillan.

Chapter 8
Prime Ministerial Management of the Actors in the European Monetary Policy Core Executive

This chapter focuses on the actors in the European monetary policy core executive. In addition to the premier, these are particularly foreign secretary and chancellor and at times trade and industry minister(s). In some cases actors responsible for a policy area not directly related to European monetary policy were involved in the decision-making process as well. This chapter addresses the question as to how far these actors impacted on the premier's political leadership. It also considers whether any of the prime ministers attempted to expand their leeway by using their right of appointment and dismissal (particularly on Foreign Office and Treasury appointments) as well as the management of the cabinet. Lastly, prime ministerial options for two-level politics are examined to analyse whether any of the premiers managed to force their cabinet to accept decisions due to their own position in the European Council.

8.1 Resource of Appointment

8.1.1 James Callaghan

An important task for James Callaghan when forming his cabinet in 1976 was to balance his party's left and right wing. Europe was one of the issues they were divided on (see Sect. 5.2.1). His decision not to appoint **Roy Jenkins** as foreign secretary suggests he took these divisions into account when putting together his cabinet. While Callaghan acknowledged that Jenkins' experience and knowledge would have recommended him for the post, he thought that due to the latter's pro-European credentials[1] the Eurosceptic backbenchers would never trust him.

[1]In 1972 Jenkins had opposed the official party line and voted with the Conservative government for Britain to join the EC.

B. Bujard, *The British Prime Minister in the Core Executive*, Contributions to Political Science, https://doi.org/10.1007/978-3-319-89953-4_8

Therefore he decided he "could not risk the uneasy truce that then prevailed in the Party by appointing someone who would be accused of tilting the balance, however scrupulous he might be" (Callaghan 2006: 399). Yet according to accounts by contemporaries the relationship between the two men was not without problems (e.g. Owen 2009: 97, 182; Donoughue 2009: 343). Jenkins had challenged Callaghan for the party leadership. Thus, the latter might also have wanted to restrict a rival's influence. Nonetheless, until he became President of the European Commission in autumn 1976, Jenkins remained in cabinet, albeit as home secretary away from European policy.[2] Callaghan appointed **Tony Crosland** to the FCO who "was not nearly as committed as Roy Jenkins to Community membership and would not arouse as much suspicion when he took the necessary decisions, as he must, that would link Britain more closely with the Community" (Callaghan 2006: 399). Crosland was an agnostic on Europe (Healey 2006: 329–330). When Crosland[3] died in 1977, Callaghan decided to appoint a young successor and fresh face to the cabinet. Moreover, he wished to strengthen the group of young ministers in the cabinet, hoping they would contribute innovative ideas (Callaghan 2006: 447–448). He chose 38-year old **David Owen**. His cabinet colleague Denis Healey considered this too early a promotion, arguing Owen tried to conceal his insecurity with arrogance and as a result was not well liked by FCO staff (Healey 2006: 458; see also Bruce-Gardyne 1986: 60). Owen's stance in the core executive was weak. He was not a member of the Labour Party's National Executive Committee (NEC), the party's governing body. His influence in cabinet was limited, particularly compared to Chancellor Healey, who was seen as the obvious candidate to head the FCO, if he had left the Treasury. Owen's position depended mainly on his appointment by the PM (Dickie 1992: 107, 108). He was a self-declared supporter of EC membership but opposed the establishment of a single European state. This view led to difficulties with senior FCO officials, who did not share his view that it was sometimes important to robustly present Britain's stance in European level discussions. In his opinion such a strategy did not signify anti-European sentiment but an essential defence of UK interests (Owen 2009: 33, 157). On the ERM, he sided with the sceptics. Michael Franklin (2013: 762), then head of the COES, thought this was because Owen hoped to become party leader and might have wanted to accommodate the party left by not presenting himself as too pro-European. Yet Bernard Donoughue (2009: 373) considered Owen an agnostic on the ERM from the start.

Denis Healey, chancellor since 1974, remained in his post. Due to his ministerial experience he was seen as an important cabinet member with a power base independent of the new PM. According to Donoughue (1987: 14) it would have been very difficult for Callaghan to dismiss Healey from the cabinet. In his view Healey played a considerable role as chancellor in cabinet and "neither of his Prime

---

[2]The decision not to promote Jenkins to the Foreign Office raised criticism e.g. from Callaghan's advisers Tom McNally and Bernard Donoughue (Donoughue 2009: 16, 17).

[3]As the EMS discussion began in 1978 Crosland's tenure as foreign secretary is not further considered.

Ministers [Wilson and Callaghan] found it easy to impose upon him changes of economic policy. They had to convince him intellectually and politically" (Donoughue 1987: 33). On Europe, he was a self-declared agnostic and pragmatist (Healey 2006: 329–330). He saw the ERM as a tool for Germany to expand its competitiveness at the expense of countries with weaker currencies. While initially agnostic about membership, Healey (2006: 438–439) noted that discussions with people such as Manfred Lahnstein (German finance ministry) made him realise the likely effects of such a mechanism and he decided to oppose it.

To balance the different party wings Callaghan appointed **Michael Foot** as leader of the House of Commons (Giddings 1995: 40). Foot represented the Eurosceptic left and had close links to the trade unions (Dell and Hunt 1994: 456). The hope was that he would act in cabinet "as a moderating influence on his left-wing friends in the party and the unions" (Donoughue 1988: 17). Callaghan knew he needed Foot: "Michael and I had never worked together before, but now it was essential that we should do so if our minority Government was to survive" (Callaghan 2006: 401). **Tony Benn** was another member of the Eurosceptic left whom he appointed. Benn repeatedly opposed the government's (European) policy in cabinet and party bodies and tried to strengthen the left's influence in government (Donoughue 2009: 231, 266; Rawstorne 1978). By Donoughue's account the PM did not dismiss him because he thought that outside the cabinet Benn would organise the left and create more problems for the government than inside.[4]

Callaghan also appointed outspoken pro-Europeans to his government. Alongside Roy Jenkins these included **Harold Lever** (Chancellor of the Duchy of Lancaster), **Shirley Williams** (minister for prices and consumer protection, later for education and science) and **Edmund Dell** (trade secretary). The social democrat Dell left the government in 1978, disappointed with the development of his party (Roth 1999). Though pro-European, he was in principle opposed to a European monetary system (Dell 1994: 34). Harold Lever, who also advised Callaghan on economic policy, was one of the few cabinet ministers supporting ERM membership (Rhys 1978). Lever, despite his fairly low and non-departmental post, was an authoritative figure in the core executive, whose influence

> derived from being an internationally respected financial guru, capable of inventing monetary solutions beyond the imagination of the Treasury or Bank of England bureaucracies, and as such he was inevitably disapproved of by both of them. (Donoughue 1988: 17)

Shirley Williams supported ERM membership as well (Donoughue 2009: 393). But like Roy Jenkins she had no post in which she could influence European policy decision-making much.

Overall, Callaghan used his resource of appointment mainly for intraparty coalition building. He tried to balance pro-Europeans (e.g. Roy Jenkins, Harold Lever, Shirley Williams), Euro-agnostics (e.g. Healey, Crosland) and Eurosceptics (e.g. Foot, Benn, agricultural minister John Silkin, development minister Peter

[4]Interview with B. Donoughue, 24 March 2010.

Shore). According to his Political Secretary Tom McNally, Callaghan's cabinet was about a third pro-European, a third pragmatic on Europe and a third Eurosceptic.[5] In charge of a minority government he could not do without representatives of the different sections of the party. But, as Donoughue (2009) noted, he tried to limit the left's influence by using his resource of appointment: "Jim said that neither John Silkin [Minister for Agriculture] nor Stan Orme [Minister of Social Security] were really Cabinet material, but he had to have people from the left and they were the 'least harmful'" (68). Callaghan used his resource of appointment neither to form a more pro-European nor a more Eurosceptic government, but tried to strike a balance between the different wings of the party to avoid tilting the balance of power too much to either side.

8.1.2 *Margaret Thatcher*

When Margaret Thatcher became prime minister she had not yet consolidated her position as party leader. To secure it she had to appoint party colleagues into cabinet, who were no close political confidantes. Several members of her first cabinet accepted but did not share her political views (Parkinson 1992: 8). One was her first foreign minister **Peter Carrington**, who from the start held a more influential position in the core executive than his predecessor David Owen had ever done. He had extensive government experience (Dickie 1992: 110). Politically he and Thatcher were not close (Carrington 1988: 280). She appointed him because of his foreign policy experience but did not fully trust him. She allowed him to select his ministerial team but insisted on the inclusion of Nicholas Ridley, whose views on economics were in line with hers (Thatcher 2011: 27; Dickie 1992: 110–111). The pro-European Carrington (1988: 310–311) thought that due to the UK's limited military and economic capabilities it should embrace Europe and try to be influential in the EC. The ERM issue, though, had no priority for him. He was neither particularly interested nor had much expertise in economic policy (Thompson 1996: 17).

When Carrington resigned at the beginning of the Falklands war in spring 1982, Thatcher appointed **Francis Pym** as his successor.[6] Their relationship was difficult (Hurd 2009: 270). Therefore, she took the next chance available, which came after winning her second general election, to dismiss Pym from cabinet in June 1983 (Giddings 1995: 37). With his replacement **Geoffrey Howe**, she, for the first time, sent a political confidante to the FCO. Howe had reliably handled the economy as chancellor during her first term (Dickie 1992: 115). In the words of his successor at the Treasury Nigel Lawson (1992) he was "one of the principal architects and most

[5]Interview with T. McNally, 22 March 2010.

[6]Pym's role is not further analysed here as the ERM only became an issue of significant interest in the government from the mid 1980s.

articulate expositors of Thatcherism" (653). Yet Thatcher (2011) later criticised Howe's foreign policy objectives, which she thought were highly influenced by the Foreign Office and identified them as "a reluctance to subordinate diplomatic tactics to the national interest and an insatiable appetite for nuances and conditions which can blur the clearest vision" (309). She considered Howe's attitude to European integration "an almost romantic longing for Britain to become part of some grandiose European consensus" (Thatcher 2011: 309). On the ERM, he had shown support for the principle of a European monetary system in 1978 (HC Deb 29 November 1978, c474). But when the Conservatives came into government in 1979 he opposed immediate entry: "Some months at the Treasury persuaded me that the oil-induced volatility of the pound sterling created difficulties for our immediate membership of the Exchange Rate Mechanism of the EMS" (Howe 1995: 111). It is unclear when Howe changed his mind on ERM membership. According to Helen Thompson (1996: 25, 41) he gradually shifted his stance to again supporting ERM membership between autumn 1981 and his move to the Foreign Office in 1983. Yet only from October 1984 were there press reports suggesting he had changed his view. By Howe's own account he began to see membership as potentially desirable only after he had been at the FCO for a time. His change of position had been for economic and not for foreign or European policy reasons. He did not attribute it to the department he now headed (Howe 1995: 276). He saw monetary union as an acceptable medium term goal (Howe 1995: 534). Sharing sovereignty with others was no problem for Howe, if it meant that the UK could expand its influence in the world. The only alternative to European integration for him was isolation and loss of influence (Stephens 1997: 113). Howe and Thatcher became increasingly divided over European policy from the mid 1980s. This came to a head before the Madrid European Council (see Sect. 8.2.2). In July 1989 she responded by dismissing him from the FCO and replacing him with **John Major** (Dickie 1992: 122).

When she sent Major to the Treasury 3 months later, Thatcher appointed **Douglas Hurd** as foreign secretary. Hurd had been FCO minister under Carrington and Pym, Northern Ireland Minister and Home Secretary and as a former diplomat appeared to be perfect for the post (Dickie 1992: 125–126; Hurd 2009: 285). He was not close to Thatcher.[7] According to her foreign policy adviser Percy Cradock (1997) she remained wary of Hurd and considered him "ideologically unreliable" (23). Initially, she did not appear to have much confidence in his expertise on European policy and did not believe that he had a robust negotiating style with the other member states at the European level (Dickie 1992: 127–128). But he became an influential figure in her last cabinet and was not afraid to emphasise his independence from her (Stephens 1997: 154–155). Hurd was a convinced but pragmatic pro-European, who did not believe in the eventual establishment of a European state (Hurd 2009: 261, 478). Upon becoming foreign secretary he did not show much interest in campaigning for ERM membership as Howe had done before him (Thompson 1996: 154). But he

[7]As Edward Heath's former Political Secretary Hurd had supported him in the 1975 leadership competition not Thatcher (Hurd 2009: 266).

came to see membership as sensible, particularly for political reasons. When in December 1989 the European Council decided to set up an Intergovernmental Conference (IGC) on monetary union, he concluded—as had his department—that Britain would lack influence on the further development of European monetary policy without ERM membership (Stephens 1997: 149). He did not support EMU but thought Thatcher's negotiating strategy on it was wrong and that her brusque style did not achieve the right results as it only alienated the European counterparts. Unlike her he did not think that Britain could keep the other member states from going through with EMU (Hurd 2009: 438–439, 458).

As mentioned, **Geoffrey Howe** was the first chancellor Thatcher appointed (1979–1983). When he moved to the FCO in 1983 she appointed **Nigel Lawson** to lead the Treasury.[8] He was seen as a chancellor with economic expertise and was therefore respected by most of his departmental officials (Stephens 1997: 135). For a long time he held a strong position in the core executive, not least because he had no ambitions to become prime minister, which Thatcher knew (Thatcher 2011: 755). On the ERM, he was initially an agnostic but around late 1984/early 1985 began to see membership as desirable (Thompson 1996: 41). He claims to have taken this view as early as 1981, when he had been Financial Secretary at the Treasury, but that due to opposition from officials he had to wait for the right opportunity to put the issue back on the department's agenda (Lawson 1992: 484–485). Despite his support for ERM membership he opposed a single currency (Lawson 1992: 892). His appointment also illustrates the fact that placing a political companion in an influential department is no guarantee that he or she will take the same view on key policies. Thatcher and Lawson grew apart over the ERM. With it came his decision to let sterling shadow the Deutschmark even though Britain was no ERM member—a policy which Thatcher opposed (see also Chap. 3). She considered it a loss of trust that he implemented this policy without her consent. Yet she did not dismiss him in 1988 due to his influential position as

> he was widely—and rightly—credited with helping us win the 1987 election. He had complete intellectual mastery of his brief. He had the strong support of Conservative back-benchers and much of the Conservative press. (Thatcher 2011: 703)

She wanted him to solve the problem of rising inflation for which she made him responsible (Thatcher 2011: 715).

When Lawson resigned in October 1989, Thatcher replaced him with **John Major**. Major also supported ERM membership for economic reasons but had strong reservations about EMU (see Sect. 5.1). The PM had initially wanted to appoint **Nicholas Ridley** as chancellor, but due to his limited diplomatic abilities she settled for Major (Thatcher 2011: 717). She instead made Ridley Trade and Industry Secretary in 1989. His position on Europe was one reason for it (Thatcher 2011: 758). He had begun his political career as a supporter of European integration but had become a Eurosceptic (Hurd 2009: 426). He was one of Thatcher's staunchest

[8]Moore (2015: 66) suggests Thatcher might not have chosen Lawson, if her majority at the 1983 general election had been smaller, as it was considered a daring choice.

supporters on the ERM (Lawson 1992: 943). He also supported her in her opposition to monetary union (Dyson & Featherstone 1999: 569). Particularly at the end of her premiership he played a significant role, as he was the last remaining ally in her cabinet (Stephens 1997: 167).

On European policy, Thatcher was able to use her resource of appointment only to a limited extent to strengthen her influence in the core executive. But as the Conservatives in the early 1980s were not yet split over the issue, balancing different attitudes to European integration was not a crucial aspect on cabinet appointments such as it had been for Callaghan. Intraparty divisions over Europe only came to the fore in the late 1980s—a development to which Thatcher contributed by becoming increasingly Eurosceptic. Geoffrey Howe's resignation in 1990, for example, revealed these divisions in party and government, as he specifically referred to the divisions between him and Thatcher over Europe in his resignation speech (Howe 1995: 697–703). Yet it was John Major, Thatcher's successor, who had to take these divisions more strongly into account when appointing his cabinet to secure his political survival and party unity.

8.1.3 John Major

Upon becoming prime minister, John Major made few changes to the cabinet. As a general election was close, he did not want to make too many alterations before (Major 2000: 205). Yet, due to his move to No. 10, a new chancellor was needed. Major chose **Norman Lamont**, whom he had already worked with at the Treasury (Seldon 1998: 135). The Eurosceptic Lamont[9]—had not been involved in the decision to take sterling into the ERM at the end of the Thatcher government. He was an agnostic about the ERM, yet accepted the policy. Initially, when he became chancellor, Lamont did not see it as his task to reverse a decision taken by the previous government but to implement it (Lamont 1999: 8, 36–37). He strongly opposed EMU believing a single currency would require a European state. By his account he had held this view since the early 1970s (Lamont 1999: 112). After the UK left the ERM, Major decided to dismiss Lamont, albeit not immediately, but 8 months later. Major's critics argued that he had left Lamont in the post for so long because to have dismissed him right after the exit would have threatened his own position. They thought so because joining and remaining in the ERM had been Major's policy while Lamont had gradually become ever more opposed to it (Seldon 1998: 375). But Douglas Hurd thought Major had been right neither to have dismissed Lamont nor to accept his resignation directly after the ERM exit. In his view Lamont and Major had together executed the policy, thus if one of them had resigned, the other one would have had to do so as well (Hurd 2009: 470).

[9]For Lamont's view on Europe, see Lamont (1999: 10–11).

Lamont's successor was **Ken Clarke**, until then Home Secretary. He was a pro-European, who supported monetary union because he thought the single market would work better with a single currency (Clarke 2016: 346, 347). At the time of his appointment as chancellor Clarke was at the height of his popularity in the Conservative Party. Despite his pro-European views the party's Eurosceptics were in general not hostile to him until the mid 1990s (Seldon 1998: 377–378). He had his own authority, which did not depend on having been appointed by Major (Thomas 1998: 44).

Major left **Douglas Hurd** in charge of the Foreign Office. His role in the Major government was even more important than it had been in the previous one. His relationship with the new premier was close and dated back to Major's days as chancellor. Hurd's seniority in the party ensured that he had sufficient political authority to champion his policies in cabinet despite possible criticism from party colleagues (Dickie 1992: 127). Hurd resigned for personal reasons in 1995 (Hurd 2009: 563–564).

Major then chose **Malcolm Rifkind** as new foreign secretary. Rifkind had been Minister for Europe in the early 1980s and later Defence Secretary (Major 2000: 514). He took over at a time when calls for a more Eurosceptic foreign secretary became louder in the party. He did not appear to fit this role and was seen to have a view on Europe similar to Hurd. Upon becoming foreign secretary he was cautious to insist that he had not been particularly pro-European in the past (Young 1999: 460). Rifkind, a self-proclaimed "moderate Eurosceptic" (Rifkind 2016: 364), opposed the euro as he thought it would require a European government, which was something he did not think desirable.

An appointment which signalled that the new PM set other priorities than those of his predecessor was that of **Michael Heseltine**. Heseltine was a well-known pro-European who had resigned in 1986 from the government over the Westland affair.[10] In 1990 he had challenged Thatcher for the party leadership, which led to her resignation and Major's election as party leader. Heseltine was an early supporter of ERM membership for which he had campaigned from the backbenches before the Hanover European Council in 1988 (Dyson and Featherstone 1999: 564). Major knew that he needed to include Heseltine in his government as the latter had been widely supported in the leadership race. Major also saw him as an important factor to win the next general election (Major 2000: 207). He became environment minister and after the 1992 general election moved to the DTI (Hogg and Hill 1996: 8–9). Heseltine was an important actor in the core executive, because he had his own authority, which was not based on the appointment by the premier. This was further strengthened when he became Deputy Prime Minister in 1995 (Thomas 1998: 44). The promotion raised criticism from those sections of the party which demanded a more Eurosceptic European policy (Major 2000: 646).

---

[10]It had been an argument in the cabinet particularly between Thatcher and Heseltine (Defence Secretary) over the sale of the British helicopter company Westland; for more see Dunleavy (1995).

Alongside the pro-Europeans Major also appointed Eurosceptics to his cabinet such as **Michael Howard**, **Michael Portillo**, **Peter Lilley**, and **John Redwood**. The latter three were initially in junior government posts, yet this did not keep them from making their views on Europe known (Young 1994: 26; Young 1999: 444, 446–447). Portillo, a well-known opponent of EMU, for instance, in his position as Chief Secretary to the Treasury in May 1994 opposed official government policy by publicly dismissing a European single currency. This created dismay in the government and with Tory backbenchers over intraparty divisions over Europe (Stephens 1994). He later joined the cabinet as employment secretary and became defence secretary when Rifkind moved to the FCO. Michael Howard moved from the department of employment to environment and then to the Home Office. With his appointment as Home Secretary in May 1993 (and Redwood as Welsh Secretary) Major tried to placate his party's Eurosceptics, because Ken Clarke became chancellor in the same reshuffle. This meant that key cabinet posts were now held by pro-Europeans: Major, Hurd, Heseltine, Clarke and Norman Fowler as Party Chairman (Seldon 1998: 378).

The divisions between pro-Europeans and Eurosceptics in the cabinet only really came to the fore after the 1992 election. By appointing pro-Europeans (e.g. Clarke, Heseltine, Hurd) and Eurosceptics (e.g. Portillo, Howard, Lilley), Major tried to balance the different party wings and to secure party and government unity. Yet over time the Eurosceptics extended their reach in the party. By 1995–6 the majority of cabinet and many junior ministers were Eurosceptics. The Eurosceptic David Davis, for example, was appointed Minister for Europe in 1994. His function was seen as keeping tabs on the generally pro-European FCO (Gowland and Turner 2000: 295).

Overall, Major initially used his resource of appointment like Callaghan had done to strike a balance between pro-Europeans and Eurosceptics. Yet over time the Eurosceptics became more numerous in his cabinet.

8.1.4 Tony Blair

Tony Blair's decision to make **Gordon Brown** chancellor was probably the appointment with the largest effect on his government's European monetary policy: Brown was a leading member of the party, having been shadow chancellor since 1992. When party leader John Smith died in 1994, he had wished to succeed him. But when Blair's campaign for the leadership took off, Brown decided not to compete with him (Anderson and Mann 1997: 84, 98). Brown and Blair were held to be close friends at the beginning of Blair's premiership, but they were also contestants for power in the government (Rawnsley 2001: 19). In office Brown was seen as one of the most successful chancellors Labour had ever had (Scott 2004: 30). In exchange for having stepped aside from the party leadership he expected Blair to guarantee that he would not only be responsible for the government's economic but also social policy. Blair allowed Brown to chair the economic policy cabinet committee—a post which had last been held by a chancellor in 1964. In contrast to Blair, Brown considered the government to be under dual leadership (Rawnsley 2001: 20). Due to increasing conflicts between them over the course of his premiership, Blair considered in 2003 to move Brown or to limit his influence by splitting the Treasury in two departments. According to his political confidante Peter Mandelson (2010: 369–371) neither happened because Blair lacked the authority to do either. This was after the Iraq war which had politically weakened Blair, who had used up much of his political capital to secure acceptance from parliament and public for his course on Iraq (Liddle 2014: 157). Blair (2010: 499) argued he never moved Brown because he remained the best qualified individual for the post of chancellor despite their problems. Like Callaghan had done with Benn, Blair decided that keeping Brown in government created fewer problems. He thought that Brown could have established himself as a much bigger counterforce outside the cabinet (Blair 2010: 500). Brown's appointment had implications for the government's euro policy. This was because as chancellor he was much involved in the policy-making process. Moreover, at the start of Blair's premiership he was widely held to be more pro-European and more pro-euro than Blair (Rawnsley 2001: 74).[11] Yet his position changed (or appeared to do so) later (see Sect. 8.2.4).

With **Robin Cook** Tony Blair appointed a representative of Old Labour as his first foreign secretary. Cook was then influential in the party as he was seen as a leader of the left (Kerr 2004). But his difficult relationship with Gordon Brown[12] as well as the extensive media coverage of his private life[13] shortly after Labour came into office meant that he became a less influential foreign secretary than might have been expected on account of his standing in the party. Particularly due to the extensive media coverage surrounding his private life Cook became dependent on the premier's support instead of a counterforce to him (Rawnsley 2001: 56, 58). He was not close to Blair, which might have helped to extend his influence in the core executive. The premier, for instance, in 1997 rejected all of his suggestions for Minister of Europe and instead chose Doug Henderson, a candidate who had been promoted by Gordon Brown, but had no experience on European policy (Rawnsley 2001: 21–22). In opposition Cook had opposed joining the euro, but shortly after his arrival at the FCO he became an avid supporter of European integration and of joining the Eurozone (Liddle 2014: 170–171). His diary of the years 2001–2003 documents an enthusiastic campaign to join the euro (Cook 2004). By then, however, he was Leader of the House of Commons and no longer part of European policy-making in the core executive. After re-election in May 2001 Blair replaced Cook with **Jack Straw**, who until then had been home secretary. Straw was less enthusiastic about Europe than Cook. In the 1975 referendum on EC membership he had supported the 'No'-side, which had championed leaving the EC (Straw 2011). He was a self-declared "practical European", who thought that "the euro was fundamentally flawed" (Straw 2012: 326). Blair believed that—once at the FCO—Straw would conform to his European

[11] Interview with S. Wall, 8 January 2010.

[12] On the divisions between Brown and Cook, see Anderson and Mann (1997: 117).

[13] Cook's extramarital affair was exposed by the press in summer 1997 (Mandelson 2010: 230).

policy stance including that on the euro. Also, if Straw—known to be a sceptic about Europe—argued for joining the euro this would carry more weight with the public, the media and other MPs (Mandelson 2010: 336). This argument echoes Callaghan's reason for appointing Tony Crosland as foreign secretary. In May 2006 Blair replaced Straw with **Margaret Beckett**.[14] With the reshuffle he wanted to prove his government's vitality. Yet in hindsight he saw it as a mistake to have moved Straw, who was well-liked by his foreign secretary peers. Moreover, Blair (2010: 594) concluded that Straw was disappointed about losing the post and Beckett bewildered.

An important pro-European member of the core executive early in Blair's premiership was **Peter Mandelson**. Already in the early 1990s he had shown his support for Britain to join the single currency (Anderson and Mann 1997: 369). He was close to Blair and had been to Brown until he had backed Blair for the party leadership in 1994.[15] He had hoped to become Minister of Europe, but the new premier appointed him as minister without portfolio in the Cabinet Office to ensure that the government ran smoothly and was re-elected. Blair argued that at the FCO Mandelson would only have been "caught in between" (Mandelson 2010: 216) him and Cook. Yet Mandelson did receive some responsibilities on Europe as Blair made him his "roving European ambassador" (James 2009: 609). This was not wholly unproblematic with the foreign secretary. Jonathan Powell (2010: 245), Blair's chief of staff, recalled that Cook complained to him in May 1998 that Mandelson was trying to transform the Cabinet Office into a department for Europe. Stephen Wall, head of the COES from 2000 to 2004, agreed that the European Secretariat became more important during Mandelson's period at the Cabinet Office. He did, however, not attribute this only to Mandelson but also to the fact that the foreign secretary was distrusted by Blair and Mandelson alike and that they to a degree disregarded his influence on European issues.[16] In July 1998 Blair made Mandelson trade and industry secretary. Now he could engage more fully in European policy-making. Yet, as he had to resign already in December,[17] he could not use it much to influence decision-making on the euro in the core executive. After having to resign a second time in 2001 as Northern Ireland minister,[18] Mandelson did not return to the cabinet for the remainder of Blair's premiership.

Another pro-European voice in the Blair cabinet was, for instance, Stephen Byers, who succeeded Mandelson at the DTI in 1998. He publicly spoke up in

[14]She is not further taken into account here, as in 2006 the government no longer actively considered the euro issue.

[15]For details on their relationship until 2004, see Seldon (2005: chapter 14).

[16]Interview with S. Wall, 8 January 2010.

[17]Before the election he had received a loan from Labour colleague Geoffrey Robinson, whose business activities the DTI was investigating. Mandelson had kept the loan secret. When it became public, Blair insisted for him to leave the cabinet, not to damage the government (Rawnsley 2001: 219–230).

[18]His second resignation concerned accusations he had used his previous position at the DTI to influence passport applications. There was an inquiry which found no wrongdoing on his part, but by then he had already resigned due to pressure from Blair (Seldon 2005: 169–173).

support of joining the euro and thus openly challenged the chancellor. After the 2001 election Blair moved him from this position (James and Oppermann 2009: 290). His replacement at the DTI, Patricia Hewitt, was also pro-European (Rawnsley 2001: 508; Liddle 2014: 169).

For Tony Blair, like for his predecessors, the resource to appoint and dismiss the members of his government was a limited one. Gordon Brown, for instance, was an important politician in his own right with his own party base. Later in his premiership Blair lacked the authority to move him to another position or to dismiss him from government all-together. His claim to have left Brown in his post only due to his competence should be viewed sceptically as it is not to be expected for a former prime minister to publicly admit that he was not able to dismiss an influential colleague due to the existing power balance in the core executive. Furthermore, Blair initially only had limited latitude in exerting his resource of patronage as due to the Labour party rules then in force elected members of the shadow cabinet had to be promoted to cabinet once the party was elected into government (Powell 2010: 24). During his premiership European policy was a much less controversial issue in his party than it had been during Callaghan's (see Sect. 5.2.1). Nonetheless, Blair did not set up his cabinet with respect to this policy field exclusively based on his wishes, for instance, by promoting party members to it, who shared his view on the euro. Other cleavages in the party and in cabinet were more significant than those between euro supporters and opponents such as initially between Old and New Labour[19] and increasingly between Blair and Brown and their supporters.

8.2 Prime Ministerial Cabinet Management and Political Decision-Making on ERM and EMU

8.2.1 The Callaghan Government

Contemporaries such as Bernard Donoughue (1987: 15) viewed James Callaghan as a chairman who had his cabinet under control. According to David Owen (2009: 160), Callaghan's cabinet management fostered trust among the members of cabinet and the premier supported his ministers even if they had made a mistake. Having been part of the cabinet for a long time as a minister, Callaghan was a vehement supporter of its collective responsibility and saw it as essential to involve his cabinet in taking decisions on the key issues facing the government (Donoughue 1987: 35).

On European policy, Callaghan was cautious to avoid an open conflict between pro- and anti-Europeans in his cabinet. For example, while preparing a meeting of cabinet and Chief Whip on European policy on 29 July 1977, his Principal Private

[19]An example was the first London mayoral election in 2000, when the New Labour leadership tried to prevent the candidacy of Ken Livingstone, who was seen to represent Old Labour. For more see Shaw (2004: 63–65).

Secretary Kenneth Stowe asked whether Eurosceptic ministers John Silkin and Peter Shore should be invited to hand in papers for the session to set out their views on a European policy more focused on the country's national interest, which they had previously demanded. The premier rejected this by replying it would be "too confrontational" (TNA, PREM 16/1492, 1 July 1977). Yet by including leading members of the left in his cabinet, Callaghan made them take responsibility for European policy decisions such as on the EMS and ERM. But this strategy failed in the case of Tony Benn, who continually criticised and distanced himself from the government's (European) policy. The fact that he was not dismissed in spite of this breach of collective responsibility was seen as a lack of authority on the part of the prime minister (Rutherford 1978).

In late 1976 the prime minister set up a 'seminar' to discuss monetary policy, which met 14 times in 1977 and 78 (Kavanagh and Seldon 2000: 129). Alongside Callaghan, Chancellor Healey, Harold Lever, the Governor of the Bank of England, Bernard Donoughue, the Cabinet Secretary John Hunt and the premier's Principal Private Secretary Kenneth Stowe participated regularly (Donoughue 1987: 101). The discussion in a small group prevented leaks of decisions which were sensitive to the financial markets. Callaghan repeatedly complained at cabinet meetings that information on cabinet discussions had been leaked to the press, damaging the government's standing, the efficiency of governance and the solidarity of cabinet (TNA, CAB 128/59, CM (76) 3rd Conclusions, 6 May 1976, 3; TNA, CAB 128/59, CM (76) 7th Conclusions, 25 May 1976, 4; TNA, CAB 128/63, CM (78) 2nd Conclusions, 26 January 1978, 3). It can be assumed that non-disclosure was an aim of the seminar. The seminar was integrated into the cabinet committee structure, which according to Donoughue (2009) was completed by October 1977 when he noted in his diary: "it has now become a Cabinet committee... This is an important constitutional development if maintained. For the first time, monetary policy has become part of collective Cabinet government" (254). Callaghan discussed the European Monetary System in the seminar before the Bremen European Council (6/7 July 1978), at which the German-French proposal for the system was presented. The seminar on 3 July was attended by staff from No. 10, the Treasury (Ken Couzens) and the Bank of England as well as Governor Gordon Richardson, Denis Healey, Harold Lever and David Owen. While Healey and Lever then appeared to support the scheme, Callaghan noted he could see little use for the UK (Donoughue 2009: 343).

In the full cabinet the premier addressed the EMS for the first time in its regular meeting on 6 July. He informed his colleagues that a significant part of the summit discussions was likely to be devoted to creating greater exchange rate stability between EC member currencies. To avoid speculative attacks on sterling, he argued, it was essential that the summit's outcome should neither suggest that Britain was isolated on the issue nor committed to join such a scheme after devaluation. He wanted to make clear at Bremen that the UK had always been in favour of more exchange rate stability and would constructively debate such a project. But he listed conditions which, from a British perspective, needed to be in place for such a scheme to work. These included that the pressure to adjust should not only be placed with the weaker currencies but also with the stronger ones. Also, resource transfers from the richer to the poorer countries would be necessary (TNA, CAB 128/64, CM (78) 25th Conclusions, 6 July 1978, 2–3). In the discussion it became clear that not only the Eurosceptics objected to the plan, but also the pro-European trade secretary Edmund Dell. Harold Lever argued in support of membership (Dell 1994: 34, 35). The cabinet agreed on the need to avoid a summit outcome which might result in speculative attacks on the pound. Moreover, the PM summed up that at the summit he "did not intend to go beyond agreeing to further studies of the conditions which would have to be satisfied before any agreement could be reached. There would then be a later opportunity to consider whether a satisfactory bargain could be struck" (TNA, CAB 128/64, CM (78) 25th Conclusions, 6 July 1978, 4).

After the Bremen European Council the EMS proposal was discussed in full cabinet on 13 July. Callaghan explained that his stance at the summit had been in line with what the cabinet had agreed the previous week. He proposed to set up a ministerial group which was to analyse the proposal in detail to which the cabinet agreed (TNA, CAB 128/64, CM (78) 26th Conclusions, 13 July 1978, 3, 4). In the subsequent discussion the Eurosceptics and Edmund Dell remained opposed to the scheme while Chancellor Healey and Harold Lever argued that the key question now was whether Britain wanted to influence the project by participating in it, not whether it wanted it all, since at least six member states intended to go through with the project in 1979 (Dell 1994: 37). Tony Benn, as Secretary of State for Energy with no responsibility for European monetary policy, had submitted a paper on the EMS for the session. In it he set out his opposition to the scheme, demanding a British veto of the EMS, which he called a "British 'non' of Gaullist clarity and resonance" (Benn 1978: 1). At the end of the discussion Callaghan concluded

> that a major policy decision would in due course be needed. At this stage however the Cabinet were concerned with procedure rather than substance. He would appoint a small Ministerial group, under the chairmanship of the Chancellor of the Exchequer, to consider the proposals for European monetary co-operation as they had emerged from the Bremen meeting and also the line to be taken at the forthcoming Finance Council on 24 July which would itself only be concerned with determining the lines of the studies to be undertaken by officials. The group should take into account the paper by the Secretary of State for Energy (CP(78)80). (TNA, CAB 128/64, CM (78) 26th Conclusions, 13 July 1978, 4)

GEN 136, the new cabinet committee, met four times between 18 July and 10 October 1978. The first three meetings were chaired by the chancellor, the last one by the prime minister.[20] By setting up the cabinet committee, Callaghan was able to tilt the balance of opinion towards a rejection of membership. He appointed almost exclusively colleagues who were either against joining the ERM or neutral to it and herewith ensured that the committee took the decision he wanted (Dell and Hunt 1994: 465). Alongside the chancellor, Foreign Secretary David Owen, Industry Secretary Eric Varley, Agriculture Minister John Silkin and Trade Secretary Edmund Dell as well as Harold Lever were members. Thus, the committee included

[20]For the details of the discussion in the first three meetings, see Dell (1994: 38–43).

all cabinet ministers handling European policy. Not all supported European integration: Varley and Silkin had strongly opposed joining the EC altogether, while Owen, Lever and Dell had supported it (Dell 1994: 39). Kenneth Couzens was also appointed to this ministerial committee, which was unusual as he was a Treasury official and not a minister (Franklin 2013: 762). By including Lever, Callaghan ensured that the former was able to voice his support for membership in the discussion and thus minimised the risk that Lever could resign from government because his arguments remained unheard. Meanwhile, the premier attempted to persuade him to take a more sceptical view on the ERM (Donoughue 2009: 374). Yet at the same time Callaghan excluded other ministers from the committee who would have had a strong view on the issue such as Bill Rodgers (Transport and for ERM entry) and Peter Shore (Environment and against ERM entry) (Ludlow 1982: 219, 220).

For GEN 136's last meeting, which was chaired by Callaghan, papers from the Treasury and the DTI, but none from the Foreign Office, provided the basis for discussion. The Department of Industry's paper was more positive on membership than the Treasury's and suggested that Britain would have more chances to influence the setup of the EMS, if it took part from the start (Franklin 2013: 762). The chancellor argued that it would be wrong to join the ERM under the current terms and in the form the system was likely to be realised. Most of those present agreed. It was also what Callaghan summed up at the end of the meeting, adding that for tactical reasons Britain should constructively take part in the negotiations until the December European Council (Dell 1994: 49, 50; Franklin 2013: 762). While Dell's report indicates a marginal role of the Foreign Office in the discussions, Donoughue's account differs. He also points to Callaghan's role in the discussions:

> It was a good discussion with Owen excellent, advising the PM not to take too hard a line with [Helmut] Schmidt next week, but to say that, *as it stands*, the EMS scheme has no attractions for us and so we won't join, but we will if it is amended [emphasis in the original]. Healey said the EMS would collapse in six months, with the French and Italians pulling out. The PM gave a firm steer against throughout, clearly influenced by the Party politics—he does not want a Cabinet split over something which won't last anyway. (Donoughue 2009: 372)

The issue then went to the full cabinet for further discussion and decision-making.[21] The first detailed discussion took place on 2 November. Then the government's negotiating strategy for the European Council in Brussels in early

[21]It was shortly addressed on 12 October when the PM informed the cabinet about the final GEN 136 meeting, promising extensive discussions in the full cabinet soon (TNA, CAB 128/64, CM (78) 34th Conclusions, 12 October 1978, 1). On 26 October Healey brought the cabinet up to date on the developments on EMS/ERM. The PM explained the cabinet would in the following week discuss the issue in detail on the basis of a paper by Healey setting out the implications of membership and non-membership (TNA, CAB 128/64, CM (78) 36th Conclusions, 26 October 1978, 3–4).

December was decided, but no decision was reached on whether Britain would join the ERM. Callaghan concluded:

> It was premature however for the Cabinet to reach a decision at the present stage. There was no objection in principle to a European zone of monetary stability provided our criteria were met and provided it was not to the detriment of the world monetary system. The Chancellor of the Exchequer should continue to negotiate within the framework previously agreed. The Cabinet would resume their discussion probably after the meeting of the Finance Council on 20 November and before the European Council meeting on 4 December. (TNA, CAB 128/64, CM (78) 37th Conclusions, 2 November 1978, 11)

According to Edmund Dell (1994: 51) the cabinet debate was without tension as the outcome was already clear. But the party left feared a last minute U-turn and demanded that any commitment made at the European Council would be subject to approval from cabinet and parliament. At the time Callaghan did not want to agree to this.

The full cabinet returned to the issue on 16 November. Again no formal decision was taken. When summing up the discussion, Callaghan stated that he would give more thought as to when the cabinet was to decide but suggested it would have to be at its 30 November meeting (TNA, CAB 128/64, CM (78) 39th Conclusions, 16 November 1978, 1–2). On 23 November the cabinet discussed the government's Green Paper on the EMS which was about to be published. Again no decision on membership was taken and Callaghan anew stressed the importance of keeping it open for tactical reasons. At the meeting the chancellor briefly introduced the idea of joining the EMS but not the ERM arguing this would give the UK the option to influence the setup of the system (TNA, CAB 128/64, CM (78) 40th Conclusions, 23 November 1978, 6–7). David Owen claims he had initially proposed the idea to Callaghan in September based on a paper he had received. The PM then had instructed him to get his officials to persuade the Treasury officials of it. According to Owen, Healey later agreed to the proposal (Owen 2009: 217–218). The claim cannot be validated as no further mention of it has been found in other sources. Yet several sources, including Butler himself[22], cite Michael Butler, handling economic policy at the FCO, as the originator of this idea (Franklin 2013: 762; Wall 2008: 81). In its 30 November meeting the full cabinet formally agreed to the negotiating line for the European Council laid out by Callaghan and Healey, which included the option of signing up to be part of the wider mechanism but not the ERM (TNA, CAB 128/64, CM (78) 41st Conclusions, 30 November 1978, 6–9; for the chancellor's memorandum on the proposed negotiating line, see Healey 1978). The cabinet conclusions of the meeting extensively document Tony Benn's stance. He argued it was "a mistake for us to enter the EMS in any form. We would do better to use our influence in the Community to delay its implementation" (TNA, CAB 128/64, CM (78) 41st Conclusions, 30 November 1978, 7). He rejected the plan to stay out of the ERM but join the EMS as it would lead to an "unstable two-tier community" (TNA, CAB 128/64, CM (78) 41st Conclusions, 30 November 1978, 7). He did not manage to persuade his colleagues to completely reject any form

[22]Interview with M. Butler, 22 March 2010.

of European monetary policy cooperation. But it is striking that the cabinet conclusions set out his position in such detail. While they report cabinet discussions in general, they tend not to present in detail a particular minister's stance. At the meeting Callaghan pledged in Brussels neither he nor Healey would go beyond the agreed course and "if there were any unexpected developments at the Council he would reserve his position and consult the cabinet again before modifying the United Kingdom stance" (TNA, CAB 128/64, CM (78) 41st Conclusions, 30 November 1978, 9). Thus he did bow to the party left's demands made at the 2 November session. According to Dell (1994: 52) Harold Lever still tried to gain support for ERM entry. It is unclear, however, at which specific cabinet meeting Lever argued that Britain would be more influential in European monetary policy, if it was part of it. Moreover, Lever said, Britain would be more influential in discussions on other EC issues such as the Common Agricultural Policy or the European budget, if it was member of the scheme.

Immediately after the Brussels summit (4/5 December), the cabinet revisited the EMS/ERM issue twice: on 7 December the premier reported that all UK goals had been achieved at the European Council and that there had been no crisis at the foreign exchange markets due to the announcement that Britain would not join the ERM on 1 January 1979 (TNA, CAB 128/64, CM (78) 42nd Conclusions, 7 December 1978, 1). On 14 December the chancellor brought the full cabinet up to date on further developments on the EMS (TNA, CAB 128/64, CM (78) 43rd Conclusions, 14 December 1978, 2).

Overall, when looking at the decision-making process on EMS and ERM the pivotal role of the chancellor is striking—albeit not surprising given the Treasury's key role in monetary policy-making. He chaired the GEN 136 committee Callaghan had set up to address the issue, except for the last meeting. He was also the leading minister on the issue in the full cabinet. The foreign secretary's role appears to have been rather marginal. Owen was part of GEN 136 and also laid out his arguments in cabinet, but, as the cabinet conclusions in question illustrate, he never introduced the issue in cabinet. This was done either by the prime minister or the chancellor (TNA, CAB 128/64, CM (78) 25th Conclusions, 6 July 1978 to CM (78) 43rd Conclusions, 14 December 1978).

The question whether the UK should join the ERM appears to have been decided quite early, even though the cabinet officially did not do so until the Brussels summit, with Callaghan repeatedly stating it was too early for cabinet to take a decision for fear of how the foreign exchange markets might react (Dell 1994: 51). Most cabinet ministers either opposed entry or were neutral to it, and supporters such as Harold Lever could not persuade others of the merits of ERM membership (Dell and Hunt 1994: 465). By Peter Ludlow's account Callaghan had already ruled out immediate membership by early October, thus before the cabinet debated the issue in detail. This was because he had realised at the previous Labour Party conference how strong the opposition to such a scheme was in much of his party. Yet as he was aware of the political arguments for joining the ERM—among other things the fear of being demoted to a second division in a two-speed Europe—he pressed for the closest thing possible to full membership (Ludlow 1982: 217–218, 224).

Callaghan's cabinet management on EMS and ERM was collective, yet in the sense that the decision-making process was focused on a selected group of ministers not on the full cabinet. Callaghan prepared the ERM-decision to secure his preferred outcome by establishing a cabinet committee. He appointed to it those ministers, who would ensure that the committee would decide against joining the ERM. This verdict he could then present to the full cabinet for agreement. At the same time he ensured that colleagues such as Lever or Benn had options to voice their opinions on the issue. Nonetheless, Peter Ludlow argues that by keeping other ministers with strong views (either pro- or anti-ERM membership) on the issue from the committee, Callaghan gave the impression he wanted to prevent a real debate on the EMS, supposedly because it was clear to him that it would be fierce and indecisive. Thus his approach was intended to reduce the chances of a conflict on an issue, of which he apparently had already decided that it was not likely to happen immediately. Yet, Ludlow argues, this strategy was not successful as it exacerbated existing suspicion about the EMS and fostered resentment on the part of several cabinet members about their treatment by the prime minister (Ludlow 1982: 219). Nevertheless, Callaghan did manage to avoid a full blown conflict over the issue of ERM membership. His cabinet management shows that, whatever he personally thought of membership, he valued party (in this case cabinet) unity as more important than furthering Britain's European integration in the area of monetary policy.

8.2.2 The Thatcher Government

Margaret Thatcher's cabinet leadership was from the outset dominant, although Nigel Lawson (1992) states that in the early years of her premiership she had "developed neither the delusion of self-sufficiency nor the distrust of any colleague who was not a yes-man which were in time to make her so difficult and to contribute so much to her downfall" (123). Key decisions were taken in cabinet committees which she chaired, in bilaterals with a departmental minister or in ad hoc meetings with few ministers but not in the full cabinet. The main function of the latter, Lawson (1992) observed, was "to rubber stamp decisions that had already been taken, to keep all colleagues reasonably informed about what was going on, and to provide a forum for general political discussion if time permitted" (125; see also Hurd 2009: 403). A reason for Thatcher's limited use of the full cabinet in the decision-making process was initially the strong presence of the 'Wets' between 1979 and 1981. This was the section of her party which opposed a number of Thatcherite policies—particularly on economics (Thomas 1998: 38). While Lawson (1992) considered decision-making in small groups to be effective, he also noted that Thatcher later came to use this form of cabinet management "to fragment any dissident voices... More and more, decisions were effectively taken in small groups in which she had hand-picked the balance of membership to ensure the outcome she sought. Her conduct of meetings also became increasingly authoritarian" (128). It meant, as Douglas Hurd (2009: 402) noted, that decisions of the government and discussions in the cabinet very often differed.

During Thatcher's first term as prime minister (1979–83), her government reviewed the previous administration's decision to stay out of the ERM several times, yet did not change the policy. Shortly after coming into office, Thatcher and Chancellor Geoffrey Howe confirmed at a meeting on 17 October 1979 with Foreign Secretary Peter Carrington, Trade and Industry secretaries John Nott and Keith Joseph, Bank of England Governor Gordon Richardson and Cabinet Office staff that ERM membership was out of the question at this time. The government had devised the formula that Britain should join the mechanism when the "time was right" (Thatcher 2011: 692) and the view was that it was not (Howe 1995: 274; Thatcher 2011: 691–692). The Treasury remained, as it had been in 1978, opposed to membership. Chancellor Howe appeared to have no greater interest in pursuing the issue either, while leading FCO officials saw economic and political advantages in it for Britain. They thought that ERM membership could be helpful in the context of the ongoing discussions over the UK's European budget contribution (Thompson 1996: 17, 18). However, chancellor and Treasury regarded the ERM as their area of responsibility and attempted to keep the FCO at a distance (Thompson 1996: 18, 27). Since the issue had no priority for the foreign secretary, his officials lacked the ministerial support for their course (Thompson 1996: 17). Carrington's position on the ERM, however, appears to have been somewhat unclear. According to Philip Stephens (1997: 15), Carrington spoke in support of keeping ERM membership as a real option, though did not argue for immediate entry at the October meeting. Bruce Jock-Gardyne, on the other hand, claims that the foreign secretary read out a presentation he had received from his officials in support of immediately entering the ERM at an undated meeting with the PM. Carrington concluded: "that, Prime Minister, is what I was told to say, and it seems to me a load of rubbish"[23] (Carrington quoted in Bruce-Gardyne 1986: 61). According to Thatcher (2011: 692), Howe complained in December 1979 that Carrington in a speech had shown too much support for the ERM. Thatcher's opposition to membership in any case remained strong and according to Howe (1995: 274) she decided at the October 1979 meeting that the issue was not to be further discussed in the Overseas and Defence Cabinet Committee. As a result it slipped off the government's agenda for the next 2 years. Yet by Thatcher's account she chaired another meeting on the ERM in March 1980 at which it was again concluded that Britain should not join it in the near future (Thatcher 2011: 692). There was a further meeting in January 1982 attended by Thatcher, Howe, Carrington, the Governor of the Bank of England and leading officials. According to Howe (1995: 275), the foreign secretary and the Governor favoured joining the ERM then, while he and Thatcher were still unconvinced of its merit.[24] Until the 1983 election there was no change of policy on the ERM.

[23]Bruce-Gardyne, J. (1986), *Ministers and Mandarins, Inside the Whitehall Village*, London: Sidgwick & Jackson. © Jock Bruce-Gardyne (1986). Reproduced with permission of The Licensor through PLSclear.

[24]Yet Thompson (1996: 28) cites an unnamed source, who placed Carrington's rejection of his officials' pro-entry ERM brief above-mentioned at this meeting.

Looking at the different accounts of the discussions between 1979 and 1983, the ERM did not appear to have been a priority during Thatcher's first term. Like Thatcher, Howe remained opposed (at least) to immediate membership. Though he claimed he saw ERM entry as a medium-term goal in late 1979 (Howe 1995: 274). Carrington's position might have been ambiguous, but with PM and chancellor opposing entry, a change of policy was unlikely.

The nature of the ERM debate changed during Thatcher's second term (1983–1987) and became a divisive issue in the core executive. Chancellor Nigel Lawson decided shortly after the 1983 election to review the government's monetary policy, but again no change of policy was made (Lawson 1992: 414; Thompson 1996: 37–38). Anew the issue slipped off the government's agenda, but during a sterling crisis in early 1985 Lawson, who was then redefining his position on membership, put the issue back onto the Treasury's agenda (Thompson 1996: 40, 45; Lawson 1992: 485). By autumn he had persuaded his leading officials to support entry, though they did not share his enthusiasm for it (Stephens 1997: 47).

To persuade Thatcher of ERM membership, the chancellor initially addressed the issue in their weekly bilaterals. Like Geoffrey Howe before him he was keen to keep Foreign Office and foreign secretary as well as the European Secretariat from the debate. Lawson thought support by the FCO and Howe would not be helpful in persuading Thatcher given her increasingly fraught relationship with the foreign secretary. Moreover, the Treasury continued to view the issue as part of its area of responsibility (Lawson 1992: 653; Thompson 1996: 49).[25] In February 1985 Lawson proposed to the PM to hold a seminar on the issue with officials from the Bank, the Treasury, Howe and Thatcher's economic adviser Alan Walters (Lawson 1992: 488). She agreed, though by her account Lawson's arguments for membership did not persuade her (Thatcher 2011: 694–695). At the meeting on 13 February Lawson, Howe and the Governor of the Bank of England, Robin Leigh-Pemberton, argued that Britain should join the ERM at some stage though not immediately (Thompson 1996: 46). Thatcher (2011: 695) claimed she was most surprised by Howe's change of view which she attributed to the FCO's influence on him. According to Lawson (1992: 489) she failed to see that most attendants expected accession in the foreseeable future. Looking at her summary of the meeting's outcome, one tends to agree: "since no one was arguing for immediate entry, there was no other decision to take. The meeting ended amicably enough" (Thatcher 2011: 695). She agreed, however, that the issue was to be reviewed again at a later date (Thompson 1996: 46).

Once more proposed by Lawson to Thatcher, the issue was again discussed at a meeting on 30 September 1985. Participants were Lawson, Thatcher, Treasury and Bank officials, the Bank's Governor, Howe and Brian Griffiths, the new head of Thatcher's Policy Unit. This time Lawson made the case to join the ERM immediately to support the government's strategy to battle inflation. He was supported by

[25]Lawson did, however, discuss the issue with the foreign secretary (Lawson 1992: 486–487).

the Governor and Howe (Lawson 1992: 491, 494–495). Thatcher remained sceptical and said there should be further discussion (Stephens 1997: 48). To Lawson it was clear that she had realised that she was becoming isolated with her position on the ERM. Thus, she set up another meeting with colleagues she selected to ensure they would support her stance (Lawson 1992: 496). On 13 November 1985 the meeting took place. It was not a formal cabinet committee but an ad hoc meeting attended by several cabinet ministers. Apart from Lawson, Howe, the Governor of the Bank of England Robin Leigh-Pemberton and Bank, Treasury and No. 10 staff, the premier invited Willie Whitelaw (Deputy Prime Minister), Norman Tebbit (Party Chairman), Leon Brittan (Trade and Industry Secretary), John Biffen (Leader of the House of Commons) and John Wakeham (Chief Whip). Thatcher had to include Whitelaw, Howe and Brittan due to their cabinet posts, but she had chosen Tebbit, Biffen and Wakeham in the hope that they would support her in opposing entry. The chancellor had met all ministers before, with the exception of Biffen, whom he thought a lost cause (Lawson 1992: 497–498). The prime minister's staff had not briefed the other ministers about her interests to try to persuade them to support her stance (Moore 2015: 419). Together with the Bank, the Treasury had drafted the papers which formed the basis for the meeting's discussion (Stephens 1997: 48). Lawson, Howe and Leigh-Pemberton again stated their arguments for joining the ERM, and the other participants with the exception of Biffen voiced their support (Stephens 1997: 49–50). As Leader of the House, Biffen's view did not carry much weight on this issue (Moore 2015: 419). In backing membership Leon Brittan echoed his officials' view on the issue. They supported entry, but the DTI was not much included in the core executive ERM debate (Thompson 1996: 59). Whitelaw spoke last and, according to Lawson's account, said that he would follow the recommendations of Lawson, Leigh-Pemberton and Howe that the UK should join the ERM (Lawson 1992: 499; for a similar report see Howe 1995: 450; Moore 2015: 420). According to Lawson Thatcher begged to differ, telling her ministers that if they wanted Britain to join the mechanism, they would have to do so without her (Thatcher quoted in Lawson 1992: 499; for a similar report see Howe 1995: 450; Moore 2015: 420). She herself later only stated that the meeting

> did not advance us any further than the earlier meetings. We went over the same ground and at the end I repeated that I had not been convinced by the arguments I had heard. However, I agreed that we should strictly maintain the line we had taken so far, namely that Britain would join the ERM 'when the time was right'. (Thatcher 2011: 697)

But at least in hindsight Thatcher appeared to have been aware of her position, noting that she knew she was in minority in cabinet on the issue. She also believed that apart from Howe and Lawson most cabinet members had no strong views on it (Thatcher 2011: 698).

Lawson, together with Howe, could then have demanded a full cabinet discussion. They would reportedly have been backed by Deputy Prime Minister William Whitelaw (Thompson 1996: 63). It is unclear why the chancellor did not do so. He might not have wanted to establish an alliance with Howe for the same reason that he and the Treasury had been keeping FCO and foreign secretary from the debate.

Moreover, it is unclear whether Howe and Lawson viewed the cabinet as the adequate forum in which to persuade Thatcher to agree to change policy. It is also debatable whether they believed her veto to be final (Thompson 1996: 63–64). Howe, for instance, thought she would have to adjust her position eventually. Yet for now the issue was off the agenda of the core executive (Howe 1995: 450).

Lawson again tried to discuss the issue with Thatcher at their bilateral on 21 October 1986, but she refused. Newspapers on that day reported that there was no British intention to enter the ERM before the next election. Lawson (1992: 663) believed No. 10 had been their source.

From the mid-1980s it became increasingly clear that prime minister and foreign secretary took opposing views, particularly on foreign policy. Howe's focus on ensuring Britain's influence in Europe stood in contrast to Thatcher's growing belief that the UK's major interest was close collaboration with the US (Stephens 1997: 100–101). According to Howe (1995) their relationship changed significantly while he was at the FCO. He thought that this was initially not "for personal reasons but largely because of Margaret's profound antipathy towards the Office" (394). But the divisions had a personal side to them, too, with her belittling Howe in front of colleagues (Stephens 1997: 101).

As the PM continued to veto ERM membership, Lawson began his policy of letting sterling shadow the Deutschmark in early 1987 (Lawson 1992: 682–683). Thatcher (2011: 701) later denied any knowledge of the policy at the time. Yet it is questionable that this was the case. The Bank's intervention policy on the currency markets to keep sterling below 3.00 DM was easy to spot and the press reported it (Stephens 1997: 76, 78). No. 10 also received the Treasury's daily market report, which indicated the degree of British intervention (Thompson 1996: 89; Lawson 1992: 784). In any case, until the 1987 general election nothing changed with regard to the ERM because Thatcher did not withdraw her veto.

During Thatcher's third term in office (1987–1990) the divisions inside the core executive over the ERM reached their climax and eventually led to the key actors' exit from government. Lawson, who remained chancellor, had hoped Thatcher would change her stance on the ERM after winning the 1987 election. But at a bilateral on 27 July 1987 she rejected his request for an early discussion of the issue. There would be none before the next year. According to Lawson she was also adamant that there should be no new meetings similar to the one in autumn 1985, when she had been in a minority with her rejection of ERM entry (Lawson 1992: 732; for her recollection, see Thatcher 2011: 700). The chancellor realised that he could not force her to agree to membership. While he was aware of his powerful position in the core executive due to being widely held responsible for the Conservative election victory, he knew that Thatcher, who had just secured her third consecutive election victory, was at the height of her authority (Lawson 1992: 732–733). He continued to support ERM membership in public (Stephens 1997: 81–82) as well as his policy of shadowing the Deutschmark. Over time the intervention costs to keep the pound below 3.00 DM rose. Thatcher became ever more concerned. In March 1988 she insisted that Lawson should end the policy, which he did (Lawson 1992: 830; Thompson 1996: 112–114). Thatcher's and Lawson's working relationship became increasingly strained and their divisions over exchange rate policy ever more public. This was also because Thatcher became more and more vocal of her rejection of ERM entry which found its way into the press (Stephens 1997: 100, 104).

Meanwhile the discussions about establishing economic and monetary union in the European Community went ahead. At the Hanover European Council in June 1988 the setup of the Delors group, which was to develop a plan for EMU, was agreed (Thompson 1996: 121). Lawson and Thatcher were united in their opposition to monetary union (Lawson 1992: 892; Thatcher 2011: 691). Both, however, like the rest of the government, underestimated the other EC member states' determination to go through with the project (Thompson 1996: 122). The Delors group's report, published on 17 April 1989, was not what either wanted. Lawson commented that the transfer of sovereignty which the report proposed was unacceptable to Britain. It would only be willing to accept the plan's first stage and block any moves to convene an intergovernmental conference on the issue. Lawson concluded at the same time that the UK could only successfully move against EMU, if it finally joined the ERM (Thompson 1996: 130–131, 134). This he addressed at a bilateral with Thatcher in May 1989. She again disagreed (Lawson 1992: 917–918; Thatcher 2011: 709). Lawson felt that the prime minister by then did not care about the economic and political arguments concerning ERM membership anymore, but saw the issue as a "battle of wills" (Lawson 1992: 918) between herself and her chancellor, which she intended to win.

Prior to the Madrid European Council in June 1989, Lawson finally decided to join forces with Howe to increase the pressure on Thatcher. They mapped out their strategy in several bilaterals during the first half of 1989. Like Lawson, Howe had concluded that Britain would only have sufficient political leverage to prevent the move towards EMU, if it finally joined the ERM (Stephens 1997: 114). Howe proposed to send Thatcher a joint memo setting out the advantages of ERM membership for the EMU negotiations. Lawson was sceptical about the plan's chances of success. While a memo by two ministers was no act of conspiracy, he was not sure how Thatcher would take it, particularly as she increasingly isolated herself from her ministers (Lawson 1992: 923–930). He was right as she felt ambushed by her senior ministers (Thatcher 2011: 710). She reluctantly agreed to meet them on 20 June. At the meeting she only accepted that they could discuss the issue further but showed no willingness to change her position. By Lawson's account Howe afterwards received a memo of the meeting written by Thatcher's Foreign Affairs Private Secretary Charles Powell. It included a different course of action on the ERM from the one they had proposed. They sent Thatcher another memo on 23 June in which they rejected the alternative course and demanded another meeting with her (Lawson 1992: 931–932). Thatcher reluctantly agreed. She had tried to see them separately, but the ministers had insisted on meeting together. She again refused to give in to their demands despite their threat to resign if she did not (Stephens 1997: 118). Thatcher saw Howe as the driving force on the Madrid memo and suggested that he had written it out of personal spite to create problems for her where- and whenever he could (Thatcher 2011: 710, 712). Howe rejected her charge that his actions were personal and argued he had only wanted to go ahead with the policy (Howe 1995: 575).

At Madrid Thatcher for the first time announced detailed conditions under which the UK could join the ERM. She did not mention a timetable for entry as her ministers had demanded (Thompson 1996: 141). She also announced that Britain would prepare its own EMU proposal. This took the Treasury by surprise as she had not informed them of this before. Nonetheless, the chancellor began working on options with his officials (Lawson 1992: 938–940).

Lawson's and Howe's ultimatum before the summit provided Thatcher with the choice of either keeping them in their posts and surrendering or trying to end their alliance and asserting her position. She chose the latter and dismissed Howe from the Foreign Office on 24 July 1989 (Stephens 1997: 125). Meanwhile, the media continued to run stories highlighting the divisions between her and Lawson. Over the summer there were press reports that the PM's economic adviser Alan Walters, who had returned to No. 10 in May, had criticised Lawson's exchange rate policy at meetings in the City. Walters rejected the accusations and claimed Lawson had fabricated them (Thompson 1996: 153). Despite the controversy around him Thatcher refused to dismiss Walters to prove there were no divisions between her and Lawson (Stephens and Holberton 1989). Lawson had cautioned her against reappointing Walters due to his well-known opposition to several government policies which the chancellor argued would create problems for the government. She had ignored his objections (Lawson 1992: 842). The situation became more difficult when the *Financial Times* on 18 October published excerpts of an article by Walters in which he had called the ERM "half-baked"[26] (Walters quoted in Holberton 1989). Thatcher did not publicly distance herself from him and Lawson informed her on 26 October that he could not remain chancellor if Walters stayed in his post (Thompson 1996: 154). The chancellor considered Walters to be the most prominent example of the PM's continuous attempts to emphasise their differences over exchange rate policy (Lawson 1992: 958). Thatcher (2011: 716) claims she was taken off guard by Lawson's announcement but still refused to dismiss Walters. Lawson resigned. In his resignation speech on 31 October he criticised Thatcher's political leadership:

> for our system of Cabinet government to work effectively, the Prime Minister of the day must appoint Ministers whom he or she trusts and then leave them to carry out the policy. When differences of view emerge, as they are bound to do from time to time, they should be resolved privately and, whenever appropriate, collectively. (HC Deb 31 October 1989, c208)

Lawson's successor John Major, having been foreign secretary for just 3 months, was barely known outside Westminster and many believed that from now on economic policy would be made from No. 10 (Stephens 1997: 140). As a result of Lawson's resignation the case for ERM membership temporarily slipped off the

[26]Holberton, S. (1989), PM's economist adds his guarded support, *Financial Times*, 18 October 1989. Used under licence from the Financial Times. All Rights Reserved.

government's agenda again. While the new chancellor on 31 October confirmed his support for the conditions set out in Madrid, neither he nor the new foreign secretary Douglas Hurd showed much interest in furthering this cause as their predecessors had done (Thompson 1996: 154). After the Strasbourg meeting in December 1989, at which the European Council had decided that Intergovernmental Conferences (IGCs) on EMU and on political union were to be convened, Hurd adopted the FCO's view: without ERM membership the UK would not be able to influence the discussions on EMU (Stephens 1997: 149). In early 1990 Hurd persuaded Major that ERM entry before the start of the IGCs would be helpful to the UK's negotiating position. In March the foreign secretary and the chancellor publicly announced their support of ERM entry (Thompson 1996: 161). Hurd encouraged Major to promote membership with the prime minister with economic instead of political arguments. Major agreed. After what had happened before Madrid, proposals connected with the FCO were not taken into account anymore by No. 10 (Stephens 1997: 150; Major 2000: 156). Like his predecessor had done, Major decided—though most government ministers would have supported him—to try to persuade Thatcher to agree to ERM membership bilaterally and not in the full cabinet (Thompson 1996: 162). Discussions were difficult because Thatcher was partly cooperative and partly backtracked on what she had agreed to before (Stephens 1997: 153). Major's position in government was comparably strong at this stage because the prime minister was weak. The Conservatives trailed the Labour Party in the polls. Also, they had begun with the collection of the deeply unpopular poll tax.[27] Moreover, at the annual party leadership election Thatcher had been challenged for the first time. There were backbencher demands for a change of policy on the ERM. Thus, the PM could not risk losing another chancellor over the issue (Thompson 1996: 162). Meanwhile in spring/summer 1990 DTI minister Nicholas Ridley continuously pushed her to ignore the proposals in support of joining the ERM made by Hurd and Major. Ridley by then attended all cabinet committees covering European policy and was an important supporter in Thatcher's quest against membership (Stephens 1997: 153–154, 130). But due to the external and internal pressure Thatcher finally began to modify her position (Stephens 1997: 156). Major persuaded her to show willingness that Britain would join the ERM by the end of 1990. In May she announced that the conditions for ERM membership were close to being fulfilled (Thompson 1996: 162, 163). At a bilateral on 13 June Major secured her agreement to joining the ERM, which he announced in early July. He had tried to persuade her to agree to accession in July, but she had insisted to wait until autumn (Stephens 1997: 157). In July Ridley had to resign because of an interview in which he had claimed that EMU was a German plan to take over Europe (Gowland et al. 2010:

[27]It was a local tax, which "was to be a flat-rate one and payable by all to some degree, even students and the unemployed... Thatcher's personal support, defiant style and the pusillanimous nature of many MPs and ministers... let a clearly flawed law on to the statue book. In March 1990 polls showed a huge majority opposed it and on 7 April a riot erupted in London. When John Major succeeded Thatcher he quickly replaced the measure with one more closely resembling the old-property-based rates." (Jones 2001: 537).

114–115; for the interview see Lawson 1990). His statements were given particular prominence as some interpreted them as Thatcher's. Nigel Lawson, for example, recalled that he had heard her make similar remarks in private conversations (Lawson 1992: 900, see also Howe 1995: 632). With Ridley gone Thatcher had lost her last political confidante in government and a key supporter against ERM entry.

In October Major managed to persuade Thatcher that it was time to join the ERM. Discussions continued to be difficult as it was unclear whether she would stand by her agreement. On 4 October at a meeting attended by her, Major, Treasury officials and Eddie George, the Bank's Deputy Governor, she appeared to have decided spontaneously to join the ERM immediately. The Treasury had originally planned to join on 12 October. Yet Major wanted to minimise the risk of a last minute U-turn by Thatcher and pushed for earlier entry (Stephens 1997: 170–171; Thompson 1996: 172–173). On 5 October 1990 Major announced that Britain would join the ERM the following Monday (8 October) with an exchange rate of 2.95 DM. She had set this rate without consulting the other ERM members as stipulated by ERM rules. As a result Hurd and the FCO could not use ERM membership as leverage in the IGC negotiations as the other members were angry that the UK had set its exchange rate without consultation (Thompson 1996: 174, 175).

With regard to policy-making on EMU the full cabinet was marginalised (as were the relevant cabinet committees). It was briefed about the early European level deliberations on EMU, but there were no in-depth discussions in the cabinet about it. Instead the core executive discussions were restricted to prime minister, chancellor and foreign secretary (Dyson and Featherstone 1999: 595). In June 1990 Major published another alternative to the Delors plan: the 'hard Ecu' plan (Thompson 1996: 166). This was the second British proposal. The first had been Lawson's competing currencies plan, which he had developed after the Madrid summit (Lawson 1992: 939–942). In April Major had tried to persuade Thatcher to change her negotiating stance for the upcoming IGC. He proposed to agree to a treaty change to put into effect the Delors plan under the condition that there was an opt-in mechanism for all member states. In that case, only if the single currency became a reality, would the EC members need to take a decision about taking part. Major saw this as an advantage because the government would only have to decide in the future whether it wanted to join the single currency. A month later he sent Thatcher a memo warning her that France and Germany were willing to isolate the UK on the issue and would push the other members to agree to a new treaty. She did not share his assessment (Stephens 1997: 162–163). Major (2000) recalled later:

> The Prime Minister simply wanted to say no. I knew this would be useless. It would not stop our partners going ahead, and would only deprive the UK of any influence over their plans. Margaret was dismissive, even scornful, of this argument. She did not grasp that I was not asking her to change her policy on the single currency—because I agreed with her on that—but to be more subtle in her opposition to it. (142)

Douglas Hurd wanted the government to take a constructive role in the negotiations. Like Major he thought Britain would have to accept the aim of EMU in its alternative proposal to the Delors Plan, if it wanted to have any influence on the negotiations (Stephens 1997: 179–180).

At the first IGC in Rome in October 1990, Thatcher announced that she would oppose any efforts to force the establishment of a single currency and insisted that this be noted in the summit conclusions (Stephens 1997: 181). In her subsequent parliamentary statement despite addressing the 'hard ECU' plan, she commented that "a single currency is not the policy of this Government" (HC Deb 30 October 1990, c871). Major (2000: 152) thought her comments made in parliament ensured that the plan was not seen as a realistic alternative to the Delors Plan but as a British diversionary tactic. Her statement also triggered Geoffrey Howe's resignation. His resignation speech on 13 November was the prelude to the Conservative party leadership contest which led to Thatcher's resignation on 22 November 1990 (Gowland et al. 2010: 115–116).

Overall, looking at the discussions on the ERM in the core executive in the early 1980s, these were limited to a few ministers (foreign secretary and chancellor) as well as representatives of the Bank of England, Thatcher's Policy Unit and advisers like Alan Walters. Between 1979 and late 1988 the issue only appeared four times on the full cabinet's agenda as the cabinet conclusions show (TNA, CAB 128/66 to TNA, CAB 128/92).[28] Three times they concerned realignments in the ERM but no discussion whether Britain should join the mechanism (TNA, CAB 128/73, CC (82) 7th Conclusions, 25 February 1982, 3; TNA, CAB 128/74, CC (82) 34th Conclusions, 17 June 1982, 9; TNA, CAB 128/76, CC (83) 11th Conclusions, 24 March 1983, 5–6). One time a speech by the UK's European Commissioner Christopher Tugendhat in support of Britain joining the ERM was addressed. The cabinet noted this, but did not discuss whether this required a change of policy (TNA, CAB 128/70, CC (81) 8th Conclusions, 24 February 1981, 4). When it became clear that support in the core executive to join the ERM was rising in the mid-1980s, Thatcher realised that she could no longer avoid a larger meeting of ministers to discuss it. Once she realised that she was in a minority on the issue, she decided to veto the project altogether, refusing to discuss it any further. By doing so she managed to keep the issue off the government's agenda. In subsequent years there were no wide-ranging discussions on it in the core executive which included the full cabinet. Thatcher might have kept the issue from the full cabinet because she did not view it as a valid forum in which to take government decisions anyway, as Lawson (1992: 125) suggested. Moreover, she knew that most senior cabinet ministers held a different position on it than she did. By keeping the issue off the full cabinet's agenda and curtailing other options for a wider discussion in the core executive, she managed to veto entry for years. Paradoxically, she was supported in this by those senior ministers who opposed her on the ERM. Howe and Lawson, too,

[28]It was also referred to at least twice in connection with other issues, e.g. the negotiations about the British contribution to the EC budget (e.g. TNA, CAB 128/67, CC (80) 12th Conclusions, 20 March 1980, 5; TNA, CAB 128/73, CC (82) 6th Conclusions, 18 February 1982, 3).

kept the issue from the full cabinet. They also did not form any alliances with other ministers/departments such as the DTI. Major, as well, did not choose the full cabinet as the forum in which to convince Thatcher of ERM entry, though he did form a coalition on the issue with Foreign Secretary Hurd. The decision to join the ERM was not made after a discussion of the full cabinet. Therefore it was not collective decision-making. Other ministers apparently heard about it in the news instead of in cabinet (Blair 1999: 163). The fact that Thatcher eventually decided to join the ERM despite no apparent change of mind on the desirability of membership had to do with her reduced standing in the core executive. Around 1985 she was in a predominant position and thus able to veto ERM membership. By 1989/90 she had lost this predominance, and to survive politically had to accept a policy her senior ministers and a number of her backbenchers supported.

On EMU, the situation was different. Thatcher opposed it as well, but senior cabinet ministers such as chancellor and foreign secretary supported her stance. However, Major and Hurd thought Thatcher pursued the wrong negotiating strategy and that by refusing to accept that EMU was going to happen, she damaged British chances to influence further decision-making on it. With her resignation in November 1990, she left the issue to her successor John Major.

8.2.3 The Major Government

John Major's cabinet management differed much from that of his predecessor.[29] He moved government decision-making to a larger extent back into the cabinet. While Thatcher had used ad hoc committees or bilateral meetings with ministers to take decisions, Major did this to a lesser degree and more issues were handled in cabinet committees (Thomas 1998: 44). In his first 2 years in office he, moreover, often liked to take final decisions in the full cabinet. From 1992/93 decision-making was increasingly moved to cabinet committees (Seldon 1994: 163). Major provided ministers with more options to raise issues in the full cabinet. Particularly in the first 2 years of his premiership the feeling in his cabinet was collegial. After Thatcher ministers appreciated the fact that there were again extensive cabinet discussions before decisions were taken (Kavanagh and Seldon 2000: 224, see also Hogg and Hill 1996: 13). The *Guardian* noted on Major's first anniversary as prime minister:

> As for Europe, which is debated within the powerful Overseas Policy and Defence (OPD) committee, everyone is invited and most of the Cabinet seems to turn up. One session lasted three hours and was resumed next day. As a result, gut Euro-sceptics, Howard and Lilley ..., remain committed to the Maastricht endgame. (White and Pick 1991)

Major gave every minister a chance to speak and present his arguments without foreclosing the debate by stating his own view at the start of a session as Thatcher

[29]Background information for this chapter was taken from an interview with N. Wicks, 1 November 2010.

had done. It gave him the possibility to pin ministers down to decisions such as the Eurosceptics over the Maastricht negotiations in December 1991 (Kavanagh and Seldon 2000: 224). Major (2000) said about his cabinet management: "I... preferred to let my views be known in private, see potential dissenters ahead of the meeting, encourage discussion, and sum up after it... I chose consensus in policy-making, if not always in policy" (209). His cabinet management resembled that of Callaghan, who also included his cabinet's Eurosceptic members in the decision-making process, so they would defend decisions to their followers. It was shaped by Major's pragmatic political outlook and particularly after 1992 by his diminished power base. Agency was also relevant: it seems that "consultative" (Kavanagh and Seldon 2000: 225) cabinet management was more to his liking than Thatcher's style.

Until after the 1992 election Major's collective cabinet management style was not perceived as weakness but as strength. Only later was his preferment of consensus criticised as indecisiveness (Stephens 1997: 198). There was also criticism that Major later avoided discussing controversial issues such as European policy in the full cabinet (Kavanagh and Seldon 2000: 225). Sarah Hogg and Jonathan Hill (1996: 13–14) from his No. 10 staff thought the form of decision-making was adequate in light of the fragile party Major had to lead. Moreover, they argued, it helped him survive the ERM exit and the intraparty conflicts over the Maastricht Treaty ratification.

Particularly after the ERM exit in autumn 1992, cabinet unity declined markedly. The media increasingly published internal government information, which often concerned the Conservatives' divisions over Europe. Ministers, worried that the content of cabinet discussions might later be read in the press, stopped speaking openly in cabinet (Kavanagh and Seldon 2000: 225). Major was disappointed that cabinet members were not willing to only discuss their differences internally and that accounts of cabinet discussions over Europe regularly found their way into the press. All the while, it was impossible to trace who was responsible for the leaks (Major 2000: 699).

Immediately upon coming into office, the Major government had to deal with the plans for EMU as the European negotiations culminating in the Maastricht Treaty in December 1991 were progressing. In January 1991 Chancellor Lamont published a draft treaty on monetary union in which he set out how the 'hard ECU', proposed by the UK government the previous autumn, could be established and managed (Thompson 1996: 184). Like Major, the new chancellor saw the 'hard ECU' as a more realistic proposal for the establishment of monetary union than the Delors plan. But while Conservative backbenchers welcomed it, the European partners were scarcely interested. According to Lamont the prime minister nonetheless wanted him to continue promoting the plan with the other EC members, and it was difficult to persuade him to accept that it was useless (Lamont 1999: 113, 114). Eventually, however, the government ended its attempts to use the concept as negotiation strategy. The question now appeared to be whether to veto any treaty on EMU negotiated at the IGC or to sign up to monetary union. The former would have undermined Britain's EC membership and the latter would have risked the break-up of the Conservative Party and "would have been contrary to ministers' own preferences" (Thompson 1996: 184). Despite officially supporting the 'hard ECU' plan until summer 1991, the British government had already shifted its prime concern on EMU by late February to ensuring that the UK would not be forced to join (Blair 1999: 177). The idea of a British opt-out from EMU had initially been proposed by Nigel Wicks, Second Permanent Secretary to the Treasury, when Major was still chancellor (Lamont 1999: 110–111). According to Lamont, Major saw it as a device to keep Britain at the centre of European integration and the Conservative Party united despite not committing the country to join the single currency. The chancellor, more hostile to a European single currency than the PM, also supported the idea of an opt-out from EMU (Lamont 1999: 111–112). Yet, in contrast to Major, he believed that such an opt-out with the option to eventually opt-in to EMU would soon become a definite opt-out (Blair 1999: 174). When European Commission President Jacques Delors in May 1991 proposed an extra treaty clause allowing the UK to decide later about EMU membership, Major and Lamont supported this (Thompson 1996: 184–185). The treaty, later finalised at Maastricht, included a specific protocol, which had been drafted in London, securing Britain's EMU opt-out (Stephens 1997: 200).

Major ensured that the full cabinet was informed about the plans on monetary union and discussed the general British stance at the Maastricht Treaty negotiations. In the period before the IGC on EMU began, Lamont kept the full cabinet posted about the content of the draft treaty on the 'hard ECU'. But it was not much discussed. The key policy decisions on it had already been made by the prime minister, the chancellor and the foreign secretary. Similarly, the chancellor regularly informed the full cabinet about the development of the EMU negotiations during the IGC. Yet Lamont tended not to say much and there was hardly any debate on it (Dyson and Featherstone 1999: 595–596). Ahead of the negotiations Major had established a cabinet committee chaired by Douglas Hurd to handle the treaty proposals. Major himself chaired further discussions on the issue in the cabinet committee on overseas and defence policy (Seldon 1998: 245; Major 2000: 271). It was important to him "to ensure that every cabinet member was consulted and able to have a serious input into our deliberations" (Major 2000: 271), because "I needed all of them to be committed to my negotiating position" (Major 2000: 271). Yet, at least on EMU, consulting the cabinet did not mean that the policy was collectively decided. It appears more to have been the case that the cabinet members felt they were included in the decision-making process, while decisions were taken by a small group of ministers. However, with regard to the treaty in general, the PM promoted extensive debate on its outline and paid close consideration to the views of the Eurosceptics in his cabinet. On 5 December 1990 the full cabinet agreed to his general negotiating stance for Maastricht (Stephens 1997: 202). With help from Douglas Hurd Major managed to convince sceptical cabinet members like Michael Howard (Employment) and Peter Lilley (DTI) in one-to-one talks to support his general negotiating line on Maastricht (Major 2000: 276). Cabinet colleagues praised Major's approach in the run up to the European negotiations because of his attempts to involve all relevant sections of the government in drawing up the British negotiating position through discussions at cabinet committee level (Seldon 1998: 245). However, for Major this form of cabinet management had a very practical advantage. By including the Eurosceptics in the deliberations, he ensured that they were part of the settlement and could not claim to have been kept out of the discussions. For instance, Major had got Howard and Lilley to agree to his negotiating line and he had stuck to it in Maastricht. So when he returned with the agreement reached at the summit, they were part of it (Jay 2007). At the same time Major's way of cabinet management gave individual cabinet ministers greater influence. Important in this respect was that four of the then five Eurosceptic cabinet ministers were in charge of policy fields directly relevant to the negotiations. These included on EMU Lamont (Treasury) and to a lesser extent Lilley (DTI).[30] Meanwhile most of the pro-European and neutral cabinet ministers, of which there were about 17, did not head departments crucial to the negotiations. Michael Heseltine's return to the cabinet did not much affect policy-making on Europe during the Maastricht negotiations either as he was preoccupied with the poll tax and was unpopular among fellow cabinet ministers for having made Thatcher fall (Blair 1999: 203–204). Nevertheless, Heseltine was one of the few ministers who showed a keen interest in the negotiations and when Lamont or Hurd reported on the progress regularly asked questions (Dyson and Featherstone 1999: 564). EMU was discussed by an extended Overseas Policy and Defence Cabinet Committee with Major in the chair, as the Treasury and Lamont did not want the issue to be discussed in a committee chaired by the foreign secretary and the FCO. Yet, as mentioned, crucial meetings on EMU took place elsewhere and included chancellor and prime minister and sometimes the foreign secretary. They happened more often than cabinet committee meetings on Maastricht—particularly shortly before the summit (Dyson and Featherstone 1999: 596). Both policy priorities the Major government advocated during the European negotiations on EMU—the 'hard ECU' and the opt-out—were devices to keep the cabinet (and the party) together. Pro-Europeans as well as Eurosceptics could support the 'hard ECU' proposal. To the former it could be presented as way for the UK to eventually join EMU and to the latter as a device to derail the EMU plans without coming across as anti-European. Similarly the opt-out proposal could be presented to the pro-Europeans as a possibility that Britain would join EMU, if the conditions were right. To the Eurosceptics it could suggest that the government had no intention to effectively sign the UK up to a single currency (Forster 1999: 54–55, 63, 71).

However, the Maastricht Treaty later became more controversial in Major's cabinet and party as the difficulties to ratify it in parliament showed (see Sect. 9.3). When the Danes voted against the treaty in a referendum in June 1992, Major faced calls from inside his cabinet (Michael Howard, Peter Lilley and Michael Portillo) to consider abandoning the treaty. But the premier insisted on ratification with support from ministers like Ken Clarke (then Home Secretary) and Michael Heseltine (President of the Board of Trade). Yet he agreed that it would not be concluded until after a second successful Danish referendum (Gowland and Turner 2000: 281).

---

[30]The other two, Kenneth Baker (Home Office) and Michael Howard (Employment), were less relevant on EMU.

While the full cabinet had been regularly informed about Britain's position on EMU and the negotiations in the run up to Maastricht, sterling's ERM membership was less of an issue. Discussions on it in the core executive were limited to chancellor and prime minister. In the time leading up to the exit from the mechanism in autumn 1992, there had been no extensive cabinet discussions about the pressure sterling was facing and what the options were (Stephens 1997: 264–265; see also Hurd 2009: 468). Lamont argued that he had already realised in late 1991 that the ERM rules constrained his options to conduct an exchange rate policy which would be conducive to revive the economy. Sometime before May 1992, he claimed, he had attempted to speak to the prime minister about his doubts over membership but was turned down. He decided to continue the policy until the end of the year, when he wanted to discuss it again (Lamont 1999: 154, 209; Major (2000) makes no reference to this conversation in his memoirs). In late July Major and Lamont met for an economic policy seminar at No. 10 at which the option to leave the mechanism came up, but was ruled out (Lamont 1999: 217; Major 2000: 317–318). Sterling's situation in the ERM became even more difficult. On 14 August the pound was only 3 pfennigs above its floor in the mechanism. The Treasury discussed whether a temporary suspension of membership could be helpful (Stephens 1997: 224–225). But Lamont stated publicly on 26 August: "We are going to maintain sterling's parity and we will do whatever is necessary"[31] (Lamont quoted in Stephens 1997: 226). Speculative pressure on the pound and other currencies did not subside (Stephens 1997: 228–229). On 14 September Major and Lamont met with members of staff and discussed the possibility of an ERM exit. Initially the focus of the meeting had been the upcoming French referendum on the Maastricht Treaty and its likely effect among other things on the financial markets. The chancellor suggested that taking sterling out of the mechanism should be considered, though, according to Philip Stephens (1997: 241–243), he did not insist that this was done immediately. Lamont (1999: 242) contradicted this in his memoirs. Major (2000: 328) claimed that the chancellor then argued that they would need to discuss remaining in the ERM if the economic situation did not improve by early 1993 and that it was Major himself, who said they might have to return to the issue even earlier. Lamont (1999) again contradicted:

> I can categorically say that the Prime Minister never at any time in my presence made any such remark implying any sympathy with the idea of leaving the ERM. The only remarks he made about withdrawal to me were to the effect that he wasn't prepared to discuss it. (242)

Whatever happened, sterling fell beneath its ERM floor of 2.7780 DM the next day (Stephens 1997: 245).[32]

---

[31]Stephens, P. (1997), *Politics and the Pound, The Tories, the Economy and Europe*, 2nd edition, London/Basingstoke: Papermac.

[32]A statement by the president of the Bundesbank contributed to the slide (Stephens 1997: 244–245).

The decision to leave the ERM was taken on 16 September 1992 at a ministerial meeting. It also had been scheduled to discuss the upcoming French referendum on the Maastricht Treaty, but became a crisis meeting on ERM membership. Apart from Major and Lamont, Foreign Secretary Douglas Hurd, Home Secretary Ken Clarke, President of the Board of Trade Michael Heseltine and Chief Whip Richard Ryder attended. Later the Governor of the Bank of England Robin Leigh-Pemberton, his deputy Eddie George, leading Treasury official Terence Burns, and Sarah Hogg, Head of Major's Policy Unit, joined as well (Thompson 1996: 196). An interest rate rise agreed by the ministers in the morning had failed and around lunch time chancellor and Treasury, opposed to another increase, proposed to suspend membership. But Hurd, supported by Clarke and Heseltine, argued against it. Major sided with them (Seldon 1998: 316). Hurd thought everything should be done to avoid the impression that Britain left the ERM as soon as things became difficult. Together with Heseltine and Clarke he argued for another interest rate rise (Stephens 1997: 251–252, see also Clarke 2016: 305). He explained the difficulties he and the other ministers faced:

> We were told late in the morning that every minute of discussion cost the reserves £18 million, that every remedy had been tried and that we should immediately suspend British membership of the ERM. We were none of us in any position to gainsay this advice. I argued, and others agreed, that if this was to happen our partners should be told and the rules of the ERM followed. It could not be sensible to act in a way which would destroy trust in all our other decisions. (Hurd 2009: 468–469)

But later that day the decision was taken to temporarily suspend membership. Lamont and Major discussed it one-to-one. Yet the final decision was taken with all key ministers (Seldon 1998: 317). Lamont (1999: 250) later criticised Major's strategy to include the others. He thought it made decision-taking more difficult, when in a financial crisis swift decisions were essential. According to Ken Clarke they were there, because they "were additional doctors brought in at the last moment simply to witness the death of the patient" (Clarke quoted in Hurd 2009: 469).

A day later, on 17 September 1992, the issue was addressed in the regular full cabinet meeting which lasted three hours. The cabinet supported the course. Yet they did not extensively discuss the events of the previous days and some cabinet members did not fully understand them (Seldon 1998: 319). According to Ken Clarke (2016) none of the cabinet ministers "seemed to have any strong views on what to do or say: instead they simply appeared to agree to what had happened" (308). However, by then it was already clear that ERM re-entry was politically highly unlikely and would economically only be sensible after a reform of the mechanism. Yet to admit that a return was doubtful would have placed sterling again under pressure. Moreover, pro-Europeans such as Heseltine and Clarke wanted to keep this option open (Seldon 1998: 320; Stephens 1997: 265).[33] They argued that sterling would not last long outside the mechanism, while the chancellor

[33] Clarke (2016: 308) claimed he already knew then that re-entry was unlikely but thought it important keep up the impression that the government had a policy, which was re-entry to the ERM.

welcomed that Britain could now make its economic and exchange rate policy outside of the ERM framework. Major came to share Lamont's view, though during the autumn both continued to formulate conditions under which Britain would re-join the ERM (Thompson 1996: 198–199). Douglas Hurd was urged by his officials to argue at the 17 September cabinet meeting for a quick return to the ERM which he, however, thought was not a realistic option (Hurd 2009: 469). The Eurosceptics Michael Howard, Michael Portillo and Peter Lilley concluded, like Major and Lamont, that re-entry was not feasible for political reasons (Stephens 1997: 265). Howard reminded his colleagues at the cabinet meeting that support from Conservative MPs for a return to the ERM was highly unlikely (Seldon 1998: 320).

While the working relationship between Major and Lamont had initially been relaxed and they had regularly met for bilaterals (Lamont 1999: 35), it deteriorated during and after the ERM crisis. The chancellor increasingly retreated into the Treasury (Thompson 1996: 201–202). According to Lamont (1999: 318) their relationship suffered because they had different views on what to do after the ERM exit. He also criticised that governmental decision-making became increasingly difficult, with presentation being more discussed than policy. Eight months after leaving the ERM Major, in an attempt to re-establish his government's credibility, dismissed Lamont as chancellor and appointed Ken Clarke as his successor. While Clarke had demanded re-entry at the time of the ERM exit, he said in one of his first TV interviews as chancellor that he principally wanted sterling to re-enter the ERM, but that this would not be possible in the current parliament (Thompson 1996: 202). Clarke and Major worked well and closely together. According to Major (2000: 604) their only difference was that Clarke was more pro-European than he was. They regularly met once or twice a week informally (Clarke 2016: 321). Clarke was not afraid to publicly challenge the views of his Eurosceptic colleagues, which led to conflicts with them.[34]

Meanwhile, the preparations to establish EMU went ahead. To the new chancellor it was important that Britain kept all options open on monetary union. In September 1994 he accepted that the European Commission could publish specific macroeconomic convergence aims for the UK and used these as framework for his own budget (Thompson 1996: 210). In December, divisions between prime minister and chancellor became apparent, because Major had said in an interview he was considering a referendum on EMU. Clarke opposed a referendum and had tried to persuade Major to reject the idea (Thompson 1996: 214). But the prime minister hoped to ease the tensions within his party with the referendum proposal. He managed to persuade his initially reluctant foreign secretary to back it. Hurd remained sceptical, but felt it

[34]E.g. in February 1995 Clarke denied in a speech that joining the single currency would have critical constitutional ramifications. Michael Portillo criticised his senior colleague publicly which showed the degree of division over EMU in the Major cabinet at the time (Stephens 1997: 314–315).

was important to support the prime minister on this. Major enlisted Hurd to try to convince other cabinet ministers to agree, but not only pro-Europeans such as Heseltine and Clarke, also Eurosceptics like Michael Portillo remained opposed (Hurd 2009: 566). In 1996 the question of a referendum before Britain entered EMU was extensively discussed in the full cabinet. Major claimed he decided to mention that the issue was under discussion at the next Prime Minister's Questions in parliament to avoid a leak of the discussions. Opponents of a referendum in the cabinet such as Clarke and Heseltine felt coerced and were cross (Major 2000: 687–688). The chancellor remained particularly opposed to a referendum and in March there were press reports he might be willing to resign over the issue. His resignation would have been a disaster, with a general election looming, as he was seen as an important electoral asset for the Conservatives. Yet the rest of the cabinet by now at least accepted a referendum. After a number of meetings between Major and Clarke, the cabinet endorsed a referendum in early April 1996. However, there was not going to be a pre-emptive referendum as many Eurosceptics had favoured. Instead the Conservative election manifesto was to include the promise of a referendum only if and when cabinet and parliament had agreed to Britain joining the Eurozone (Gowland and Turner 2000: 307–309). But pressure in cabinet to take a more anti-EMU line did not subside and the remaining pro-European ministers apart from the chancellor were becoming less outspoken on the issue. On 23 January 1997 the cabinet agreed to a more sceptical stance on the single currency despite strong opposition from Clarke. This signified the low point of the relationship between chancellor and prime minister, while many in the core executive were angry with Clarke for preventing the cabinet from fully ruling out to join the euro in the next parliament almost on his own (Seldon 1998: 697–698). Major stated the agreed stance of cabinet in parliament that day:

> We have concluded, on the basis of that detailed examination of the criteria and on the basis of the information currently available, that it is very unlikely, although not impossible, that a single currency will be able to proceed safely on 1 January 1999. I am talking not just about Britain's participation, but about the single currency itself. If it did proceed without reliable convergence, we would not, of course, be part of it. (HC Deb 23 January 1997, c1071)

On the whole, avoiding a split in the party was Major's priority in cabinet management on European monetary policy. Yet this became increasingly difficult to deliver over the course of his premiership, with a rising number of Eurosceptics in his cabinet who opposed the government line by a mixture of publicly dissenting and coded messaging (Gowland and Turner 2000: 295). However, on EMU in the context of the Maastricht negotiations, Major skilfully gave the impression that the cabinet was much involved, when in fact policy and strategy was decided by a small group of ministers led by himself, the foreign secretary, the chancellor and the minister for Europe (Tristan Garel-Jones) (Dyson and Featherstone 1999: 564). And when the decision to leave the ERM had to be taken Major again resorted to taking the decision with a small group of key ministers and not the full cabinet. Major gave his foreign secretary, particularly Douglas Hurd, a key role in European policy-making. Other ministers such as from Trade and Industry, for instance, were not particularly influential on the monetary union dossier. This also applied to Michael Heseltine. Norman Lamont as chancellor was not as influential as, for instance, Nigel Lawson had been. This might have been related to the fact that Lamont on EMU (as well as on the ERM) initially executed a policy which his predecessor at the Treasury—John Major—had developed, and Major was still very much up to date on Treasury issues. Moreover, the relationship between Lamont and Major became increasingly strained throughout 1991 and Lamont was seen as less effective in the European level negotiations on EMU than, for instance, the foreign secretary on those on political union (Forster 1999: 167–168). Ken Clarke, on the other hand, was a highly influential figure on UK European policy. Despite becoming increasingly isolated in cabinet over the years with his strong support for joining EMU, he was not afraid to stand his ground against ever more Eurosceptic sentiment. Therefore he made Major's cabinet management, which particularly later in his premiership appeared to be set more on accommodating than opposing the Eurosceptics, more difficult.

8.2.4 The Blair Government

During his premiership Tony Blair seldom used the full cabinet for decision-taking. Robin Cook (2004) noted in his diary his astonishment when a full cabinet meeting was convened to discuss the government's Iraq policy. He went on: "Tony does not regard the Cabinet as a place for decisions. Normally he avoids having discussions in Cabinet until decisions are taken and announced to it" (115). Informal meetings of ministers and officials and cabinet committees were Blair's preferred decision-making fora (Powell 2010: 60). Yet key decisions were often taken in bilaterals of Blair with the responsible minister (Rentoul 2001: 544). On economic policy he had regular meetings with the chancellor and on other subject areas he chose to work directly with other ministers. But there were also issues which he liked to discuss exclusively with his No. 10 staff and the Cabinet Office without involving the responsible minister—although the Treasury sometimes took part. European policy was one example (Kavanagh and Seldon 2000: 279).

Right at the beginning of Blair's first term in office (1997–2001) it became clear that the decision-making on the single currency would be limited to a few actors in the core executive. The first meeting in government on the euro in July 1997 was attended by the ministers Gordon Brown, Peter Mandelson and the prime minister with Nigel Wicks (then Second Permanent Secretary and responsible for the policy on the euro in the Treasury) laying out the pros and cons of the single currency. Foreign Secretary Robin Cook was not invited, which according to Roger Liddle (2014: 76) was because the PM wanted to decide on the line to take with Brown and Mandelson before discussing it more broadly in the core executive. Thus it became soon clear that the foreign secretary was kept out of the loop on the government's euro policy: when one of his FCO officials asked him in summer 1997 "about rumours of a development, Robin Cook replied: 'That's the first I've heard of it'" (Rawnsley 2001: 76).

Chancellor Gordon Brown was considered to be the most resolute supporter of EMU membership in the cabinet when New Labour came into government (Gowland and Turner 2000: 330). This impression was reinforced when shortly after the election he announced the Bank of England's operational independence, a precondition for joining the Eurozone (see Chap. 3). Brown found that the Treasury was very sceptical of the single currency. Senior officials with the exception of Nigel Wicks opposed it. Early on Brown instructed his department to review all options available on the euro: joining between 1999 and 2001, in the next parliament or postponing entry ad infinitum (Seldon 2005: 318–319). By autumn 1997 the chancellor, his advisers and most Treasury officials agreed that entry was neither feasible nor desirable in the first wave (thus by January 1999) as well as during the current parliament. Yet Brown considered that a euro referendum could take place shortly after the next election provided the new currency turned out to be a success. When, however, in September/October the press increasingly speculated that a pro-euro chancellor was trying to bounce a sceptical prime minister to accept entry to the euro, Brown pressed Blair for a clear statement that the government had no intention to join immediately (Seldon 2005: 321–322). Blair (2010: 537) later claimed that it was Brown who had wanted to take a more pro-euro position in 1997 than he did. Eventually the premier accepted that there should be a statement from the government, and on 18 October 1997 an interview with Brown was published in *The Times* with a headline stating that the chancellor dismissed joining the Eurozone for the rest of the parliament (Seldon 2005: 322–323). The details of the publication had been coordinated by Blair's press secretary Alastair Campbell, Brown's press secretary Charlie Whelan and Ed Balls, Brown's adviser. According to Campbell (2007: 252–253) Charlie Whelan and Ed Balls proposed that the chancellor take part in an interview in which he would make clear that while the government's euro policy remained the same, Britain would not join the single currency immediately, i.e. probably not within the present parliament. Campbell agreed with Whelan's suggestion, though expressed surprise that the resulting headline announced that Blair had excluded the possibility of joining the single currency for the current parliament. Campbell also noted that although he and Whelan believed they were carrying out Blair's and Brown's wishes which both had discussed earlier, he was under the impression that neither had really discussed the positioning with each other in detail. This turned out to be the case, because when the interview came out, Blair called Campbell and told him that he and Brown had not agreed this (Campbell 2007: 253). Peter Mandelson (2010) thought it was more the presentation of the chancellor's announcement than its content which was problematic, as Brown's words had only been a little more guarded than what Blair would have said: "What mattered was the headline put over the story... What mattered even more was that Charlie, without consulting Alastair, briefed a similarly explicit message for *Newsnight*, ITN and the following day's *Sun*" (238). If the turn of events suggested by Mandelson and Campbell is accurate, the policy change from keeping all options open on euro entry to ruling it out for the immediate future was no deliberate move by the chancellor to bounce the PM into accepting a policy Blair had not agreed to. Instead it was a communication debacle for which Brown and Blair were responsible because they had neither clearly agreed the policy nor its presentation. In any case, the episode showed that neither the full cabinet nor other key ministers were involved in the decision-making process. Blair had agreed that there should be a statement from the government on the evening of 16 October. The cabinet had met that day but had not discussed the issue. Senior ministers, handling policy areas affected by this, such as Foreign Secretary Cook or DTI Minister Margaret Beckett had not been informed about what was going on (Seldon 2005: 324). This had also happened before: by the end of the summer 1997 the cabinet had on no occasion discussed EMU since Labour had come to power in May (Rawnsley 2001: 76).

Brown made a parliamentary statement on the government's euro policy on 27 October 1997 (HC Deb 27 October 1997, cc583–588). The chancellor set out the five tests on which the decision was to be based. He said that the government in principle supported Britain's joining a successful euro. Yet currently it was not in the UK's economic interest to enter on 1 January 1999. He went on:

> Barring some fundamental and unforeseen change in economic circumstances, making a decision in this Parliament to join is not realistic. To give ourselves a genuine choice in the future, it is essential that Government and business prepare intensively during this Parliament so that Britain will be in a position to join a single currency, should we wish to, early in the next Parliament. (HC Deb 27 October 1997, c588)

This time there had been a full cabinet discussion before the announcement. According to Campbell (2007: 255–256) most cabinet members argued for keeping the option open on the euro at the meeting on 23 October. He found it astonishing how pro-euro most of the cabinet was. Brown briefed the other ministers on the five tests and the backdrop to the planned euro assessment. The exact content of the parliamentary statement had then again been decided only by Blair and Brown. Yet, while the majority of the cabinet around that time might have been supportive of the euro and a referendum in the second term, several senior ministers had doubts such as Margaret Beckett (DTI) and Jack Straw (Home Office). The pro-euro ministers apart from the foreign secretary, on the other hand, were only middle-ranking ministers such as Peter Mandelson and Stephen Byers, then Minister of State for Schools (Seldon 2005: 330).

With the announcement that the euro decision would be taken on the basis of the five tests, the prime minister had given his chancellor a veto over Britain's policy on the single currency (Riddell 2005: 366). With time Brown concluded that joining was not desirable—neither immediately nor in the medium term. He took this view not only because it would have meant a loss of control on the part of the Treasury, but also because it would have compromised his success as guardian of the economy. The veto option Brown had been provided with also helped him put stake to his claim that he fully controlled the government's economic policy (Seldon 2005: 328). Jack Straw (2012: 326–327) thought it had been obvious early on that Brown would not recommend joining the euro. As he had developed the five tests and was responsible for their assessment, it had to be expected that he would never conclude that the tests had been met, Straw argued. According to Anthony Seldon (2005: 327) Blair in autumn 1997 underestimated Brown's growing opposition to joining the euro and assumed that, with the next election out of the way, the five tests would be met and a referendum would be called. Roger Liddle (2014: 79–80) thought that Blair until summer 2003 (see below)—even after the statement on the negative assessment of the five tests—believed Brown could eventually be persuaded to agree to entry.

Brown and the Treasury prevented a wide ranging discussion of the euro issue in Whitehall. The FCO tried to facilitate a debate on it from early 1998, yet the Treasury made it clear that only it would decide on the five tests and thus whether the UK should join the euro (Seldon 2005: 331). Blair, on the other hand, wanted to keep the support of his pro-euro ministers and, for instance, supported Robin Cook and Beckett's successor at the DTI, Stephen Byers, at a meeting with Brown at No. 10 in January 2000, after they had become frustrated about the government's inactivity on the euro (Seldon 2005: 332). Brown tended to react in a highly irritated way when other ministers made positive remarks about the single currency. He felt they were trespassing on his area of responsibility. In May 2000, for example, Peter Mandelson (then Northern Ireland minister) and Byers publicly addressed the disadvantages of staying outside the euro. Cook followed in June. Brown was furious and complained to Blair that his authority was being compromised. The PM then told the full cabinet on 15 June that they should get behind the statement Brown would make on the policy in his Mansion House speech that evening (Rawnsley 2001: 387–388).

In late 2002 the assessment of the tests was finished. Twenty-five Treasury officials had been involved in putting together 18 studies. From January 2003 No. 10 and the Treasury discussed the outcome in six meetings (Rawnsley 2010: 192, 193). No. 10 gained the impression that Brown put the assessment in a negative light, though the Treasury declared that the tests were scientific and unbiased (Seldon 2008: 209). The last seminar on 1 April 2003 was attended by Blair, Jeremy Heywood (Principal Private Secretary), Jonathan Powell (Chief of Staff) and Stephen Wall (PM's European policy adviser) from No. 10. Attendants from the Treasury were Ed Balls, Gus O'Donnell (Permanent Secretary), Jon Cunliffe (responsible for International Finance), and David Ramsden (head of economic and monetary policy) alongside the chancellor. At the meeting Brown and his staff announced that it was not in Britain's current national economic interest to join the euro (Rawnsley 2010: 194). Blair stated that he did not share the Treasury's assessment. Brown insisted that there would be no changes to his department's report. But due to prime ministerial pressure changes were made to it which the Treasury held to be of marginal importance. Throughout April Blair and Brown negotiated their strategy on the announcement of the outcome of the tests in several meetings. Brown had initially wanted to announce it in his upcoming Budget speech, which Blair found unacceptable during the ongoing Iraq war without a full cabinet debate. He eventually prohibited Brown from mentioning it in the Budget for fear the government could be accused of a cover up, if it announced such a key decision in this way during the war. Blair and Brown met alone without staff and no records were taken. In May the issue reached the full cabinet (Seldon 2008: 210–212). Again the Foreign Office (like the other departments) had not been included in the decision-making process before the issue reached the cabinet. There are different accounts as to how the cabinet was consulted at the time. According to Peter Riddell (2005: 373) the chancellor debated the assessment and its conclusions in bilaterals with ministers, which was followed by a long discussion in the full cabinet. Andrew Rawnsley (2010: 195–196) claims that there was no discussion in the full cabinet, but that the ministers were invited to discuss the assessment individually with the chancellor and the prime minister. By Anthony Seldon's account Brown had wanted to talk to each minister individually, which the prime minister had not agreed to. He does not explicitly state whether there was a discussion in the full cabinet, only that ministers were invited to "tutorials" (Seldon 2008: 212) with Blair and Brown on the assessment. According to Derek Scott (2004: 225) the cabinet discussed the issue in a group as well as in smaller meetings with Blair and Brown. By Jonathan Powell's account Brown had wanted to discuss the issue only in the cabinet's economic subcommittee which he chaired. Yet Blair had insisted on discussion with all cabinet members, knowing that most would support his position. These discussions were then with individual ministers (Powell 2010: 255; see also Liddle 2014: 167–168). In any case, when the cabinet was consulted on the issue, key ministers such as David Blunkett (Home Office) and Jack Straw (FCO) opposed a referendum. Deputy Prime Minister John Prescott was sceptical as well (Rawnsley 2010: 196; Seldon (2008: 212) claims Prescott was neutral on this). On 9 June 2003 a parliamentary statement was given on the outcome of the tests. Again Blair and Brown had been divided—this time over who would announce it. Brown prevailed (Rawnsley 2010: 196). The chancellor's statement de facto marked the end of serious discussions on EMU in the core executive as the issue was effectively dead for the remainder of Blair's premiership.[35]

Tony Blair's handling of the euro policy was marked, on the one hand, by a strong focus on his own office as well as the European Secretariat and, on the other hand, on his chancellor. Particularly No. 10 and the Treasury handled the policy. The FCO and other departments such as the DTI were not much involved. The full cabinet as a place for discussion let alone as decision-making body was marginalised. As mentioned, the governmental statement on the euro with the interview in *The Times* in autumn 1997 was neither based on a discussion in the full cabinet nor had senior ministers been informed of it at the time. There is not much indication—neither before nor after Brown in 2003 effectively ruled out Britain's accession to the Eurozone for the foreseeable future—that Blair had much interest in looking for support from the full cabinet or systematically forging alliances with other senior ministers to exert pressure on the chancellor.[36] While he did insist that the outcome of the five tests was discussed with other cabinet ministers prior to Brown's parliamentary statement in 2003 (according to Jonathan Powell

[35]For the reasons why the issue did not return to the government's agenda after 2003 until Blair's resignation in 2007, see Wall (2008: 171).

[36]Rawnsley (2010: 196) cites Jonathan Powell referring to Blair's lack of coalition building in cabinet.

(2010: 255) because he knew the cabinet was in majority supportive of the euro), this did not help Blair's cause much. Senior ministers such as Jack Straw opposed a referendum. Thus, Blair had either underestimated Straw's opposition to the euro, which had been a key reason why he had appointed him (see Sect. 8.1.4), or had overestimated his own ability to persuade others of the merits of joining the euro (which appears to be same in the case of the chancellor). A reason for his marginalisation of the full cabinet on the euro issue might have been that Blair (like Thatcher) did not see it as a decision-making forum in the core executive as Robin Cook (2004: 115) suggested. Jonathan Powell (2010: 255) claims that most cabinet ministers in 2003 supported Blair's position that joining the euro should not be fully ruled out after the assessment of the five tests had been completed and that the ultimate reason for not joining the euro was the lack of change to the British exchange rate. Had the balance of view been clearly as pro-euro as Powell suggested and had included the other senior ministers, Blair might have been able to use the full cabinet to put pressure on the chancellor. By choosing to limit the decision-making process to himself and Brown and their respective offices/departments, however, there was no chance for the PM to build up pressure in the core executive on the chancellor to change his policy. At the same time Blair curtailed his own influence on the decision-making process by emphasising that the decision was entirely an economic one. Thus, he gave his chancellor a veto on the policy which Brown exercised until the end of Blair's premiership. In his memoirs Blair (2010: 70–71) rejected the implication he had given Brown a free hand in economic policy and argued that, at least for the first two terms, he was very much in control of economic policy. Even if this was his assessment of the power balance on economic policy-making in the core executive, on the euro it was the chancellor who decided the policy, not the prime minister. Moreover, even if he wanted to, by 2003 Blair was not in a position to move Brown to another post or from the government. He needed Brown's support on his Iraq policy, which divided the Labour Party (Liddle 2014: 158). Apart from Brown, other ministers only had marginal influence on the decision-making on the euro. The foreign secretaries Cook and Straw had limited roles in the core executive on European policy-making in general—on European monetary policy their involvement was perhaps more limited than it had been the case in earlier administrations (for example Howe under Thatcher or Hurd under Major). According to Jonathan Powell (2010: 286) Cook and Straw complained about Blair taking much influence on foreign policy decision-making and that they were required to check most policy decisions with No. 10. The trade and industry secretaries—among them euro-supporters Peter Mandelson and Stephen Byers—had even less impact on the issue. The exclusion of pro-euro ministers from the policy-making process in the core executive had the effect that they tended to voice their views in public instead. This created rifts in the core executive, because the ministers openly defied Brown (see above). Yet it did not lead to an expansion of the group of decision-makers on the euro. This remained limited to PM and chancellor, with the latter in the decisive position.

8.3 Prime Ministerial Two-Level Politics in European (Monetary) Policy

Whether British objectives can be secured in the negotiation process in the European Council depends to a large extent on the individual prime minister and his negotiating style. This is because the negotiating style in the European Council, as explained in Sect. 6.1.4, is more direct and personal than in other EC/EU bodies such as the Council of the European Union (Wessels and Schäfer 2014: 238). When looking at the negotiating strategies pursued by the prime ministers analysed here, differences can be detected.

The different sources provide only limited information on James Callaghan's handling of European Council negotiations. Roy Denman (1997), head of the COES from 1975 to 1977, painted quite a negative picture. On the Labour government's demeanour in general at the European level he noted: "in the large majority of cases, from the Prime Minister down, the attitude, both to the Community's aims and its institutions, varied from the hostile to the contemptuous" (258). Yet Callaghan had better relations with German Chancellor Helmut Schmidt and other leaders than, for instance, his predecessor Harold Wilson had had (Gowland and Turner 2000: 216). Schmidt (1990: 116), for example, characterised Callaghan as a person focused on reconciliation, who was dependable and not deceitful. In any case, Callaghan (2006) himself noted the advantages of regularly meeting with other EC leaders, particularly during the informal parts of the summits: "The exchanges [between the European leaders] enabled all of us to gain insight into the view of the other leaders and to profit from their experience and their contacts" (317).

On the ERM James Callaghan did not use his position in the European Council to conduct two-level politics. He instead focused on maintaining the cohesion of his cabinet and his party. With regard to the negotiations at the Brussels European Council in December 1978, the prime minister had committed himself before the summit to adhere to the negotiating line laid down by his cabinet. Should a change of position become necessary, he had agreed only to do so after consulting his cabinet (TNA, CAB 128/64, CM (78) 41st Conclusions, 30 November 1978, 9). However, on the issue his stance corresponded with that of the majority of his cabinet: EMS but not ERM membership. Thus, he had no reason to force his cabinet colleagues into accepting a different decision by exerting pressure on them through striking another deal with his European counterparts.

Despite acknowledging that Margaret Thatcher's lack of a conciliatory negotiating style was a key reason for her success in achieving a solution on Britain's EC budget contribution, her first foreign secretary Peter Carrington (1988: 318–319) pointed out that it made the relationship between Britain and the European partners more difficult. Thatcher's way of arguing in the European Council alienated her counterparts.[37] John Major (2000: 265) recalled his shock upon realising at his first European Council that Thatcher's will power was not considered as positive by her European counterparts as it was in the UK. To her European colleagues the PM was a unifying force, but in the sense that she united them against her. Percy Cradock (1997) thought her lack of understanding of her opposites was problematic in negotiations:

> She had on the whole a poor view of foreigners, other than Anglo-Saxons, just as she had little time for European traditions or statesmen. This lack of imagination about the other side was a real defect. Too often it meant a one-dimensional policy, the assertion of British claims in a vacuum, with inevitable surprises and rebuffs when the other party failed to fit into our preconceptions. (21–22)

Nigel Lawson (1992) considered Thatcher's negotiating style to be counterproductive:

> For her, unanimity meant she had a veto; and if you had a veto you used it... For everyone else, unanimity gave them a card that could from time to time be played to secure a national objective. Once the others realized that Margaret was playing by quite different rules, there ceased to be any reason, in any of the fields where unanimity prevailed—or in any other field for that matter—to make any concessions to the UK, since nothing could be secured in return. (898–899)

Margaret Thatcher could have pursued a two-level strategy in European policy. But it remains questionable that she, who according to a ministerial colleague severely disliked European Council meetings (Thompson 1996: 60) and at the end of her period in office was unable to find consensus with her European counterparts,[38] would have been inclined to use her membership of the body to pressure her cabinet into accepting a decision it opposed. On the ERM Thatcher neither shared the aims of most European partners nor of her senior ministers. On EMU she and her senior ministers were united in their opposition to it (with the possible exception of Geoffrey Howe), while her European counterparts supported it. In either case she would not have gained anything from striking a deal with her colleagues in the European Council to overcome resistance from her ministers on the issue in question.

John Major's negotiating strategy in the European Council differed considerably from his predecessor's. His assessment of Thatcher's negotiating style (see above) suggests that his decision to pursue another strategy might not entirely have been guided by personal preferences but also by the conclusion that her strategy had been unhelpful. His advisers Sarah Hogg and Jonathan Hill argued: "Understanding both the issues and the psychology of the players is the key to European Council

[37]E.g. Roy Jenkins (1989: 530), then European Commission President, suggested, that Thatcher at the Dublin summit in November 1979 did not bring the discussion about the UK's budget contribution forward by insisting on 'her money', but antagonised her European counterparts.

[38]At the Rome European Council in 1990 she insisted that Britain's dissent from the other EC members' plans on EMU was included in the summit conclusions (Dyson and Featherstone 1999: 632).

negotiations: John Major possesses that rare combination of skills to a high degree" (Hogg and Hill 1996: 146). Before the Maastricht European Council he met his European counterparts to discuss the topics of the summit. According to the *Financial Times* this was a marked contrast to Thatcher's relationship with her European partners which had not included any "special effort in advance of summits"[39] (Stephens 1991). Major (2000) acknowledged the difficulties due to the different decision-making processes of the European and the domestic level because "when British ministers spoke the language of Westminster in Brussels it was like spitting in church. Others shied away from our 'non-consensual' approach, and the club closed ranks against us. Britain was isolated again. It was immensely frustrating" (583). Major's relations with his European counterparts became more difficult over the years and those with German Chancellor Helmut Kohl and French President Jacques Chirac, for example, never fully mended after his government's policy of non-cooperation in EU decision-making in retaliation for the ban on British beef during the 1996 BSE crisis (Seldon 1998: 650).

While John Major did conduct two-level politics, for instance, on the EU budget,[40] on the EMU negotiations he did not do so. To keep the support of the Eurosceptics in his cabinet he had made much effort to get them to agree to his negotiating stance (see Sect. 8.2.3). This meant that he could not put forward to his cabinet colleagues deals with his European counterparts he had not previously consulted them on (Blair 1999: 46). Moreover, as the negotiating objective on EMU—achieving an opt-out—was something Eurosceptics and pro-Europeans in the party alike could support, a different deal at Maastricht would not have been in Major's interest.

Tony Blair's initial advantage on the European level was that he was not John Major. With his charisma and his negotiating style he elicited much goodwill from his European counterparts. At the Amsterdam Treaty negotiation a month after coming into office, for instance, small concessions, like more cooperation in defence and foreign policy, reinforced the impression that he was a pro-European willing to compromise (without having to give up significant sovereignty rights e.g. on border controls) (Seldon 2005: 319–320). According to Robin Cook (2004), Blair's negotiating style in the European Council significantly affected the UK's influence:

> It is to Tony Blair's credit that in his first term in office he transformed Britain's relations with Europe. This was very much his personal achievement, and I saw how he came to command attention in the European Council, where his intervention was often pivotal in

---

[39]Stephens, P. (1991), Major's charm offensive promises summit dividend, *Financial Times*, 29 November 1991. Used under licence from the Financial Times. All Rights Reserved.

[40]During Britain's 1992 EC presidency Major chaired the Edinburgh European Council and achieved a compromise on the European budget, which had to be recalculated with implications for the UK rebate. Chancellor Lamont opposed taking a decision on the budget during the presidency. He argued that the government, due to its obligation to chair the negotiations, would be too constrained to receive the best possible result. But Major thought that particularly during the presidency a decision in the country's interest was achievable because Britain controlled the agenda (Wall 2008: 151).

> determining which view would come out on top. For the first time since Britain joined the European Council, it had a government that was taking the initiative in Europe, rather than responding to the agendas of others. (131)

While Blair did conduct two-level policy, for instance, on the EU budget,[41] on EMU his position in the European Council did not help at home. With the announcement of the five tests the chancellor held the key to the policy. Moreover, the government had decided that the public would have to agree to membership in a referendum. Therefore, Blair would not have gained anything from striking a deal with his European counterparts in the European Council as it did not give him any leverage on domestic policy-making on the euro.

8.4 Actors in the European Monetary Policy Core Executive and Prime Ministerial Political Leadership

In this chapter the agency and behaviour of other actors in the European monetary policy core executive apart from the prime minister were analysed. It was also considered how the prime ministers in question managed these actors. With regard to the prime ministerial resource of appointment, the analysis showed that all four were constrained in their use of it. All had to compromise to an extent on their appointments due to cleavages in their parties. Yet differences in European policy attitudes were only relevant on appointments in the cases of James Callaghan and John Major as their parties were divided on this issue. On ERM and EMU, there are examples of the four leaders using their prerogative on appointment in an attempt to further a particular policy. There is, for instance, Margaret Thatcher, who after the Madrid European Council attempted to reassert her position in the core executive and break the alliance between foreign secretary and chancellor. Thus she dismissed Geoffrey Howe from the FCO to exclude him from the European (monetary) policy core executive. Another example is Tony Blair's appointment of Jack Straw as foreign secretary. Blair had hoped to convince Straw of the merit of joining the euro, because he thought that if the known EMU-sceptic Straw supported euro membership this would persuade more citizens to support this as well. Both examples, however, show that using the right of appointment does not result in a PM being able to determine a particular policy. For instance, despite Howe's dismissal from the European monetary policy core executive, Thatcher only managed to postpone the decision to join the ERM but not to foreclose it. Blair, on the other

[41]During the UK's 2005 presidency Blair used a two-level policy to pressure Brown to acquiesce to a course Brown did not want on the EU budget negotiations. Blair thought the best chances for agreement were as long as the negotiations were conducted under British chairmanship – particularly as Britain was the only EU member wishing to keep the UK rebate. Yet the Treasury argued a better deal could be struck, if the UK did not hold the presidency. Blair prevailed over Brown and secured a budget agreement under his chairmanship of the European Council (Wall 2008: 150–151; Blair 2010: 535, 542–543).

hand, was not able to convert Straw, who remained opposed to euro membership. Thus, instead of a pro-euro foreign secretary who would further his intended policy the premier had appointed one who did not support it.

On prime ministerial cabinet management with regard to European monetary policy, parallels can be drawn between the cases of James Callaghan and John Major as well as those of Margaret Thatcher and Tony Blair. In the case of the first two the collective leadership thesis applies. Yet the leadership was collective in the sense that the decision-making process was focused on a selected group of ministers not on the full cabinet. With regard to the divisions over Europe in their parties both included all senior core executive actors in the decision-making process on ERM membership (Callaghan) and ERM exit (Major) to ensure either decision was widely supported. Callaghan prepared the ERM-decision to secure his preferred outcome by establishing a cabinet committee. He appointed to it those ministers who would ensure that the committee would decide against joining the ERM. This verdict he could then present to the full cabinet for agreement. Major took the decision to suspend Britain's ERM membership not only with his chancellor but also with other senior ministers (President of Board of Trade/DTI, foreign and home secretary). In the context of the Maastricht Treaty negotiations Major took the key decisions on EMU in a small group of ministers consisting of him, the chancellor and the foreign secretary. Yet he ensured that the full cabinet felt included in the decision-making process by being regularly briefed. In Callaghan's and Major's case the state of their parties on Europe much influenced their form of cabinet management, as safeguarding cabinet and party unity was the most important factor on it. Yet their cabinet management can probably not only be attributed to the (party) political context of the time as both men were also known to be in favour of collective decision-making in general.

In the cases of Margaret Thatcher and Tony Blair the analysis showed that both intended to conduct a predominant leadership. They limited the decision-making process in the core executive on ERM and EMU, for instance, by preventing wide-ranging debates on the issue in the core executive, such as in the full cabinet. Yet they were not able to be predominant or at least not for long. Blair restricted core executive decision-making to himself and his chancellor on monetary union. By arguing that the basis of the euro decision was economics he gave Brown a veto on the policy. Moreover, by failing to secure alliances with other pro-euro ministers, let alone placing them in senior posts in his cabinet, he had no opportunity to exert pressure on Brown to achieve a policy change once it became clear that the chancellor took a different view on the issue. Thatcher for several years managed to veto joining the ERM (at times by refusing to discuss the issue with her ministers) and thus defied her foreign secretary and her chancellor. Hence, she achieved prime ministerial predominance, but it was temporary. Her dismissal of Howe from the FCO, Lawson's resignation and other issues such as the poll tax weakened her position in the core executive so much that she eventually had to succumb to the pressure from her new chancellor and foreign secretary, Major and Hurd, on the ERM. Thus, she only postponed the implementation of a policy she opposed. On EMU Thatcher again limited the decision-making process to chancellor and foreign secretary, while marginalising the full cabinet. Though the ministers agreed that EMU was undesirable, they disagreed on the UK's negotiating strategy on it. Yet Thatcher again attempted to be predominant by opposing EMU at the Rome IGC and effectively destroying the government's alternative to the Delors plan with her subsequent parliamentary statement. This, however, was no strategy her foreign secretary and chancellor supported. Limiting the decision-making process to a few core executive actors had a key disadvantage: ministers who took a dissenting stance on the issue did not feel that they were able to voice it in the core executive. So they carried the debate about the ERM in Thatcher's case and EMU in Blair's case into the public sphere by setting out their opposing view there (e.g. Howe and Lawson, Cook and Mandelson).

Conducting two-level politics on European policy was an option available to all four leaders. Yet none of them chose it on ERM or EMU as they would not have achieved anything domestically by making deals in the European Council to pressure the actors in their domestic core executive to agree to another policy. For Callaghan and Major party unity was the key. Neither PM would have strengthened their domestic leadership position by discarding their compromise policy drafted to be acceptable to pro-Europeans and Eurosceptics alike (joining EMS but not ERM or the EMU opt-out) in favour of siding with their fellow leaders in the European Council. For Thatcher this was similar over ERM and EMU, particularly as she neither agreed with her European counterparts nor with the key actors in the domestic core executive on the issue or the UK's strategy in the negotiations. In Blair's case, too, two-level politics did not help achieve his policy goals domestically. As he had agreed that the five tests would decide whether the UK should join the euro, siding with his European counterparts would not have granted him greater leverage at home on the policy.

Considering the other actors in the core executive who might constrain a premier's leeway, the most important on European monetary policy decision-making was the chancellor. This is hardly surprising as monetary policy in general was a key area which the Treasury handled (and still handles). If the chancellor's view was in line with that of the PM (e.g. Callaghan and Healey on the ERM), other ministers had slim chances to force a change of policy. In cases where the PM's and the chancellor's views differed, the head of government might have been able to uphold his position for a while. But when divisions between the two became too deep and public knowledge—as was the case with Thatcher and Lawson—it had a destabilising effect on the government. At the same time a premier's option to take a veto position was temporary and highly dependent on the political context. Thatcher was able to defy Lawson's wish for immediate ERM entry even when he threatened resignation together with Howe. But when a year later Major proposed entry, she was no longer in a position to risk another chancellor's resignation over a policy she did not want.

Of somewhat lesser importance to the decision-making process on European monetary policy was the foreign secretary. If his view was in line with the PM's and the chancellor's the policy was practically unchangeable for other members of the core executive. An example of this is the Callaghan government's decision on

EMS and ERM, which was supported by Callaghan, Healey and Owen. Tony Benn, for instance, was not able to persuade the cabinet of his view that Britain should not be part of the EMS at all, nor was Harold Lever with his view that the UK should join the ERM. At the same time a prime minister's leeway could be influenced, if a foreign secretary collaborated with the chancellor to achieve a policy change. Hurd and Major were able to do this with regard to Thatcher on the ERM. However, as successive chancellors tended to ensure that European monetary policy remained their preserve, this collaboration did not happen often. The Chancellors Geoffrey Howe and Nigel Lawson on the ERM as well as Gordon Brown on EMU, for example, tried to keep either issue away from debate in the core executive. On ERM and EMU the foreign secretaries were more limited in their influence on the decision-making process than might be the case in other areas of European policy. This is due to the policy field as the Treasury was and is the key department in monetary policy-making. The foreign secretary with significant influence on the prime minister was Douglas Hurd on John Major. This was partly due to his foreign policy expertise, his standing in the core executive and in the party, but most importantly because he was close to Major. At moments other actors influenced the monetary policy debate in the core executive, for example, the trade and industry secretary, but they were in general even less influential than the foreign secretary.

The analysis in this chapter has shown that individual ministers could strongly impact on policy decisions depending on their standing in the core executive, their relationship with the prime minister as well as the PM's strategy in managing his cabinet. At the same time prime ministerial cabinet management was much affected by the state of the party in government—whether it was unified or divided on the policy field in question. This also had implications for the behaviour of the party in parliament, which is considered in the next chapter.

References

Anderson, P., & Mann, N. (1997). *Safety first: The making of New Labour*. London: Granta Books.

Benn, T. (1978, 13 July). Britain, Germany and the proposed monetary system, In The National Archives [hereafter TNA]. *Records of the Cabinet Office [hereafter CAB] 129/203*, CP (78) 80.

Blair, A. (1999). *Dealing with Europe: Britain and the negotiation of the Maastricht Treaty*. Aldershot: Ashgate.

Blair, T. (2010). *A journey*. London: Hutchinson.

Bruce-Gardyne, J. (1986). *Ministers and mandarins: Inside the Whitehall village*. London: Sidgwick & Jackson.

Callaghan, J. (2006). *Time and chance*. London: Politico's.

Campbell, A. (2007). *The Blair years: Extracts from the Alastair Campbell diaries*. London: Hutchinson.

Carrington, P. A. (1988). *Reflect on things past: The memoirs of Lord Carrington*. London: Collins.

Clarke, K. (2016). *Kind of blue: A political memoir*. London: Macmillan.

Cook, R. (2004). *The point of departure: Diaries from the front bench* (2nd ed.). London: Pocket Books.

Cradock, P. (1997). *In pursuit of British interests: Reflections on foreign policy under Margaret Thatcher and John Major*. London: John Murray.
Dickie, J. (1992). *Inside the Foreign Office*. London: Chapmans.
Dell, E. (1994). Britain and the origins of the European Monetary System. *Contemporary European History, 3*(1), 1–60.
Dell, E., & Lord Hunt of Tanworth (= J. Hunt). (1994). The failings of cabinet government in mid to late 1970s. *Contemporary Records, 8*(3), 453–472.
Denman, R. (1997). *Missed chances: Britain and Europe in the twentieth century* (2nd ed.). London: Indigo.
Donoughue, B. (1987). *Prime minister: The conduct of policy under Harold Wilson & James Callaghan*. London: Jonathan Cape.
Donoughue, B. (1988). The prime minister's day. *Contemporary British History, 2*(2), 16–19.
Donoughue, B. (2009). *Downing Street diary: With James Callaghan in No. 10* (2nd ed.). London: Pimlico.
Dunleavy, P. (1995). Reinterpreting the Westland affair: Theories of the state and core executive decision making. In R. A. W. Rhodes & P. Dunleavy (Eds.), *Prime minister, cabinet and core executive* (pp. 181–218). London: Macmillan.
Dyson, K., & Featherstone, K. (1999). *The road to Maastricht: Negotiating economic and monetary union*. Oxford: Oxford University Press.
Forster, A. (1999). *Britain and the Maastricht negotiations*. London: Macmillan.
Franklin, M. (2013). Could and should Britain have joined the European Exchange Rate Mechanism in 1979? A personal memoir. *Journal of Contemporary European Research, 9*(5), 759–766.
Giddings, P. (1995). Prime minister and cabinet. In D. Shell & R. Hodder-Williams (Eds.), *Churchill to Major: The British prime ministership since 1945* (pp. 30–70). Armonk: M.E. Sharpe.
Gowland, D., & Turner, A. (2000). *Reluctant Europeans: Britain and European integration 1945–1998*. Harlow: Longman.
Gowland, D., Turner, A., & Wright, A. (2010). *Britain and European integration since 1945: On the sidelines*. London: Routledge.
HC Deb. (1978, November 29), Vol 959, c474.
HC Deb. (1989, October 31), Vol 159, c208.
HC Deb. (1990, October 30), Vol 178, c871.
HC Deb. (1997, January 23), Vol 288, c1071.
HC Deb. (1997, October 27), Vol 299, cc583–588.
Healey, D. (1978, November 28). European Monetary System, in TNA. *CAB 129/204*, CP (78) 122.
Healey, D. (2006). *The time of my life* (2nd ed.). London: Politico's.
Hogg, S., & Hill, J. (1996). *Too close to call: Power and politics - John Major in No. 10* (2nd ed.). London: Warner Books.
Holberton, S. (1989, October 18). PM's economist adds his guarded support. *Financial Times*.
Howe, G. (1995). *Conflict of loyalty* (2nd ed.). London: Pan Books.
Hurd, D. (2009). *Memoirs*. London: Abacus.
James, S. (2009). Taming the 'awkward state'? The changing face of European policy-making under Blair. *Public Administration, 87*(3), 604–620.
James, S., & Oppermann, K. (2009). Blair and the European Union. In T. Casey (Ed.), *The Blair legacy: Politics, policy, governance and foreign affairs* (pp. 285–298). Basingstoke: Palgrave Macmillan.
Jay, M. (2007, January 4). *British Diplomatic Oral History Programme (BDOHP) interview*. Cambridge: Churchill Archives Centre, Churchill College.
Jenkins, R. (1989). *European diary 1977-1981*. London: Collins.
Jones, B. (2001). The policy-making process. In B. Jones, D. Kavanagh, M. Moran, & P. Norton (Eds.), *Politics UK* (4th ed., pp. 527–542). Harlow: Longman.

Kavanagh, D., & Seldon, A. (2000). *The powers behind the prime minister: The hidden influence of Number Ten* (2nd ed.). London: HarperCollins.
Kerr, J. (2004, January 6). *British Diplomatic Oral History Programme (BDOHP) interview*. Cambridge: Churchill Archives Centre, Churchill College.
Lamont, N. (1999). *In office*. London: Little, Brown.
Lawson, D. (1990, July 14). Saying the unsayable about the Germans. *The Spectator*.
Lawson, N. (1992). *A view from No. 11: Memoirs of a Tory radical*. London: Bantam.
Liddle, R. (2014). *The Europe dilemma: Britain and the drama of EU integration*. London: I.B. Tauris.
Ludlow, P. (1982). *The making of the European Monetary System*. London: Butterworth.
Major, J. (2000). *The autobiography* (2nd ed.). London: HarperCollins.
Mandelson, P. (2010). *The third man: Life at the heart of New Labour*. London: Harper Press.
Moore, C. (2015). *Margaret Thatcher: The authorized biography, Volume two: Everything she wants*. London: Allen Lane.
Owen, D. (2009). *Time to declare: Second innings*. London: Politico's.
Parkinson, C. (1992). *Right at the centre: An autobiography*. London: Weidenfeld and Nicolson.
Powell, J. (2010). *The new Machiavelli: How to wield power in the modern world*. London: The Bodley Head.
Rawnsley, A. (2001). *Servants of the people: The inside story of New Labour* (2nd ed.). London: Penguin.
Rawnsley, A. (2010). *The end of the party* (2nd ed.). London: Penguin.
Rawstorne, P. (1978, December 5). New moves to boost left-wing influence. *Financial Times*.
Rentoul, J. (2001). *Tony Blair: Prime minister*. London: Warner Books.
Rhys, D. (1978, December 9). Lever gives strong support for new monetary system. *Financial Times*.
Riddell, P. (2005). Europe. In A. Seldon & D. Kavanagh (Eds.), *The Blair effect 2001-5* (pp. 362–383). Cambridge: Cambridge University Press.
Rifkind, M. (2016). *Power and pragmatism: The memoirs of Malcolm Rifkind*. London: Biteback.
Roth, A. (1999, November 4). Edmund Dell. *The Guardian*.
Rutherford, M. (1978, December 8). A time of uncertainty. *Financial Times*.
Schmidt, H. (1990). *Die Deutschen und ihre Nachbarn: Menschen und Mächte II* (2nd ed.). Berlin: Siedler.
Scott, D. (2004). *Off Whitehall: A view from Downing Street by Tony Blair's adviser*. London: I. B. Tauris.
Seldon, A. (1994). Policy making and cabinet. In D. Kavanagh & A. Seldon (Eds.), *The Major effect* (pp. 154–166). London: Macmillan.
Seldon, A. (with Baston, L.) (1998). *Major: A political life* (2nd ed.) London: Phoenix.
Seldon, A. (with Ballinger, C., Collings, D., & Snowdon, P.) (2005). *Blair* (2nd ed.). London: Free Press.
Seldon, A. (with Snowdon, P., & Collings, D.) (2008). *Blair unbound* (2nd ed.). London: Pocket Books.
Shaw, E. (2004). The control freaks? New Labour and the party. In S. Ludlam & M. J. Smith (Eds.), *Governing as New Labour: Policy and politics under Blair* (pp. 52–69). Basingstoke: Palgrave Macmillan.
Stephens, P. (1991, November 29). Major's charm offensive promises summit dividend. *Financial Times*.
Stephens, P. (1994, May 4). Backbench dismay over in-fighting on EMU. *Financial Times*.
Stephens, P. (1997). *Politics and the pound: The Tories, the economy and Europe* (2nd ed.). London: Papermac.
Stephens, P., & Holberton, S. (1989, June 15). Thatcher rejects calls to dismiss economic advisor. *Financial Times*.

Straw, J. (2011, December 6). *Britain and Europe*. Speech at the European Institute, University College London. https://www.ucl.ac.uk/european-institute/analysis-publications/analysis/straw/Jack_Straw_061211.pdf. Accessed October 19, 2016.

Straw, J. (2012). *Last man standing: Memoirs of a political survivor*. London: Macmillan.

Thatcher, M. (2011). *The Downing Street years*. London: Harper Press.

Thomas, G. P. (1998). *The prime minister and cabinet today*. Manchester: Manchester University Press.

Thompson, H. (1996). *The British Conservative government and the European Exchange Rate Mechanism, 1979-1994*. London: Pinter.

TNA. (1976, May 6). *CAB 128/59*, CM (76) 3rd conclusions.

TNA. (1976, May 25). *CAB 128/59*, CM (76) 7th conclusions.

TNA. (1977, July 1). *Records of the Prime Minister's Office [hereafter PREM] 16/1492*, Kenneth Stowe to the prime minister.

TNA. (1978, January 26). *CAB 128/63*, CM (78) 2nd conclusions.

TNA. (1978, July 6). *CAB 128/64*, CM (78) 25th conclusions.

TNA. (1978, July 13). *CAB 128/64*, CM (78) 26th conclusions.

TNA. (1978, October 12). *CAB 128/64*, CM (78) 34th conclusions.

TNA. (1978, October 26). *CAB 128/64*, CM (78) 36th conclusions.

TNA. (1978, November 2). *CAB 128/64*, CM (78) 37th conclusions.

TNA. (1978, November 16). *CAB 128/64*, CM (78) 39th conclusions.

TNA. (1978, November 23). *CAB 128/64*, CM (78) 40th conclusions.

TNA. (1978, November 30). *CAB 128/64*, CM (78) 41st conclusions.

TNA. (1978, December 7). *CAB 128/64*, CM (78) 42nd conclusions.

TNA. (1978, December 14). *CAB 128/64*, CM (78) 43rd conclusions.

TNA. (1980, March 20). *CAB 128/67*, CC (80) 12th conclusions.

TNA. (1981, February 24). *CAB 128/70*, CC (81) 8th conclusions.

TNA. (1982, February 18). *CAB 128/73*, CC (82) 6th conclusions.

TNA. (1982, February 25). *CAB 128/73*, CC (82) 7th conclusions.

TNA. (1982, June 17). *CAB 128/74*, CC (82) 34th conclusions.

TNA. (1983, March 24). *CAB 128/76*, CC (83) 11th conclusions.

Wall, S. (2008). *A stranger in Europe: Britain and the EU from Thatcher to Blair*. Oxford: Oxford University Press.

Wessels, W., & Schäfer, M. (2014). Europäischer Rat. In W. Weidenfeld & W. Wessels (Eds.), *Europa von A bis Z: Taschenbuch der Europäischen Integration* (pp. 233–240). Bonn: Bundeszentrale für Politische Bildung.

White, M., & Pick, H. (1991, November 28). Mr Nice Guy and his chums. *The Guardian*.

Young, H. (1994). The prime minister. In D. Kavanagh & A. Seldon (Eds.), *The Major effect* (pp. 18–28). London: Macmillan.

Young, H. (1999). *This blessed plot: Britain and Europe from Churchill to Blair* (2nd ed.). London: Papermac.

Chapter 9
Prime Ministerial Management of the Parliamentary Party in European Policy

In this chapter the behaviour of the governmental parliamentary party in European policy is analysed. How did it vote on this subject area? Did it mainly support the incumbent government and prime minister or were there regular rebellions? The parliamentary party's voting record on European policy in general is addressed in this chapter with particular reference to the ERM and EMU case studies. A broader view of the parliamentary party's behavioural pattern and its impact on the PM's political leadership is taken, because it can be assumed to form the trajectory for the parliamentary party's likely behaviour on the specific cases ERM and EMU. The party's general behaviour in the policy field can also give an indication as to what the prime minister might have expected it to look like on ERM or EMU specifically. This is important as in some cases parliament did not vote on European monetary policy issues as the government did not introduce legislation on it. Therefore no voting records can be used to assess the parliamentary party's view on the issue. Take for example the Blair government and EMU: as it took no decision to join the euro, the parliamentary party did not vote on whether Britain should enter the Eurozone. Yet as the decision remained under consideration at least until 2003, the PM had to take the view of his parliamentary party into account. This also had implications for the management of his parliamentary party, which is considered in this chapter as well. This concerns issues such as the prime minister's relationship with his backbenchers and whether he tends to compromise with them on policy or to use measures to force them to adhere to the whip. How a PM handles his parliamentary party is, of course, also related to the parliamentary arithmetic. A slim or non-existent majority requires a different kind of management than a decisive majority. Therefore the parliamentary arithmetic is also considered in this chapter.

B. Bujard, *The British Prime Minister in the Core Executive*, Contributions to Political Science, https://doi.org/10.1007/978-3-319-89953-4_9

9.1 James Callaghan

On becoming prime minister in April 1976 James Callaghan had already been a Member of Parliament (MP) for 31 years (Rose 2001: 133). As prime minister he was respected in the House of Commons and often appeared self-assured and in control (Thomas 2004: 18).

Callaghan regularly spent time in parliament and often worked there instead of at Downing Street. He thought it important to be seen in the Tea Room, to speak with members of the Parliamentary Labour Party (PLP) and he often dined in the Commons. Apart from informal meetings with Labour MPs, he attended the weekly PLP meetings, those of the National Executive Committee (NEC), the party's governing body, and of the PLP-TUC Liaison Committee, the link between the PLP and the trade unions. Moreover, it was important to him that every Labour MP who wished to speak to him personally could do so (Kavanagh and Seldon 2000: 128, 130).

James Callaghan had to lead a minority government. Of the 319 seats Labour had won at the autumn 1974 general election the PLP had shrunk to 306 members by April 1979 due to by-election losses and defections (Norton 1980: XXI–XXII). From March 1977 to July 1978 Labour governed with the help of the Lib-Lab pact (Marsh 1990: 292). The Liberal Party had agreed to support the government in case of a confidence vote. In return the government had agreed to consult the Liberals on key issues. On European policy this meant the introduction of a parliamentary bill for proportional voting in the first elections to the European Parliament, set to take place in 1978. This proposal was controversial in the Labour Party. Cabinet members such as Tony Benn and Peter Shore opposed it. On 13 December 1977 it was rejected in the Commons (Butler and Kavanagh 1980: 20, 34–35). The Lib-Lab pact affected the management of the PLP: while it secured that the government stayed in power, it forced it to balance Liberal Party interests and goals with what it wanted to do and what their own backbenchers were willing to accept (Norton 1980: 445). On the ERM, however, the pact did not pose a constraint. The proposal to establish a European Monetary System came up in summer 1978 and a decision had to be taken on it by December. By then Callaghan had ended the pact with the Liberals and continued his minority government.

Callaghan took the management of the parliamentary party very seriously. It was a regular feature in cabinet discussions[1] and the debate on how to manage the parliamentary minority extended as part of Cabinet business over the course of his premiership (Donoughue 2009: 43–44). The PM regularly met the Chief Whip to discuss government business and all whips when controversial parliamentary votes had to be prepared (Donoughue 1987: 27–28, 2009: 115). Callaghan (2006: 442) considered it the success of his whips and of the Leader of the House of Commons

[1]'Parliamentary Affairs' was on the cabinet agenda in 15 of the 24 cabinet conclusions between 8 June and 19 December 1978 (TNA, CAB 128/64, CM (78) 21st Conclusions, 8 June 1978, to TNA, CAB 128/64, CM (78) 44th Conclusions, 19 December 1978).

Michael Foot that the government managed to survive for more than 3 years without a majority. Although, according to Bernard Donoughue (2009: 54), early in Callaghan's premiership Chief Whip Michael Cocks as well as Foot found it difficult to correctly read and assess the backbenchers' mood.

Leadership of the PLP was difficult. Between 1976 and 1979 Labour MPs voted on 233 occasions against the government. This meant that at 23.4% of all parliamentary votes, so-called divisions, Labour MPs voted against their own side. Between 1976 and 1979 236 Labour MPs voted at least once against their government which was about 77% of the PLP (own calculation based on data from Norton 1980; House of Commons Library 2016).[2] The percentage of divisions in which at least one Labour MP voted against the government increased during Callaghan's premiership and therefore made his management of the PLP increasingly difficult. The number of divisions, in which at least one Labour MP rebelled, expressed as a percentage of all divisions in which Labour MPs were not given a free vote, increased over the course of Callaghan's premiership (1976–77 session: 30%; 1977–78 session: 36%; 1978–79 session: 45%) (Norton 1980: 437). Subject of the intraparty rebellions was among other issues European policy. 34 cases of dissension were specifically on the EC. This equalled 14.6% of the 233 occasions in which Labour MPs cast dissenting votes during Callaghan's premiership (own calculation based on data from Norton 1980). These rebellions were, for example, related to the decision about the electoral system to be used for the first European Parliament election (Norton 1980: 429).

There was considerable hostility against European monetary cooperation at the Labour Party conference in September 1978, when the party adopted a motion rejecting the European Monetary System (Goodman 1978a). The majority of the PLP was hostile as well. In November 1978, 120 MPs—which was more than half of the PLP members not holding a ministerial post—supported a motion which rejected any effort to gain control of domestic policies with the help of the planned monetary system on the part of the European Community, its institution or member states (Ludlow 1982: 220). To the government it was clear that the issue had to be addressed in parliament. In the cabinet conclusions of the 30 November 1978 meeting it was noted that

> it would be wrong to force any necessary European instruments through the House of Commons in a hurry before Christmas at a time when the Party might still be divided in its attitude to the EMS. However, the regulations in question were likely to be only permissive, and raised no serious issues of policy for the United Kingdom as such. Provided it was clear that the House had an opportunity to debate fully any decisions which directly affected the United Kingdom and had proper explanatory memoranda in good time, this should be sufficient. (TNA, CAB 128/64, CM (78) 41st Conclusions, 30 November 1978, 8)

[2]The 1st division on Callaghan's first day as PM was division No. 106 of the 1975–6 parliamentary session on 5 April 1976 (HC Deb 5 April 1976, cc29–164).

The prime minister concluded the discussion noting:

> The Lord President of the Council should arrange for a debate in the House of Commons on those Community instruments which might be needed to give effect to the decisions to the European Council. This should take place before the Finance Council meeting on 18 December. (TNA, CAB 128/64, CM (78) 41st Conclusions, 30 November 1978, 9)

A day before the cabinet meeting there had been a parliamentary debate on the government's Green Paper on the EMS. Chancellor Healey had opened the debate on behalf of the government and explained that early ERM membership was not going to happen unless the concept of the mechanism was adjusted (Rawstorne 1978). This he had also announced in the same week at a meeting of the PLP (Goodman 1978b). Before, two committees of the National Executive Committee (NEC), which were dominated by the party left, had demanded that the government vetoed the establishment of the EMS at the European level altogether, no matter whether the UK would join it at all. Thus they rejected the government's position to keep all options open for now on EMS and ERM membership (Goodman 1978a). On 30 November the cabinet also discussed the NEC's view on the EMS noting that "it was a mistake to be too influenced by the views expressed by the NEC, which was unrepresentative, and the members of whose committees on this subject were relatively inexperienced" (TNA, CAB 128/64, CM (78) 41st Conclusions, 30 November 1978, 8). The cabinet on 7 December concluded that it wanted to conduct a debate on the EMS that month:

> It would arise on a Motion to take note of a document covering two draft regulations which were required to provide for the European Monetary System to be established. Its scope would not cover all aspects of the European Monetary System, but it would be set in the context of the meeting of the European Council which had taken place in Brussels on the previous Tuesday and should therefore be wide enough to fulfil the Government's undertaking to provide a further opportunity for debate. (TNA, CAB 128/64, CM (78) 42nd Conclusions, 7 December 1978, 1)

As the prime minister on 6 December 1978 in his statement on the European Council had announced that Britain would not join the ERM at this time (see Sect. 10.1), the parliamentary debate on 13 December functioned as planned as an opportunity for debate but was no factor in the decision-making process on the issue.[3]

Callaghan attempted to avoid an open conflict between the government and the party over Europe as it would have severely harmed both (Gowland et al. 2010: 87). He knew that the PLP and other party sections constrained the government's scope in making political decisions on this subject area. Already at a cabinet meeting on 25 February 1977, when the provisions for the first direct elections to the European Parliament had been discussed, he had concluded:

> The Government had a need to carry the Parliamentary Party, the National Executive Committee and the Party in the country with it as far as possible, and could not be expected

---

[3]For the debate, see HC Deb 13 December 1978, cc811–844.

> to carry legislation against the wishes of a majority in the Government Party. (TNA, CAB 128/61, CM (77), 8th Conclusions, 25 February 1977, 4)

There is no indication that he changed his view later. Moreover, the divisions between party and government—as the rebellions in parliament illustrated—were not restricted to Europe. They particularly concerned those issues which divided Labour's left and social democratic wing. For instance, the left regularly opposed the mainly social democratic government's economic and defence policies (Gowland et al. 2010: 87–88; Norton 1980: 432).

The assumption that slim or non-existent majorities tend to have a disciplining effect on the government's parliamentary party cannot be applied to explain the PLP's behaviour under Callaghan (Norton 1980: 460). It showed little unity and solidarity with the government. The possibility that a government defeat in parliament might trigger a snap election appears not to have resulted in MPs showing greater loyalty to the government.

The government's difficult position in parliament, however, had a unifying effect at another political level. According to Callaghan (2006), it strengthened the cohesion of the cabinet:

> I would claim that the Labour Cabinet of 1976 to 1979 would stand comparison with most as a good-tempered body, with a minimum of personal backbiting, very little malicious leaking and a strong feeling of solidarity. Perhaps this was helped by the absence of a Parliamentary majority, the knowledge that our collective life usually hung by a thread and that we ourselves could end it. (444)

To Callaghan the parliamentary party was a constraining factor on European policy. Due to its behaviour, for example, on the European Parliament elections, it was clear that the government could not be sure that its MPs would not defy the whip when voting on this subject area. A decision to join the ERM would have resulted in the introduction of a parliamentary bill on it by the government. It might have failed to gain the necessary parliamentary support due to intraparty protests and could have deepened the split between Labour's pro- and anti-Europeans. As most of the cabinet did not see membership as desirable either, a decision to join the ERM was not to be expected by the government. In his memoirs Callaghan (2006) gave his assessment of the situation also referring to the limits his party put on his leeway:

> I favoured the general idea as likely to bring more order into the currency markets of Europe and the world, but quite apart from my technical concerns I could not travel fast. Many people in the Labour Party remained suspicious of what they thought was too close an entanglement with Europe, and this, coupled with my own and the Treasury's belief that sterling was standing too high to make our entry advantageous, led me some days later to tell Schmidt and Giscard that we could not enter the European Monetary Scheme at the outset. (493)

While there were many rebellions by members of the PLP, Callaghan proved to be a skilful party leader balancing various intraparty interests on Europe. As his own position on European integration was pragmatic and his European policy mainly reactive, he was able to balance the opposing blocks of pro- and anti-Europeans and postponed an open confrontation between those sections of the party. After

Callaghan's resignation from the party leadership, tensions increased and contributed to the decision of a number of social-democratic members to leave Labour to form the Social Democratic Party (SDP) in the early 1980s.

The ERM decision is a fitting example of Callaghan's party management: the government officially supported the EMS, but did not join the ERM, its centre piece. Hence Britain showed support for European integration in principal without adopting significant binding responsibilities in EC monetary integration. Because of this the government neither antagonised the pro-Europeans nor the anti-Europeans in its party on this issue. The compromise to join the EMS without the ERM shielded the government from controversial and dragged-out parliamentary debates on the issue and kept opponents of the government's European policy from gaining a forum in parliament in which they could promote their views.

On the whole, the parliamentary party did constrain James Callaghan's leeway on European monetary policy-making and—equally important—he perceived it to do so, which in turn influenced his strategies and policy decisions in this subject area.

9.2 Margaret Thatcher

When she became prime minister in May 1979, Margaret Thatcher had less parliamentary experience than her predecessor Callaghan had had when he had become head of government. Yet she had already been a MP for 20 years (Rose 2001: 133).

In 1975 Conservative MPs were open to Thatcher as new party leader because she allocated posts based on the competence and capability of a particular MP and looked for direct contact with the members of her party (Norton 1980: 451). Thatcher's position as party leader then was not secure. Her only success so far had been defeating Edward Heath as leader (Clark 1999: 471). She was keen to keep in touch with fellow Tory MPs. She frequently met them for dinner at the House and regularly met members of the party's backbench committees (Norton 1985: 39). Unlike Callaghan, though, she did not regularly visit the Tea Room or the bars of the House of Commons (Kavanagh and Seldon 2000: 196). Over the years Thatcher lost touch with her MPs. Philip Norton, for instance, as early as 1985 suggested in a study on Conservative backbench behaviour that there were signs that she moved away from her party management style of the early 1980s due to the large parliamentary majority she had won at the 1983 general election (Norton 1985: 39). This impression grew over the years: when she had started out as party leader she had wanted to avoid Edward Heath's aloofness from the Parliamentary Conservative Party (PCP), yet many Tory MPs elected after 1987 maintained they had neither met her personally nor had been to Downing Street (Dunleavy and Jones 1993: 288).

Thatcher, too, regularly worked with the Whips to manage the party. In her view a government could only successfully get its planned legislation through parliament, if there was a good working relationship between the Whips' Office, the '1922 committee' of Tory backbenchers, the Leader of the House as well as the prime minister and his office (Thatcher 2011: 34).

Parliamentary majorities were no problem for Thatcher. At the 1979 general election the Conservatives gained a majority of 43 seats, which they expanded at the 1983 general election to 144. In 1987 they achieved a majority of 102 seats (Butler and Butler 2006: 108).

Yet Tory MPs were by no means deferential to the prime minister. A month after the 1983 general election, for instance, Conservative backbenchers took several decisions which were not in line with her preferences: they elected a speaker, whom Thatcher did not approve of. They voted for an increase of their pay, which she did not support. Moreover, they voted against the death penalty, which she advocated (Butler and Kavanagh 1988: 11). Between 1979 and 1983 there were 159 intraparty rebellions. Between 1983 and 1987 there were 203 and between 1987 and 1992 Conservative MPs voted on 198 occasions against their government (Cowley and Stuart 2003: 317).[4] Concerning intraparty opposition Thatcher's premiership was quieter than Callaghan's. He had had to deal with 233 intraparty rebellions in parliament between April 1976 and May 1979. Yet the PCP during Thatcher's second term (1983–1987) turned out to be more rebellious than the one under John Major's leadership between 1992 and 1997. Then Conservative MPs voted in 13% of the divisions against their own government. Between 1983 and 1987 this was 16%. Even during Thatcher's first term as prime minister the degree of rebellions was with 12% only marginally below the percentage of the rebellions between 1992 and 1997 (Cowley and Norton 1999: 86). However, during Thatcher's term in office fewer MPs were involved in these rebellions. Between 1979 and 1992 just 9% of the rebellions included 20 or more MPs. This rose to 25% in the 1992–1997 parliament. Most consisted of one to ten MPs casting dissenting votes—this was the case for 68% of all rebellions during that time (Cowley and Norton 1999: 87). The government lost one important vote in each of its three terms due to an intraparty revolt. Yet none concerned European policy (Cowley and Norton 1996: 15–17).[5] Apart from this, Tory rebels only seldom managed to block parliamentary bills through rebellions, because the government's majority created a large threshold that had to be overcome to succeed (Cowley and Norton 1996: 17–18, 20).

European policy had no particular significance in the intraparty revolts during Thatcher's premiership. For instance, on important Conservative backbench rebellions in the time period 1979–1983, Philip Norton only lists one referring to European policy. It was in June 1982 when 9 Conservative MPs dissented (by voting against the government or by abstention) on a motion criticising the EC

[4]Cowley and Norton (1996: 16) list marginally different numbers: 1979–83: 158 rebellions, 1983–87: 202, 1987–1992: 199.

[5]1982: 23 MPs voted against the government and 28 abstained at a vote on the immigration bill. 1986: 72 MPs voted against the government at the second reading of the Shops Bill. 1990: 23 MPs voted against the government and many MPs abstained on a vote on a clause of the National Health Service and Community Care Bill (Cowley and Norton 1996: 15–17).

and European Union. Other policy areas such as employment and immigration were much more contested and here Conservative MPs rebelled in higher numbers against the government (Norton 1985: 30).[6]

The Thatcher administration, nevertheless, was not willing to take risks on European policy legislation it wanted to enact. During the ratification of the Single European Act in 1986, for example, a 'three-line whip'[7], the highest level of pressure on MPs to take part in a vote and to vote in line with the government, and a 'guillotine' were issued (Miller 2008: 2). The latter is a mechanism "used by governments to limit the amount of time that MPs can spend debating a particular stage of a Bill in the House of Commons" (UK Parliament 2016a). This indicates that the government wanted to ensure that the treaty was ratified soon and not postponed by continuous amendments brought in by its opponents. Furthermore, the PM and not the foreign secretary was sponsor of the bill in the House of Commons, which increased the pressure on Conservative MPs not to dissent from the government's position. While there was some opposition on the Tory back-benches against the SEA, the government achieved that only 17 of their MPs revolted (Wall 2008: 73–74).

Moreover, in her first term Thatcher, despite a clear majority, regularly altered policies to avoid a rebellion by Tory MPs. Thus the government anticipated dissent on its backbenches and changed its policy accordingly (Cowley and Norton 1996: 40; Norton 1985: 28–29).

On the question of British ERM membership the PM initially did not have to take her parliamentary party much into account. There was no wide-ranging debate of the issue. Discussions were limited to the core executive, more specifically to Chancellor Lawson, Foreign Secretary Howe and her. The issue was not on the full Cabinet's agenda and only few members of the government and officials knew about the dispute. David Hannay, for instance, the UK's Permanent Representative in Brussels from 1985 to 1990, said that he was not aware of the discussions between the three at the time.[8] While it is clear that Chancellor Major and Foreign Secretary Hurd later effectively applied pressure on Thatcher to agree to ERM membership (see Sect. 8.2.2), it cannot be assessed in how far she felt pressured by Conservative MPs to agree to the policy change. There was, in any case, dissent on the Tory backbenches over Europe in general as well as over ERM membership with MPs calling for a more positive approach to European integration (Thompson 1996: 162; Stephens 1989).

Thatcher's European policy interests and strategies—in particular with regard to plans for monetary union—did at the end of her premiership lead to increased

[6]Cowley and Norton (1996) in their analysis of Conservative MPs' voting behaviour between 1979 and 1992 do not mention any European policy vote as problematic during that time either.

[7]Definition: "A 'three-line whip', when an item is underlined three times, indicates that attendance is required and pairing is not normally allowed. This is imposed on important occasions, such as second readings of major Bills and motions of no confidence" (Miller 2008: 2).

[8]Interview with D. Hannay, 29 March 2010.

discontent and divisions in the party. This was prominently illustrated by Geoffrey Howe's resignation as Leader of the House of Commons. In his resignation speech on 13 November 1990 he explained his decision to leave the government with the incompatibility of his European policy view and strategy with hers. He particularly referred to European monetary policy (HC Deb 13 November 1990, cc461–465). Howe pointed out how problematic Thatcher's attitude to European integration was for Britain and for the party:

> The tragedy is—and it is for me personally, for my party, for our whole people and for my Right Hon. friend herself, a very real tragedy—that the Prime Minister's perceived attitude towards Europe is running increasingly serious risks for the future of our nation. It risks minimizing our influence and maximizing our chances of being once again shut out. (HC Deb 13 November 1990, c465)

His appeal that it was time for other Tory MPs to assess their position towards the premier and whether her political aims were in Britain's interest (HC Deb 13 November 1990, c465) formed the prelude for Michael Heseltine's candidacy for the party leadership as a challenge to Thatcher. The fact that Howe's speech had such an effect indicates that European policy then played a greater role for the parliamentary party than at the beginning of Thatcher's premiership. Moreover, with two intergovernmental conferences coming up, leading party members concluded that Thatcher was no longer the right person to safeguard British interests in this context. Yet Europe was not the only reason why she lost the support of her parliamentary party as there were also, for instance, worsening economic conditions and the unpopular poll tax (George 1998: 230). In the first round of the leadership contest in November 1990, 204 Tory MPs voted for her, while 152 chose Heseltine. Thatcher would have needed four more votes to avoid a second ballot. She initially had wanted to put her name down for the second ballot, but decided to resign after a number of senior Tories—including most of her cabinet—told her she would not win (Seldon 1998: 122–123).

However, for the major part of Thatcher's premiership Europe posed no significant problem with regard to her parliamentary party management. Although significant European policy decisions were taken during her premiership, such as on the SEA/Common Market, the government did not have to face strong opposition on its European policy from its parliamentary party. Yet over the course of Thatcher's premiership the discontent with the prime minister, who increasingly exhibited a Eurosceptic attitude, grew as did diverging views on European integration in the party. This particularly concerned EMU.

9.3 John Major

John Major, in comparison with his predecessors, had less parliamentary experience upon becoming prime minister in 1990, having been an MP for only 11 years (Rose 2001: 133). But from 1983 to 1985 he had worked in the Whips' Office and had displayed a particular talent in understanding the mood of Tory MPs. He was considered "one of the shrewdest and most effective whips in recent memory" (Riddell 1994: 47). Yet over the course of his premiership there were claims that he lost touch with his fellow MPs (Kavanagh and Seldon 2000: 233).

The balance of power in parliament presented Major with greater problems than Margaret Thatcher. At the 1992 general election the Conservatives were returned to office under his leadership, albeit with a reduced majority of 21 seats (Butler and Butler 2006: 109). 54 first-time Conservative MPs had been elected, many of whom were Thatcher supporters and Eurosceptics (Seldon 1998: 285). As a result there was now a fairly large and comparably united group of Eurosceptic MPs on the Conservative backbenches (Thomas 1998: 45). Already in the 1980s there had been highly rebellious MPs, yet then these had hardly any influence. This was different now and they could no longer be ignored (Seldon 1998: 286). This was also because this group of MPs, who did not hesitate to vote against the government's European policy, was larger than the government's parliamentary majority.[9] The Conservative majority further declined over the course of the parliament due to by-election losses and defections. Between the 1992 general election and the dissolution of parliament in March 1997 the Conservatives lost 15 seats (House of Commons Information Office 2003: 2). In parliament Major also had to rely on support from other parties such as the Ulster Unionists to get legislation enacted (Alderman 1996: 9, 11).

The increasing loss of public support—as seen in opinion polls, by-elections as well as regional and European elections—helped to make the management of the Conservative parliamentary party more difficult as Major's status in the party declined (Kavanagh and Seldon 2000: 236). Particularly the ERM exit in autumn 1992 contributed to a massive loss of public support for the Major government. The Tories lost their reputation for being competent managers of finances and the economy, and Major's approval ratings declined sharply (Seldon 1998: 322–323; Geddes 2013: 234). Disputes over the government's European policy caused much trouble in the parliamentary party with continuous infighting. Major wanted these fights to stop. In a bid to silence his intraparty critics he decided in 1995 to resign from the party leadership and force a leadership election (Major 2000: 608, 610, 626). Although he won, the outcome suggests that the result was less based on support for his political course than on a lack of alternatives. 89 MPs had voted against him and there were abstentions (Bale 2016: 53–54). It was obvious that there was still discontent among MPs. Thus Major's plan to reassert his authority by re-election failed (Rose 2001: 20).

Due to the unstable parliamentary position as well as the declining majority during the 1992 parliament, a close working relationship with the Whips' Office, particularly the Chief Whip, was similarly important for Major as it had been for Callaghan (Kavanagh and Seldon 2000: 233).

The Conservative Party under John Major gained a reputation for being extraordinarily rebellious, in particular after the 1992 election. Yet this is not accurate.

[9]Interview with S. Wall, 8 January 2010.

Between 1992 and 1997 Tory MPs rebelled in 174 parliamentary divisions against the government. This amounted to 13% of all divisions—a lower number than during Thatcher's second term in office (1983–1987), which had seen dissension in 16% of all divisions (Cowley and Norton 1999: 84–86). But the number of Conservative MPs voting against the government had risen compared to the Thatcher era: between 1992 and 1997 20 or more MPs took part in 25% of the rebellions. Between 1979 and 1992 this had merely been 9%. At 66% of the intraparty revolts between 1992 and 1997 up to nine MPs took part. During Thatcher's premiership this had been 68% (Cowley and Norton 1999: 87). Between 1992 and 1997 175 MPs voted against their government at least once. This amounted to a little more than half of the Parliamentary Conservative Party. But of these 175 only 8 (2% of Tory MPs) voted at least 50 times against the government during the parliament. Meanwhile, 48% of Conservative MPs did not even once vote against their government. For the period 1979–1992 it had been 42% (Cowley and Norton 1999: 88, 89). Thus, Conservative MPs under Major's leadership in general were not much more rebellious than they had been under Thatcher during the 1980s. But the intraparty revolts focused much on one policy field: European policy.

When the Maastricht Treaty negotiations were concluded it had not been foreseen that the subsequent ratification process would become a significant problem for the Major government. Before the final European level negotiations the PM had laid out in detail in the House of Commons on 20 November 1991 what he was willing to accept at these negotiations. Only six Eurosceptics on the Conservative benches had then voted against the government's negotiating position. Nine had abstained.[10] With a majority of 101 votes Major considered his negotiating stance accepted (Seldon 1998: 244–245). After the Maastricht summit and his parliamentary statement on the outcome of it on 11 December 1991 (see Sect. 10.3), a 2-day debate on the treaty began on 18 December. Major once again explained the outcome and at the end of the debate only seven Tory MPs voted against the government's line, while three (including Margaret Thatcher) abstained. Although the treaty was signed on 7 February 1992, the government decided to postpone its ratification until after the next general election which had to be called by spring 1992. It was feared that Thatcher and her supporters might oppose ratification, and Major wanted to avoid the governmental party to appear divided ahead of a general election. If ratification took place after the election, it was assumed there would be sufficient time until the next one in 1996/7 for the public to forget about eventual Conservative party divisions due to the Maastricht Treaty (Seldon 1998: 250–251). Thus, the ratification process began after the general election. However, when the Danes voted against the treaty in a referendum in June 1992, Major decided to follow his Whips' advice and temporarily suspended the ratification process (Major 2000: 348–349). The subsequent treaty ratification in spring and summer 1993 cost a lot

[10]Abstentions cannot automatically be seen as opposition as the parliamentary records do not state why someone did not vote, e.g. the MP might have been ill (Cowley and Stuart 2003: 330).

of time and was often frustrating for the government (Kavanagh and Seldon 2000: 236).[11] The support which the government had received by its MPs on the outcome of the negotiations at the end of 1991 gave way to increasing criticism. For several the Danish vote had been a catalyst which resulted in them showing increasing hostility to the treaty in public (Seldon 1998: 295). 84 of them signed a 'Fresh Start' Early Day Motion on 3 June, demanding the government to use the Danish referendum outcome to renegotiate Britain's relationship with the EC (Baker et al. 1999: 82). Like the Thatcher government on the ratification of the Single European Act in the 1980s, the Conservative leadership decided to enforce a 'three-line whip' on the Maastricht Treaty bill. This was to ensure that all Tory MPs voted, so that the government could achieve the necessary majority to ratify the treaty (Miller 2008: 2). While the Whips had considered allowing a free vote on the treaty, Major refused. He argued that it was the party's obligation to ratify the treaty, which the government had agreed to after having consulted parliament on the negotiating position beforehand (Major 2000: 351). At the treaty bill's second reading on 21 May 1992, 22 Conservative MPs voted against the government and several abstained. This vote marked the beginning of a series of 62 intraparty rebellions against the Maastricht bill. During these 62 rebellions more than 1100 votes were cast by members of the PCP against their own government. These votes amounted to 60% of all votes against the government in the 1992 parliament by the ruling party. Additionally, a high number of Conservative MPs abstained. The government faced the largest intraparty rebellion during the third reading of the bill on 20 May 1993 when 41 Tory MPs voted against it (Cowley and Norton 1999: 90–91). Only by linking the vote on the *European Communities (Amendment) Bill* to a vote of confidence did the government manage to successfully complete the ratification process (Major 2000: 383–384).

Comparing the intraparty revolts during the ratification of the Maastricht Treaty with those over other issues between 1992 and 1997, it becomes clear that at 51% of the Non-Maastricht-rebellions only one government MP rebelled. Yet at almost half of the Maastricht rebellions (48%) between 20 and 29 MPs voted against their own government. But the largest series of rebellions in the 1992 parliament was not related to Europe. It was over the *Firearms (Amendment) Bill* in late 1996. Spread over eight rebellions more than a third of the PCP (120 MPs) then voted against their government (Cowley and Norton 1999: 91, 93).

The Conservative MPs' behaviour in the 1992 parliament was compared to that of the PLP at the end of Callaghan's government. Yet this claim does not hold when looking at the number of government defeats in parliament because ruling party MPs had voted against the government. In the 5 years of the Labour administration (1974–1979) the government had been defeated 23 times in parliament due to backbencher revolts. 21 of these defeats had taken place between January 1978 and March 1979. Under Major the government introduced 195 bills in the 1992

[11]Between the second and third reading of the bill there were 210 hours of parliamentary debate (Cowley and Norton 1996: 25).

parliament. Only one did not make it onto the statute book (Cowley and Norton 1996: 45, 1999: 101–102).

On the question of ERM membership it became apparent that the government's freedom of movement was constrained by the PCP. On 17 September 1992, a day after the ERM exit, the cabinet announced after its weekly meeting that the pound should re-join the ERM as soon as possible (Stephens 1997: 264). Yet during the parliamentary debate on the issue on 24 September, the PM said that he did not see a chance for sterling to return into the ERM any time soon (HC Deb 24 September 1992, c4). This statement has also to be seen in the context of a motion supported by more than 70 Tory MPs demanding the government to refrain from attempting to put sterling back into the ERM. Under the impression of the difficult ratification process of the Maastricht Treaty it was clear to Major and his pro-European cabinet colleagues that requesting an early return into the ERM did not make much sense (Stephens 1997: 272–273).

The management of the parliamentary party on European policy was also so difficult for Major, because the so-called 'Maastricht rebels' did not oppose the government's European policy for the same reasons. Nonetheless, they made up a cohesive group. They had their own 'whipping'-system in parliament (Major 2000: 365; Cowley and Norton 1999: 91). Moreover, the rebels also used the media to publicise their differences from the government, which made the Tories' intraparty divisions more obvious than had been the case before (Cowley and Norton 1999: 102). This also helps to explain why the party appeared so much more rebellious during Major's premiership than, for instance, during Thatcher's. Major attempted to secure backbencher support by making deals with them and altering policy to avoid dissension. If this was not possible, such as on the Maastricht Bill, the government tried to avoid rebellions by accepting parliamentary motions they had before rejected or by refraining from taking a vote on an issue at all (Cowley and Norton 1996: 40–41). Major's attempts to anticipate his MPs' voting behaviour and to avoid revolts by adjusting policy led to criticism. Norman Lamont in his resignation speech in June 1993, for example, criticised the fact that the government paid too much attention to the views of party managers when making policy (HC Deb 9 June 1993, cc284–285).

But the government also actively tried to discipline Eurosceptic backbenchers to vote in line with the government. Major, for instance, attempted to convince party activists to press the Maastricht rebels to follow the government's line. As the activists were often more Eurosceptic than their MPs, this strategy failed (Cowley 2005: 64).

The PM also used the tool of withdrawing the whip from MPs to discipline rebellious party colleagues. This means that an MP is excluded from the parliamentary party, though he keeps his seat in parliament (UK Parliament 2016c). In autumn 1994 eight MPs had the whip withdrawn, because they had dissented from the government line by abstaining during the legislative process of the *European Communities (Finance) Bill*. The bill referred to a decision to increase the European budget. The decision had been taken under Major's chairmanship at the Edinburgh European Council in December 1992, when the UK had held the EU presidency. It now had to be transposed into national law. Major had already made clear in the Queen's Speech at the beginning of the 1994–95 parliamentary session that his government was not willing to compromise on this bill. Instead, it saw the successful legislative process on this as a question of confidence for the government. The government planned to combine the vote on the bill with a question of confidence to avoid any opposition on it by the parliamentary party. To secure a quick legislative process for the *European Communities (Finance) Bill,* the government set a tight timetable. The bill was also short to avoid the possibility of many amendments, which would prolong the legislative process. The parliamentary party, however, was critical of the bill from the start. The government's strategy of combining it with a vote of confidence was also opposed by several backbenchers (Alderman 1996: 5). The Whips put strong pressure on Tory MPs to vote in line with the government. For instance, ill MPs were asked to take part in the divisions to ensure a majority. Yet on the bill's second reading vote on 28 November 1994 eight Conservative MPs abstained. Their abstention did not risk the government's majority which was helped by Labour MPs who voted against their party line. Nevertheless the government withdrew the whip from these Tory MPs. Another voluntarily resigned the whip a day later (Alderman 1996: 7–9).

By withdrawing the whip Major wanted to make clear to his MPs that the government would not accept a lack of support and discipline on European policy in parliament. Yet, at the same time, he reduced his parliamentary majority to a very slim one as the government was continuously losing seats in by-elections (George 1998: 237). The strategy of withdrawing the whip for disloyal behaviour turned out to be unsuitable, because the whipless MPs still had support for their actions from large sections of their constituencies. Moreover, they remained in close contact with other Eurosceptics in the PCP. Meanwhile, it became more difficult for the Whips to calculate division outcomes in parliament, as the party leadership did not have any influence anymore on the whipless MPs. Furthermore, these MPs were able to present themselves as martyrs and to further highlight the existing intraparty conflicts over Europe (Alderman 1996: 18). In late 1994 the *European Communities (Finance) Act* was passed in the third reading with 25 Conservative abstentions (including the whipless MPs). But the government's intraparty problems over Europe did not end as there were further parliamentary revolts by Tory MPs such as over fisheries policy. Moreover, the Ulster Unionists, on whose backing the government had counted since 1993, ended their arrangement to support the government in parliament in early 1995 due to the latter's Northern Ireland policy (Alderman 1996: 10–11). Because of the government's weak position in parliament Major was soon under pressure to readmit the eight MPs into the PCP without gaining any concessions from them. This meant that they made no promises that they would support the government's European policy in parliament in the future (Thomas 1998: 47). Major later justified his decision to readmit them by arguing that the whipless MPs had suggested that they wanted to work with the government. His parliamentary private secretary Graham Bright shared this assessment. However, the Whip's Office was more sceptical and only reluctantly agreed to the MPs' readmission. It soon became clear that their judgement had been more accurate, as the MPs in question immediately after readmission to the parliamentary party explained publicly that they were not willing to support the government on its European policy (Major 2000: 605–606).

Considering the circumstances Major faced at the time, he showed much sensibility in his party management. Through the positions he took on Europe in general and on the single currency, Major attempted to avoid a split of his party (Kavanagh and Seldon 2000: 239). He considered this as one of his key achievements: "I was pleased to keep Britain in Europe and to prevent the Conservative Party from splitting" (Major 2000: XXI). Yet his attempts to balance entirely opposing European policy attitudes resulted in a lack of clear leadership of the Conservatives from their party leader on European policy. Moreover, his positioning on Europe to avoid a party split affected his standing with the party's pro-Europeans as well as the Eurosceptics as it "diminished him in the eyes of both sides" (Kavanagh and Seldon 2000: 239). Furthermore, the limits of Major's strategy to gain parliamentary support by compromising with intraparty rebels and making concessions to them became apparent, as some parts of the European legislation were not open to negotiation (Cowley and Norton 1996: 44).

Yet in spite of the intraparty conflicts over Europe, the PCP in the later years of Major's premiership voted in a fairly united way in parliament. In the first parliamentary session 1992–93—when the Maastricht Treaty was ratified—there were 93 rebellions by Conservative backbenchers against their own government. Yet the remaining four sessions until the 1997 general election saw altogether merely 81 rebellions by Conservative MPs (Cowley and Norton 1999: 99). Thus it is likely that the decline in the government's majority did in fact have a disciplining effect on the voting behaviour of Conservative MPs in the 1992 parliament. However, European policy, as, for example, illustrated by the difficulties of passing the *European Communities (Finance) Bill* into law in 1994, remained an area where backbenchers were willing to rebel. This damaged Major and his government politically as the parliamentary debates on Europe highlighted the intraparty divisions over the issue and fostered the public's assessment that the Conservatives were generally divided and at odds with each other (Cowley and Norton 1996: 27).

9.4 Tony Blair

When Tony Blair became prime minister in 1997 he had been an MP for 14 years. Yet, in contrast to his three predecessors, he had never held a ministerial post in those years (Rose 2001: 133).

The parliamentary arithmetic posed no problem for the government during Blair's time in office (1997–2007). In 1997 Labour gained a parliamentary majority of 179. At the 2001 and 2005 general elections as well, the Conservatives were not able to present themselves as a convincing alternative, as Labour retained a majority of 167 in 2001 and 66 in 2005 (Butler and Butler 2006: 109).

On the management of his parliamentary party Blair, like his predecessors, worked with the Whips' Office. Due to the significant parliamentary majorities at least early in his premiership, it was not necessary for the Chief Whip to visit No. 10 Downing Street as often as had been the case during Callaghan's or Major's premiership (Kavanagh and Seldon 2000: 284). Blair met weekly after Prime Minister's Question Time the Labour Party's Parliamentary Committee. It consisted of six backbenchers and the chairman of the Parliamentary Labour Party (PLP). Like the Whips, this body informed the PM about matters of interest to fellow Labour MPs. Additionally, Blair regularly invited small groups of MPs to No. 10 for talks. He tried to meet each Labour MP personally at least once a year, yet did not regularly visit the Tea Room to meet MPs like Callaghan had done (Powell 2010: 141; Kavanagh and Seldon 2000: 284–285). According to his chief of staff Jonathan Powell (2010: 161), Blair felt that a stronger presence in parliament was less profitable as he, for instance, thought that the participation in parliamentary debates resulted only in the media highlighting the opposition leader's performance rather than that of the prime minister. Yet being less present in the Commons meant that there were fewer occasions for MPs to speak to him. Similarly, his decision to reduce Prime Minister's Question Time to once per week early in his premiership (see Sect. 6.2.1) also meant that MPs had less opportunity to meet their party leader and to talk to him informally.

Initially Labour MPs gained a reputation for being obedient, though the 1997 parliament saw 96 rebellions. Considering that the Major government during the 1992–93 session had to deal with 94 intraparty revolts over the ratification process of the Maastricht Treaty alone (see Sect. 9.3), the low number of intraparty rebellions during Blair's first term is remarkable. Yet on average the rebellions were larger than those during the Conservatives' period in office between 1979 and 1997. The average size of a rebellion by government MPs was 15 in the 1997 parliament. In the 1992 parliament, for instance, it had been 11. Moreover, 133 MPs voted at some time in the 1997 parliament against the government, which was about half of the Labour backbenches (Cowley and Stuart 2003: 315, 317–319). During Blair's second term the PLP showed itself to be much more rebellious. This included more than 200 Labour MPs, who voted in 259 cases against the government. Thus between 2001 and 2005 Labour backbenchers rebelled on 20.8% of all votes (Cowley 2005: 5–6). During the last 2 years of Blair's premiership parliamentary revolts became even more frequent: between the May 2005 general election and Blair's resignation in 2007 there were intraparty rebellions on 130 votes. This was at 26% of all votes (own calculation based on data from Cowley and Stuart 2006; Cowley and Stuart 2007a) Overall, Blair's period in office (May 1997 to June 2007) saw 6520 dissenting votes cast by Labour MPs. In comparison, during Thatcher's premiership (May 1979 to November 1990) there had been 4259 rebellious votes by MPs of the governing party. Labour MPs under Blair revolted on a range of issues such as defence and foreign policy or immigration (Stuart 2009: 182).

Yet European policy was no issue which featured significantly in Labour backbencher rebellions. Considering that Labour MPs had often rebelled against the European policy line taken by their leadership in the 1990s—e.g. during the ratification of the Maastricht Treaty in 1992/3 around 40 times—this development is remarkable. However, between 1997 and 2007 MPs rebelled in only 19 cases against their government's European policy. Three took place in the first term, 13 in the second and another three in the last 2 years of his premiership. Overall, they made up only 4% of all intraparty rebellions during Blair's period in office. Moreover, the number of revolting MPs is hardly comparable with that during Callaghan's or Major's premiership. Between 1997 and 2007 in total 19 MPs were involved in these rebellions over Europe. At the largest revolt in July 2003, 15 MPs voted against a government resolution supporting the Convention on the Future of Europe's draft treaty (Cowley and Stuart 2007b: 1–2).

Looking at these numbers, particularly in comparison with the rebellions on European policy his predecessor John Major had faced, it is clear that Europe was not a subject area on which Blair needed to fear that his parliamentary party might not support him. Instead, the issue appeared to be of little interest to Labour backbenchers or as Philip Cowley (2008) put it: "If there's anything that unites Labour MPs nowadays it's this: most of them find the subject of Europe boring." This assessment appears even more plausible if one takes into account that Labour MPs were willing to oppose the government on other policies. Blair's Iraq policy, for instance, saw the largest rebellion by governing party MPs in over 150 years, when in March 2003 139 Labour MPs voted against the government (Stuart 2009: 185).

Although Europe did not appear to be a highly sensitive issue in the PLP, Tony Blair did not want to take any risks on important European policy votes. For the ratification of the Nice Treaty in 2004, for example, a 'three-line whip' for government MPs was issued just as it had been the case with the SEA under Thatcher and the Maastricht Treaty under Major. While 100 Labour MPs abstained from the vote and thereby ignored the 'three-line whip', the government managed to ratify the treaty with a large majority. For the ratification of the later abandoned Constitutional Treaty the Blair administration again put down a 'three-line whip' and a 'programme motion', which allowed the government to allocate the time to be spend on debate at each stage of the bill's legislative process (Miller 2008: 2–3; UK Parliament 2016b).

Blair wanted the Parliamentary Labour Party to be disciplined and united. This was to be one of the key differences between Old and New Labour as well as between Labour and Conservative Party. In his first speech to the PLP after the 1997 election, he emphasised the need for the party to be disciplined (Cowley 2007: 25–26). That Labour had been in opposition for 18 years and had lost four consecutive general elections initially helped to discipline MPs. When Labour came into government their MPs desperately wanted to avoid doing anything which could send them back into opposition. The wish to present the party as united—also in the context of the experience of the previous Conservative government and their divisions over Europe—significantly contributed to Labour MPs rebelling comparably rarely against their own government in Blair's first term. But the self-discipline of Labour MPs declined over the course of the 1997 parliament. Particularly, once they realised that the Conservative opposition remained weak in the opinions polls, rebellions against their government were no longer viewed as that much of a problem (Cowley 2005: 58–60). Moreover, by the end of 2001 almost a quarter of the PLP had been in government but had already left it again. Thus a number of MPs had personal reasons to be unhappy with the leadership, for example, for having been dismissed from ministerial office. There were also those who realised that they would never gain a government post and who began to rebel because of that (Cowley and Stuart 2005: 25).

According to Jonathan Powell the prime minister, by way of personal conversations with rebellious MPs, tried to persuade them to follow the government line and appealed to their loyalty to the party. At the same time, Powell claimed that a large degree of intraparty rebellions against Blair's policies was organised by an unofficial whipping organisation controlled by Chancellor Gordon Brown, over which Blair at times was not able to prevail (Powell 2010: 156–157). The Labour party leadership also tried—as Major had before—to pressure the PLP to discipline. Shortly before Labour entered the government in 1997, the guidance rules for members of the PLP were tightened. In the case of repeated rebellions against the leadership there was the threat of losing the whip or even being suspended from the party. Yet no Labour MP was suspended from the PLP or lost the whip due to repeatedly rebellious behaviour in parliament during Blair's premiership (Cowley 2005: 63). There had been considerations to do so in the case of particularly rebellious MPs, but the party leadership decided not to go through with it, because they did not want to do the same error as John Major had done when he withdrew the whip from several Eurosceptic backbenchers in 1994 (Powell 2010: 156) (see Sect. 9.3). The party leadership also attempted to discipline MPs by informing the local constituency parties of their MPs' voting behaviour in the hope they would discipline particularly rebellious ones. This strategy was as unsuccessful as the attempts of the Major government had been, because the local party often expected their MPs in parliament to be rebellious rather than deferential (Cowley 2005: 63). Additionally, the government increasingly compromised over several bills to avoid rebellions by the PLP—particularly in Blair's third term when Labour's majority had declined from 167 to 66 (Stuart 2009: 186).

On the whole, the Parliamentary Labour Party particularly after Blair's first term did trouble him, but not on European policy. It should also be taken into account that on the issue of joining EMU no legislation was brought into parliament. This was because Blair could not achieve a breakthrough on it in cabinet, particularly with respect to his chancellor. Thus it remains unclear how the PLP would have reacted, if they actually had had to vote on euro membership, particularly as the issue was a contested one in the Labour Party (see Sect. 5.2.1).[12]

[12]Gamble and Kelly (2000) provide a detailed survey of the various attitudes on EMU in the Labour Party at that time.

Table 9.1 Size of the governmental party and position on Europe 1976–2007 (own illustration)

Prime Minister	Parliamentary arithmetic	Parliamentary party position on Europe
J. Callaghan (1976–1979)	Lack of a parliamentary majority	Strong intraparty divisions over Europe
M. Thatcher (1979–1990)	Clear majority, particularly large in 2nd and 3rd term	Increasing intraparty tension over Europe at the end of her premiership
J. Major (1990–1997)	Sharp decline of the majority in 1992, then small and further declining majority	Strong intraparty divisions over Europe
T. Blair (1997–2007)	Large, but declining majority particularly in the 3rd term	Weak intraparty tension over Europe

9.5 The Parliamentary Party and Prime Ministerial Political Leadership

Looking at their parliamentary party with regard to size and position on Europe, as Table 9.1 shows, each prime minister analysed here faced a different situation.

Considering the theses on prime ministerial and collective leadership, the latter can be applied to Major's premiership with regard to the parliamentary party and his management of it—but only on European policy. Major's leeway here was constrained by the controversial debate about it among his fellow Conservative MPs. He had to take into account the diverging attitudes in his parliamentary party when trying to enact his legislative programme in this area such as on the ratification of the Maastricht Treaty. To avoid an intraparty split which could have endangered his power base, he opted for policies which were acceptable to pro-Europeans as well as Eurosceptics such as the opt-out on EMU. The intraparty discussions focused on EMU, the future European Union, Britain's role in it and the ERM exit in autumn 1992. But as the number of revolts by Conservative MPs between 1992 and 1997 have illustrated, the parliamentary party was overall not much more rebellious than it had previously been under Thatcher's leadership (see Table 9.2). Their dissenting behaviour predominately focused on European policy. Therefore, with regard to this subject area, one can assume a constraining effect of the parliamentary party on Major's political leadership and his possibilities to shape his government's decisions.

Looking at James Callaghan and the PLP during his premiership, it can also be concluded that his leeway in European policy was constrained by his parliamentary party. Therefore in his case the collective leadership thesis applies with regard to his party in parliament. Like Major, Callaghan had to take into account the diverging attitudes in his parliamentary party when trying to enact his legislative programme in this area such as on the legislation on the electoral system for the European Parliament elections. To avoid an intraparty split which could have endangered his power base, he also opted for policies which were acceptable to pro-Europeans as well as Eurosceptics, such as joining the EMS but not the ERM. This was even more

Table 9.2 Rebellions by the parliamentary party in government 1976–2007 (Cowley and Stuart 2003: 317, 2006, 2007a; Cowley 2005: 5; House of Commons Library 2016)

Parliament	No. of rebellions by government MPs	No. of all votes	Rebellions as a percentage of all votes[a]	Prime Minister
1976–1979	233	995	23.4%	Callaghan
1979–1983	159	1295	12.3%	Thatcher
1983–1987	203	1264	16.1%	Thatcher
1987–1992	198	1596	12.4%	Thatcher/ Major
1992–1997	174	1294	13.4%	Major
1997–2001	96	1279	7.5%	Blair
2001–2005	259	1246	20.8%	Blair
2005–2007[b]	130	500	26%	Blair

[a]Percentage values are own calculation based on the sources above-mentioned
[b]These do not include votes cast under PM Gordon Brown between 27 June and the end of the session on 30 October 2007

important for him since he led a minority government. In Callaghan's case, however, European policy was merely one of the issues on which his backbenchers dissented. In contrast to Major's parliamentary party, whose rebellions focused mainly on Europe, the backbencher rebellions on European policy between 1976 and 1979 only accounted for 14.6% of all rebellions by Labour MPs against their government (see Sect. 9.1). The PLP's voting behaviour between 1976 and 1979 showed how deeply split the party already was. Yet it also has to be taken into account that Callaghan himself did not show particular ambition to further Britain's European integration. However, he neither pursued the goal to take the UK out of the European integration process. But according to his Political Secretary Tom McNally, after the 1975 referendum on EC membership Callaghan "was quite ready to park Europe as an issue. Not least because it had been very divisive within the party and therefore he wanted to put it on the backburner and that is where it was."[13] Party unity was his priority and not forcing through political decisions against resistance from his party.

With regard to the suggestion that slim or non-existent majorities can have a disciplining effect on the government's parliamentary party (Cowley and Norton 1996: 41), there are also differences between the premierships of Callaghan and Major. The PLP under Callaghan did not exhibit much discipline despite lacking a majority. At the risk of bringing down the government it voted on 233 occasions against it (see Table 9.2). This was different with the PCP under Major. After the difficult ratification of the Maastricht Treaty and under the impression of a declining majority, Tory MPs did not vote much against the government in the following parliamentary sessions (1993/94–1996/97) (see Sect. 9.3). Yet as the comparably low number of backbencher revolts included European policy issues such as the expansion of the European budget and as they were accompanied by controversial intraparty debates, it did not change the public impression that the Conservative parliamentary party was at odds with each other and lacked solidarity.

[13]Interview with T. McNally, 22 March 2010.

In the cases of Margaret Thatcher and Tony Blair, one can speak of a form of prime ministerial predominance with regard to their parliamentary party. While both might not have been able to persuade their fellow MPs to adopt their attitude to Europe, the revolts by members of their parliamentary parties on Europe were limited.

Thatcher, for instance, was fairly unconstrained by her parliamentary party and managed to enact her legislative programme—such as on the EC's Common Market programme and the Single European Act—without much opposition from it. Whether this would have been the case on monetary union, which she wanted to reject altogether, remains open as she was no longer in office when the Maastricht Treaty was negotiated and ratified. In any case, at least at the end of her premiership she appears to have shown little consideration for her fellow Tory MPs' views on Europe. Yet, as Geoffrey Howe's resignation for example showed, intraparty divisions over Europe came increasingly to the fore and contributed to her losing office.

Looking at Tony Blair's premiership, the particularly low number of revolts by PLP members over their government's European policy supports the assumption of prime ministerial predominance in that policy area. Yet on other (foreign) policy issues this was not the case. The PLP's opposition to Blair's Iraq policy, for instance, was strong, which was also illustrated by the resignations of members of the government like Robin Cook or Clare Short. Moreover, on the PLP's influence on the government's European policy during Blair's premiership, it also has to be noted that no decision to join the euro was taken in the core executive. Hence there was no parliamentary bill on which Labour MPs, who were opposed to or sceptical of EMU, might have dissented. Thus on EMU it remains open whether Blair would have been more constrained by his parliamentary party than on other issues of European policy.

For the four leaders it has to be assumed that on European policy decision-making (as on other policy areas), they took a certain form of backbench behaviour into account, and this at least to a degree influenced their strategies and their policy decisions on the issue in question. Moreover, potential party rebellions in parliament over issues might have been avoided with the government compromising, for example, by watering down legislation or refraining from taking a decision at all. This gave governing party MPs influence over government policy, which was, however, mainly exerted behind the scenes (Stuart 2009: 186). As such behaviour by the prime minister, the government and the parliamentary party cannot be measured as, for instance, the number of parliamentary rebellions, these processes cannot be verified empirically.

In this chapter the behaviour of the parliamentary party and their management by the four prime ministers in European policy and particularly on ERM and EMU was taken into view to analyse how far the parliamentary party played an enabling or constraining role with regard to the PM's political leadership. In the following chapter the prime ministers' political communication and media management on ERM and EMU are studied to find out to what extent the media as a communication channel with the public affected prime ministerial political leadership and how far either prime minister was able to shape it.

References

Alderman, K. (1996). The passage of the European Communities (finance) Act (1995) and its aftermath. *Contemporary British History, 10*(3), 1–20.

Baker, D., Gamble, A., Ludlam, S., & Seawright, D. (1999). Backbenchers with attitude: A seismic study of the Conservative Party and dissent on Europe. In S. Bowler, D. M. Farrell, & R. S. Katz (Eds.), *Party discipline and parliamentary government* (pp. 72–93). Columbus: Ohio State University Press.

Bale, T. (2016). *The Conservative Party: From Thatcher to Cameron* (2nd ed.). Cambridge: Polity.

Butler, D., & Butler, G. (2006). *British political facts since 1979*. Basingstoke: Palgrave Macmillan.

Butler, D., & Kavanagh, D. (Eds.). (1980). *The British general election of 1979*. London: Macmillan.

Butler, D., & Kavanagh, D. (Eds.). (1988). *The British general election of 1987*. New York: St. Martin's Press.

Callaghan, J. (2006). *Time and chance*. London: Politico's.

Clark, A. (1999). *The Tories: Conservatives and the nation state 1922-1997* (2nd ed.). London: Phoenix.

Cowley, P. (2005). *The rebels: How Blair mislaid his majority*. London: Politico's.

Cowley, P. (2007). Parliament. In A. Seldon (Ed.), *Blair's Britain, 1997-2007* (pp. 16–34). Cambridge: Cambridge University Press.

Cowley, P. (2008, January 21). This will not be like Maastricht. *The Guardian*.

Cowley, P., & Norton, P. (1996). Are Conservative MPs revolting? Dissension by government MPs in the British House of Commons 1979-1996, University of Hull: Centre for Legislative Studies, *Research Papers in Legislative Studies*, No. 2/96.

Cowley, P., & Norton, P. (1999). Rebels and rebellions: Conservative MPs in the 1992 Parliament. *British Journal of Politics and International Relations, 1*(1), 84–105.

Cowley, P., & Stuart, M. (2003). In place of strife? The PLP in Government, 1997-2001. *Political Studies, 51*(2), 315–334.

Cowley, P., & Stuart, M. (2005). Parliament. In A. Seldon & D. Kavanagh (Eds.), *The Blair effect 2001-5* (pp. 20–42). Cambridge: Cambridge University Press.

Cowley, P., & Stuart, M. (2006, November). *Dissension amongst the Parliamentary Labour Party, 2005-2006: A data handbook*. http://www.revolts.co.uk/Dissension%20data%20handbook%202005-06%20Final.pdf. Accessed August 29, 2016.

Cowley, P., & Stuart, M. (2007a, November). *From Blair to Brown: Dissension in the Parliamentary Labour Party, 2006-2007: A data handbook*. http://www.revolts.co.uk/Dissension%20handbook%202006-7%20web%20version.pdf. Accessed August 29, 2016.

Cowley, P., & Stuart, M. (2007b, September 12). *Europe: The dog that hasn't barked (yet?)*. http://www.revolts.co.uk/The%20dog%20that%20didnt%20bark.pdf. Accessed August 29, 2016.

Donoughue, B. (1987). *Prime minister: The conduct of policy under Harold Wilson & James Callaghan*. London: Jonathan Cape.

Donoughue, B. (2009). *Downing Street diary: With James Callaghan in No. 10* (2nd ed.). London: Pimlico.

Dunleavy, P., & Jones, G. W. (with Burnham, J., Elgie, R., & Fysh, P.) (1993). Leaders, politics and institutional change: The decline of prime ministerial accountability to the House of Commons, 1868-1990. *British Journal of Political Studies, 23*(3), 267–298.

Gamble, A., & Kelly, G. (2000). The British Labour Party and monetary union. *West European Politics, 23*(1), 1–25.

Geddes, A. (2013). *Britain and the European Union*. Basingstoke: Palgrave Macmillan.

George, S. (1998). *An awkward partner: Britain in the European Community* (3rd ed.). Oxford: Oxford University Press.

Goodman, E. (1978a, November 28). EMS veto sought. *Financial Times*.

Goodman, E. (1978b, November 29). We won't join EMS yet—Healey. *Financial Times*.

Gowland, D., Turner, A., & Wright, A. (2010). *Britain and European Integration since 1945: On the sidelines*. London: Routledge.

HC Deb. (1976, April 5), Vol 909, cc29–164.

HC Deb. (1978, December 13), Vol 906, cc811–844.

HC Deb. (1990, November 13), Vol 180, cc461–465.

HC Deb. (1992, September 24), Vol 212, c4.

HC Deb. (1993, June 9), Vol 226, cc284–285.

House of Commons Information Office. (2003, September). *By-election results: 1992-1997.* Factsheet M14 Members series, revised edition.

House of Commons Library. (2016, May 23). *Number of House of Commons divisions*, Standard Note No. SN/PC/04670.

Kavanagh, D., & Seldon, A. (2000). *The powers behind the prime minister: The hidden influence of Number Ten* (2nd ed.). London: HarperCollins.

Ludlow, P. (1982). *The making of the European Monetary System.* London: Butterworth.

Major, J. (2000). *The autobiography* (2nd ed.). London: HarperCollins.

Marsh, I. (1990). Liberal priorities, the Lib-Lab-Pact and the requirements for policy influence. *Parliamentary Affairs, 43*(3), 292–321.

Miller, V. (2008, January 22). *EU treaty bills: The whip and referendum clauses.* House of Commons Library Standard Note No. SN/IA/4650.

Norton, P. (1980). *Dissension in the House of Commons 1974-1979.* Oxford: Clarendon Press.

Norton, P. (1985). Behavioural changes, backbench independence in the 1980s. In P. Norton (Ed.), *Parliament in the 1980s* (pp. 22–47). Oxford: Basil Blackwell.

Powell, J. (2010). *The new Machiavelli: How to wield power in the modern world.* London: The Bodley Head.

Rawstorne, P. (1978, November 30). Britain not to join EMS without changes—Healey. *Financial Times.*

Riddell, P. (1994). Major and parliament. In D. Kavanagh & A. Seldon (Eds.), *The Major effect* (pp. 46–63). London: Macmillan.

Rose, R. (2001). *The prime minister in a shrinking world.* Cambridge: Polity Press.

Seldon, A. (with Baston, L.) (1998). *Major: A political life* (2nd ed.). London: Phoenix.

Stephens, P. (1989, December 12). Thatcher says Britain may join ERM ahead of general election. *Financial Times.*

Stephens, P. (1997). *Politics and the pound: The Tories, the economy and Europe* (2nd ed.). London: Papermac.

Stuart, M. (2009). The role of parliament under Blair. In T. Casey (Ed.), *The Blair legacy: Politics, policy, governance and foreign affairs* (pp. 178–189). Basingstoke: Palgrave Macmillan.

Thatcher, M. (2011). *The Downing Street years.* London: Harper Press.

Thomas, G. P. (1998). *The prime minister and cabinet today.* Manchester: Manchester University Press.

Thomas, G. P. (2004). United Kingdom: The prime minister and parliament. *The Journal of Legislative Studies, 10*(2/3), 4–37.

Thompson, H. (1996). *The British Conservative government and the European Exchange Rate Mechanism, 1979–1994.* London: Pinter.

The National Archives [hereafter TNA]. (1977, February 25). *Records of the Cabinet Office [hereafter CAB] 128/61*, CM (77), 8th Conclusions.

TNA. (1978, June 8). CAB 128/64, CM (78) 21st Conclusions.

TNA. (1978, November 30). CAB 128/64, CM (78) 41st Conclusions.

TNA. (1978, December 7). CAB 128/64, CM (78) 42nd Conclusions.

TNA. (1978, December 19). CAB 128/64, CM (78) 44th Conclusions.

UK Parliament. (2016a). Allocation of time motions. http://www.parliament.uk/site-information/glossary/allocation-of-time-motion/. Accessed September 28, 2016.

UK Parliament. (2016b). Programme motion. http://www.parliament.uk/site-information/glossary/programme-motion/. Accessed September 28, 2016.

UK Parliament. (2016c). Whips. http://www.parliament.uk/about/mps-and-lords/principal/whips/. Accessed August 28, 2016.

Wall, S. (2008). *A stranger in Europe: Britain and the EU from Thatcher to Blair.* Oxford: Oxford University Press.

Chapter 10
Prime Ministerial Political Communication and Media Management in European Monetary Policy

To find out whether a premier can shape public debate as an opinion leader and contribute to his position as a predominant prime minister, it is helpful to analyse (a) his public statements on an issue and (b) their coverage by the media. In this chapter this is done by taking a single example for each of the four PMs with reference to a specific European (monetary) policy event or initiative. This is because the scope of the study does not allow for a long-term analysis of the media management of the incumbents in question during their entire periods in office. As such an approach would cover 31 years it would constitute a research project of its own.

It is not assumed that a head of government can shape his country's news coverage by merely one statement. However, it can be expected that such speeches tend to be much considered by the media as they are a key element of the government's overall communication strategy on the event or policy initiative in question. Therefore it is instrumental to analyse how the media responded to a prime ministerial statement on such an issue. To investigate (a) if any of the media outlets adopted the prime minister's arguments and (b) whether there was a change in the news coverage of the government's European monetary policy decision in question, the news coverage 2 weeks before and 2 weeks after the specific event is analysed for each case. To systematically analyse the media coverage, a summarising qualitative content analysis ('zusammenfassende qualitative Inhaltsanalyse') (Mayring 2010: Sect. 5.5.2) is conducted, using inductively developed categories. These categories are derived from each prime minister's statement. To develop categories which can be used to analyse the media coverage, the various arguments presented in the prime ministers' statements have to be identified. These individual arguments then have to be generalised and bundled together to identify a small number of key arguments from each prime minister's statement, which can be used in the further analysis (Mayring 2010: 67–70, 83). These remaining arguments or categories are then used to structure the content of the media coverage to extract from it the material for the case study analysis and summarise it (Mayring 2010: 98). It is analysed whether the

B. Bujard, *The British Prime Minister in the Core Executive*, Contributions to Political Science, https://doi.org/10.1007/978-3-319-89953-4_10

media outlets adopt and agree with those arguments. By studying this data, the following question is to be answered:

> Can the prime minister influence the media coverage of the event or policy initiative in question through his statement on it?

Only print media coverage is analysed here. As mentioned in Sect. 5.3, British broadcasters have to cover political news in a cross-partisan and balanced manner in accordance with their programme mandate. This is also regulated by laws and codices. UK newspapers on the other hand explicitly voice political views and are expected to do so (McNair 1999: 51). While the question whether the press can significantly influence public opinion is contested in communication and public opinion research, it is clear that politicians tend to assume that the press can actively impact on the public's attitude on an issue (Temple 2008: 200–203). Thus it can be presumed that a prime minister will attempt to use any parliamentary statement not only to rally support in parliament but also to shape the media coverage on the issue. It can further be assumed that if a premier is able to influence the media this should be identifiable in the press coverage. This means that the PM's arguments on the issue in question appear in the coverage as they are picked up and supported by the media.[1] To review a wide range of print media coverage the following national newspapers have been selected for the analysis: the *Financial Times*, the *Guardian*, the *Independent*, the *Daily Mail* and the *Sun*.[2] The first three are broadsheets or quality papers with a mainly highly educated readership (Temple 2008: 87–88). The *Daily Mail* can be counted as a mid-market paper particularly representing readers (and thus voters) of Middle England (Temple 2008: 90–91). Despite massively losing readers since the 1980s, the *Sun* still has an important voice in political reporting because it "understands populist issues" (Cole 2007). As to its readership: by 2007 more than two-thirds of its readers belonged to lower social groupings such as skilled manual workers and below (Cole 2007). This selection covers pro-European and Eurosceptic newspapers as well as varying partisan attitudes. By 2001, for instance, the *Daily Mail* and the *Sun* belonged to the Eurosceptic section of the print media while the *Financial Times*, the *Guardian* and the *Independent* were pro-European (Seymour-Ure 2002: 136). With regard to partisanship the *Daily Mail* in particular was a Tory newspaper supporting the Conservatives at every general election between 1979 and 2005. The *Financial Times* and the *Independent* traditionally presented themselves as independent, though the latter supported Labour at the 1997 and 2001 general elections (in 2001 with the Liberal Democrats). In 2005 it only supported the Liberal Democrats. The *Guardian* was on the left of the political spectrum and supported Labour at each general election

---

[1]The Internet is not addressed here as it only from the 1990s became an increasingly used source of political information. Moreover, a study from 2007 found that even then only around 10% of British people with Internet access used it to gather political information (Gavin 2007: 5).

[2]In the case of the *Independent* and the *Daily Mail* (for the Blair case study) the Sunday editions (*Independent on Sunday* and *Mail on Sunday*) were researched as well, as they are included in the Nexis database.

between 1979 and 2005 with the exception of the one in 1983. It often did so in combination with the Liberal Democrats. The *Sun*'s partisanship was more variable. It was a Labour paper until the end of the 1970s. From 1979 to 1992 it supported the Conservatives and from 1997 to 2005 Labour (Butler and Butler 2006: 269, 273; Butler and Sloman 1980: 443, 449). The newspapers were examined for each case study except for the *Independent*. It could not be considered for the Callaghan case as it was only established in the 1980s.

The newspaper articles were digitally researched using the Nexis database for the *Guardian* and the *Independent* as well as the *Daily Mail* for the Blair case study. The *Financial Times* was also researched digitally using the Financial Times Historical Archive. The searches were conducted using several keywords and keyword combinations.[3] Press coverage from the *Daily Mail* for the Callaghan, Thatcher and Major case studies and the *Sun* for all cases as well as parts of the *Guardian* for the Callaghan case study were researched at the British Library Newspaper Archive in Colindale/London.[4]

The following cases were selected for analysis: for James Callaghan it was the European Council on 4/5 December 1978, at which the establishment of a European Monetary System (EMS) was agreed. On 6 December he made a statement in parliament on the summit. In Margaret Thatcher's case the European Council in Madrid on 26/27 June 1989 and her parliamentary statement on it on 29 June were analysed. In Madrid Thatcher announced that sterling would join the ERM as soon as several conditions were fulfilled. She also accepted the first stage of EMU as laid out in the Delors report. For John Major the European Council in Maastricht on 9/10 December 1991 and his statement in parliament on it on 11 December were considered. At Maastricht the EC heads of state and government settled the remaining questions on the European Union Treaty and Major negotiated an EMU opt-out for the UK. In Tony Blair's case his parliamentary statement on 23 February 1999 on the national changeover plan was analysed. The plan was intended to prepare Britain to join the euro as soon as possible, if the public voted for it in a referendum (on which no date was given). These cases were selected because they represent key meetings or policy initiatives during each prime minister's period in office. On all occasions, the government made important decisions on European

[3]The following keywords were used: Callaghan: 'Callaghan and Brussels', 'Callaghan and EMS', 'Callaghan and Europe', 'European and Summit' and 'Prime Minister and Europe'. Keywords Thatcher: 'Delors Report', 'ERM', 'Madrid Summit', 'Thatcher and EMS', 'Thatcher and EMU', 'Thatcher and Madrid'. Keywords Major: 'European Council', 'Major and EMU', 'Major and Maastricht', 'Major and Single Currency', 'opt out'. Keywords Blair: 'EMU and Blair', 'Euro and Blair', 'National Changeover Plan' and 'Single Currency'.

[4]Newspaper reports on the perspectives of other actors such as EC member states, European institutions or the domestic opposition with regard to the prime ministerial statements or the events/initiatives in question were not included in the analysis. Press reports only mentioning the issue of the case studies but focusing on different topics were also excluded.

monetary policy.[5] In each case the print media coverage is considered 2 weeks before and 2 weeks after the prime ministerial statement in parliament. The aim is to find out whether the coverage changed after the speech and whether the papers adopted the prime minister's arguments.

10.1 James Callaghan: European Council in Brussels, December 1978

In 1978 the European Community discussed the establishment of a European Monetary System (EMS) centring on an Exchange Rate Mechanism (ERM) (see also Chap. 3). The British government debated the project (see Sect. 8.2.1) and in late November published a Green Paper on the scheme, but did not indicate whether it intended to join it (for a reprint of the Green Paper, see Financial Times 1978a). At the Brussels European Council on 4/5 December 1978 the EC members formally agreed to establish a monetary system, although Britain, Ireland and Italy initially decided not to join the ERM. Ireland and Italy revised their decisions shortly after, leaving the UK as the only country outside the ERM upon its introduction in 1979.

In his parliamentary statement on the summit on 6 December 1978 (HC Deb 6 December 1978, cc1421–1438) Prime Minister James Callaghan announced that the EC heads of state and government had decided to establish a European Monetary System on 1 January 1979. Britain would not join the system's core, the Exchange Rate Mechanism, but take part in the establishment of a European Currency Unit (ECU) and the European monetary fund. However, he explained, the EC members had agreed that the UK could join the ERM at a later date, if it wished to do so (HC Deb 6 December 1978, c1421).

In his statement on the decision on ERM and EMS and the subsequent answers to questions from MPs, Callaghan focused on four aspects: (a) national interest and sovereignty, (b) economic policy, (c) monetary policy and (d) British influence in Europe.

On national interest and sovereignty Callaghan stated that he in principle supported giving up national sovereignty for an international monetary system, provided the system contributed to better trading relations between the participating countries, more growth and less unemployment (HC Deb 6 December 1978, cc1427–1428). On the current scheme he declared that the decision against joining the ERM had been a result of having "defended British interests on this occasion" (HC Deb 6 December 1978, c1427). Yet in his speech the PM did not explicitly

[5] A European Council meeting in Blair's case would have been preferable for better comparability of the cases. But as the government in 1997 announced that the UK would not yet join the euro (which it confirmed in 2003), there were no European Council's between 1997 and 2007 at which questions of European monetary policy were discussed which were relevant to the UK to the same degree as was the case at the summits selected for the other three case studies.

define what he meant by Britain's national interest. From the context it can be assumed that his views on economic and monetary policy as well as British influence in Europe were all part of what he understood as Britain's national interest.

On economic policy Callaghan said that economic convergence was necessary for the ERM to function successfully. This was currently not the case as the EC members' economies had not converged. Consequently, it was "imprudent to join the exchange rate mechanism" (HC Deb 6 December 1978, c1426). The government had concluded that for the UK the system's potential benefits were currently outweighed by its disadvantages, which might include more unemployment and unneeded deflation (HC Deb 6 December 1978, cc1436–1437). But he had stressed at the summit the significance of EC policies to achieve convergence between the members' economies, the PM explained (HC Deb 6 December 1978, c1422).

The third aspect he addressed concerned monetary policy. Callaghan argued that exchange rate stability in Europe as well as globally was in the country's interest (HC Deb 6 December 1978, cc1429, 1434). He regarded effective international monetary cooperation as a helpful supporting measure under certain conditions, but argued that it depended on Britain's own domestic policy after all to have a stable currency and stay competitive (HC Deb 6 December 1978, cc1423–1424). Therefore, on the question whether a country should contribute to exchange rate stability by policies set externally or by the country itself, he declared: "Our future lies in our own hands" (HC Deb 6 December 1978, c1437).

The fourth aspect of Callaghan's argument related to Britain's influence in Europe. According to him the country had played a constructive role in the EMS negotiations (HC Deb 6 December 1978, c1423). Equally, the UK would continue to be a key influence on further development and direction of the project by being part of the decision-making process on it, even without ERM membership (HC Deb 6 December 1978, c1438). Despite staying out of the ERM, Britain was neither isolated at the European level nor had the EC partners questioned Britain's loyalty, Callaghan declared (HC Deb 6 December 1978, cc1430, 1437).

The following section analyses to what extent the press adopted the four aspects of Callaghan's argument on the ERM decision and whether he can be seen as an opinion leader on the issue. Firstly, the newspapers' view on EMS/ERM is considered in the 2 weeks before his statement. In a second step each paper's stance is analysed after it to assess (a) how it considered the PM's arguments to remain outside the ERM and (b) whether it changed its position.

The ***Financial Times*** covered the EMS plans in much detail and particularly looked at the scheme's monetary and economic policy implications. Thirty-nine articles, published in the 4 weeks between 22 November and 20 December 1978, were considered here.[6] Twenty-two appeared before Callaghan made his

[6]Other articles in the published time period not considered here covered the position of other member states and Labour party committees on EMS/ERM and technical questions on the EMS without reference to the government's stance on the issue.

parliamentary statement. Three were published on the day of it. While the articles were mainly descriptive accounts of the scheme's technical aspects as well as the negotiations on it, in two the paper explained its position in support of ERM membership. In both articles it criticised the fact that the government, as it expected and repeatedly mentioned (e.g. Marsh 1978; Riddell 1978; Goodman and Riddell 1978), was set to reject entry entirely rather than considering the option to join the mechanism with a wider band of fluctuation of 6 instead of 2.25%. This had been offered to Italy during the negotiations. With a wide band sterling would be able to float sufficiently, the paper argued (Brittan 1978a; Financial Times 1978c). Such a course would give the government the chance to take part in the scheme without being bound to a rigid exchange rate. Moreover, Britain would be able to influence the EMS's further development more than was possible outside the ERM (Financial Times 1978c). The *FT* saw the idea that wide margins signified economic weakness not as a sufficient reason to reject such a policy (Brittan 1978a; Financial Times 1978c). On 1 December it concluded on the ERM that "the political case for being in at the start is overwhelming"[7] (Financial Times 1978c).

On Britain's role in Europe the paper on 24 November acknowledged that the government wanted to avoid the UK to be marginalised in Europe (Goodman and Riddell 1978). In late November the *FT* declared that the government had shown with its EMS Green Paper that it had taken a significant step in a pro-European direction. It had indicated that EC membership was not a burden but an advantage, and in the document had struck a positive tone on the UK's European integration, which was "a world of difference from the previous approach that Britain was somehow a member of Europe rather against her will"[8] (Financial Times 1978b). But with an earlier change of heart it could have had more influence on EMS planning, the paper believed. Therefore, it saw the document as "evidence of lost opportunities as well as of an eleventh-hour conversion"[9] (Financial Times 1978b).

Overall, where the *Financial Times* did voice an opinion on the ERM in the 2 weeks before Callaghan's statement, it supported joining it—albeit with a wider fluctuation margin than envisioned in the current ERM plan. It also supported a more constructive approach in European policy than the government had previously adopted. Yet it saw its EMS Green Paper as a step into the right direction.

After Callaghan's parliamentary statement of 6 December, the ***Financial Times*** returned in its coverage to a mainly descriptive account of events. But in a few articles it addressed its own view showing that it still considered ERM membership desirable. It was critical of the government's approach to Europe, for instance,

---

[7]Financial Times (1978), Why we should join the EMS, 1 December 1978. Used under licence from the Financial Times. All Rights Reserved.

[8]Financial Times (1978), On the Road to EMS, 27 November 1978. Used under licence from the Financial Times. All Rights Reserved.

[9]Financial Times (1978), On the Road to EMS, 27 November 1978. Used under licence from the Financial Times. All Rights Reserved.

calling its policy of the past months "minimalist and even obstructive"[10] (Financial Times 1978d). It saw the reason for this approach mainly in Callaghan's attempts to appease the Labour left (Financial Times 1978d).

On the economic aspects of the ERM, which Callaghan had addressed in parliament, the *Financial Times* returned to its position in support of wide margins for the pound in the mechanism and criticised the government again for not seriously considering this (Brittan 1978b). After Callaghan's statement the *FT* much discussed Britain's role in Europe. In contrast to the premier, who had argued that the UK remained an important actor on further ERM discussions, the paper saw the risk it could become a member state on the second tier in a Europe made up of two tiers. It took this view even after it became clear that Ireland and Italy were not going to join the ERM either: on 7 December it argued that if a "two-tier Europe"[11] (Brittan 1978b) became a reality, Callaghan was to be credited as one of its architects. This the paper attributed to his refusal to consider ERM membership with a wide 6% margin for sterling's exchange rate. The *Financial Times*, moreover, argued such a move would have been the more 'European' solution to the EMS problem while not making much difference to the current situation. Yet it might have contributed to a little more British influence over the EC's budget and agricultural policy (Brittan 1978b). Thus the *FT* echoed its stance on the ERM from before Callaghan's speech, stating it would have been a sensible position with regard to Britain's role in Europe to have been in the ERM from the start. As before Callaghan's speech the *Financial Times* stated critically that one reason why the government had not wanted to join with a wide margin had been the fear to then be a second rate member state. Outside the ERM the country was now just this, the paper believed (Brittan 1978b). On 8 December it criticised with regard to the PM's parliamentary speech the fact that "what the Government seems to have done is to have gained time rather than to have asserted any particular authority"[12] (Rutherford 1978). The *FT* anew discussed Britain's role in Europe on 13 December in the context of Italy's U-turn on ERM membership. The paper believed the shift by the Italians could "heighten the sense of isolation of Britain"[13] (Financial Times 1978e) and increase the pressure on the government to revise its decision to remain outside the ERM as well. The paper suggested that the assumption it would be easier to achieve improvements of the ERM inside rather than outside might have contributed to the Italian change of mind and noted: "This is a point of view which the British government, too, might have taken into account"[14] (Financial Times 1978e).

---

[10]Financial Times (1978), A divided Europe, 7 December 1978. Used under licence from the Financial Times. All Rights Reserved.

[11]Brittan, S. (1978), The architects of a two-tier Europe, Financial Times, 7 December 1978. Used under licence from the Financial Times. All Rights Reserved.

[12]Rutherford, M. (1978), A time of uncertainty, Financial Times, 8 December 1978. Used under licence from the Financial Times. All Rights Reserved.

[13]Financial Times (1978), Italy decides to join the EMS, 13 December 1978. Used under licence from the Financial Times. All Rights Reserved.

[14]Financial Times (1978), Italy decides to join the EMS, 13 December 1978. Used under licence from the Financial Times. All Rights Reserved.

On the whole, Callaghan does not appear to have been able to influence the *Financial Times* much with his parliamentary statement as the paper did not shift its view from supporting ERM membership (albeit with a wide margin for sterling). On Britain's influence in Europe the paper remained of the opinion that a more constructive approach in its European policy was needed. The *FT* had hoped for this when the government had published its EMS Green Paper in November. Yet it did not consider it being realised at the Brussels summit.

Like the *Financial Times*, the ***Guardian*** extensively covered the EMS and ERM discussions in the 4 weeks between 22 November and 20 December 1978. Twenty-nine articles were considered here.[15] Twenty-one appeared before Callaghan's statement on the summit. Two were published on the day of it. They were mainly descriptive accounts of events with the paper early expecting that Britain would not join the ERM from the start (Palmer 1978; Hoggart 1978a; White 1978). But in an article from 29 November the *Guardian* did indicate its view on ERM membership, showing that unlike the *Financial Times* its position was close to that of the government. The paper declared that full EMS membership would bring Britain no more advantages than the government's soft-landing plan of joining the EMS but not the ERM. Moreover, it acknowledged that the UK had raised important questions with regard to potential problems of the scheme which, however, made Britain appear very sceptical. But if these issues were addressed, the system could function better than in its currently planned form, the paper believed (The Guardian 1978). Unlike Callaghan, who would stress the economic and monetary implications of the ERM in his statement, the paper seemed to consider the government's prime motive on the ERM to be political. In the context of the Green Paper it noted on 25 November that at least half of Labour's MPs had already signalled their opposition to the ERM. Thus it would split the party, close to an upcoming general election on a key issue, if the PM announced that Britain would join the ERM (Hoggart 1978a). On the summit's second day the paper again suggested it was a political decision not to join the ERM (Jenkins 1978b).

With regard to monetary policy the *Guardian* suggested that if Britain joined the ERM, sterling would first of all have to be devalued. It thought Callaghan would not be willing to accept this ahead of a general election (Jenkins 1978a).

On Britain's role in Europe the paper after the summit referred to the risk of a two-tier Europe and asked on which tier Britain would place itself, particularly if the EMS still existed after the next general election (Jenkins 1978c).

Overall, the *Guardian*, where it did refer to its own view, tended to support the government's stance that there were no greater advantages for Britain in joining the ERM than in joining only the EMS but without the ERM. At the same time it was aware of the risk of Britain losing influence in Europe due to the ERM decision.

[15]Further articles published in the time period not covered here addressed the position on the EMS by e.g. the British chambers of commerce or the parliamentary budget committee.

After Callaghan's parliamentary statement of 6 December 1978, the ***Guardian*** returned to its descriptive coverage of events in the remaining six articles, without setting out its own view on ERM and EMS. Yet on 7 December it noted that the European Council in Brussels had politically been successful for Callaghan. Aided by Italy's and Ireland's reluctance to join the ERM as well, the prime minister had managed to receive praise from the anti-Europeans in his party and even from some Conservative MPs (Aitken 1978).

But in another commentary from the same day the paper was highly critical of Callaghan's statement, albeit referring to its presentation not its content. It argued that the prime minister had been careful not to relish in his triumph which according to the paper had been styled as a personal achievement of the PM. This behaviour it criticised as showing "high self-regard" (Hoggart 1978b).

On the reasons why the government had decided to stay out of the ERM the paper changed its view: while it had suggested in November that joining would split the Labour Party (Hoggart 1978a), it noted after the statement that it had not been due to the Labour left's opposition to the ERM but because of short-term economic and political reasons. The paper believed the calculation was that inside a system of fixed exchange rates sterling would be more exposed than if it remained outside it (Keegan and Stephens 1978).

On Britain's role in Europe, the *Guardian* after Callaghan's speech suggested that assessments of a Europe made up of two tiers might have been too hasty, but that despite this, the UK together with Ireland and Italy had already been classified as one of the poorer countries in the European Community (Jenkins 1978d). The *Guardian* noted that the government was not interested in isolation due to staying out of the ERM, yet it did not mention whether it did think the UK was isolated (Jenkins 1978d). The paper stated on 10 December that the summit, at which two other countries had decided not to join the ERM, had gone very well for the premier, because "so far from being the sole dissident on trial again for un-European activities, Callaghan was almost a member of the jury—or at least a smug suspect assured of his immunity through a bargain with the prosecution" (Keegan and Stephens 1978).

Overall, the *Guardian* appeared to be partly critical of Callaghan in its coverage after his speech, yet it did not set out its own view on ERM and EMS or the government's policy. Thus there is no indication that it shifted its position from before his statement, when it had supported the government's policy of joining EMS but not the ERM.

The ***Daily Mail*** covered the debate on the European Monetary System far less extensively than the two broadsheets. Seven articles, published between 22 November and 20 December 1978, were considered in the analysis.[16] Four

[16]Further articles published in the time period not considered here addressed Thatcher's EMS stance and that of Labour party bodies, e.g. the Labour executive's international and home policy committees.

appeared before Callaghan's speech and one on the day of it. During and after the Brussels summit the paper appeared critical of ERM membership in some of its coverage. It argued, for instance, on 5 December there was no reason to return to a system of fixed exchange rates. It also referred to the EMS as a first step to economic and monetary union (Alexander 1978).

On the economic policy implications of the EMS, the *Daily Mail* referred to Callaghan's focus on pursuing his own economic policy. The paper drew attention to the disadvantages of the policy for Britain's role in Europe and stated that the prime minister's hesitation to give up the government's options to bring down unemployment and curb inflation might once again result in Britain being an outsider in Europe (Dickie 1978a).

With regard to monetary policy the paper argued on 4 December that the ERM posed a significant dilemma for the government. A decision against joining the ERM could lead to increased pressure on the pound's exchange rate, and the financial markets could conclude the decision meant that sterling was too weak to compete with the other currencies in the ERM. Yet should the government decide to fully join the EMS, a devaluation of the pound could be necessary to be able to stay in the prescribed margin, the paper stated (Dickie 1978a).

On Britain's role in Europe the *Daily Mail* noted potential disadvantages if Britain did not join the ERM. It stated on 4 December that a decision against membership could make the UK a second rate member of the Community. This could result in it being excluded from the decision-making process on the monetary system (Dickie 1978a). A day later the paper suggested that without full EMS membership it was to be expected that the government would be consulted on decisions about the system but not be able to vote on them (Dickie 1978b). Yet the paper did not indicate whether it saw this as a problem or a price worth paying to stay out of the ERM.

Overall, the *Daily Mail* took a somewhat paradox position. One the one hand, it was critical of the monetary system and saw no merit in adopting a fixed exchange rate. Yet, on the other hand, it pointed out potential disadvantages to Britain's role in the EC if it did not join the ERM. Yet it did not mention how problematic it thought they were. It also did not refer to what it thought of the government's policy.

After Callaghan's parliamentary statement the ***Daily Mail*** addressed the ERM decision in only two articles in the time period considered here. It appears that external factors such as Ireland's shift on ERM membership had a larger influence on the paper's assessment than the premier's arguments. After Callaghan's appearance in parliament the *Daily Mail* showed that it was content with the summit outcome, stating that the premier had not left the negotiating table as a loser. In the view of the paper this role had been taken up by the Irish and the Italian heads of government. At the same time, the paper suggested that Ireland's and Italy's non-participation in the ERM reduced the risk for Callaghan of being presented as an unsuccessful prime minister, who had decided against joining the ERM, because it would have meant devaluating sterling in an election year. Secondly, Britain had not been reduced to being a second rate member state as there were two other countries that had decided not to join the ERM either, the paper argued (Dickie 1978c). But when it became clear by mid-December that Italy and Ireland would join the ERM, the *Daily Mail* reported that there were doubts in the EC institutions whether the UK could afford to remain the only country outside it (Kennedy 1978). Yet it did not comment whether it shared these doubts.

While it is difficult to assess the *Daily Mail's* view on the ERM from only two articles, they include no indication that it had changed it from before Callaghan's statement. The paper rated the summit's outcome—at least as long as Ireland and Italy also remained out of the ERM—as a success for Callaghan.

The ***Sun***'s coverage of EMS and ERM was also lower than that of the broadsheets. Ten articles, published between 22 November and 20 December 1978, were considered in the analysis.[17] Four were published before Callaghan's speech, one on the day of it. The tabloid characterised the government's ERM position as giving the impression of intending to join despite not actually wanting to be a part of it (Shrimsley 1978a). It did not explicitly state its view on the mechanism in these articles. Yet it found that Britain deserved the criticism of the UK's EMS stance made by Luxembourg's Prime Minister Gaston Thorn, but did not elaborate on this (Shrimsley 1978a).

On the economic implications for Britain the *Sun* took a different focus than Callaghan, who would state on 6 December that full EMS membership in the existing form would not be economically advantageous for the country. The tabloid instead suggested 2 days earlier that the premier was aware that the British economy was so weak that it would be very difficult for sterling to compete with the other currencies in the ERM (Terry 1978a).

On Britain's (and the PM's) role in Europe the paper reported on 5 December that the other EC members had been hostile to Callaghan at the European negotiations. It also suggested that he was ridiculed for his stance of principally welcoming the EMS but waiting for the right time to join (Terry 1978b). A day later the *Sun* argued that the premier, who had been expected to be the big loser at the summit, was a winner instead. Moreover, the EMS plan had failed not only because the UK had decided not to join the ERM, but also because Italy and Ireland had decided to abstain (Terry 1978c).

Overall, while the *Sun* did not explicitly voice its own view on EMS and ERM, it assumed that due to the weakness of the British economy the pound would have difficulties to compete with the other currencies in the ERM.

As it had done before Callaghan's statement, the ***Sun*** differed in its assessment of the economic implications of the EMS for Britain from that of the prime minister after his appearance in parliament. While he had stated that full EMS membership in the existing form would not be economically advantageous for the country, the

[17]Another article published in the time period not included here considered the EMS view by opposition politician Enoch Powell.

tabloid thought the main reason for not joining the ERM had been that the UK economy was too weak for it and declared that this was shameful and not to be celebrated (The Sun 1978a). On 8 December it stated that the UK's economic problems had been vividly illustrated by what the paper called the "humiliating experience in Brussels" (Shrimsley 1978b). As Callaghan had to take the decision to reject membership because the British currency was too weak to compete in the ERM, it could not be said that he had done a brave thing, the *Sun* criticised (Shrimsley 1978b).

The tabloid changed its opinion on Britain's (and the PM's) role in Europe during the 4 weeks considered here. While it had complimented Callaghan on 6 December on the outcome of the summit (Terry 1978c), it complained a day later that the premier had returned from Brussels with the confirmation that British citizens were second rate (The Sun 1978a). Once it became clear that Italy and Ireland would join the ERM, the paper considered the UK isolated in Europe (The Sun 1978b) and Callaghan the outsider of the European Monetary System. While he had left the summit the previous week as a winner, this was not the case any longer (Woosey 1978).

The *Sun*'s coverage between 22 November and 20 December does not suggest it found ERM membership desirable, yet it saw non-participation as a sign of weakness of the British economy, which it resented. Thus the paper did not support the government's EMS/ERM policy. As it did not explicitly state its view on the EMS and the ERM, there is no indication that it changed its view on the issue after Callaghan's statement.

Looking at the four papers' coverage of the EMS/ERM discussion and the government's decision on it (Table 10.1), Callaghan does not appear to have had much success in framing the debate with his arguments against joining the ERM as

Table 10.1 Newspapers' attitudes to EMS/ERM and support for government policy 1978 (own illustration)

	Financial Times	The Guardian	Daily Mail	The Sun
Before the speech				
Attitude to EMS and ERM	Support	Soft-landing	Mixed	Unclear
Support for government policy	Mixed	Support	Unclear	Unclear
After the speech				
Attitude to EMS and ERM	Support	Unclear	Unclear	Unclear
Support for government policy	No support	Unclear	Unclear	No support

Key: Support = support of EMS and ERM membership or support of the government's policy on EMS and ERM; No support = no support of EMS and ERM membership or no support of the government's policy on EMS and ERM; Soft-landing = support of soft-landing position: EMS membership without ERM membership; Mixed = different views are expressed, e.g. by different authors, or opposition to ERM but at the same time fear to be left out of European integration or assessment of government's policy is mixed; Unclear = unclear whether newspaper supports EMS and ERM membership or the government's policy on EMS/ERM; Change = change of attitude on ERM and EMS or of the government's policy on ERM and EMS in the considered time period expressed in his parliamentary statement. By contrast, Italy's and Ireland's U-turns on ERM membership affected the debate. Immediately after the summit, at least the *Guardian*, the *Daily Mail* and the *Sun* considered the Brussels summit to have been a success for the PM. The *Sun*, at least, revised its assessment once it became clear that Italy and Ireland would join the ERM and Britain alone would stay outside the mechanism. It is striking that neither the *Daily Mail* nor the *Sun* picked up Callaghan's attempts to frame the decision against entry as patriotic by arguing that it was not in the country's national interest. Instead the *Sun*, for instance, saw Britain's economic decline (which it considered to be shameful) at the heart of the decision against joining the ERM and therefore criticised the government's decision. The papers in general did not appear to pick up the arguments Callaghan had made to explain his decision on the ERM in greater degree. Instead at least some saw the decision to remain out of the ERM as entirely motivated by short-term political calculations and party-political considerations.

10.2 Margaret Thatcher: European Council in Madrid, June 1989

After the completion of the Single European Act calls for closer monetary integration increased. In 1988 an expert group consisting of the heads of the national central banks led by European Commission President Jacques Delors was set up to develop a plan for a European monetary and economic union. It published its plan in a report in April 1989 (see Chap. 3). On 26 and 27 June 1989 the European Council met in Madrid and decided when to begin with stage one of the Delors plan.[18] On 29 June Prime Minister Margaret Thatcher gave a statement in parliament on the outcome of the meeting followed by questions from MPs (HC Deb 29 June 1989, cc1109–1124).

Thatcher said that the European Council had confirmed its intention to realise economic and monetary union. The Delors report was to form the basis for further discussion though other proposals were to be considered as well. The European Council had also agreed to begin the first stage of the Delors plan on 1 July 1990 while no decision had been reached on stages two and three. The premier furthermore informed the parliament that she had confirmed in Madrid that Britain would join the Exchange Rate Mechanism once a number of conditions were in place, which included reducing UK inflation, the scrapping of foreign exchange controls and the implementation of free capital movement in the EC (HC Deb 29 June 1989, cc1109–1110).

Thatcher focused on three aspects when explaining the decisions taken at the summit: (a) cooperation in monetary and economic policy, (b) sovereignty and (c) national interest.

[18] Apart from the Delors report on EMU, the summit also discussed the plan to give the European Community a social dimension. This analysis only covers EMU.

On the first aspect she acknowledged that closer cooperation in monetary and economic policy between EC member states was desirable to the UK (HC Deb 29 June 1989, cc1109, 1110). Particularly economic liberalisation should be intensified by "cutting constraints on enterprise and free competition" (HC Deb 29 June 1989, c1111). At the same time, she demanded that vital aspects of economic policy should remain to be decided at member state level (HC Deb 29 June 1989, c1109). European monetary and economic union should be based on voluntary cooperation (HC Deb 29 June 1989, cc1112–1113). Establishment of EMU was to be an incremental process not "a sudden thing" (HC Deb 29 June 1989, c1124). Therefore, her government would present suitable alternative proposals (HC Deb 29 June 1989, c1116).

Related to this view of European cooperation in monetary and economic policy was the second aspect Thatcher focused on in her speech: sovereignty. She considered the Delors report's stages two and three unacceptable as they included a massive transfer of national sovereignty rights to the European level (HC Deb 29 June 1989, c1109). With regard to the report she reiterated her refusal to "give up fundamental functions of monetary, fiscal economic policy to a group of central bank governors who are not democratically accountable" (HC Deb 29 June 1989, c1116).

Thatcher thirdly referred to Britain's national interest. She considered it to be safeguarded by the agreement to begin the Delors plan's first stage from 1 July 1990, in which Britain would take part. According to her, the measures encompassed in this stage included "completion of the single market, abolition of all foreign exchange controls, a free market in financial services and strengthening the Community's competition policy by reducing state aids" (HC Deb 29 June 1989, c1109). All provisions were in the interest of UK industry and the City of London. Moreover, decision-making rights of the British parliament were fully secured in this context (HC Deb 29 June 1989, c1110).

The following section analyses how far Prime Minister Thatcher managed to influence the print media debate on ERM and EMU policy. Again the analysis comprises coverage 2 weeks before the summit and 2 weeks after (15 June to 14 July 1989). The five newspapers' views on ERM and EMU prior to Thatcher's speech are set out in a first step. In a second one their views after the parliamentary statement are analysed. Coverage by the *Independent*, which by then had existed for a few years, is studied here as well.

The ***Financial Times*** extensively covered the summit, the plans for EMU, British ERM membership and Thatcher's parliamentary statement. Thirty-four articles, published between 15 June and 14 July 1989, were considered here.[19] Twenty-

[19]Further articles published in the time period not considered here covered the issues discussed at the summit from the perspective of the other European states, other British politicians, industry and academia.

four appeared before Thatcher's speech and four on the day of it. Many were descriptive reports of the developments around ERM, EMU and the summit. But the paper also set out its own view on ERM and EMU.

On the ERM the *Financial Times* argued that committing the country to membership would provide Britain with a better negotiating position at the European Council. More importantly, it noted, the "domestic arguments for commitment to full membership of the EMS have become overwhelming"[20] (Financial Times 1989b). Britain should join soon. Instead of waiting for inflation to come down, ERM membership should be used to reduce it (Financial Times 1989b). Directly after the summit the *FT* suggested that Thatcher had named membership conditions which could lead to Britain remaining outside the ERM for several years. According to the paper this delay could mean more inflation than necessary and a deeper recession for Britain (Financial Times 1989c; for the delay argument see also Stephens 1989a; Brittan 1989).

On EMU the *Financial Times* wrote shortly before the summit that Thatcher was domestically and internationally under strong pressure to soften her opposition to it (Buchan et al. 1989). It supported this and argued that EMU was going to be realised and thought the premier would do well to accept this and respond accordingly:

> After 40 years of experience it should be burnt into the consciousness of a British prime minister that she may slow down an evolution on which all other members of the EC are resolved; she may influence its form; but she will not stop it. It is true that in this case obdurate resistance can make it difficult for the others to proceed (since an amendment of the treaty will be required), but they can—and ultimately will—find a way around British opposition. The only issues are how moves towards monetary union will occur and whether they will happen with the UK or without it.[21] (Financial Times 1989b)

Nevertheless, while the paper thought it important that Britain was part of further planning on EMU, which suggests it did not oppose monetary union per se, it did have reservations over the Delors plan. It noted there were "elements in the proposals—notably the attempt to impose tight control over the fiscal policies of member countries—that are at best unnecessary and at worst dangerous"[22] (Financial Times 1989b). Prior to the summit it also argued that it would be difficult for the UK to point out these flaws of the plan, because of Thatcher's isolation at the European level. As a result of her opposition to joining the ERM, "she will be in a poor position to criticise the genuine weak points in the report"[23] (Financial Times 1989a). The *Financial Times* disapproved, saying that through her stance on European monetary policy, Thatcher was risking "total isolation on a vital matter

[20]Financial Times (1989), Isolation in Madrid, 23 June 1989. Used under licence from the Financial Times. All Rights Reserved.

[21]Financial Times (1989), Isolation in Madrid, 23 June 1989. Used under licence from the Financial Times. All Rights Reserved.

[22]Financial Times (1989), Isolation in Madrid, 23 June 1989. Used under licence from the Financial Times. All Rights Reserved.

[23]Financial Times (1989), Spain enters the ERM, 19 June 1989. Used under licence from the Financial Times. All Rights Reserved.

among the group of countries that holds the key to the UK's future"[24] (Financial Times 1989b). During the summit it suggested that the "momentum towards eventual monetary union may prove unstoppable"[25] (Stephens 1989a). After the European Council the *FT* continued to voice doubts over parts of the Delors report such as its stance on fiscal policy which it called "flawed"[26] (Financial Times 1989c) with regard to the process of its stages two and three.

On national sovereignty the *Financial Times* assumed that there would be transfers. It shared this assessment with Thatcher, who would make a statement to similar effect in her speech in parliament. In contrast to the PM, however, the paper did not explicitly state that it also thought those sovereignty transfers unacceptable. On the day of Thatcher's statement it noted that the European Council had taken a significant decision which would most likely result in a considerable transfer of national sovereignty rights to EC institutions in the future—a development in the European Community the paper called "a watershed in its political history"[27] (Davidson 1989). The paper went on to argue with regard to the upcoming EMU negotiations that "the purpose of the negotiation will be to transfer sovereignty to Community institutions"[28] (Davidson 1989). It also questioned whether Thatcher actually comprehended the direction in which the European Community was moving. According to the *Financial Times* this was political integration rather than intergovernmental cooperation (Davidson 1989).

Overall, the *Financial Times* strongly supported immediate ERM membership not only for economic but also for political reasons to strengthen Britain's stance in the EMU negotiations. On EMU the paper focused on Britain not being left out, thus suggesting that it supported the idea of monetary union. Yet it showed doubts over how it was to be realised because it thought the Delors report to be problematic.

After Thatcher's statement on 29 June 1989 the ***Financial Times*** does not appear to have changed its views on ERM and EMU. Many articles published in the remaining time period analysed here were descriptive accounts of the negotiations and decisions.

In an article on Thatcher's Commons speech the paper returned to its assessment that despite her announcement, ERM membership was not going to happen soon. The *FT* thought that it was out of the question that Thatcher would let Sterling join the ERM before the next general election. It suggested that her parliamentary

24Financial Times (1989), Isolation in Madrid, 23 June 1989. Used under licence from the Financial Times. All Rights Reserved.

25Stephens, P. (1989), Thatcher ceases to thump the table over monetary union, Financial Times. 27 June 1989. Used under licence from the Financial Times. All Rights Reserved.

26Financial Times (1989), Compromise in Madrid, 28 June 1989. Used under licence from the Financial Times. All Rights Reserved.

27Davidson, I. (1989), Clear path for European Community emerges through the fog, Financial Times, 29 June 1989. Used under licence from the Financial Times. All Rights Reserved.

28Davidson, I. (1989), Clear path for European Community emerges through the fog, Financial Times, 29 June 1989. Used under licence from the Financial Times. All Rights Reserved.

statement had been designed to indicate that she had taken a more constructive tone during the Madrid negotiations, but that she had not "ceded any ground on the major issues of principle"[29] (Stephens 1989b).

On EMU the *Financial Times* remained convinced of the view it had taken before Thatcher's statement: it was going to happen and the concept of the Delors plan was flawed. With regard to Britain's role in the further negotiations on EMU it argued:

> the challenge for the UK is to accept the essential preconditions of Emu, while doing everything possible to ensure that both the goal and the path towards it lacks [sic] the "airy-fairyness" despised by the prime minister. The point on which the UK must insist is that Emu is an economically risky and difficult course, which must not be rushed.[30] (Financial Times 1989d)

The paper did not change its view on sovereignty. In contrast to Thatcher, who had called the Delors report stages two and three unacceptable as they would include a massive transfer of national sovereignty rights to the European level, the *FT* held this argument to be irrelevant: "EMS and Delors report do not seek the transfer of sovereignty. They are an expression of a political power already conceded to the Community"[31] (Financial Times 1989e). It had been ceded when the UK had accepted the primacy of community law upon joining the European Community in the early 1970s, the paper argued (Financial Times 1989e).

Overall, a change of position by the *Financial Times* due to Thatcher's statement cannot be detected. In the period after the PM's speech, the paper no longer discussed whether the UK should join the ERM but focused on when this would possibly be the case. The *FT* thought that it would not happen any time soon. As the paper called for Britain's engagement in the negotiations, it suggests that it remained supportive of the idea of monetary union. Yet it continued to be wary of the process set out in the Delors plan.

The ***Guardian*** reported much but not as extensively as the *FT* about the summit and the UK's response to the EMU plan and ERM membership. Twenty-five articles were analysed here. Twenty were published before the PM's parliamentary statement and one on the day of it.[32]

Like the *Financial Times* the *Guardian* supported ERM membership. It, for instance, argued that Spain's decision to join the ERM shortly before the summit was proof of a sensible economic policy from which Britain, behaving so timidly, could learn much (The Guardian 1989a). To the *Guardian*, being a member of the

---

[29]Stephens, P. (1989), Thatcher pledges to counter Delors plan, Financial Times, 30 June 1989. Used under licence from the Financial Times. All Rights Reserved.

[30]Financial Times (1989), Mrs Thatcher and the Emu, 1 July 1989. Used under licence from the Financial Times. All Rights Reserved.

[31]Financial Times (1989), EC legal limits on British sovereignty, 3 July 1989.

[32]Further articles published in the analysed time period not considered here, covered the topics of the summit from the perspective of the other European states, the European Commission, other British politicians and companies. At the beginning of the time period the paper also addressed the outcome of the European elections.

ERM was part of the policy to reduce inflation, not a reward after inflation had been curbed. The paper also questioned whether the UK would be able to reduce inflation on its own (The Guardian 1989a). It suggested that ERM membership, in the worst case, was a policy not attempted before but which seemed to have worked well for all the other ERM members. Moreover, in the best case, it would end Britain's indecisiveness about its place in Europe (The Guardian 1989a). Like the *Financial Times* the paper supported ERM membership not only for economic, but also for political reasons. On 20 June, for example, it criticised Thatcher saying that with her opposition to joining the ERM she was risking isolation at the European level and keeping Britain from influencing future EC development (Milner 1989; The Guardian 1989a). After Thatcher's announcement in Madrid that Britain would join the ERM, the *Guardian* argued that she had become realistic. Membership, it went on, would increase British options to influence developments in Europe (Young 1989). All the while it remained critical of Thatcher's handling of the negotiations asking whether her ERM concession in Madrid was too late to have any impact on the other members (Palmer and Hooper 1989).

On EMU the *Guardian* argued on the first day of the summit (26 June) that Britain had a choice between taking part in European integration or pursuing a "Little Englander policy" (The Guardian 1989b). It questioned which future the country would have outside a new economic zone with a single currency, thus indicating it preferred the former option. Similar to the *Financial Times* the *Guardian* believed that EMU was going to happen despite Thatcher's opposition to it (The Guardian 1989b). However, the paper's support for EMU was not unqualified. It considered the Delors plan inadequate on a number of aspects. This included, for instance, that its concept of a central bank based on the German Bundesbank lacked democratic and political control. Nevertheless, if Britain joined the EMU process it would be in a better position to improve it from the in- than from the outside, the paper argued (The Guardian 1989c). It saw political, economic and democratic problems in the context of EMU which it thought should be debated not just at home but also at the European level (Palmer 1989). At the same time, it criticised the government for having only scorned the Delors plan but not having presented an alternative proposal (Young 1989).

The *Guardian* took a different view on sovereignty than Thatcher, as her subsequent parliamentary speech showed. The paper suggested that the government had already given up significant parts of sovereignty in financial matters when it had taken the decision in 1979 to abolish exchange controls. Moreover, on Thatcher's position on the ERM it questioned that she was actually surrendering something that Britain could still give up. The paper argued that whether one liked it or not, the UK belonged to Europe. This meant that its economic and political future would be much influenced by the EC. Thus the *Guardian* asked whether the UK might not gain more influence over its own future, if it accepted what was going on around it instead of plainly rejecting it (Milner 1989).

Overall, the *Guardian* took a similar stance as did the *FT* before Thatcher's parliamentary speech. It supported immediate ERM membership. It did so for economic and political reasons to strengthen the UK's position at the European level. On EMU it seemed to focus on Britain not being left out. It had doubts over how EMU was to be realised as set out in the Delors report. But it thought these could be remedied if the UK was part of the process from the start.

Three of the four articles published by the ***Guardian*** after Thatcher's statement of 29 June considered here, were mainly descriptive accounts of her appearance in parliament (Rawnsley 1989; White 1989; Knewstub 1989). The paper did not elaborate on its own stance on ERM and EMU, thus it cannot be detected that it changed its view on either as a result of Thatcher's speech. On EMU it noted that the premier, who had said she would vote against treaty change, would not be able to keep the other EC members from negotiating a treaty on monetary union without the UK (The Guardian 1989d). Yet the *Guardian* did not reveal whether it saw this as a threat.

Similar to the other two broadsheets, the ***Independent*** reported much on the summit, ERM membership and the British position on EMU. Twenty-four articles were considered in the analysis. Twenty-one appeared before Thatcher's parliamentary statement and one on the day of it.[33] Like the other broadsheets, the *Independent* supported ERM membership. Before the summit it noted that if the PM announced ERM entry it would (a) persuade the markets that she supported her chancellor and (b) signal a more constructive European policy (Jenkins 1989a). On 22 June it argued that committing to quick ERM entry would ensure that the UK was part of further developments on EMU and would probably be able to slow them down (Usborne and Cottrell 1989). On the economic implications of membership the *Independent* estimated that the current inflation level in Britain would not have been as high had the UK joined the ERM in 1985 (Rees-Mogg 1989). This is re-addressed in another article which, however, leaves open whether lower inflation in ERM member states was a result of their ERM membership (Wilson-Smith 1989). The paper, moreover, suggested that the government would sooner achieve lower inflation, if the country joined the ERM now (The Independent 1989a). After the summit it remained critical of Thatcher's handling of the negotiations on European monetary policy, saying her decision against fully joining the EMS was a mistake, because ERM membership would have meant curbing inflation and would have emphasised the notion that Britain was "an advocate of pragmatic progress" (The Independent 1989b).

On EMU the *Independent* reported on 27 June that Thatcher had committed the UK to it, but not to the process suggested by the Delors report. The paper supported this and welcomed her approach, because if the prime minister could convince her European counterparts to revise the Delors plan's stages two and three according to

---

[33]Further articles published in the time period not considered here dealt with the Conservative's results at the European election and with the position of the other member states, business associations and the opposition on the topics of the summit. There were also a few overview articles marginally covering the Madrid summit.

her suggestions, this would make the EC's approach to EMU "more practical and open-minded" (Jenkins 1989b).

The *Independent* suggested that Thatcher's arguments had achieved weight in the European debate, because she no longer rejected EMU all-together and instead had called for alternative approaches to EMU. As long as one wanted to go somewhere, there was nothing wrong with proposing a step-by-step approach, it noted. Its outlook was positive arguing that the UK might finally have found its place in the European integration project (Jenkins 1989c).

The paper argued for a constructive approach to European integration at the summit, because, as it suggested on 27 June, this would mean that Britain would not just complain from the sidelines but would be an important architect of a significant European integration project (Jenkins 1989b).

Overall, the *Independent* supported immediate ERM membership for economic and political reasons, as Britain would so be included in the discussions on EMU. It, moreover, supported EMU but not the process set out in the Delors report. It also supported the policy Thatcher indicated at the summit because the UK could help making the process more practical.

After Thatcher's statement the ***Independent*** with just two articles scarcely reported on EMU and ERM until the end of the analysed time period. In both articles the paper reported what Thatcher had said in parliament without stating its own view on ERM and EMU (Goodwin 1989; Bevins 1989). Thus there is no indication that her speech led to a change of view on the part of the *Independent*.

The coverage of the ***Daily Mail*** of the summit, EMU and ERM and Thatcher's statement in parliament was less extensive than that of the broadsheets. Thirteen articles were considered here. Ten were published before her speech in Parliament and one on its day.[34]

In contrast to the broadsheets the *Daily Mail* took a more sceptical view of European monetary integration. Its position on ERM membership appeared to change in the time period analysed here. On 19 June the paper noted that the premier had good reason to be uneasy about her chancellor's proposal to join the ERM. The last time she had allowed him to decide monetary policy his decision to shadow the Deutschmark had led to rising inflation, the paper argued (Alexander 1989a). But once it became clear that Thatcher at Madrid would commit the UK to ERM membership, the paper showed support for it. It welcomed the conditions she would name in parliament on 29 June as necessary for Britain to join the ERM, such as an end to exchange controls in other European countries and lower inflation in Britain, as sensible (Johnson 1989; see also Alexander 1989b).

[34]Further articles published in the analysed time period not considered here dealt with the bad European election outcome for the Conservatives and with the stance of the opposition and other European actors on the summit's topics.

The *Daily Mail* did not explicitly mention its view on EMU. On 28 June it stated that the current plans would fail just as the Werner-Plan in the 1970s had failed (Alexander 1989c). It did, however, support Thatcher's negotiating stance on EMU. In a portrait of her published on the first day of the summit it demanded more appreciation of her approach to the negotiations, as she was right in looking at the long-term effects on European economic and financial policy (Johnson 1989). On the day of her speech it noted that the PM would today be able to celebrate her triumph over the Brussels technocrats, who were trying to get their hands on the UK's funds (Deans 1989a).

Overall, the *Daily Mail* appeared to shift its view on the ERM in line with the PM from scepticism to support, provided the conditions she would mention in her parliamentary statement were in place. On EMU the paper supported Thatcher's stance. It did not explicitly set out its own view of the project but in some of its coverage gave the impression that it at least had reservations about EMU.

A day after Thatcher's statement, the ***Daily Mail*** wrote that the premier had been celebrated by Tory MPs for hindering plans for a European single currency and a federal Europe (Deans 1989b). Only two articles were published after the PM's appearance in parliament. In neither did the paper express its own view of ERM or EMU or of the government's policies on it. Consequently no change in its coverage after Thatcher's speech, if there was any, could be detected.

The ***Sun*** covered the summit and Thatcher's statement less extensively than the other papers. Eight articles, published between 15 June and 14 July, were considered in the analysis. Seven appeared before the prime minister's speech and one on the day of it.[35]

Similar to that of the *Daily Mail*, the *Sun*'s position on the ERM appeared to change. On day one of the summit the tabloid was alarmed over suggestions Thatcher might compromise on the ERM and agree to join. It hoped she would not do so (The Sun 1989a). But a day later the *Sun* highlighted the advantages of membership using a British company producing products for the gas and oil industry as an example. The paper then suggested that membership would make sterling's exchange rate more stable and be helpful to UK exports (Reid 1989). On the day of Thatcher's parliamentary statement it argued her agreement to ERM entry would lead to more stability (albeit without explaining of what exactly) (The Sun 1989b).

On EMU the *Sun* had a clear opinion: It opposed it and welcomed Thatcher's refusal to accept the scheme to abolish sterling and adopt a single currency (Kemp 1989a). It complained that UK prices appeared higher in ECU due to the exchange rate between sterling and ECU. Only holiday makers would welcome a single currency as they would no longer have to exchange money, the paper argued (Kay 1989). On the day of Thatcher's speech it argued that she had delayed plans to

[35]Further articles published in that time period not considered here dealt with the position of others on the issues like Commission President Delors and the discussion of a social dimension of the EC.

establish full economic union which it saw as the aim of "Euro fanatics" (The Sun 1989b) and suggested such a move was now unrealistic.

The tabloid shared Thatcher's argument that the transfer of sovereignty rights in economic and monetary policy to the European level as devised in the later stages of the Delors Plan was unacceptable. On 26 June the *Sun* commented that it feared she might yield to the wishes of others who wanted Britain to give up power over sterling and its economy (The Sun 1989a). The tabloid hoped that Thatcher would not change her stance and would follow her intuition which, it argued, had so often been good for Britain (The Sun 1989a). On 27 June it argued that Thatcher had fought the other Europeans the previous day over the control of the British economy (Kemp 1989a). And even in the article in support of ERM membership the *Sun* reiterated that such membership should not mean giving up Britain's independence. This was an issue on which the paper noted that it agreed with the prime minister (Reid 1989). On 28 June it argued that the results she had achieved in Madrid were a triumph which secured the further existence of the pound (Kemp 1989b).

Overall, the *Sun*'s view on EMU and ERM was in line with Thatcher's arguments. Like her, the tabloid particularly opposed EMU because of its implications for British sovereignty. On the ERM it shifted its stance from opposition to tentative support along with the prime minister, just as the *Daily Mail* had done.

As the ***Sun*** did not address ERM and EMU after Thatcher's appearance in parliament until the end of the analysed time period, it cannot be evaluated whether her statement had any impact on the paper's view of the issues. Yet as the analysis of the coverage prior to her statement has indicated, her actions at the summit with regard to the ERM did.

Looking at the five newspapers' coverage of the decisions taken at the Madrid summit (Table 10.2), Thatcher does appear to have had limited success in framing the debate with her arguments on ERM and EMU as expressed in her parliamentary statement. Unlike the prime minister, the analysed broadsheets supported the principle of EMU although they saw significant problems with the concept envisioned in the Delors plan. There is no indication that any of the papers changed their view on this due to Thatcher's more sceptical attitude to a common European monetary policy, which she set out in parliament after the summit. The three newspapers, moreover, supported ERM membership which they saw as an important element in securing Britain's influence in the upcoming EMU negotiation. In contrast to Thatcher they supported immediate membership. The *Sun*'s and the *Daily Mail*'s opinion appeared to be more in line with Thatcher's view on European monetary policy. On the ERM both had voiced opposition in the beginning, but when Thatcher shifted her stance and announced in Madrid that Britain would join, they altered their positions as well. Thus, in this case the premier appears to have been able to shape either paper's stance, albeit not through her parliamentary statement but through her previous announcement at the summit. The *Sun* explicitly and the *Daily Mail* at least in tendency opposed EMU, which was also in line with Thatcher's view. The *Financial Times* and the *Guardian* on the other hand, argued that sovereignty rights

Table 10.2 Newspapers' attitudes to ERM, EMU and support for government policy 1989 (own illustration)

	Financial Times	The Guardian	The Independent	Daily Mail	The Sun
ERM					
Before the speech					
Attitude to ERM	Support	Support	Support	Change to support	Change to support
Support for government policy	No support	Mixed	No support	Support	Support
After the speech					
Attitude to ERM	Unclear	Unclear	Unclear	Unclear	–
Support for government policy	Unclear	Unclear	Unclear	Unclear	–
EMU					
Before the speech					
Attitude to EMU	Support	Support	Support	Unclear	No support
Support for government policy	No support	No support	Support	Support	Support
After the speech					
Attitude to EMU	Support	Unclear	Unclear	Unclear	–
Support for government policy	Unclear	Unclear	Unclear	Unclear	–

Key: Support = support of ERM/EMU membership or support of the government's policy on ERM/EMU; No support = no support of ERM/EMU membership or no support of the government's policy on ERM/EMU; Mixed = different views are expressed, e.g. by different authors or opposition to ERM/EMU but at the same time fear to be left out of European integration or mixed assessment of government's policy; Unclear = unclear whether paper supports the government's policy on ERM/EMU or ERM/EMU in general; Change = change of attitude on ERM/EMU or of the government's policy on ERM/EMU in the considered time period

in economic and monetary policy had already been transferred to the European level and were no longer anything the premier could secure.

10.3 John Major: European Council in Maastricht, December 1991

At the Maastricht European Council on 9 and 10 December 1991 the heads of government and state settled the remaining open points of the European Union treaty. Britain had campaigned for a general opt-out clause on Economic and Monetary Union. When Denmark, the only other country supporting a general opt-out, withdrew its support in early December, an opt-out limited to the UK became likely (Buchan 1991). The summit ended with the conclusion of the treaty. Prime Minister John Major had achieved an opt-out from EMU's third stage and one from the Social Chapter.[36] In his parliamentary statement on the summit on 11 December 1991 and the subsequent questioning from MPs (HC Deb 11 December 1991, cc859–878), Major announced that the European Council had agreed a treaty to establish a European Union. It had also decided to introduce a single currency by the end of the decade, if sufficient member states met the agreed convergence criteria. A special provision had been included for the UK allowing it to decide later whether it wanted to join stage three of EMU, the PM clarified (HC Deb 11 December 1991, c859).

In his statement Major explained the summit results focusing on three aspects: (a) Britain and EMU, (b) national interest and (c) Britain's role in Europe.

On Britain and EMU the PM clarified that a protocol to the European Union treaty, drafted by Britain, stipulated that the country was not obliged to join EMU's third stage. But it would be part of decision-making on EMU (HC Deb 11 December 1991, c859). This meant that the UK would be able to decide whether to join EMU's third stage at a time when the actual conditions were clear, Major said (HC Deb 11 December 1991, c864).

He also referred to the country's national interest, which, he said, had been secured and advanced through the treaty (HC Deb 11 December 1991, c863). While not giving an explicit definition of what he meant by the country's national interest, his speech suggests that he saw it in terms of preserving Britain's national sovereignty through (a) intergovernmental decision-making and (b) British opt-outs from supranational decision-making. On European foreign policy decision-making, for instance, he noted: "We have... preserved unanimity for all decisions where we decide that we need it" (HC Deb 11 December 1991, c860). Also, Britain had not agreed to co-decision-making between European Parliament and Council of Ministers as "the Council of Ministers must be the body that ultimately determines the Community's laws and policies" (HC Deb 11 December 1991, cc860–861). Moreover, the principle of 'subsidiarity' was included in the treaty, which meant that "the Community should only be involved in decisions which cannot more effectively be taken at national level" (HC Deb 11 December 1991, c861).

On Britain's influence in Europe, Major argued that the country had "played a leading role" (HC Deb 11 December 1991, c862) in the treaty negotiations. It had made practical proposals, particularly when suggestions by other members had been too ambitious. Where it had considered those unworkable, it had proposed alternatives. A British influence could be detected throughout the treaty, Major claimed (HC Deb 11 December 1991, c862). The UK would be involved in all decisions on Economic and Monetary Union (HC Deb 11 December 1991, c864). It was not "semi-detached from the decisions that will be made in Europe. It will be part of all the decisions made in Europe" (HC Deb 11 December 1991, c865).

[36]In the following analysis his statement on the treaty and the press coverage 2 weeks before and 2 weeks after the summit are studied focusing on EMU.

The following section analyses to what extent John Major managed to influence the print media debate on the outcome of the treaty negotiations particularly on EMU. Again the analysis comprises coverage 2 weeks before the summit and 2 weeks after (28 November to 24 December 1991). The first part of the analysis covers the time period ending with the day of Major's speech. In a second step the media coverage after the speech is analysed.

The ***Financial Times*** extensively covered the negotiations and the summit. Forty-one articles, published between 28 November and 24 December 1991, were considered in the analysis.[37] Twenty-two were published before Major's statement and four on the day. Before Major's appearance in parliament the paper reported much on the EMU negotiations and the government's stance, but did not specifically express its own view on monetary union.

On the country's national interest the premier would say in parliament that it had been safeguarded by the treaty. The *Financial Times* took a different view. On 4 December it referred to diverging definitions of national interest, noting that in Britain it "continues to be measured almost entirely according to criteria relating to independence and sovereignty, rather than in terms of the benefits to the nation and its people, which could be derived from a pooling of sovereignty"[38] (Mauthner 1991). To the *FT* it was more in the UK's national interest to be integrated in a European Community of prosperity and stability than preserving sovereignty in policy fields where it had been diminished already anyhow (Mauthner 1991).

On Britain's role in Europe the *Financial Times* came to a mixed conclusion and consequently took a different view from Major's. He would state in parliament that Britain was a key actor in Europe. The *FT* in contrast called the UK isolated on the EMU negotiations when Denmark withdrew support for a general opt-out clause in early December (Buchan and Stephens 1991). On 3 December it criticised that European integration in the past 40 years had only progressed because of the other EC members, while Britain had tried to prevent it or keep out. The *FT* complained that the current administration conducted the same policy and noted that Major "is determined not to be left out, but he will do his best to limit the damage"[39] (Davidson 1991a). It argued that the proposal for a general EMU opt-out gave the EC partners the impression that Britain was trying to sabotage the project. Moreover, the paper viewed the government's stance on the treaty as unconstructive:

> Being "at the heart of Europe", to use Mr John Major's phrase, certainly does not mean accepting every proposal for further monetary and political integration, made even by a

---

[37]Further articles published in the analysed time period not considered here covered the negotiations on European social policy, the views of the other EC countries and the opposition on EMU and Major's negotiating style in general.

[38]Mauthner, R. (1991), The persistent odd man out, Financial Times, 4 December 1991. Used under licence from the Financial Times. All Rights Reserved.

[39]Davidson, I. (1991), New era for EC family, Financial Times, 3 December 1991. Used under licence from the Financial Times. All Rights Reserved.

majority of the other member states. It does, however, require more than a purely negative stance. What has been lacking on the British side are constructive suggestions on how European integration can be taken forward.[40] (Mauthner 1991)

As mentioned, the *Financial Times* did not specifically lay out its own view on EMU in the analysed time period leading up to Major's statement. Yet its position on Britain's national interest, its role in Europe and the government's European policy showed a strong support for European integration in general. Moreover, the paper was critical of the government's policy in the context of the EMU negotiations.

After Major's parliamentary statement of 11 December the ***Financial Times*** indicated its support for EMU. It noted: "The agreement of the Community countries to adopt a single currency, with a binding timetable, is a momentous achievement"[41] (Brittan 1991). The paper criticised the fact that Major had not "felt politically strong enough to embrace the single currency to the extent that Germany has"[42] (Brittan 1991). It found it hard to believe that Britain would eventually opt-out of a single currency because the economic risks of not joining were too large. Also, as ERM member, the UK already had to fulfil all the obligations of monetary union without receiving all the advantages, the *FT* noted (Brittan 1991). Elsewhere the *Financial Times* (1991) again questioned that Britain would remain outside once EMU was realised.

On Britain in Europe, the *Financial Times* stated critically a day after Major's speech that Britain had itself at Maastricht introduced the start of a "two-tier Europe in which it is in a minority of 1"[43] (Davidson 1991b). It acknowledged that Major had done much to bring the UK into the European mainstream but at the same time had kept a distance to several crucial decisions taken at Maastricht. Through this he had taken the country to the edge of Europe, it criticised (Thompson-Noel 1991). It, moreover, condemned the fact that Britain had lost its influence on the EMU timetable due to its insistence on an opt-out. In the paper's opinion the government's EMU objective had been "to delay and if possible prevent any Community commitment to a single currency"[44] (Davidson 1991b). This contrasted with Major's argument that the opt-out would give the UK further choice on EMU. It appears that the *Financial Times*' view on the treaty and on the EMU decisions was not much influenced by Major's framing of events. The

[40]Mauthner, R. (1991), The persistent odd man out, Financial Times, 4 December 1991. Used under licence from the Financial Times. All Rights Reserved.

[41]Brittan, S. (1991), A victory, but not quite a triumph, Financial Times, 12 December 1991. Used under licence from the Financial Times. All Rights Reserved.

[42]Brittan, S. (1991), A victory, but not quite a triumph, Financial Times, 12 December 1991. Used under licence from the Financial Times. All Rights Reserved.

[43]Davidson, I. (1991), Hollow victory for Britain as it launches two-tier Europe, Financial Times, 12 December 1991. Used under licence from the Financial Times. All Rights Reserved.

[44]Davidson, I. (1991), Hollow victory for Britain as it launches two-tier Europe, Financial Times, 12 December 1991. Used under licence from the Financial Times. All Rights Reserved.

FT, which called European monetary union a "momentous achievement"[45] (Brittan 1991), seems to have seen the opt-out, the key element of Major's policy on EMU in the negotiations as futile as it expected Britain to join the single currency because it thought the economic risks of remaining outside were too large.

The ***Guardian*** also reported extensively on the treaty negotiations, the summit and Major's parliamentary statement on it. Thirty-five articles, published between 28 November and 24 December 1991, were included in the analysis.[46] Twenty-two appeared before the premier spoke in parliament and four on the day of his speech. Like the *Financial Times*, the *Guardian* focused in its coverage before Major's statement on reporting the government's negotiating stance on EMU as well as the negotiations of the treaty. The paper did not indicate explicitly whether it supported joining monetary union. Yet it showed on 9 December in the context of the draft treaty's proposals on EMU that it had reservations about how it was to be achieved, because it found the provisions in the draft incomplete on this. The paper criticised that there was no explanation how the other member states could imitate Germany's behaviour on wages, rates of growth and productivity as it thought this was necessary, if EMU was to succeed (Kelly and Elliott 1991).

On Britain in Europe the paper's assessment was critical. In contrast to Major, who in parliament would argue that the UK was a key actor in Europe, the *Guardian* instead wrote on the day of his Commons speech that the treaty with the opt-outs pointed to the establishment of a two-speed Europe with Britain on the slower path (Palmer 1991, Hutton 1991b also refers to a two-speed Europe due to the EMU decision). In another article it referred to the main concession Major had had to make to be granted an opt-out from the third stage of EMU: the acceptance of the irreversibility of the process of economic and monetary union. To the *Guardian* this meant that Britain had agreed to have neither veto nor any other tool to slow the process of EMU down. It would also have no influence on the selection of the leadership of the European Central Bank (Hutton 1991a).

Overall, the *Guardian* did not explicitly state whether it supported monetary union, but it showed that it was sceptical of the path the EC members intended to embark on to realise it. In any case, it was critical of the government's policy on EMU.

After Major's parliamentary statement, the ***Guardian*** elaborated more on EMU in its coverage of the negotiation outcome than it had done before the speech. According to the paper Britain was on the path to join the single currency despite the opt-out. It argued that Major had managed to disguise the far reaching decisions

[45]Brittan, S. (1991), A victory, but not quite a triumph, Financial Times, 12 December 1991. Used under licence from the Financial Times. All Rights Reserved.

[46]Further articles published in the analysed time period not considered here very marginally related to the negotiations or reported on other topics of the treaty e.g. social policy. The views of the opposition, other EC members and the British public on the issues were addressed, too.

on EMU with the Social Chapter opt-out which had overshadowed all other decisions taken at Maastricht. Yet the momentum towards EMU was now unstoppable. There was a date for it. Despite the opt-out the UK no longer had a veto and remaining outside of EMU was increasingly unlikely. Moreover, the paper argued, Britain had agreed to a deal which meant that—like the other member states—it would effectively conduct an economic policy throughout the next decade as if it was joining the single currency (Young 1991). Unlike Major who had argued that the opt-out gave the country an additional option on EMU, the *Guardian* suggested that Britain would be under pressure to join EMU and that the agreement at Maastricht had not interrupted but rather hastened this process (Young 1991). It estimated that the single currency could replace sterling in 6–7 years and suggested that it was impossible to imagine that when the time would come to take a decision the UK would exercise its EMU opt-out. Even if there was still a conservative government by then, the paper argued, the City of London would make this government agree to adopt the single currency (Aitken 1991). Thus like the *Financial Times*, the *Guardian* thought the opt-out might turn out to be useless.

On Britain in Europe the *Guardian* considered the UK strongly integrated in Europe, while lamenting Major's lack of explicit support for Britain's European integration. It noted on 12 December that he had placed the UK at the centre of European integration as he had promised to do—albeit without publicly admitting how close, which the paper regretted (Young 1991). As it had done before his speech, the paper argued that while Major had secured an opt-out, he had conceded the opportunity to be part of the decision-making on future personnel of a European Central Bank. A further concession by the UK had been the acceptance of a specific timetable on EMU (White 1991).

Overall, the coverage of the *Guardian* in the period after Major's speech does not seem to be much influenced by the PM's framing of events. Despite not explicitly setting out its own position on EMU, the paper saw it as an inevitable process—unlike Major who argued that Britain had a choice about taking part. The *Guardian*, moreover, did not believe that the UK would eventually opt-out of EMU.

Like the other two broadsheets, the ***Independent*** extensively covered the negotiations and the decisions taken at Maastricht. Thirty-eight articles, published between 28 November and 24 December 1991, were considered in the analysis.[47] Eighteen appeared before Major spoke in parliament and three on the day of it.

Prior to the PM's statement, the *Independent* showed that it supported EMU, a position which differed from Major's cautious stance. As early as 28 November, the paper suggested that if Britain did not join EMU, sterling would probably stand in the shadow of the stronger ECU. If it then joined later, the conditions for

[47]Further articles published in the time period not considered here dealt with the Social Chapter and other issues of the treaty. They also covered the negotiation stance of other EC member states, the interpretation of opinion poll data concerning the government's European policy and the role of the Foreign Office in European policy.

membership would already have been set by the other members. Without immediate and complete EMU participation, the *Independent* argued, the influential role of the City of London was at risk. This in turn, it believed, would have negative economic consequences for the country (The Independent 1991a). It also questioned parliament's freedom of choice on the single currency. The financial markets, the paper warned, would move their business from the UK, if they felt the opt-out could lead to Britain losing the economic advantages it had due to its single market membership. This could result in negative economic consequences for the UK (Usborne et al. 1991b). Because of the agreement of an EMU timetable, the *Independent* suggested on the day of Major's speech that the UK would not be able to remain outside of EMU, if a single currency was established. The government should instead soon clear up doubts over participation in order to be able to influence further EMU development. On EMU, it noted, that the UK had underrated the other member states' resolution to realise the project (The Independent 1991c).

The *Independent* urged constructive engagement with Europe and criticised the government's negotiating strategy, calling it "negative and reactive" (The Independent 1991b). With the outcome on EMU becoming clearer during the summit and the expectation of a definite timetable for the single currency, the paper again criticised the government's policy. According to the *Independent* the idea that the UK could agree to an EMU treaty had in parts been based on the belief that monetary union was not very likely to be realised. Now, however, it looked quite certain to happen at the end of the decade. Staying out of the single currency could be a huge risk for Britain leaving UK companies without the benefits of EMU as well as risking a run on the pound, the paper argued. It concluded that Britain should not have focused so much on achieving the opt-out, because, if it had not done so, it might have been able to secure better conditions on the process towards a single currency (Marshall 1991). Due to the planned timetable for EMU, the paper concluded on the second day of the summit that the introduction of the single currency by 1999 was all but certain which would also make it the date by which Britain would have to decide about joining the project (Marshall and Usborne 1991).

From the *Independent*'s position on EMU it can be gathered that in contrast to Major it did not see the opt-out (and thus the provisions of the treaty) to be in the country's national interest. On 11 December it criticised that the government had pursued its opt-out policy to appease its party's right wing. This was wrong because governments were meant to take difficult decisions and not delay them—particularly if such a postponement might hurt the interests of the nation (The Independent 1991c). The paper argued that to consider EMU membership to include a loss of sovereignty was too simple. Instead a single currency would mean that there were shared rules. Therefore, in important areas there would be an increase instead of a loss of sovereignty (The Independent 1991c).

On Britain's role in Europe the *Independent* suggested before the summit that the fear of European level isolation had dominated Major's European policy—at least in public. Meanwhile, it noted, an opt-out might lead to greater marginalisation. Moreover, it saw the risk that the UK could lose influence in the world due to a marginalised position in Europe, with negative economic effects for the country (The

Independent 1991a). Once it was clear that there would be no general EMU opt-out which would apply to all member states, the paper argued that the UK at Maastricht had lost the opportunity to prevent its own isolation on EMU (Usborne et al. 1991a). This differed from Major's view that despite the opt-out the UK would be fully involved in the decision-making on EMU.

Overall, the *Independent* supported joining EMU which it saw as more or less inevitable anyway. Like the other broadsheets it feared Britain would be isolated due to the opt-out. It opposed the government's opt-out policy, because it thought it had kept the government from securing better terms on the passage to a single currency.

After Major's parliamentary statement on the summit, the ***Independent*** showed a mixed assessment of the decisions on EMU. A day after Major's speech the paper viewed the opt-out in a positive light seeing it as giving Britain two options: either joining a monetary union which looked convincing or staying away from a project which appeared dubious (Jenkins 1991). At the same time it suggested—as it had done before Major's statement—that the opt-out was something Major had inherited from Thatcher, something which was necessary politically to manage his party but not representative of the UK's actual position on Europe (Jenkins 1991).

It returned to its criticism of the government's opt-out policy which it had already exhibited before Major's statement. On 12 December it noted that it was regrettable that Major due to the political restrictions he faced at home, which had been his predecessor's legacy, had to present Britain's view mostly in a negative way and felt it necessary to have the opt-out which might damage Britain. According to the paper it was not good that Britain insisted on a special deal on something which would have repercussions for decisions on investments now and in the future (The Independent 1991e).

On 15 December the paper suggested it was not economically sensible to remain outside a currency zone of which Germany and France were part. It criticised that the government had used up political capital to achieve an EMU opt-out only to postpone a confrontation with its own party's right wing over Europe (Huhne 1991). The paper had already warned of this before the summit (MacIntyre 1991). At the same time the *Independent* was, at least in one article, highly critical of EMU, calling it "the stupidest [sic] economic decision for the past 50 years" (Rees-Mogg 1991).

On the country's national interest, which Major had said had been safeguarded by the provisions in the treaty, the *Independent* remained of a different view. It thought Maastricht was not a victory in that respect. Instead, with a possible introduction of a single currency by 1999, it was in the country's interest to be part of it—economically and to safeguard the City of London's position as key financial hub in Europe, it believed (Huhne 1991).

On Britain's influence in Europe the paper again did not share the PM's view, which was that the country remained fully involved in the decision-making process on EMU despite the opt-out. The *Independent* noted a day after Major's statement that the UK had achieved two key objectives with the EMU and the Social Chapter opt-outs. But due to them, the country was now isolated on two key areas of European integration (The Independent 1991d). In another article on the same day, however, it took a positive view on Britain's future role in Europe, saying that the treaty with its aim of monetary and a mostly intergovernmental political union would ensure that Britain would gain a place at the centre of European integration. There it would be able to belatedly join France and Germany, whose close relationship, the paper argued, was a result of Britain's decision to stay away for so long (Jenkins 1991).

Overall, the coverage of the *Independent* in the analysed time period showed a mixed assessment of the EMU decisions taken at Maastricht. There were articles suggesting that the paper viewed EMU more positively than the government and was worried the country might once more be left without a voice on a European project which it would probably have to join later anyhow. The paper had already held this position before Major's statement. Thus, it did not adopt his arguments on EMU after his parliamentary speech. Yet in other articles the paper also showed opposition to EMU and support for the government's opt-out policy.

The ***Daily Mail*** extensively covered the EMU negotiations and results. Twenty-one articles, published between 28 November and 24 December 1991, were analysed. Eleven appeared before Major's speech and one on its day.[48]

The paper supported adopting the single currency, provided it turned out to be a success. On the summit's first day it argued Britain would not be able to and should not block moves to a single currency. If Germany decided to give up the Deutschmark for something else, this alternative would be something the City of London and anyone travelling abroad would want to use. Consequently the *Daily Mail* argued that Major was right to ensure that (a) the UK remained part of Europe's financial centre, (b) the government was involved in the development of the single currency and (c) parliament would be able to take a decision about joining in the future. It explicitly endorsed the PM's European policy and wished the prime minister the best for the negotiations. The summit would be a test to his negotiation skills as well as to Britain's intentions to help develop a more resilient and secure European Community. This, the paper argued, could only be done, if Britain was part of the EC (Daily Mail 1991a). Major and his government were less concerned with placating intraparty critics of their European policy than with safeguarding the UK currency in the negotiations, the paper believed (Deans and Doughty 1991).

On Britain in Europe the *Daily Mail* tended to take a more sceptical view than Major. While he would later say in parliament that the country had played a leading part in the negotiations, the paper before the summit warned that an EMU opt-out limited to the UK would not only make the establishment of a single currency more likely, but also Britain appear isolated (Doughty and Greig 1991). On 4 December it

[48]Further articles published in the time period not considered here were on the Social Chapter discussions and the negotiating position of other European politicians or other heads of government and state. It also referred to public opinion polls on Major and his performance and Thatcher's view of the negotiation results.

noted that on a general EMU opt-out Britain was in a minority of one against eleven (Doughty 1991).

Overall, the view on EMU expressed by the *Daily Mail* was mixed. Despite stating support for the adoption of the single currency, if successful, the paper also exhibited reservations about EMU. On the day of Major's speech, for example, it stated that the opt-out meant that Britain would not be pushed to abolish sterling in order to adopt the European single currency (Greig and Doughty 1991) The paper displayed support for Major's policy on the negotiations and EMU. Yet it also expressed doubts about an EMU opt-out limited to the UK.

After Major's statement on the summit, the ***Daily Mail*** confirmed its agreement with the government's EMU policy. It remained supportive of joining the single currency should it turn out to be a success. As before the PM's speech, it argued that the UK would want to adopt a single currency, if Germany eventually decided to replace the Deutschmark with it. It argued that Major had achieved that Britain was part of the negotiations on further EMU development. The paper welcomed this, stating that this achievement should be supported by the electorate and unite the Tory Party (Daily Mail 1991b). On EMU, it noted, Britain had gained the option to take a decision on the issue when it wanted to do so without being excluded from the decision-making on the project in the meantime (Greig and Deans 1991).

The paper agreed with Major that the treaty was in the national interest, although it omitted to set out explicitly what it thought such interest was. On 12 December it mentioned in two articles that he had reached an agreement which secured British interests (Johnson 1991; Daily Mail 1991b).

The *Daily Mail* supported Major's argument that the treaty safeguarded British influence in Europe. While it had worried before the summit that Britain might be isolated or outnumbered on the EMU opt-out (e.g. Doughty and Greig 1991, Doughty 1991), the day after his speech it claimed that Major had achieved an agreement which secured that the UK was not isolated (Johnson 1991). Moreover, his handling of the negotiations had been a significant move towards keeping the UK at the centre of European integration (Greig and Deans 1991).

Overall, the *Daily Mail* agreed with Major's line of argument on EMU. But this was not just the case after his statement. Despite some scepticism on the opt-out limited to the UK, it had already supported his stance on EMU in the run up to the Maastricht summit—particularly his aim of keeping the option to join open, should the single currency turn out to be a success.

The ***Sun*** reported less extensively on the EMU treaty negotiations and results than any of the other papers. Eleven articles, published between 28 November and 24 December, were considered in the analysis. Seven appeared before Major's parliamentary statement.[49]

[49]Further articles published in the time period not considered here covered the discussion on European social policy, the British industry's stance on EMU and Thatcher's view of the negotiation outcome.

Prior to the summit the *Sun* did not explicitly state whether it supported joining EMU. But it shared Major's view that it was essential for parliament to be able to decide independently and later whether to join a single currency. On the summit's first day it argued that the PM at Maastricht would not agree to a deal which would leave MPs without their right to decide themselves whether to join the single currency or not (Kavanagh 1991a). The tabloid tended to frame the negotiations as a dispute between Major and his European counterparts or Britain and the other EC members, for instance, with headlines such as "PM 'won't be bullied'" (The Sun 1991a). On 10 December it suggested that there had been an ambush by the other members at the summit telling the UK to abolish sterling by the end of the decade (Kavanagh and Black 1991).

Overall, the *Sun* did not explicitly express its view on EMU. Yet it did refer to the parliament's right to decide about adopting a single currency, which it—like Major—thought had to be secured.

After Major's parliamentary statement, the ***Sun*** welcomed the fact that he had not given up sterling for a single currency (Littlejohn 1991). Assessing the summit outcome, the paper called it a victory that Britain had in principle agreed to a single currency by 1999, but had secured the right to determine itself if and when to join (The Sun 1991c). It congratulated Major on his achievements saying that it was now the UK's right to decide whether or not to adopt a single currency of Europe and thus to choose what was the best course for the country (The Sun 1991b).

After his speech the *Sun* continued to report the negotiation outcome as a dispute or at least a competition between Major and his European counterparts. For example on 12 December it compared the prime minister to a one-handed poker player—one-handed because of pressure from Conservative hardliners. According to the paper Major had surprised his critics "by playing a bad hand like a professional Mississippi riverboat gambler—scooping the jackpot" (Kavanagh 1991b).

This sort of coverage suggests that the *Sun* thought it more important that Britain had succeeded in fending off pressure from the other EC members than in contributing to the outcome by making practical proposals on the treaty content, as Major argued in his speech.

The *Sun* supported the treaty outcome without addressing any of the arguments Major had presented in parliament in greater detail. According to the tabloid the PM had achieved a result which every Conservative politician (and this also meant Margaret Thatcher) should approve of (Kavanagh 1991b).

After Major's parliamentary statement the *Sun* again did not explicitly mention its position on the single currency. Yet there appears to have been no change in the paper's support for Major's EMU policy. Already before his speech it had noted particularly the necessity of securing parliament's right to decide about joining the single currency.

Overall, John Major's influence on the coverage by the five newspapers with his statement on the Maastricht Treaty appears to have been fairly limited (Table 10.3). Particularly with his argument that the opt-out on EMU was central as it ensured that

Table 10.3 Newspapers' attitudes to EMU and support for government policy 1991 (own illustration)

	Financial Times	The Guardian	The Independent	Daily Mail	The Sun
Before the speech					
Attitude to EMU	Unclear	Unclear	Support	Mixed	Unclear
Support for government policy	No support	No support	No support	Mixed	Support
After the speech					
Attitude to EMU	Support	Unclear	Mixed	Support	Unclear
Support for government policy	No support	No support	Mixed	Support	Support

Key: Support = support of EMU-membership or support of the government's policy on EMU; No support = no support of EMU-membership or no support of the government's policy on EMU; Mixed = different views are expressed, e.g. by different authors or opposition to EMU but at the same time fear to be left out of European integration or mixed assessment of government's EMU policy; Unclear = unclear whether paper supports the government's policy on EMU or EMU membership; Change = change of attitude on EMU or of the government's policy on EMU in the considered time period

the UK parliament would have a choice on the single currency he failed to persuade the broadsheets. They saw the opt-out as futile, thinking that the pressure on Britain to join would just be too great. Moreover, at least the *Independent* viewed the opt-out policy as a problem because it thought that it kept the government from negotiating better terms for the EMU process. The *Daily Mail*, however, argued that British interests (in this case sterling) were safeguarded by the opt-out. The *Sun* appeared more concerned with Major's success over the EU members in the negotiations. It is surprising that the tabloid did not address the provisions for EMU at greater length, particularly if the coverage on Maastricht and Major's statement is compared to that of Tony Blair's national changeover plan announcement, which is considered in the next section.

Apart from the opt-out the *Financial Times* and *Guardian* particularly challenged Major's claim that the negotiation outcome illustrated Britain's role as key actor in Europe. They saw Maastricht as the start of a two-speed Europe with Britain in the slower lane. The *Daily Mail* after Major's speech showed that it shared his view on Britain's position in Europe, while the *Sun* evaluated it mainly in the context of whether the UK had triumphed at the expense of the other members in the negotiations. Overall, the *Daily Mail* appears to have been most in line with Major's framing of the Maastricht results, although it had already expressed this view before his statement, albeit then with some reservations. So in the case of the *Daily Mail* Major seems to have been able to reinforce existing views with his parliamentary statement.

10.4 Tony Blair: National Changeover Plan, February 1999

Chancellor Gordon Brown had announced in autumn 1997 that Britain would not join the single currency in the first wave and that the Treasury would conduct five tests to evaluate whether joining the euro was in the country's economic interest (see Chap. 3). On 23 February 1999 Prime Minister Tony Blair announced in the House of Commons the national changeover plan. It set out how Britain could prepare to eventually join the euro (HC Deb 23 February 1999, cc179–196). In his statement the premier particularly focused on four aspects: (a) Britain and EMU, (b) the national interest, (c) the decision-making basis and (d) the referendum.

On Britain and EMU Blair explained that the government in principle supported membership provided the currency was successful and the UK met several economic conditions. He pointed out, however, that joining the euro was neither unavoidable nor automatic (HC Deb 23 February 1999, c179). To have the option to join, it was necessary "to step up our practical preparations now; hence the national changeover plan" (HC Deb 23 February 1999, c180). Following these preparations, Britain could introduce the euro 2 to 3 years after a public vote for it in a referendum, he estimated (HC Deb 23 February 1999, c181).

Like his predecessors Blair referred to the national interest. He said that it was the deciding factor in determining whether the UK would join the euro and defined it as economic interest (HC Deb 23 February 1999, c188). Entry should be put into effect, if the conditions for sustained economic convergence and the five economic tests, which Brown had announced, were satisfied (HC Deb 23 February 1999, cc191, 195). According to the PM, decision-making on the euro was based on economics. He acknowledged that there were constitutional and political arguments related to the question of membership, but these should be no obstacle to entry, if it was economically advantageous (HC Deb 23 February 1999, c179). To reject membership for reasons of sovereignty was mistaken, Blair argued, because the world was moving closer together and "sovereignty pooled can be sovereignty—or at least power and influence—renewed" (HC Deb 23 February 1999, c182). It was sensible to pool sovereignty with others, if it was in the UK's economic interest and advancing its impact and position in the world, he said (HC Deb 23 February 1999, c190).

Lastly, Blair addressed the referendum which his party had promised on the euro. The plan, he said, was an essential condition for it. Without the preparations set out in it, the UK would have no option to pursue entry, even if it wanted to: "there can be no referendum without a national changeover plan" (HC Deb 23 February 1999, c194). The plan was to achieve the necessary preparations to have a choice on euro membership, the prime minister argued (HC Deb 23 February 1999, cc186–187).

The following section analyses how far Prime Minister Blair managed to influence the print media coverage of the national changeover plan. The analysis comprises the five newspapers' coverage in the 2 weeks before the parliamentary announcement and the 2 weeks after (9 February to 9 March 1999). The first part of each paper's analysis covers the time period ending with the day of Blair's parliamentary speech. In a second step the media coverage after the speech is analysed. As several papers on the day of Blair's speech discussed its content, it can be assumed that they had been informed about it beforehand.

Of the three broadsheets the ***Financial Times*** reported the most about the changeover plan and the government's position on EMU in the 4 weeks around Blair's announcement. Eighteen articles were considered in the analysis. Four were published before the prime minister's statement and one on the day of it.[50]

The *Financial Times* supported joining the euro. One day before Blair's speech it demanded political leadership from him to persuade the public to vote for it in a referendum. While it acknowledged that there was still a gap between the UK's economic performance and the fulfilment of the chancellor's five tests, it noted that "it looks now as if it can and should be bridged. Mr Blair must say so loudly"[51] (Financial Times 1999a). The paper added another test to the ones Blair would mention in parliament: public opinion. While the economic convergence criterion was the most important, Britain would not join the euro if the public voted against entry in a referendum, the paper noted (Financial Times 1999a). With regard to the PM's policy on the euro, which it characterised as ambiguous, the *FT* supported an early referendum suggesting on 11 February that there were "powerful political and economic reasons for holding the promised referendum in the next 18 months. Blair cannot wish them away"[52] (Peston 1999a). On the day of Blair's announcement the *Financial Times* argued his speech would be a firm confirmation of policy to adopt the euro: "Blair will today end months of equivocation and signal a clear commitment to taking Britain into Europe's single currency early after the next election"[53] (Peston 1999b). But the *FT* was also critical. It considered the speech a "belated start to a campaign to persuade a largely sceptical British public to support economic and monetary union in a referendum after the next general election"[54] (Peston 1999b). It noted that Blair would not indicate when exactly the transition process was to start. In the plan he had also failed to name the date when the UK would formally join the single currency by fixing the pound's exchange rate with the euro (Peston 1999b).

[50]Additional reports published in the analysed time period not considered here addressed technical questions on the use of the euro by departments and industry. There were also articles on the views of the opposition, European institutions, lobby groups and specific branches of industry and reports on opinion polling on the question of euro membership, which were not addressed here.

[51]Financial Times (1999), On euro tiptoe, 22 February 1999. Used under licence from the Financial Times. All Rights Reserved.

[52]Peston, R. (1999), Pressure over the euro may force Blair off the fence, Financial Times, 11 February 1999. Used under licence from the Financial Times. All Rights Reserved.

[53]Peston, R. (1999), Blair will unveil UK route to EMU entry, Financial Times, 23 February 1999. Used under licence from the Financial Times. All Rights Reserved.

[54]Peston, R. (1999), Blair will unveil UK route to EMU entry, Financial Times, 23 February 1999. Used under licence from the Financial Times. All Rights Reserved.

Overall, the *Financial Times* supported joining the euro und welcomed the government's changeover plan. Yet it criticised the fact that it was late and left important questions open.

After Blair's statement on the national changeover plan on 23 February 1999, the ***Financial Times*** continued to support joining the euro and read the announcement as a sign that the PM had "put himself at the head of a cross-party campaign to take the UK into the European single currency early in the next century"[55] (Peston and Brown 1999, for a similar assessment see Peston 1999c; Financial Times 1999b). But the paper demanded that Blair's move to the top of a pro-European coalition should be followed by immediate action (Stephens 1999). A day after his speech it again lamented that Blair had not indicated when the euro transition process was to start (Brown and Sanghera 1999).

The *FT* agreed with Blair that membership was in Britain's economic interest. It suggested that his declaration of intent avoided the country again staying behind on an important EU development it could not prevent and which it would have to join eventually. It went on: "Mr Blair was right yesterday to focus on the economic issues. He was right also to conclude that Britain cannot afford to remain aloof from the grand project of its continental partners"[56] (Financial Times 1999b).

With regard to economic policy which Blair had called the basis for the government's decision on the euro, the paper again argued that the plan had left key questions in that area unanswered. This included particularly the date when the UK would formally join the single currency by fixing the pound's exchange rate with the euro (Brown and Sanghera 1999). It mentioned other economic questions the plan had not addressed either: at which exchange rate was the pound to join the Eurozone (Financial Times 1999c)? How did the government plan to fulfil the Maastricht criteria of 2 years of exchange rate stability without formally re-joining the ERM or having sterling shadow the euro (Brown and Sanghera 1999; Peston 1999d)? What would the changeover process cost (Brown and Sanghera 1999; Brown 1999)?

On sovereignty the *FT* supported pooling it with others, but noted the difficulty that this policy meant for the prime minister:

> The sharing of sovereignty, as he said explicitly on Tuesday, is designed to enhance the nation's power and prosperity—just as the unsplendid isolation of his opponents would diminish it. I cannot think of a serious politician beyond the shores of British Europhobia who would find anything remarkable in such an observation. But what is obvious to the French, the Germans or the Belgians has been a secret well-hidden from Mr Blair's electorate.[57] (Stephens 1999)

---

[55]Peston, R. & Brown, K. (1999), Blair lays groundwork for euro changeover, Financial Times, 24 February 1999. Used under licence from the Financial Times. All Rights Reserved.

[56]Financial Times (1999), Mr. Blair nails his euro to the mast, 24 February 1999. Used under licence from the Financial Times. All Rights Reserved.

[57]Stephens, P. (1999), Liberated by Europe, Financial Times, 26 February 1999. Used under licence from the Financial Times. All Rights Reserved.

As it had done before Blair's speech, the *Financial Times* addressed the referendum and the public's impact on the government's EMU policy. It considered Blair's announcement to be only the beginning of a demanding process in which the government would have to persuade the public that entry was "desirable as well as inevitable"[58] (Financial Times 1999b). In another article it concluded that Blair's "stepping up a gear"[59] (Financial Times 1999c) on EMU would not help companies and industry to prepare for the euro, as among other things there was still a referendum to be held and it was unclear how the public would decide. On 26 February the *FT* addressed the difficulties of changing the public's attitude on Europe. A reason for the public's scepticism, the paper thought, was that it had too often been told that European policy was a battle between the UK and the other EU members with the former more often on the losing than on the winning side. But the *FT* saw hope in Blair's popularity: "The pro-European case has never been put with force and consistency by a prime minister as popular as this one... Mr Blair can win"[60] (Stephens 1999).

In sum, the *Financial Times* interpreted the statement as a sign that Blair had given up his ambiguous position on the euro and supported membership (e.g. Peston 1999c). The paper welcomed this. Yet it also warned of the difficulties in connection with this policy. It pointed out (a) that the national changeover plan had left key questions of economic and monetary policy unanswered and (b) that the public remained sceptical but still had to vote to join the euro before it would become a reality. It is striking that the paper strongly focused on the person of the prime minister with regard to the government's euro policy (e.g. Stephens 1999; Peston 1999c). A change in the coverage of the changeover plan due to the statement was only discernible with regard to Blair's attitude to the euro, which the paper had called ambiguous before and pro-membership afterwards. On the issue itself no change could be traced. Both before and after Blair's speech, the *Financial Times* supported joining the euro. Thus, if anything, the paper might have seen the PM's announcement as an affirmation of its own views.

The ***Guardian*** covered the changeover plan announcement and the government's position on the euro between 9 February and 9 March 1999 less extensively than the *Financial Times*. Ten articles were considered in the analysis.[61] Prior to Blair's parliamentary statement the paper addressed the issue in only one article. Here it did not elaborate on its own view on EMU but suggested a direction in which the upcoming announcement could go. It cited a source inside the government, who

[58]Financial Times (1999), Mr. Blair nails his euro to the mast, 24 February 1999. Used under licence from the Financial Times. All Rights Reserved.

[59]Financial Times (1999), Unileverage, 24 February 1999. Used under licence from the Financial Times. All Rights Reserved.

[60]Stephens, P. (1999), Liberated by Europe, Financial Times, 26 February 1999. Used under licence from the Financial Times. All Rights Reserved.

[61]Further articles in the time period not covered here addressed public opinion on euro membership and the opposition's stance on it (inside parliament and outside in the form of anti-euro groups).

had said that after returning from an EU meeting in Germany the previous month, Blair had concluded that he wanted to convince UK voters to support joining the euro (White et al. 1999).

After Blair's changeover plan announcement, the ***Guardian*** showed that it was sceptical about the euro. It pointed to the difficulties of being part of the political left, but against the euro, as this meant you were associated with the Conservative Party's "weirdo wing" (Elliott 1999). Despite the fact that this section of the Tories had been right on certain issues it was important that a grouping was established which monetary union opponents, who were not against foreigners, could support, the paper argued (Elliott 1999).

The paper opposed joining the euro particularly for economic reasons. On 24 February, for instance, the *Guardian* argued that despite its own pro-European attitude it was very sceptical that monetary union could become a success in Europe as well as in Britain, whose economy had not converged with the other EU economies (The Guardian 1999a). On 1 March the *Guardian* argued that it thought that, when looking at the economics of it, EMU was getting ever more suspicious (Elliott 1999). This suggests that it did not support Blair's assessment that joining the euro was in the country's national interest given that its definition of the UK's economic interest differed from his. Like the *Financial Times*, but less extensively, the *Guardian* referred to the economic questions the plan had left unanswered. It noted, for instance, that Blair's announcement had not included information as to when the pound's and the euro's exchange rates would be locked with each other (Elliott and Atkinson 1999). Moreover, Blair had omitted to explain when the conditions the chancellor had set out in the five tests would be satisfied and what sort of exchange rate policy the government was planning to conduct during the transition to adopting the euro (White and Elliott 1999).

The paper considered Blair's announcement a significant step to supporting euro membership and claimed he had presented his argument with so much authority that the impression was given the issue was already decided (The Guardian 1999b). In another article the paper again referred to the discrepancies between presentation and content of Blair's statement saying that its presentation was more important than its substance as Blair had managed to implicitly suggest that a key step had been taken towards full European integration (The Guardian 1999a). This was echoed in a further commentary which argued that there was not much difference between what Blair had said the previous day and what Brown had said in October 1997. Yet the expectations had changed: while Brown's statement had appeared to signify faint-heartedness, Blair's had given the impression that it was a radical move (Young 1999).

As to Blair's argument that a referendum needed to be preceded by the changeover plan, the paper agreed by stating that a referendum without preparation was not sensible. At the same time, it suggested that the plan, coupled with an economic policy focused on achieving convergence between Britain and the members of the Eurozone, was a helpful propaganda tool for the government to generate a "self-fulfilling-prophecy" (Young 1999).

As the *Guardian* only addressed the plan once before Blair's announcement and then did not set out its own position on EMU, it cannot be evaluated whether it changed its view on it after the PM's speech. Yet it is obvious that it thought Blair supported joining the euro which the paper did not—despite the premier's arguments made in his changeover plan announcement. The paper also criticised the government's plan as a propaganda tool.

The ***Independent*** covered the changeover plan and the government's EMU policy between 9 February and 9 March 1999 more extensively than the *Guardian*. Fourteen articles were included in the analysis.[62] Two appeared before Blair's speech. In neither the paper indicated its own view on the euro but reported developments in government on the policy (Grice 1999; Coyle and Waugh 1999).

After Tony Blair announced the changeover plan on 23 February, the ***Independent*** showed its doubts over euro membership. Moreover, it was not convinced that it would happen soon. On the conditions Blair had pointed out in his speech which had to be in place for Britain to join the euro, the paper noted that these could give the government the possibility to step away from the euro should it fail to be successful or if the UK economy would not converge with the other EU economies (Grice and Coyle 1999). It did not consider the statement as proof that Blair had placed himself at the top of a campaign for speedy entry as, for instance, the *Financial Times* had suggested. The *Independent* noted that in the run-up to the announcement it had been argued that the prime minister would take a significant step towards the UK joining the euro and that there would be no alternative. Yet, the paper stated, that had not been the case as no such step had been taken and Blair had only said that before taking the decision about joining he wanted to make certain to have "very expensive equipment, just in case" (McElvoy 1999).

Moreover, the paper suggested that Blair had merely wanted to test whether a prime ministerial impulse would suffice to move public opinion far enough for him to dare risk his political authority by fully supporting euro entry (McElvoy 1999). In another article the *Independent* reiterated that Blair had not announced a change of policy but had only made clear that from now on he would personally defend the euro, which he before had left to others. This was not the same as showing leadership, it criticised (The Independent 1999a). But the *Independent* also showed other assessments: on 24 February, for instance, it stated that Blair had put Britain onto a clear course towards euro entry with the announcement. This was reinforced by the article's headline which claimed that the prime minister was preparing to abolish sterling (Grice and Coyle 1999).

The *Independent* pointed out that the government's five tests were not only important for economic reasons but could also contribute to a tactical advantage as

[62]Further articles published in the time period not considered here covered the position of anti-euro-groups, the opposition and assessments of the plan by industry representatives and reports on the views of other media outlets.

they provided the government with the option to leave the euro project (Grice and Coyle 1999). The paper further argued that the stated conditions for membership were fulfilled whenever the prime minister and the chancellor said so (Watkins 1999). It thought these conditions to be arbitrary, as it was known that Blair had already supported euro entry before his premiership and had taken steps to pursue it since then (The Independent 1999b).

On 1 March the paper questioned the assertion that the government's euro policy was based on economics, which Blair had claimed in his speech. It suggested that the government in principle had taken the decision to join but would not set a date for it as long as it was uncertain it could win a referendum. The question when the British economy would converge with those of the Eurozone countries was used to cover this up (The Independent 1999b).

The *Independent* was highly critical of the Blair administration's changeover plan. It suggested that the government was trying to establish a "fait accompli" (Watkins 1999) on joining the Eurozone by making financial contributions to the changeover process. This view was echoed in another article which stated that the announcement supported by substantive financial means to prepare for a possible entry to the euro made it seem more or less certain that the UK was to join the Eurozone (Sylvester 1999). The paper, moreover, did not support Blair's argument that the changeover plan was a necessary pre-condition for a referendum. Instead it questioned the order of things as it argued that the prime minister had pretended that spending public funds to prepare for adopting the euro was economically sensible. Yet joining the euro was only going to happen after the public agreed to it. Therefore the paper asked why the government did not call the referendum in the current parliament (The Independent 1999b).

The paper thought the government's course of action showed its fear of losing a referendum. To highlight the irrationality of this policy it likened the prime minister to a father who had promised his children that they would visit Disneyland. Yet they would only do so, if the weather was good. Meanwhile, the father thought it was a good idea to prepare for the journey, for instance, by buying the tickets for the ferry and packing up the car (Sutcliffe 1999).

From only two articles published before Blair's statement, which included no information on the paper's opinion on the euro, no conclusion can be drawn that the *Independent* changed its view on it. Yet there is no indication that Blair with his speech was able to persuade the paper that euro membership was sensible. Instead the *Independent* appeared sceptical about joining the single currency. Moreover, it questioned whether the government's argument that it would decide based on the economics was genuine. It also suggested that the government wanted to establish a 'fait accompli' with the changeover plan. It criticised this and argued that a referendum should be held before making more preparations for eventual euro membership.

The ***Daily Mail*** covered the changeover plan and the government's euro policy extensively. Seventeen articles, published between 9 February and 9 March 1999, were considered here.[63] One was published before Blair's statement and three on the day.

The paper opposed euro membership saying that it was perfectly in order to think that the UK's national interest in the long-term would by secured by joining the single currency, but thought this position was wrong (Daily Mail 1999a). Due to the euro's slide against the dollar the day before, it found the changeover plan announcement on 23 February inappropriate (Alexander 1999a).

The *Daily Mail* did not share Blair's view that the plan was a pre-condition for a referendum in order for the electorate to have a choice. Instead it argued that the changeover plan was actually part of the government's policy to join the euro (Daily Mail 1999a). It considered the Blair administration's euro policy to be authoritarian and a manipulation of the democratic process (Daily Mail 1999a). According to the paper the government took the second step before the first with the plan (It viewed the referendum as the first step). With help of the plan the government wanted Britain to develop close ties to the new currency. Thus voting against membership in a future referendum would be inconceivable, the *Daily Mail* criticised. It considered this deceitful and an insult to the voters' intelligence as they knew that the Blair administration wanted to join the euro as soon as it could (Daily Mail 1999a). Moreover, the paper warned of the costs of the transition process which, it thought, might be huge—particularly considering the fact that it was for something which might not be realised (Alexander 1999a).

Overall, the *Daily Mail* opposed joining the euro and criticised the government's decision to implement the changeover plan before a referendum. It considered the plan a device of the government to make adoption of the euro inevitable, which it condemned as deceitful.

After Blair's statement on 23 February, the ***Daily Mail*** remained opposed to EMU and called the national changeover plan a plan to take over the country (Waterhouse 1999). It likened the membership discussion to a battle and used World War II analogies. According to the paper Blair, Brown, Michael Heseltine, Ken Clarke and Edward Heath were willing to give up Britain's sovereignty. If that was going to happen, Britain should sign up to the Eurozone in Compiegne in France. Moreover, doing so, the paper argued, meant effectively joining the successor of the Third Reich (Alexander 1999b).

On 9 March the *Daily Mail* suggested that Britain was once again in a battle for its survival (Neil 1999). The argument that Blair and his government were implementing a policy of stealth to create the impression that joining the euro was inevitable, resurfaced several times in its coverage in the period after Blair's statement (e.g. Hughes 1999; Daily Mail 1999b; Massie 1999). On 24 February the paper argued that the government had already decided to join the euro as

[63]Further articles published in the time period not considered here covered the views of anti-euro-groups and the opposition. Others dealt with the state of the euro which had been introduced that year.

otherwise the changeover plan made no sense. It condemned this as the greatest fraud ever undertaken in the UK (Johnson 1999). It saw the plan as spending taxpayers' money on a policy to which the public had not yet agreed and which it in majority opposed (Hughes 1999; see also Massie 1999).

On the country's economic interest it argued that it was feasible, sensible and advantageous to be a member of the EU but not of EMU (Daily Mail 1999c). By being able to set interest rates and taxation levels independently, the UK would thrive economically. Remaining outside the Eurozone would mean keeping the flexibility needed as a global trading power. Single market membership was advantageous economically, but adopting the euro was a step too far, the paper believed. On the country's long-term economic, social and democratic goals, the *Daily Mail* thought it better if Britain did not join the euro (Daily Mail 1999c).

On pooling sovereignty, which Blair had supported in his speech, the paper suggested adopting the euro was effectively a decision to join a federal European state (Johnson 1999; see also Glover 1999). The *Daily Mail* opposed this and stated that if Britain joined the euro this would lead to a further loss of the country's sovereignty as EU taxes and a common economic policy and eventually a European government would follow (Glover 1999).

The paper argued that the British people should understand that the country was sufficiently prosperous and strong to remain independent and did not have to become part of an EU state just because it was en vogue to argue that such a development was unavoidable (Neil 1999).

In sum, the *Daily Mail* did not accept Blair's arguments as to why joining the euro was beneficial to the UK. It had already done so on the day of Blair's speech and did not change its view thereafter. In contrast to the *Financial Times*, for instance, the *Daily Mail* perceived the government's euro policy as a threat to national sovereignty. It also did not share the PM's view on what was the correct economic policy for Britain. Blair also failed to persuade the paper of the necessity to implement the plan before a referendum. It remained of the view it had taken before Blair's announcement, which was that the government wanted to make a 'no' in a referendum impossible by presenting entry as unavoidable. It was a strategy which the *Daily Mail* vehemently criticised as dishonest.

The ***Sun*** covered the government's changeover plan and euro policy extensively. Twenty-eight articles between 9 February and 9 March 1999 were considered here.[64] It addressed both topics in five articles before Blair's speech and one on the day of it.

The *Sun* opposed joining the euro. It saw Britain's economic interest not in European integration but in economic independence. On 20 February it argued that the UK should be economically independent and unburdened by the problems which might lead to the EU's demise (Kavanagh 1999a). Instead of spending money on preparing to join the euro, the *Sun* asked whether Blair should not rather spend it

[64]Further articles published in the analysed time period not considered here related to the position of the opposition, business, anti-euro-groups and citizens on euro membership.

on ensuring that Britain could survive independently (Kavanagh 1999a). It complained that millions were spent on the government's policy of pressuring the country to adopt the euro and called the changeover plan the "next step in the softening up process" (The Sun 1999a).

The *Sun* thought the introduction of the euro would impact much on national sovereignty, which it—unlike Blair would state in his speech—did not see as renewed by pooling it with others. It also did not see the decision purely based on economics as the premier would argue. According to the tabloid it was also important to note that there were voters who held Britain's sovereignty in higher regard than ensuring that international companies could more easily make profit and who rather wanted to be governed by MPs, who were accountable, instead of by EU commissioners, which no one had elected (The Sun 1999a).

The *Sun* also questioned the order of preparing for euro membership before holding a referendum. It did not share Blair's view that the changeover plan was a precondition for a referendum on euro membership. The tabloid instead demanded that Blair should admit that he wanted to adopt the euro. If this was the case, he should hold the referendum immediately (The Sun 1999a).

Overall, the *Sun* opposed joining the euro. Moreover, it considered membership as curtailing national sovereignty. It also thought the referendum should precede the national changeover plan, which it saw as a device to make the adoption of the euro inevitable. Economically, it preferred independence over European integration.

Despite Blair's announcement on 23 February, the ***Sun*** did not change its view on the euro and continued to oppose membership. It considered the national changeover plan a costly propaganda tool to trick voters into believing they could not oppose joining the single currency (The Sun 1999b; for a similar argument see Littlejohn 1999).

As before Blair's speech it saw the country's national interest in economic independence, not in European integration. Thus, in contrast to the PM, it did not consider joining the euro as being in the country's economic interest. It argued on 24 February that the UK could be a successful economic power inside the EU but outside of EMU (The Sun 1999b). It suggested the key reasons to oppose the euro were neither soft-hearted nor out of date but "based on hard economic fact" (The Sun 1999b).

As before Blair's speech the paper saw no merit in pooling sovereignty with others, which the PM had supported in parliament. On 24 February the *Sun* suggested joining the euro meant the UK would just become a small part of a federal European state (The Sun 1999b). Moreover, the tabloid thought that such a move meant that Britain would stop being an independent country (The Sun 1999c), it would become of part of a European federal mega-state (Kavanagh 1999c) and would lose the power to act only in the British public's interest (The Sun 1999d). The paper also complained that Blair wanted to abolish Britain's democracy and adopt a European technocracy ruled from Brussels (Kavanagh 1999b).

The *Sun* continued to reject the changeover plan as a precondition for the referendum and questioned Blair's argument that one had to prepare in order to

Table 10.4 Newspapers' attitudes to EMU and support for government policy 1999 (own illustration)

	Financial Times	The Guardian	The Independent	Daily Mail	The Sun
Before the speech					
Attitude to EMU	Support	Unclear	Unclear	No support	No support
Support for government policy	Mixed	Unclear	Unclear	No support	No support
After the speech					
Attitude to EMU	Support	No support	No support	No support	No support
Support for government policy	Mixed	No support	No support	No support	No support

Key: Support = support of EMU-membership or support of the government's policy on EMU; No support = no support of EMU-membership or no support of the government's policy on EMU; Mixed = different views are expressed, e.g. by different authors or opposition to EMU but at the same time fear to be left out of European integration or mixed assessment of government's EMU policy; Unclear = unclear whether paper supports the government's policy on EMU or EMU in general; Change = change of attitude on EMU or of the government's policy on EMU in the considered time period

have a choice on the euro. It, moreover, called into question that it was necessary to spend large sums of public money to prepare banks and computer systems before being able to take the decision "wither to waste it all?" (The Sun 1999b).

As it had done before Blair's speech, it questioned the order of plan and referendum, noting that due to the government's policy British industry had to cope with uncertainty. This would not be the case if a referendum was conducted immediately, the paper suggested (The Sun 1999b).

There is no indication that Blair in the analysed time period was able to persuade the *Sun* of the merits of joining the euro. Already before his speech the tabloid had strongly opposed joining, a stance which did not change. It also remained of the view that Britain's economic goal should be independence, not European integration. Moreover, it thought joining the euro would have a negative impact on Britain's sovereignty, making it part of a federal Europe.

Considering the coverage of Blair's announcement by the five newspapers in the 4 weeks analysed here (Table 10.4), it becomes evident that the prime minister persuaded all of one thing: his intention to join the euro. While the *Financial Times* welcomed it, the *Daily Mail* and the *Sun* opposed it vehemently. So did the *Guardian* and the *Independent*, albeit more moderately. Moreover, Blair was not able to persuade any of the papers that the national changeover plan was a necessary condition for a referendum. Except for the *Financial Times*, which did not mention it, the papers concluded more or less explicitly that Blair and his government, with the preparations set out in the plan, attempted to create an atmosphere which would make entry seem inevitable. The advantages of pooling sovereignty with others, which Blair had referred to in his speech, were not accepted by the *Daily Mail* and the *Sun*. They viewed the euro as a threat to national sovereignty instead. All five newspapers, albeit for different reasons, took issue with Blair's argument that the government's decision on the euro was based on economics. The *Financial Times* and the *Guardian* referred to the questions the changeover plan had left unanswered in this area. The *Independent* questioned whether economic policy was actually the basis of the government's decision on the euro. The *Daily Mail* and the *Sun* argued that the government's economic policy in this respect was completely wrong, as economic independence was to be favoured over European integration.

10.5 The Media and Prime Ministerial Political Leadership

The prime ministerial predominance thesis presumes that the increasing personalisation of political debate and the centralisation of political decision-making strengthen the PM, who becomes an opinion leader in public debate. The collective leadership thesis on the other hand assumes that he has fewer opportunities to manage the media and thereby set the agenda to try to influence public opinion, as he is only one of several government actors trying to do so.

Looking at the newspaper coverage for the prime ministers in the four case studies analysed in this chapter, it has to be concluded that none of the leaders were able to substantially influence the media coverage through their statements. As mentioned in this chapter's introduction it is not assumed that a head of government can shape his country's news coverage by merely one announcement. However, it can be expected that such speeches tend to be much considered by the media, as they are a key element of the government's overall communication strategy on the event or policy initiative in question. Yet from the analyses of the four case studies it cannot be concluded that any one of the prime ministers was able to become an opinion leader on the European monetary policy decision in question. But it does appear that prime ministerial statements, if in line with a particular paper's view on an issue, could reinforce this view. This was, for instance, the case with Tony Blair and the changeover plan which reinforced the view of the *Financial Times* that he had placed himself firmly in the pro-euro camp. Another example is the *Daily Mail* on the EMU negotiations at Maastricht. It had supported John Major's view that an opt-out was the best option on EMU already before his statement, albeit with reservations. After his speech, it fully supported Major's arguments on the outcome of the negotiations. In general, the PMs in the cases considered here tended to fail to achieve a change in the view of the papers. The only exception was Margaret Thatcher in 1989 on the ERM. The *Daily Mail* and the *Sun* changed their position on ERM membership from opposition to support. Yet they did so mainly due to her actions at the Madrid summit and not specifically because of her announcement in parliament.

As all four leaders were the key actors involved in the European level negotiations in the selected case studies and/or made the announcement on an aspect of government policy, the coverage of summit or policy initiative in question was bound to focus on them. But particularly in Blair's case the press focused much on the prime minister. This does suggest an enhancement of the PM's leadership role in the media discourse. The analysed print media appeared to consider the changeover plan to be an issue which Blair was responsible for and tended to neglect other core executive actors involved in the decision-making process such as Chancellor Brown in their coverage. An example is the *Financial Times* who argued that, if anyone could persuade the British public to become more pro-European, it was Tony Blair.

With regard to the potential role of the media as communication channels between the prime minister and the public it has to be concluded that this role appears to be minimal. Even if the press can influence public opinion, which as noted in the introduction to this chapter is a contested argument in communication and public opinion research, in the case of the leaders analysed here the effect appears to have been negligible. Although some newspapers supported the PM's position on the issue in question, this tended to be not a result of the prime minister's political communication through his speech as these papers had already taken this stance before. Other newspapers did not adopt either leader's arguments on the issue following his speech and thus did not transmit this view to their readers. Of course, prime minister and government can (and do) attempt to influence public opinion through the media also by employing other means such as television and print interviews, articles or essays in print media written by members of the government, written statements, government policy statements or the like. Yet the scope of the present study did not allow for an inclusion of such material as well in the case study analysis.

In the latter part of this study the four prime ministers' political leadership in European monetary policy was analysed. It considered to what extent the press and the party in parliament as well as other members of the core executive affected this leadership and how the premiers handled these potential constraints. In the next chapter these findings are taken together to evaluate the British prime minister's political leadership in the core executive.

References

Aitken, I. (1978, December 7). Callaghan flies patriot's flag over Commons. *The Guardian*.

Aitken, I. (1991, December 13). The Maastricht litmus test. *The Guardian*.

Alexander, A. (1978, December 5). One bank note that we can all live without... *Daily Mail*.

Alexander, A. (1989a, June 19). The duel dividing Downing Street. *Daily Mail*.

Alexander, A. (1989b, June 27). Maggie puts the rest on the spot. *Daily Mail*.

Alexander, A. (1989c, June 28). No need to flap about EMU now. *Daily Mail*.

Alexander, A. (1999a, February 23). Needless preparations for euro would waste billions. *Daily Mail*.

Alexander, A. (1999b, February 26). Selling out for price of a euro. *Daily Mail*.

Bevins, A. (1989, June 30). Summit 'has bought time to work on union'. *The Independent*.

Brittan, S. (1978a, November 30). EMS: missed chances and false traits. *Financial Times*.

Brittan, S. (1978b, December 7). The architects of a two-tier Europe. *Financial Times*.

Brittan, S. (1989, June 29). Don't sell Madrid short. *Financial Times*.

Brittan, S. (1991, December 12). A victory, but not quite a triumph. *Financial Times*.

Brown, K. (1999, February 25). Questions left unanswered on costs and attitudes. *Financial Times*.

Brown, K., & Sanghera, S. (1999, February 24). Changeover plan sets out 'critical path' for transition. *Financial Times*.

Buchan, D. (1991, December 2). Denmark leaves UK in the lurch on opt-out. *Financial Times*.

Buchan, D., & Stephens, P. (1991, December 2). UK isolated on single currency opt-out clause. *Financial Times*.

Buchan, D., Bruce, P., & Davidson, I. (1989, June 24). Thatcher faces pressure over economic union. *Financial Times*.

Butler, D., & Butler, G. (2006). *British political facts since 1979*. New York: Palgrave Macmillan.

Butler, D., & Sloman, A. (1980). *British political facts 1900–1979* (5th ed.). London: Macmillan.

Cole, P. (2007, August 27). The paradox of the pops. *The Guardian*.

Coyle, D., & Waugh, P. (1999, February 22). Spending ban on euro poll. *The Independent*.

Daily Mail. (1991a, December 9). The only bandwagon that's on the move.

Daily Mail. (1991b, December 12). Good for Europe, great for Britain.

Daily Mail. (1999a, February 23). Treat the people as grown ups.

Daily Mail. (1999b, February 27). The widening chasm in British politics.

Daily Mail. (1999c, March 1). Positive thinking to save the pound.

Davidson, I. (1989, June 29). Clear path for European Community emerges through the fog. *Financial Times*.

Davidson, I. (1991a, December 3). New era for EC family. *Financial Times*.

Davidson, I. (1991b, December 12). Hollow victory for Britain as it launches two-tier Europe. *Financial Times*.

Deans, J. (1989a, June 29). Who did win at the Euro summit? *Daily Mail*.

Deans, J. (1989b, June 30). The worst is over on inflation, says jubilant Maggie. *Daily Mail*.

Deans, J., & Doughty, S. (1991, December 2). Major puts nation before party over Europe. *Daily Mail*.

Dickie, J. (1978a, December 4). Jim faces squeeze. *Daily Mail*.

Dickie, J. (1978b, December 5). And Jim comes under market pressure. *Daily Mail*.

Dickie, J. (1978c, December 7). How the French let Jim off the hook. *Daily Mail*.

Doughty, S. (1991, December 4). Britain wins the F-word battle. *Daily Mail*.

Doughty, S., & Greig, G. (1991, December 3). Fight to salvage Euro treaty. *Daily Mail*.

Elliott, L. (1999, March 1). Let's not get stitched up in currency briefs. *The Guardian*.

Elliott, L., & Atkinson, M. (1999, February 24). Fast-track to euro in Britain. *The Guardian*.

Financial Times. (1978a, November 25). Government not ready to decide whether it is in Britain's best interest to join.

Financial Times. (1978b, November 27). On the road to EMS.

Financial Times. (1978c, December 1). Why we should join the EMS.

Financial Times. (1978d, December 7). A divided Europe.

Financial Times. (1978e, December 13). Italy decides to join the EMS.

Financial Times. (1989a, June 19). Spain enters the ERM.

Financial Times. (1989b, June 23). Isolation in Madrid.

Financial Times. (1989c, June 28). Compromise in Madrid.

Financial Times. (1989d, July 1). Mrs Thatcher and the Emu.

Financial Times. (1989e, July 3). EC legal limits on British sovereignty.

Financial Times. (1991, December 12). Multi-speed move to union.

Financial Times. (1999a, February 22). On euro tiptoe.

Financial Times. (1999b, February 24). Mr. Blair nails his euro to the mast.

Financial Times. (1999c, February 24). Unileverage.

Gavin, N. T. (2007). *Press and television in British politics: Media, money and mediated democracy*. Basingstoke: Palgrave Macmillan.

Glover, S. (1999, March 9). Forgive my glee at Germany's jitters. *Daily Mail*.

Goodman, E., & Riddell, P. (1978, November 24). MPs will get chance to vote before final EMS decision. *Financial Times*.
Goodwin, S. (1989, June 30). Thatcher claims EC support over monetary union. *The Independent*.
Greig, G., & Deans, J. (1991, December 12). Major, Master of the House. *Daily Mail*.
Greig, G., & Doughty, S. (1991, December 11). Major wins by a knock-out! *Daily Mail*.
Grice, A. (1999, February 12). Ministers are told to take pro-euro line. *The Independent*.
Grice, A., & Coyle, D. (1999, February 24). Blair gears up to ditch the pound. *The Independent*.
HC Deb. (1978, December 6), Vol 959, cc1421–1438.
HC Deb. (1989, June 29), Vol 155, cc1109–1124.
HC Deb. (1991, December 11), Vol 200, cc859–878.
HC Deb. (1999, February 23), Vol 326, cc179–196.
Hoggart, S. (1978a, November 25). EMS terms 'must suit Britain'. *The Guardian*.
Hoggart, S. (1978b, December 7). Lending authors some token support. *The Guardian*.
Hughes, D. (1999, February 24). Prepare to kill the £. *Daily Mail*.
Huhne, C. (1991, December 15). Opting out will never be an option. *The Independent*.
Hutton, W. (1991a, December 11). Major wins quest for opt-out on single European currency. *The Guardian*.
Hutton, W. (1991b, December 11). Monetary milestone reached on Europe's two-speed road. *The Guardian*.
Jenkins, P. (1978a, December 1). PM given a blank cheque. *The Guardian*.
Jenkins, P. (1978b, December 5). Joining the poker game without any cards. *The Guardian*.
Jenkins, P. (1978c, December 6). Sunny Jim all smiles amid wreckage. *The Guardian*.
Jenkins, P. (1978d, December 7). Giscard—A new tune or just the old French fiddle. *The Guardian*.
Jenkins, P. (1989a, June 20). Lessons of defeat for Mrs Thatcher. *The Independent*.
Jenkins, P. (1989b, June 27). Prime minister signals a clever compromise on EMS. *The Independent*.
Jenkins, P. (1989c, June 28). Third time lucky for Britain in Europe. *The Independent*.
Jenkins, P. (1991, December 12). Major's each-way bet pays off. *The Independent*.
Johnson, P. (1989, June 26). A battle that has Maggie baffled. *Daily Mail*.
Johnson, P. (1991, December 12). Now he can score a home victory. *Daily Mail*.
Johnson, P. (1999, February 24). This is the biggest con-trick in history. *Daily Mail*.
Kavanagh, T. (1991a, December 9). Delors blasts PM's 'shame' over F-word. *The Sun*.
Kavanagh, T. (1991b, December 12). How Major played the winning hand in Europe. *The Sun*.
Kavanagh, T. (1999a, February 20). We're diving into cauldron of discontent. *The Sun*.
Kavanagh, T. (1999b, February 24). Our rights are not Blair's to give away. *The Sun*.
Kavanagh, T. (1999c, February 25). You say no to euro by 15-1. *The Sun*.
Kavanagh, T., & Black, E. (1991, December 10). 'F' off. *The Sun*.
Kay, J. (1989, June 28). So what the 'eck does an ECU mean? *The Sun*.
Keegan, W., & Stephens, R. (1978, December 10). L'Entente de Giscard et Jim. *The Guardian*.
Kelly, R., & Elliott, L. (1991, December 9). Germany calls the monetary tune. *The Guardian*.
Kemp, D. (1989a, June 27). Just listen! I'm fighting for Britain. *The Sun*.
Kemp, D. (1989b, June 28). Maggie wins time to save the pound. *The Sun*.
Kennedy, E. (1978, December 16). Euro-cash fear for 'odd man out' Britain. *Daily Mail*.
Knewstub, N. (1989, June 30). PM 'bought time on Delors report'. *The Guardian*.
Littlejohn, R. (1991, December 12). Dud match. *The Sun*.
Littlejohn, R. (1999, March 9). Warning: Pro euro demo, no traffic delays expected. *The Sun*.
MacIntyre, D. (1991, December 8). Playing for high stakes at Maastricht. *The Independent*.
Marsh, D. (1978, November 23). Britain and Italy find common ground on EMS. *Financial Times*.
Marshall, A. (1991, December 10). Single currency comes a step closer. *The Independent*.
Marshall, A., & Usborne, D. (1991, December 10). ECU likely to take over by 1999. *The Independent*.
Massie, A. (1999, March 3). We're all doomed but not inevitably. *Daily Mail*.
Mauthner, R. (1991, December 4). The persistent odd man out. *Financial Times*.

Mayring, P. (2010). *Qualitative Inhaltsanalyse* (11th ed.). Weinheim: Beltz Verlag.
McElvoy, A. (1999, February 24). Mr Blair remains a cautious soul—And not without good reason. *The Independent*.
McNair, B. (1999). *An introduction to political communication* (2nd ed.). London: Routledge.
Milner, M. (1989, June 24). Bite the sugar-coated bullet, Mrs Thatcher. *The Guardian*.
Neil, A. (1999, March 9). To the north, separatists seek to dismember the country. To the south, federalists conspire to turn us into a province of Euroland. We must win this Battle for Britain... and to do it we must, above all, have faith in ourselves. *Daily Mail*.
Palmer, J. (1978, November 23). Premier seeks halfway house deal on EMS. *The Guardian*.
Palmer, J. (1989, June 28). Coming home weaker but not wiser. *The Guardian*.
Palmer, J. (1991, December 11). EC unites on historic treaty with Britain in the slow lane. *The Guardian*.
Palmer, J., & Hooper, J. (1989, June 27). Thatcher sets out terms for entry into EMS. *The Guardian*.
Peston, R. (1999a, February 11). Pressure over the euro may force Blair off the fence. *Financial Times*.
Peston, R. (1999b, February 23). Blair will unveil UK route to EMU entry. *Financial Times*.
Peston, R. (1999c, February 24). Government comes of age with euro pledge. *Financial Times*.
Peston, R. (1999d, February 25). Sterling will not shadow euro, says PM. *Financial Times*.
Peston, R., & Brown, K. (1999, February 24). Blair lays groundwork for euro changeover. *Financial Times*.
Rawnsley, A. (1989, June 30). Thatcher finds herself mistress of a new lingo. *The Guardian*.
Rees-Mogg, W. (1989, June 27). Listen to the young to steer clear of the political rocks. *The Independent*.
Rees-Mogg, W. (1991, December 16). The Euro-dodo that was too stupid and fat to fly. *The Independent*.
Reid, J. (1989, June 27). Euro-money is our best bet. *The Sun*.
Riddell, P. (1978, November 23). Treasury attacked for failing to reveal EMS impact. *Financial Times*.
Rutherford, M. (1978, December 8). A time of uncertainty. *Financial Times*.
Seymour-Ure, C. (2002). New Labour and the media. In A. King (Ed.), *Britain at the polls, 2001* (pp. 117–142). New York: Chatham House.
Shrimsley, A. (1978a, December 1). Britain misses the money train. *The Sun*.
Shrimsley, A. (1978b, December 8). How Britain won last place. *The Sun*.
Stephens, P. (1989a, June 27). Thatcher ceases to thump the table over monetary union. *Financial Times*.
Stephens, P. (1989b, June 30). Thatcher pledges to counter Delors plan. *Financial Times*.
Stephens, P. (1999, February 26). Liberated by Europe. *Financial Times*.
Sutcliffe, T. (1999, February 24). On a momentous day for our island race, Blair turns up. *The Independent*.
Sylvester, R. (1999, February 28). Can they save the pound? *The Independent on Sunday*.
Temple, M. (2008). *The British press*. Maidenhead: Open University Press.
Terry, W. (1978a, December 4). Lone-wolf Jim in big euro crunch. *The Sun*.
Terry, W. (1978b, December 5). Britain gets the bird at Euro talks. *The Sun*.
Terry, W. (1978c, December 6). Big Jim comes up all smiles! *The Sun*.
The Guardian. (1978, November 29). Half-way to a better Europe.
The Guardian. (1989a, June 20). Spain's conquest.
The Guardian. (1989b, June 26). Bulldog tantrums not in order.
The Guardian. (1989c, June 28). A defeat with the seeds of victory.
The Guardian. (1989d, July 11). Inflation may threaten EC monetary union.
The Guardian. (1999a, February 24). Going for the euro.
The Guardian. (1999b, February 24). Introducing Euro-Blair.
The Independent. (1989a, June 26). Crossing rubicons at Madrid.
The Independent. (1989b, June 28). Spanish rhetoric.

The Independent. (1991a, November 28). Lonely future on the margin.
The Independent. (1991b, November 29). Nothing to fear but fear itself.
The Independent. (1991c, December 11). A classic British error.
The Independent. (1991d, December 12). Maastricht summit.
The Independent. (1991e, December 12). A triumph, despite the legacy.
The Independent. (1999a, February 24). Fine words, but a change of tone does not a policy make.
The Independent. (1999b, March 1). Come on, Mr Blair: Call a referendum on the euro now.
The Sun. (1978a, December 7). Relegation.
The Sun. (1978b, December 13). Blow to Britain over Euro money.
The Sun. (1989a, June 26). Keep up the fight, Mrs T!
The Sun. (1989b, June 29). Still champ.
The Sun. (1991a, November 30). PM 'won't be bullied'.
The Sun. (1991b, December 12). Come the hour, come the man!
The Sun. (1991c, December 12). How Britain succeeded at Maastricht.
The Sun. (1999a, February 20). Is Blair taking us for granted?
The Sun. (1999b, February 24). This thing is bigger than both of us...
The Sun. (1999c, February 25). People power.
The Sun. (1999d, March 6). This is our finest hour.
Thompson-Noel, M. (1991, December 14). A turning point—Or maybe not. *Financial Times.*
Usborne, D., & Cottrell, R. (1989, June 22). The loser at the summit. *The Independent.*
Usborne, D., Bevins, A., & Lambert, S. (1991a, December 2). UK isolated on right to opt out of one currency. *The Independent.*
Usborne, D., Lambert, S., Helm, S., Bevins, A., Torday, P., & Marshall, A. (1991b, December 6). Economic Union: How EMU works. *The Independent.*
Waterhouse, K. (1999, February 25). A hundred yard start in the euro race. *Daily Mail.*
Watkins, A. (1999, February 28). Blair wants a fait accompli, not a poll. *The Independent on Sunday.*
White, M. (1978, December 2). Whitehall reassures EEC on Euro-cash. *The Guardian.*
White, M. (1989, June 30). Thatcher alert against 'Paris-Bonn domination'. *The Guardian.*
White, M. (1991, December 12). Tories hail Major triumph. *The Guardian.*
White, M., & Elliott, L. (1999, February 24). Blair 'crosses the rubicon' towards Euroland. *The Guardian.*
White, M., Ward, L., & MacAskill, E. (1999, February 20). Euro timetable to be shortened. *The Guardian.*
Wilson-Smith, P. (1989, June 27). Currency system which challenges nations to curb inflation. *The Independent.*
Woosey, B. (1978, December 16). Jim's left in the lurch. *The Sun.*
Young, H. (1989, June 29). The devil's advocate bows to reality. *The Guardian.*
Young, H. (1991, December 12). Sub plot of the social chapter. *The Guardian.*
Young, H. (1999, February 24). Caesar Blair casts the die and there's no going back. *The Guardian.*

Chapter 11
Conclusion: Prime Ministerial Political Leadership in British European (Monetary) Policy

This study examined the political leadership of the Prime Ministers James Callaghan, Margaret Thatcher, John Major and Tony Blair in European policy by analysing case studies from European monetary policy. The research questions were:

(a) Can the political leadership of the British prime minister in European policy be characterised as prime ministerial predominance or as collective leadership?
(b) Has there been a trend towards more prime ministerial predominance between 1976 and 2007?

The analysis focused on four aspects:

First of all, the premier's institutional resources were identified with regard to European policy decision-making and particularly in the area of European monetary policy. As the analysis showed, the prime ministerial institutional resources in Prime Minister's Office and Cabinet Office were extended in the time period 1976 to 2007. A particular leap came during Tony Blair's premiership. The use of these resources was affected by the context such as developments in European integration as more policy areas received a European dimension and the heads of state and government became more involved in European policy-making through regular European Council meetings and bilateral summits. The PM's personal preferences also shaped the use of these resources such as Blair's dislike of the private secretary system, which influenced his institutional reforms on European policy-making. Margaret Thatcher and Tony Blair tried to modify their institutional resources to make them more focused on the prime minister in European policy-making and to have more capabilities to exert a leadership role in this policy field. James Callaghan and John Major, however, did not introduce changes similar to those of Blair and Thatcher. Therefore, such a development was not evident in their cases. It appears that they were either content with the institutional resources at their disposal in Cabinet Office and PMO or even if on occasion they were not, they lacked the interest or the means or did not see a necessity to make similar institutional reforms to secure a stronger focus on the prime minister in European policy-making.

B. Bujard, *The British Prime Minister in the Core Executive*, Contributions to Political Science, https://doi.org/10.1007/978-3-319-89953-4_11

On European monetary policy Thatcher and Blair attempted to use their institutional resources to be predominant. For instance, the European Secretariat under Blair was specifically tasked to do planning on EMU. This suggests that Blair wanted to have his own expertise on the euro, independent of the Treasury, and not leave the issue to the department. This might also have been related to the fact that he had to work with a chancellor who himself aspired to be predominant in this area of European policy. Thatcher, on the other hand, had Alan Walters as her personal economic adviser. He would give her advice independent of chancellor and Treasury, which she could use against Lawson (and Howe), who tried to persuade her to agree to ERM entry. In the cases of Major and Callaghan there was no indication that they developed similar independent advice structures. Instead Major, for example on EMU in the run up to the Maastricht negotiations, specifically turned to the leading Treasury official on the issue, Nigel Wicks, for advice.

Secondly, the agency and behaviour of other actors in the European (monetary) policy core executive apart from the prime minister were analysed. Moreover, the PM's options in handling these actors who potentially constrain his room for action were studied and how he could attempt to broaden his leeway in that respect. The present analysis showed that individual ministers could significantly affect policy decisions depending on their status in the core executive, their relationship with the prime minister and the PM's cabinet management strategy. Meanwhile prime ministerial cabinet management was much influenced by the cohesion of the ruling party—whether it was unified or divided on the policy field in question. On the analysed European monetary policy cases the Prime Ministers Callaghan and Major did exercise collective leadership. Yet this did not mean a return to classical 'cabinet government' in the sense that the full cabinet was included. Instead it was decision-making limited to a number of key actors in the core executive. As their parties were divided over Europe, which also affected the PM's leeway on appointments and thus the composition of the core executive, Callaghan's and Major's key interest on cabinet management was to safeguard cabinet and party unity. Margaret Thatcher and Tony Blair attempted to achieve their policy goals by predominant leadership. Both limited the decision-making process on European monetary policy, for instance, by preventing a wide-ranging debate on ERM and EMU in the core executive. Thatcher from 1985, when the ERM-issue became relevant in the core executive, defied her foreign secretary and her chancellor by vetoing membership. Thus she achieved prime ministerial predominance. This, however, was temporary. Her dismissal of Geoffrey Howe from the Foreign Office, Nigel Lawson's resignation and other issues such as the poll tax weakened her position in the core executive so much that by 1989 she had to submit to the pressure of her new chancellor and foreign secretary, John Major and Douglas Hurd, to agree to ERM membership. Despite the change of context she kept up her predominant leadership strategy, which then failed to produce the intended results, as she was only able to postpone the implementation of a policy she opposed. On EMU Thatcher also limited the decision-making process to chancellor and foreign secretary and marginalised the full cabinet. While the three ministers agreed on the undesirability of EMU, they disagreed on the government's strategy for the European level negotiations on it. Thatcher again adopted a predominant leadership strategy by explicitly opposing EMU at the Rome IGC and effectively destroying the government's alternative to the Delors plan with her subsequent statement in parliament. She did this despite her ministers' opposition. Her leadership strategy failed on two levels: EMU was established despite her opposition and her parliamentary statement was the prelude to a process which led to her resignation. Tony Blair, on the other hand, limited the decision-making process on EMU to his chancellor and himself. He gave Brown a veto on the euro policy by stating that the basis of the decision was economics. Failing to secure alliances with pro-euro ministers, let alone appointing them to senior cabinet posts, he had no option to exert pressure on Brown to change policy once it became clear that the chancellor took a different stance on the issue from his own. Thus his predominance strategy also failed.

From the analysis it can be concluded that a key actor on European monetary policy, who could significantly impact on the PM's scope of action, was the chancellor. If his view was in line with the prime minister's, for instance Callaghan and Healey on the ERM, other ministers had slim chances to achieve a change of policy. If it was not, the chancellor could constrain the prime minister's leeway in policy-making on the issue in question as was the case with Blair and Brown. Of somewhat lesser influence was the foreign secretary. On ERM and EMU the foreign secretaries had a more limited impact on the decision-making process than might be the case in others areas of European policy. This is due to the policy field as the Treasury was and is the leading department on monetary policy.

Moreover, it became clear from the analysis that while all four prime ministers could have used their membership in the European Council as a means to conduct two-level politics on European monetary policy, none of them did. This was because none of them would have strengthened their domestic leadership position by making deals with their counterparts in the European Council to force actors in their core executive to a change of policy. As noted, in Callaghan's and Major's case party unity was the key. Neither PM would have strengthened their leadership position at home by dropping their compromise policy, which had been drafted to be tolerable for pro-Europeans and Eurosceptics alike (EMS but no ERM membership or the EMU opt-out), and siding with their fellow leaders in the European Council. This was similar for Thatcher over ERM and EMU—particularly as she agreed neither with the key actors in the core executive nor with her European counterparts on either issue and/or the UK's strategy in the European level negotiations. In Blair's case, as well, two-level politics did not help him achieve his policy goals domestically. After having stated that the five tests would decide whether the UK should adopt the single currency, siding with the other national leaders in the European Council would not have increased his influence on the policy at home.

Thirdly, the position of the governing party in parliament and its voting behaviour on European policy was analysed to understand how far it affected the prime minister's political leadership in the policy field. The premier's resources to influence his parliamentary party concerning European policy-making were also considered. The parliamentary party was a factor which could significantly impact on the prime minister's scope of action in European policy-making. In the present analysis this was particularly observable in the cases of John Major and James Callaghan. Both had to govern either with a non-existent or a small parliamentary majority. Moreover, their parties were split over Europe in general and over ERM and EMU in particular. Both prime ministers had to take into account the diverging attitudes in their parliamentary party when trying to enact their policy programme. To avoid an intraparty split which would endanger their power base, both adopted policies which were acceptable to pro-Europeans as well as Eurosceptics such as the opt-out from EMU or EMS without ERM membership. While Callaghan and Major were constrained, Margaret Thatcher and Tony Blair did not have to take the parliamentary party into account as a considerable constraint on their leeway in European (monetary) policy. Both governed with comfortable and at times large majorities. Although they might not have been able to persuade their fellow MPs to adopt their attitude to European integration or to ERM or EMU, there were only a limited number of revolts by members of their parliamentary parties on Europe. Hence with regard to their parliamentary parties both were able to be predominant. Yet no crucial decisions in European monetary policy, which might well have resulted in trouble with the parliamentary party, were taken during their premierships. Thatcher was already out of office when the provisions for EMU set out in the Maastricht treaty had to be ratified. In Blair's case parliament was not asked to decide about joining the euro as the government itself never agreed to adopt the single currency.

For the four office holders it has to be assumed that on policy—European and other areas—they took a certain form of backbench behaviour into account, which, at least to a degree, influenced their strategies and policy decisions. Moreover, possible rebellions in parliament might have been avoided, because the government compromised with its MPs, for instance, by watering down legislation or by refraining from taking a particular decision at all. Such behaviour by PM, government and parliamentary party cannot be measured as, for example, the number of rebellions in parliament. Therefore, such processes cannot be verified empirically.

Fourth, an analysis of parliamentary statements on particular European monetary policy decisions by the four prime ministers and their adoption by the national press was conducted. It was to be evaluated to what extent the incumbents could influence media coverage and the media's assessment of their European monetary policy. As was seen, the four premiers had to do this against a backdrop of increasing Euroscepticism in the press and a British public, which was less than unenthusiastic about Europe and also in parts Eurosceptic. The media analysis in Chap. 10 showed that the prime ministers' chances to shape the media coverage of European monetary policy were limited. From the case study analysis it could be concluded that none of the PMs was able to become an opinion leader on the European monetary policy decision in question. If they were at all able to influence newspapers, it tended to be by reinforcing existing views. Thus, if the prime ministers had hoped to use the media as a communication channel with the public on this subject area in order to influence them, they failed. Even if the press is able to shape public opinion, which as noted before, is a contested argument in communication and public opinion research, in the case of the four leaders analysed here the effect appears to have been negligible. Some newspapers supported a PM's position on the issue in question, but this tended to be no result of his political communication. These papers had already taken a similar view before his speech. Other newspapers, particularly those which did not share the prime minister's view, tended not to adopt the PM's arguments on the issue. Thus they did not transmit his arguments to their readers, which might have helped the premier to increase public support for his stance on the issue in question.

Looking at the four prime ministers' political leadership in European monetary policy in the time period 1976–2007, it can be concluded that it changed considerably (Table 11.1). There was collective as well as predominant prime ministerial political leadership. Yet a decisive trend towards more prime ministerial predominance was not observable, despite all four leaders having shown a keen interest in the policy area and the extension of prime ministerial resources over the years. Similarly there was no decisive trend towards more collective leadership. Looking at the aspects identified in Chap. 2, as to what could constitute prime ministerial predominance and collective leadership, the picture is mixed. Prime ministerial leadership fluctuated between 'collective leadership' and 'prime ministerial predominant leadership'. Which it turned out to be appears to have particularly depended on the party in government. When it lacked unity on the policy field and there were intraparty splits, there was also no prime ministerial predominance. Yet this did not mean that collective leadership in the sense of including the whole cabinet was the only feasible consequence. A case in point was John Major's leadership on the EMU negotiations at Maastricht, where he gave the impression of including the parliamentary party and the full cabinet in the decision-making process by having them discuss the government's negotiating position before the summit. Yet the policy was set in a small group which included him, the chancellor and the foreign secretary. Callaghan pursued a similar strategy by establishing a cabinet committee of which he could be sure due to the ministers he sent there, that they would decide against joining the ERM. This decision he could then present to the full cabinet for affirmation.

What is also striking, when looking at the different forms of political leadership between 1976 and 2007 on European monetary policy, is that effective prime ministerial predominance appeared to be less frequent than, for instance, presidentialization approaches have suggested. This, however, does not mean that prime ministers did not attempt to be predominant. Tony Blair actively sought to gain more capabilities in European policy-making, for instance, by making institutional reforms in PMO and Cabinet Office. He, moreover, had the European Secretariat do planning on EMU. Yet these attempts were without effect on the issue, as he could not realise his policy on the euro without the support of his chancellor (and other senior ministers). Later in his premiership he had used up too much political capital in order to secure support for his decision to join the US forces in the Iraq war to be able to forward his euro policy, for instance, by dismissing Brown as chancellor. He also failed to build alliances with pro-euro ministers. Thus his political leadership can be described as failed predominance as he adopted a predominant leadership strategy, although it did not achieve the intended results. This was because the balance of power in the core executive and—at least later in his premiership—the

Table 11.1 Prime ministerial political leadership in European monetary policy 1976–2007 (own illustration)

	Callaghan ERM	Thatcher ERM	Thatcher EMU	Major ERM	Major EMU	Blair EMU
Actors in the core executive	Alliance with C, full cabinet divided over Europe	1985–1989: unconstrained by C and FS, full cabinet marginalisation 1989–1990: con-strained by C + FS, full cabinet marginalisation	Inclusion of C + FS, full cabinet marginalisation	Inclusion of senior ministers, full cabinet divided over Europe	Alliance with C + FS, full cabinet divided over Europe	No alliances with pro-euro ministers, constrained by C, full cabinet marginalisation
	No two-level politics	No two-level politics	No two-level politics	No two-level politics	No two-level politics	No two-level politics
Parliamentary party	Constraint	Marginal constraint	Marginal constraint	Constraint	Constraint	Marginal constraint
Public and media	No opinion leader	No opinion leader	No opinion leader	No opinion leader	No opinion leader	No opinion leader
Political leadership	Collective	Predominance (1985–1989), failed predominance (1989–1990)	Failed predominance	Collective	Collective	Failed predominance

Key: *C* = chancellor, *FS* = foreign secretary

context did not allow him to be predominant on the euro policy. This was similar to Thatcher, who in 1989/1990 kept up her predominant leadership strategy on ERM and EMU, although the context and the balance of power in the core executive had changed and did not allow her to succeed with it any longer.

That no decisive trend towards prime ministerial predominance was observable in European monetary policy in the time period 1976 to 2007 might be due to the selected policy field, in which the Treasury and the chancellor had (and have) a strong influence (and at times, although to a lesser extent, the Foreign Office and the foreign secretary). Moreover, prime ministerial predominance appears rather to have been a particular image which Prime Ministers Thatcher and Blair liked to cultivate than—at least in European monetary policy—something they were able to realise. Thatcher famously said shortly before the 1979 general election that once prime minister she "could not waste time having any internal arguments" (Thatcher quoted in Hennessy 2001: 401), suggesting that her leadership would be predominant. Tony Blair said in January 2000 in an interview: "I will decide the issue of monetary union, I'm the prime minister who's got responsibility for it, according to the British national interest"[1] (Blair quoted in Newman 2000). Institutional reforms during his premiership contributed to claims that there was such a thing as a 'Blair presidency' (for a debate of the presidential analogy, see Kavanagh 2005:16). Yet as was seen on the euro policy, these reforms did not help him to be predominant. The cases of Thatcher's and Blair's political leadership analysed here thus also support the notion that a prime minister's political leadership is not determined by his personal preferences. Moreover, these personal preferences do not determine whether an adopted leadership strategy is effective. As Martin J. Smith with his approach to studying prime ministerial power has suggested, there are other factors such as the context or other actors in the core executive that affect a PM's scope of action and influence whether he can use his preferred leadership strategy effectively (Smith 1999: Chap. 4).

Yet the present analysis also showed that if the prime minister exercised collective leadership, this was not a return to classical 'cabinet government' in the sense of including the full cabinet. It was a more limited version, which was focused on prime ministerial leadership in collaboration with a few key ministers.

It has become clear from the analysis that the party in government is a very important factor in shaping the trajectory in which a prime minister's political leadership is exercised. The PM's scope of action not only in European policy-making but also in other policy fields is much affected by his party particularly in two ways: on the one hand by his cabinet ministers, who can block the implementation of policies the premier favours. As was seen in this analysis, the prime minister's options of selecting his government team are much affected by party political considerations and not necessarily based on policy or his own preferences. On the other hand, in the case of the party in parliament it was shown that rebellions

[1]Newman, C. (2000), Blair acknowledges British are opposed to euro, Financial Times, 17 January 2000. Used under licence from the Financial Times. All Rights Reserved.

against government policy are no seldom occurrence and can at times severely limit a PM's leeway and also his options for predominant leadership. This shows that, despite the suggestions that the British executive has become more 'presidentialized' and focused on the prime minister, the party in government remains a central influence on a prime minister's political leadership.

As stated in the introduction to this study, the present analysis forms part of wider assessment of prime ministerial leadership in the United Kingdom which is necessary to come to more solid findings on the role of the prime minister in the British core executive. Such a wide-ranging evaluation provides the possibility to separate prime ministerial leadership image from the actual handling of the political decision-making process. Assuming—like the core executive approach does—that a PM's political leadership varies among policy areas, a next step would be to analyse prime ministerial political leadership in other policy fields. This concerns other areas of European policy as well as completely different policy fields. In the case of the former, particularly those are of interest which will still be relevant after the UK's exit from the European Union, for instance, trade, foreign and defence policy. In this context it would also be interesting to study whether the premier's leadership is predominant or collective as well as whether collective leadership remains limited to a few actors.

The analysis here has shown that a prime minister aspiring to exercise predominant political leadership has better chances to do so effectively (though no guarantee), if he has (a) a decisive majority and (b) a united party on the policy field in question. Even if there are intraparty rebellions against his policies in parliament, he is fairly immune to them due to the parliamentary arithmetic. Therefore it would be interesting to study a prime minister who does not have a decisive majority or lead a united party on the policy field in question but still appears intent on being predominant in his political leadership. None of the prime ministers analysed here matched this category, yet David Cameron's successor as prime minister, Theresa May, initially appeared to be a possible case.

When she took over the premiership in 2016, May set up a Department for Exiting the European Union and entrusted portfolios which directly affected the exit negotiations with the EU to three 'Brexiteers': Boris Johnson (Foreign Secretary), Liam Fox (Secretary of State for International Trade) and David Davis (Secretary of State for Exiting the European Union) (Bujard 2017: 584). Despite this, the new prime minister did not give the impression that she was adopting a leadership strategy focused on much collectivity on the UK's negotiations to leave the European Union as well as on finding a new relationship with the other EU members and the European Union itself. Before the Conservative Party conference in October 2016 she distanced herself from remarks made by Fox, Johnson and Davis on the Brexit negotiations. Davis, for instance, stated in September 2016 that it was unlikely that the UK would remain part of the single market. He said this when he made a statement in parliament on the progress of the government's preparations for leaving the EU. Yet the prime minister's official spokeswoman dismissed the position as Davis's personal opinion and not government policy (Asthana 2016). However, at the Conservative Party conference in October 2016, May appeared to confirm that the government might not seek privileged access to the European single market (Elliott and Charter 2016).

What initially appeared to be the peak of her predominant leadership strategy was May's decision to call on parliament to hold a snap election shortly after the Article 50 TEU notification. However, it turned out to have the opposite effect. The June 2017 general election left May with a minority government in need of support from the Northern Irish pro-Brexit Democratic Unionist Party (DUP) to stay in office (Bujard 2017: 588–590). In addition, she led a party which was not united in its position on the most important objectives of current UK European policy: Britain's future relationship with the other EU member states as well as the EU itself and what kind of Brexit to seek (Helm 2016). European policy and the party's Eurosceptics have troubled every Conservative prime minister since John Major and have severely limited their leeway on European policy-making. Similar to John Major and her immediate predecessor David Cameron, Theresa May appeared to appease rather than to confront them. Moreover, the outcome of the June 2016 EU referendum had changed the balance of power between Pro-Europeans and Eurosceptics in the party: the latter were now in charge and if the former would "counsel compromise on migration or the single market, they [were] accused of talking Britain down or trying to refight the referendum" (Behr 2016). In May's case, as well, the strong impact of the party on the prime minister's political leadership, which was identified in the present study, was observable. Despite the decision to leave the EU being a result of a vote by the UK public, May appeared to be particularly concerned with her party's reaction. Indicative of this was, for example, her announcement just before the 2016 Conservative Party conference that the formal exit process from the EU would begin in March 2017—to pre-empt a possible rebellion from Tory MPs who might have feared that she would not go through with Brexit (Rachman 2016).

References

Asthana, A. (2016, September 6). David Davis's single market stance 'not government policy'. *The Guardian*.

Behr, R. (2016, October 5). We are witnessing nothing less than a Tory reformation. *The Guardian*.

Bujard, B. (2017). Vereinigtes Königreich. In W. Weidenfeld & W. Wessels (Eds.), *Jahrbuch der Europäischen Integration 2017* (pp. 583–592). Baden-Baden: Nomos Verlagsgesellschaft.

Elliott, F., & Charter, D. (2016, October 3). EU leaders reject May over 'hard' Brexit talks. *The Times*.

Helm, T. (2016, October 1). Bitter Tory fight over Brexit set to overshadow Conservative conference. *The Observer*.

Hennessy, P. (2001). *The prime minister: The office and its holders since 1945* (2nd ed.). London: Penguin.

Kavanagh, D. (2005). The Blair premiership. In A. Seldon & D. Kavanagh (Eds.), *The Blair effect 2001-5* (pp. 3–19). Cambridge: Cambridge University Press.

Newman, C. (2000, January 17). Blair acknowledges British are opposed to euro. *Financial Times*.

Rachman, G. (2016, October 4). May walks into a Brexit trap. *Financial Times*.

Smith, M. J. (1999). *The core executive in Britain*. Basingstoke: Macmillan.

References

Aitken, I. (1978, December 7). Callaghan flies patriot's flag over Commons. *The Guardian*.

Aitken, I. (1991, December 13). The Maastricht litmus test. *The Guardian*.

Alderman, K. (1996). The passage of the European Communities (finance) Act (1995) and its aftermath. *Contemporary British History, 10*(3), 1–20.

Alderman, R. K., & Cross, J. A. (1985). The reluctant knife: Reflections on the prime minister's power of dismissal. *Parliamentary Affairs, 38*(4), 387–408.

Alexander, A. (1978, December 5). One bank note that we can all live without... *Daily Mail*.

Alexander, A. (1989a, June 19). The duel dividing Downing Street. *Daily Mail*.

Alexander, A. (1989b, June 27). Maggie puts the rest on the spot. *Daily Mail*.

Alexander, A. (1989c, June 28). No need to flap about EMU now. *Daily Mail*.

Alexander, A. (1999a, February 23). Needless preparations for euro would waste billions. *Daily Mail*.

Alexander, A. (1999b, February 26). Selling out for price of a euro. *Daily Mail*.

Allen, D. (2013). The United Kingdom. In S. Bulmer & C. Lequesne (Eds.), *The member states of the European Union* (2nd ed., pp. 108–133). Oxford: Oxford University Press.

Anderson, P., & Mann, N. (1997). *Safety first: The making of New Labour*. London: Granta Books.

Ashford, N. (1992). The political parties. In S. George (Ed.), *Britain and the European Community: The politics of semi-detachment* (pp. 119–148). Oxford: Clarendon.

Asthana, A. (2016, September 6). David Davis's single market stance 'not government policy'. *The Guardian*.

Bache, I., & Nugent, N. (2007). Europe. In A. Seldon (Ed.), *Blair's Britain, 1997–2007* (pp. 529–550). Cambridge: Cambridge University Press.

Baker, D., & Seawright, D. (Eds.). (1998). *Britain for and against Europe: British politics and the question of European integration*. Oxford: Clarendon.

Baker, D., & Sherrington, P. (2004). Britain and Europe: Europe and/or America? *Parliamentary Affairs, 57*(2), 347–365.

Baker, D., Gamble, A., & Ludlam, S. (1993). 1846... 1906... 1996? Conservative splits and European integration. *The Political Quarterly, 64*(4), 420–434.

Baker, D., Gamble, A., & Ludlam, S. (1994). The parliamentary siege of Maastricht 1993: Conservative divisions and British ratification. *Parliamentary Affairs, 47*(1), 37–60.

Baker, D., Gamble, A., Ludlam, S., & Seawright, D. (1999). Backbenchers with attitude: A seismic study of the Conservative Party and dissent on Europe. In S. Bowler, D. M. Farrell, & R. S. Katz (Eds.), *Party discipline and parliamentary government* (pp. 72–93). Columbus: Ohio State University Press.

Bale, T. (2016). *The Conservative Party: From Thatcher to Cameron* (2nd ed.). Cambridge: Polity.

B. Bujard, *The British Prime Minister in the Core Executive*, Contributions to Political Science, https://doi.org/10.1007/978-3-319-89953-4

Bale, T., & Sanders, K. (2001). 'Playing by the book': Success and failure in John Major's approach to prime ministerial media management. *Contemporary British History, 15*(4), 93–110.

Ballinger, C., & Seldon, A. (2004). Prime ministers and cabinet. In A. Seldon & K. Hickson (Eds.), *New Labour, Old Labour: The Wilson and Callaghan governments, 1974–79* (pp. 173–189). London: Routledge.

Barber, L. (1998, July 16). Move over Metternich. *Financial Times.*

Bates, S. (1999). Brussels with the blinkers on. *British Journalism Review, 10*(1), 35–40.

Beckett, A. (2016, January 27). The most potent, permanent and elusive figure in British politics. *The Guardian.*

Behr, R. (2016, October 5). We are witnessing nothing less than a Tory reformation. *The Guardian.*

Bender, B. G. (1991). Whitehall, central government and 1992. *Public Policy and Administration, 6* (1), 13–20.

Benn, T. (1978, 13 July). Britain, Germany and the proposed monetary system, In The National Archives [hereafter TNA]. *Records of the Cabinet Office [hereafter CAB] 129/203*, CP (78) 80.

Bennister, M. (2007). Tony Blair and John Howard: Comparative predominance and 'institution stretch' in the UK and Australia. *The British Journal of Politics and International Relations, 9* (3), 327–345.

Bennister, M. (2008). Blair and Howard: Predominant prime ministers compared. *Parliamentary Affairs, 61*(2), 334–355.

Bevins, A. (1989, June 30). Summit 'has bought time to work on union'. *The Independent.*

Blair, A. (1999). *Dealing with Europe: Britain and the negotiation of the Maastricht Treaty.* Aldershot: Ashgate.

Blair, T. (2010). *A journey.* London: Hutchinson.

Blick, A., & Jones, G. (2010). *Premiership: The development, nature and power of the British prime minister.* Exeter: Imprint Academic.

Borthwick, R. L. (1995). Prime minister and parliament. In D. Shell & R. Hodder-Williams (Eds.), *Churchill to Major: The British prime ministership since 1945* (pp. 71–103). Armonk: M. E. Sharpe.

Braithwaite, R. (1998, January 28). *British Diplomatic Oral History Programme (BDOHP) interview.* Cambridge: Churchill Archives Centre, Churchill College.

Brincker, G.-S., & Wessels, W. (2012). Europäischer Rat. In W. Weidenfeld & W. Wessels (Eds.), *Jahrbuch der Europäischen Integration 2012* (pp. 65–80). Baden-Baden: Nomos Verlagsgesellschaft.

Brittan, S. (1978a, November 30). EMS: missed chances and false traits. *Financial Times.*

Brittan, S. (1978b, December 7). The architects of a two-tier Europe. *Financial Times.*

Brittan, S. (1989, June 29). Don't sell Madrid short. *Financial Times.*

Brittan, S. (1991, December 12). A victory, but not quite a triumph. *Financial Times.*

Brown, K. (1999, February 25). Questions left unanswered on costs and attitudes. *Financial Times.*

Brown, K., & Sanghera, S. (1999, February 24). Changeover plan sets out 'critical path' for transition. *Financial Times.*

Bruce-Gardyne, J. (1986). *Ministers and mandarins: Inside the Whitehall village.* London: Sidgwick & Jackson.

Buchan, D. (1991, December 2). Denmark leaves UK in the lurch on opt-out. *Financial Times.*

Buchan, D., & Stephens, P. (1991, December 2). UK isolated on single currency opt-out clause. *Financial Times.*

Buchan, D., Bruce, P., & Davidson, I. (1989, June 24). Thatcher faces pressure over economic union. *Financial Times.*

Bujard, B. (2003). *Die politische Führung des britischen Premierminister: Das "Model of Prime Ministerial Power" am Beispiel der Europapolitik Margaret Thatchers und Tony Blairs* (unpublished M.A. thesis), University of Cologne, Cologne.

Bujard, B. (2016). Vereinigtes Königreich. In W. Weidenfeld & W. Wessels (Eds.), *Jahrbuch der Europäischen Integration 2016* (pp. 591–600). Baden-Baden: Nomos Verlagsgesellschaft.

Bujard, B. (2017). Vereinigtes Königreich. In W. Weidenfeld & W. Wessels (Eds.), *Jahrbuch der Europäischen Integration 2017* (pp. 583–592). Baden-Baden: Nomos Verlagsgesellschaft.

Buller, J., & Smith, M. J. (1998). Civil service attitudes towards the European Union. In D. Baker & D. Seawright (Eds.), *Britain for and against Europe: British politics and the question of European integration* (pp. 165–184). Oxford: Clarendon.

Bulmer, S., & Burch, M. (1998). Organizing for Europe: Whitehall, the British state and European Union. *Public Administration, 76*(4), 601–628.

Bulmer, S., & Burch, M. (2005). The Europeanization of UK government: From quiet revolution to explicit step-change? *Public Administration, 83*(4), 861–890.

Bulmer, S., & Burch, M. (2009). *The Europeanisation of Whitehall: UK central government and the European Union*. Manchester: Manchester University Press.

Burch, M. (1995). Prime minister and Whitehall. In D. Shell & R. Hodder-Williams (Eds.), *Churchill to Major: The British prime ministership since 1945* (pp. 104–136). Armonk: M. E. Sharpe.

Burch, M., & Holliday, I. (1996). *British cabinet system*. Hemel Hempstead: Prentice Hall Harvester Wheatsheaf.

Burch, M., & Holliday, I. (1999). The prime minister's and cabinet offices: An executive office in all but name. *Parliamentary Affairs, 52*(1), 32–45.

Burch, M., & Holliday, I. (2004). The Blair government and the core executive. *Government and Opposition, 39*(1), 1–21.

Butler, D. (1979). Public opinion and Community membership. *The Political Quarterly, 50*(2), 151–156.

Butler, D., & Butler, G. (2006). *British political facts since 1979*. Basingstoke: Palgrave Macmillan.

Butler, D., & Kavanagh, D. (Eds.). (1980). *The British general election of 1979*. London: Macmillan.

Butler, D., & Kavanagh, D. (Eds.). (1988). *The British general election of 1987*. New York: St. Martin's Press.

Butler, D., & Kavanagh, D. (Eds.). (1992). *The British general election of 1992*. Basingstoke/London: St. Martin's Press/Macmillan.

Butler, D., & Marquand, D. (1981). *European elections and British politics*. London: Longman.

Butler, D., & Sloman, A. (1980). *British political facts 1900–1979* (5th ed.). London: Macmillan.

Cabinet Office. (2007). *European Secretariat*. Archived on July 1, 2007. http://webarchive.nationalarchives.gov.uk/20070701080507/cabinetoffice.gov.uk/about_the_cabinet_office/units.asp. Accessed September 11, 2016.

Callaghan, J. (2006). *Time and chance*. London: Politico's.

Cameron, D. (2013, January 23). *EU speech at Bloomberg*. https://www.gov.uk/government/speeches/eu-speech-at-bloomberg. Accessed May 29, 2013.

Cameron, D. (2016, February 22). *PM Commons statement on EU reform and referendum*. https://www.gov.uk/government/speeches/pm-commons-statement-on-eu-reform-and-referendum-22-february-2016. Accessed April 8, 2016.

Campbell, A. (2007). *The Blair years: Extracts from the Alastair Campbell diaries*. London: Hutchinson.

Campbell, J. (2011). *The Iron Lady: Margaret Thatcher: From Grocer's daughter to prime minister* (2nd ed.). London: Penguin Books.

Carey, S., & Burton, J. (2004). The influence of the press in shaping public opinion towards the European Union in Britain. *Political Studies, 52*(3), 623–640.

Carrington, P. A. (1988). *Reflect on things past: The memoirs of Lord Carrington*. London: Collins.

Cartledge, B. (2007, November 14). *British Diplomatic Oral History Programme (BDOHP) interview*. Cambridge: Churchill Archives Centre, Churchill College.

Christoph, J. B. (1993). The effects of Britons in Brussels: The European Community and the culture of Whitehall. *Governance, 6*(4), 518–537.

Clark, A. (1999). *The Tories: Conservatives and the nation state 1922-1997* (2nd ed.). London: Phoenix.

Clarke, K. (2016). *Kind of blue: A political memoir*. London: Macmillan.
Clifford, C. (2000). Administering the summit: The British prime minister's office. In B. G. Peters, R. A. W. Rhodes, & V. Wright (Eds.), *Administering the summit: Administration of the core executive in developed countries* (pp. 25–42). Basingstoke: Macmillan.
Cockerell, M., Hennessy, P., & Walker, D. (1985). *Sources close to the prime minister: Inside the hidden world of the news manipulators* (2nd ed.). London: Macmillan.
Cole, P. (2007, August 27). The paradox of the pops. *The Guardian*.
Conservative Party. (1983). *The Conservative manifesto 1983*. https://www.margaretthatcher.org/document/131063. Accessed March 8, 2018.
Cook, R. (2004). *The point of departure: Diaries from the front bench* (2nd ed.). London: Pocket Books.
Cowley, P. (2005). *The rebels: How Blair mislaid his majority*. London: Politico's.
Cowley, P. (2007). Parliament. In A. Seldon (Ed.), *Blair's Britain, 1997-2007* (pp. 16–34). Cambridge: Cambridge University Press.
Cowley, P. (2008, January 21). This will not be like Maastricht. *The Guardian*.
Cowley, P., & Norton, P. (1996). Are Conservative MPs revolting? Dissension by government MPs in the British House of Commons 1979–1996, University of Hull: Centre for Legislative Studies, *Research Papers in Legislative Studies*, No. 2/96.
Cowley, P., & Norton, P. (1999). Rebels and rebellions: Conservative MPs in the 1992 Parliament. *British Journal of Politics and International Relations, 1*(1), 84–105.
Cowley, P., & Stuart, M. (2003). In place of strife? The PLP in Government, 1997–2001. *Political Studies, 51*(2), 315–334.
Cowley, P., & Stuart, M. (2005). Parliament. In A. Seldon & D. Kavanagh (Eds.), *The Blair effect 2001-5* (pp. 20–42). Cambridge: Cambridge University Press.
Cowley, P., & Stuart, M. (2006, November). *Dissension amongst the Parliamentary Labour Party, 2005-2006: A data handbook*. http://www.revolts.co.uk/Dissension%20data%20handbook%202005-06%20Final.pdf. Accessed August 29, 2016.
Cowley, P., & Stuart, M. (2007a, November). *From Blair to Brown: Dissension in the Parliamentary Labour Party, 2006-2007: A data handbook*. http://www.revolts.co.uk/Dissension%20handbook%202006-7%20web%20version.pdf. Accessed August 29, 2016.
Cowley, P., & Stuart, M. (2007b, September 12). *Europe: The dog that hasn't barked (yet?)*. http://www.revolts.co.uk/The%20dog%20that%20didnt%20bark.pdf. Accessed August 29, 2016.
Cowley, P., & Stuart, M. (2012, October 30). *Europe: The gift that keeps giving misery to Conservative whips*. http://nottspolitics.org/2012/10/30/europe-the-gift-that-keeps-on-giving-misery-to-conservative-whips/. Accessed June 4, 2016.
Coyle, D., & Waugh, P. (1999, February 22). Spending ban on euro poll. *The Independent*.
Cradock, P. (1997). *In pursuit of British interests: Reflections on foreign policy under Margaret Thatcher and John Major*. London: John Murray.
Crossmann, R. H. S. (1963). Introduction. In W. Bagehot (Ed.), *The English constitution* (2nd ed., pp. 1–57). London: Collins/Fontana Library.
Curtice, J., & Evans, G. (2015). Britain and Europe: Are we all Eurosceptics now? In J. Curtice & R. Ormston (Eds.), *British social attitudes: The 32nd report*. London: NatCen Social Research. http://www.bsa.natcen.ac.uk/media/38975/bsa32_eu.pdf. Accessed September 1, 2016.
Curtice, J., & Steed, M. (2000). Appendix: An analysis of the result. In D. Butler & M. Westlake (Eds.), *British politics and European elections 1999* (pp. 240–256). Basingstoke: Macmillan.
Daddow, O. (2012). The UK media and 'Europe': From permissive consensus to destructive dissent. *International Affairs, 88*(6), 1219–1236.
Daily Mail. (1991a, December 9). The only bandwagon that's on the move.
Daily Mail. (1991b, December 12). Good for Europe, great for Britain.
Daily Mail. (1999a, February 23). Treat the people as grown ups.
Daily Mail. (1999b, February 27). The widening chasm in British politics.
Daily Mail. (1999c, March 1). Positive thinking to save the pound.

Daniels, P. (1998). From hostility to 'constructive engagement': The Europeanisation of the Labour Party. *West European Politics, 21*(1), 72–96.

Davidson, I. (1989, June 29). Clear path for European Community emerges through the fog. *Financial Times*.

Davidson, I. (1991a, December 3). New era for EC family. *Financial Times*.

Davidson, I. (1991b, December 12). Hollow victory for Britain as it launches two-tier Europe. *Financial Times*.

De Jonquieres, G. (1978, December 4). Shaky path to monetary union. *Financial Times*.

De Vreese, C. H. (2001). 'Europe' in the news: A cross-national comparative study of the news coverage of key EU events. *European Union Politics, 2*(3), 283–307.

Deans, J. (1989a, June 29). Who did win at the Euro summit? *Daily Mail*.

Deans, J. (1989b, June 30). The worst is over on inflation, says jubilant Maggie. *Daily Mail*.

Deans, J., & Doughty, S. (1991, December 2). Major puts nation before party over Europe. *Daily Mail*.

Dell, E. (1994). Britain and the origins of the European Monetary System. *Contemporary European History, 3*(1), 1–60.

Dell, E., & Lord Hunt of Tanworth (= J. Hunt). (1994). The failings of cabinet government in mid to late 1970s. *Contemporary Records*, *8*(3), 453–472.

Denman, R. (1997). *Missed chances: Britain and Europe in the twentieth century* (2nd ed.). London: Indigo.

Denman, R. (1999, May 4). *British Diplomatic Oral History Programme (BDOHP) interview*. Cambridge: Churchill Archives Centre, Churchill College.

Department for Business, Innovation & Skills. (2010). *Introduction to history of BERR*, archived on February 22, 2010. http://webarchive.nationalarchives.gov.uk/20100216092443/http://www.berr.gov.uk/aboutus/corporate/history/outlines/page19795.html. Accessed September 11, 2016.

Dickie, J. (1978a, December 4). Jim faces squeeze. *Daily Mail*.

Dickie, J. (1978b, December 5). And Jim comes under market pressure. *Daily Mail*.

Dickie, J. (1978c, December 7). How the French let Jim off the hook. *Daily Mail*.

Dickie, J. (1992). *Inside the Foreign Office*. London: Chapmans.

Donoughue, B. (1987). *Prime minister: The conduct of policy under Harold Wilson & James Callaghan*. London: Jonathan Cape.

Donoughue, B. (1988). The prime minister's day. *Contemporary British History, 2*(2), 16–19.

Donoughue, B. (2009). *Downing Street diary: With James Callaghan in No. 10* (2nd ed.). London: Pimlico.

Doughty, S. (1991, December 4). Britain wins the F-word battle. *Daily Mail*.

Doughty, S., & Greig, G. (1991, December 3). Fight to salvage Euro treaty. *Daily Mail*.

Dover, R. (2005). The prime minister and the core executive: A liberal intergovernmentalist reading of UK defence policy formulation 1997–2000. *British Journal of Politics and International Relations, 7*(4), 508–525.

Dunleavy, P. (1995). Reinterpreting the Westland affair: Theories of the state and core executive decision making. In R. A. W. Rhodes & P. Dunleavy (Eds.), *Prime minister, cabinet and core executive* (pp. 181–218). London: Macmillan.

Dunleavy, P., & Jones, G. W. (with Burnham, J., Elgie, R., & Fysh, P.) (1993). Leaders, politics and institutional change: The decline of prime ministerial accountability to the House of Commons, 1868-1990. *British Journal of Political Studies*, *23*(3), 267–298.

Dunleavy, P., & Rhodes, R. A. W. (1990). Core executive studies in Britain. *Public Administration, 68*(1), 3–28.

Dyson, K. (1994). *Elusive union: The process of economic and monetary union in Europe*. London: Longman.

Dyson, K., & Featherstone, K. (1999). *The road to Maastricht: Negotiating economic and monetary union*. Oxford: Oxford University Press.

Edmonds, T. (2001, July 2). *The European Communities (Finance) Bill, Bill 1 2001–02*, House of Commons Library Research Paper No. 01/62.

Elgie, R. (1995). *Political leadership in liberal democracies*. Basingstoke: Macmillan.
Elliott, L. (1999, March 1). Let's not get stitched up in currency briefs. *The Guardian*.
Elliott, L., & Atkinson, M. (1999, February 24). Fast-track to euro in Britain. *The Guardian*.
Elliott, F., & Charter, D. (2016, October 3). EU leaders reject May over 'hard' Brexit talks. *The Times*.
European Commission. (1995, Autumn). *Eurobarometer: Public opinion in the European Union*, Report No. 43.
European Commission. (1996, December). *Eurobarometer: Public opinion in the European Union*, Report No. 45.
European Commission. (1999, March). *Eurobarometer: Public opinion in the European Union*, Report No. 50.
European Commission. (2016). *Public opinion: Eurobarometer interactive search 1976–2007*. http://ec.europa.eu/COMMFrontOffice/publicopinion/index.cfm/Chart/getChart/chartType/gridChart/themeKy/3/groupKy/3/savFile/10000. Accessed September 10, 2016.
European Parliament. (2016). *Turnout by country (in %)*. http://www.europarl.europa.eu/elections2014-results/en/turnout.html. Accessed September 12, 2016.
Evans, G. (1998). Euroscepticism and Conservative electoral support: How an asset became liability. *British Journal of Political Science, 28*(4), 573–590.
Financial Times. (1976, April 6). Men and matters, McCaffrey's day too.
Financial Times. (1978a, November 25). Government not ready to decide whether it is in Britain's best interest to join.
Financial Times. (1978b, November 27). On the road to EMS.
Financial Times. (1978c, December 1). Why we should join the EMS.
Financial Times. (1978d, December 7). A divided Europe.
Financial Times. (1978e, December 13). Italy decides to join the EMS.
Financial Times. (1989a, June 19). Spain enters the ERM.
Financial Times. (1989b, June 23). Isolation in Madrid.
Financial Times. (1989c, June 28). Compromise in Madrid.
Financial Times. (1989d, July 1). Mrs Thatcher and the Emu.
Financial Times. (1989e, July 3). EC legal limits on British sovereignty.
Financial Times. (1991, December 12). Multi-speed move to union.
Financial Times. (1999a, February 22). On euro tiptoe.
Financial Times. (1999b, February 24). Mr. Blair nails his euro to the mast.
Financial Times. (1999c, February 24). Unileverage.
Fliegauf, M. T., Kießling, A., & Novy, L. (2008). Leader und Follower – Grundzüge eines interpersonalen Ansatzes zur Analyse politischer Führungsleistung. *Zeitschrift für Politikwissenschaft, 18*(4), 399–421.
Foley, M. (1993). *The rise of the British presidency*. Manchester: Manchester University Press.
Foley, M. (2000). *The British presidency: Tony Blair and the politics of public leadership*. Manchester: Manchester University Press.
Foley, M. (2004). Presidential attribution as an agency of prime ministerial critique in a parliamentary democracy: The case of Tony Blair. *British Journal of Politics and International Relations, 6*(3), 292–311.
Forster, A. (1999). *Britain and the Maastricht negotiations*. London: Macmillan.
Forster, A., & Blair, A. (2002). *The making of Britain's European foreign policy*. Harlow: Longman.
Franklin, M. (2013). Could and should Britain have joined the European Exchange Rate Mechanism in 1979? A personal memoir. *Journal of Contemporary European Research, 9*(5), 759–766.
Gamble, A. (1990). Theories of British politics. *Political Studies, 38*(3), 404–420.
Gamble, A. (2002). Political memoirs. *British Journal of Politics and International Relations, 4*(1), 141–151.
Gamble, A., & Kelly, G. (2000). The British Labour Party and monetary union. *West European Politics, 23*(1), 1–25.

Gavin, N. T. (2007). *Press and television in British politics: Media, money and mediated democracy*. Basingstoke: Palgrave Macmillan.

Geddes, A. (2013). *Britain and the European Union*. Basingstoke: Palgrave Macmillan.

George, S. (1998). *An awkward partner: Britain in the European Community* (3rd ed.). Oxford: Oxford University Press.

Giddings, P. (1995). Prime Minister and Cabinet. In D. Shell & R. Hodder-Williams (Eds.), *Churchill to Major: The British prime ministership since 1945* (pp. 30–70). Armonk: M. E. Sharpe.

Gilmour, I. (1992). *Dancing with dogma: Britain under Thatcherism*. London: Simon & Schuster.

Glover, S. (1999, March 9). Forgive my glee at Germany's jitters. *Daily Mail*.

Goodman, E. (1978a, November 28). EMS veto sought. *Financial Times*.

Goodman, E. (1978b, November 29). We won't join EMS yet—Healey. *Financial Times*.

Goodman, E., & Riddell, P. (1978, November 24). MPs will get chance to vote before final EMS decision. *Financial Times*.

Goodwin, S. (1989, June 30). Thatcher claims EC support over monetary union. *The Independent*.

GOV.UK (2016). *European and Global Issues Secretariat (EGIS)*. https://www.gov.uk/government/groups/european-global-issues-secretariat. Accessed September 11, 2016.

Gowland, D., & Turner, A. (2000). *Reluctant Europeans: Britain and European integration 1945–1998*. Harlow: Longman.

Gowland, D., Turner, A., & Wright, A. (2010). *Britain and European integration since 1945: On the sidelines*. London: Routledge.

Grant, C. (2009). *Cameron's Europe: Can the Conservatives achieve their EU objectives?* London: Centre for European Reform.

Greenslade, R. (2003). *The press gang: How newspapers make profits from propaganda*. London: Macmillan.

Greig, G., & Deans, J. (1991, December 12). Major, Master of the House. *Daily Mail*.

Greig, G., & Doughty, S. (1991, December 11). Major wins by a knock-out! *Daily Mail*.

Grice, A. (1999, February 12). Ministers are told to take pro-euro line. *The Independent*.

Grice, A., & Coyle, D. (1999, February 24). Blair gears up to ditch the pound. *The Independent*.

Hay, C. (1995). Structure and agency. In D. Marsh & G. Stoker (Eds.), *Theory and methods in political science* (pp. 189–206). Basingstoke: Macmillan.

Hay, C. (2009). The Winter of Discontent thirty years on. *The Political Quarterly, 80*(4), 545–552.

Hayes-Renshaw, F., & Wallace, H. (1997). *The Council of Ministers*. New York: St. Martin's Press.

HC Deb. (1976, April 5), Vol 909, cc29–164.

HC Deb. (1978, February 7), Vol 943, cc463–464W.

HC Deb. (1978, November 29), Vol 959, c474.

HC Deb. (1978, December 6), Vol 959, cc1421–1424.

HC Deb. (1978, December 13), Vol 906, cc811–844.

HC Deb. (1981, November 4), Vol 12, c68.

HC Deb. (1982, November 12), Vol 31, c782.

HC Deb. (1989, June 29), Vol 155, cc1109–1124.

HC Deb. (1989, October 31), Vol 159, c208.

HC Deb. (1990, October 30), Vol 178, c871.

HC Deb. (1990, November 13), Vol 180, cc461–465.

HC Deb. (1991, December 11), Vol 200, cc859–878.

HC Deb. (1992, September 24), Vol 212, c4.

HC Deb. (1993, June 9), Vol 226, cc284–285.

HC Deb. (1997, January 23), Vol 288, c1071.

HC Deb. (1997, October 27), Vol 299, cc583–588.

HC Deb. (1999, February 23), Vol 326, cc179–196.

HC Deb. (2003, June 9), Vol 406, cc407–415.

Healey, D. (1978, November 28). European Monetary System, in TNA. *CAB 129/204*, CP (78) 122.

Healey, D. (2006). *The time of my life* (2nd ed.). London: Politico's.

Heath, A. F., Jowell, R. M., & Curtice, J. K. (2001). *The rise of New Labour: Party policies and voter choices*. Oxford: Oxford University Press.

Heffernan, R. (2003). Prime ministerial predominance? Core executive politics in the UK. *British Journal of Politics and International Relations, 5*(3), 347–372.

Heffernan, R. (2005a). Exploring (and explaining) the British prime minister. *British Journal of Politics and International Relations, 7*(4), 605–620.

Heffernan, R. (2005b). Why the prime minister cannot be a president: Comparing institutional imperatives in Britain and America. *Parliamentary Affairs, 58*(1), 53–70.

Heffernan, R. (2006). The prime minister and the news media: Political communication as a leadership resource. *Parliamentary Affairs, 59*(4), 582–598.

Helm, S. (1991, December 13). Whitehall's battle for Europe. *The Independent*.

Helm, T. (2016, October 1). Bitter Tory fight over Brexit set to overshadow conservative conference. *The Observer*.

Helms, L. (2000). "Politische Führung" als politikwissenschaftliches Problem. *Politische Vierteljahresschrift, 41*(3), 411–434.

Helms, L. (2005a). Politische Führung. In D. Nohlen & R.-O. Schultze (Eds.), *Lexikon der Politikwissenschaft, Part 2* (3rd ed., pp. 737–738). Munich: Verlag C.H. Beck.

Helms, L. (2005b). *Presidents, prime ministers and chancellors: Executive leadership in western democracies*. Basingstoke: Palgrave.

Helms, L. (2005c). *Regierungsorganisation und politische Führung in Deutschland*. Wiesbaden: VS Verlag für Sozialwissenschaften.

Hennessy, P. (1986). *Cabinet*. Oxford: Basil Blackwell.

Hennessy, P. (1990). *Whitehall* (2nd ed.). London: Fontana.

Hennessy, P. (2001). *The prime minister: The office and its holders since 1945* (2nd ed.). London: Penguin.

Hillenbrand, O. (2008). Die Wirtschafts- und Währungsunion. In W. Weidenfeld (Ed.), *Die Europäische Union: Politisches System und Politikbereiche* (pp. 402–433). Bundeszentrale für Politische Bildung: Bonn.

Hogg, S., & Hill, J. (1996). *Too close to call: Power and politics - John Major in No. 10* (2nd ed.). London: Warner Books.

Hoggart, S. (1978a, November 25). EMS terms 'must suit Britain'. *The Guardian*.

Hoggart, S. (1978b, December 7). Lending authors some token support. *The Guardian*.

Holberton, S. (1989, October 18). PM's economist adds his guarded support. *Financial Times*.

House of Commons Information Office. (2003, September). *By-election results: 1992-1997*. Factsheet M14 Members series, revised edition.

House of Commons Library. (2016, May 23). *Number of House of Commons divisions*, Standard Note No. SN/PC/04670.

Howe, G. (1995). *Conflict of loyalty* (2nd ed.). London: Pan Books.

Hübner, E., & Münch, U. (1999). *Das Politische System Großbritanniens: Eine Einführung* (2nd ed.). Munich: Verlag C.H. Beck.

Hughes, D. (1999, February 24). Prepare to kill the £. *Daily Mail*.

Huhne, C. (1991, December 15). Opting out will never be an option. *The Independent*.

Hurd, D. (2009). *Memoirs*. London: Abacus.

Hutton, W. (1991a, December 11). Major wins quest for opt-out on single European currency. *The Guardian*.

Hutton, W. (1991b, December 11). Monetary milestone reached on Europe's two-speed road. *The Guardian*.

Ingham, B. (2003). *Kill the messenger… again* (2nd ed.). London: Politico's.

James, S. (2009). Taming the 'awkward state'? The changing face of European policy-making under Blair. *Public Administration, 87*(3), 604–620.

James, S. (2011). *Managing Europe from home: The changing face of European policy-making under Blair and Ahern*. Manchester: Manchester University Press.

James, S., & Oppermann, K. (2009). Blair and the European Union. In T. Casey (Ed.), *The Blair legacy: Politics, policy, governance and foreign affairs* (pp. 285–298). Basingstoke: Palgrave Macmillan.

Jay, P. (1994). The economy 1990–94. In D. Kavanagh & A. Seldon (Eds.), *The Major effect* (pp. 169–205). London: Macmillan.

Jay, M. (2007, January 4). *British Diplomatic Oral History Programme (BDOHP) interview*. Cambridge: Churchill Archives Centre, Churchill College.

Jenkins, P. (1978a, December 1). PM given a blank cheque. *The Guardian*.

Jenkins, P. (1978b, December 5). Joining the poker game without any cards. *The Guardian*.

Jenkins, P. (1978c, December 6). Sunny Jim all smiles amid wreckage. *The Guardian*.

Jenkins, P. (1978d, December 7). Giscard—A new tune or just the old French fiddle. *The Guardian*.

Jenkins, R. (1989a). *European diary 1977-1981*. London: Collins.

Jenkins, P. (1989b, June 20). Lessons of defeat for Mrs Thatcher. *The Independent*.

Jenkins, P. (1989c, June 27). Prime minister signals a clever compromise on EMS. *The Independent*.

Jenkins, P. (1989d, June 28). Third time lucky for Britain in Europe. *The Independent*.

Jenkins, P. (1991, December 12). Major's each-way bet pays off. *The Independent*.

Johnson, P. (1989, June 26). A battle that has Maggie baffled. *Daily Mail*.

Johnson, P. (1991, December 12). Now he can score a home victory. *Daily Mail*.

Johnson, P. (1999, February 24). This is the biggest con-trick in history. *Daily Mail*.

Jones, B. (2001a). The mass media and political communication. In B. Jones, D. Kavanagh, M. Moran, & P. Norton (Eds.), *Politics UK* (4th ed., pp. 177–204). Harlow: Longman.

Jones, B. (2001b). The policy-making process. In B. Jones, D. Kavanagh, M. Moran, & P. Norton (Eds.), *Politics UK* (4th ed., pp. 527–542). Harlow: Longman.

Kaiser, A. (2001). Die politische Theorie des Neo-Institutionalismus: James March und Johan Olsen. In A. Brodocz & G. S. Schaal (Eds.), *Politische Theorien der Gegenwart II: Eine Einführung* (pp. 253–282). Opladen: Leske + Budrich.

Kassim, H. (2000). The United Kingdom. In H. Kassim, B. G. Peters, & V. Wright (Eds.), *The national coordination of EU policy: The domestic level* (pp. 22–53). Oxford: Oxford University Press.

Kavanagh, T. (1991a, December 9). Delors blasts PM's 'shame' over F-word. *The Sun*.

Kavanagh, T. (1991b, December 12). How Major played the winning hand in Europe. *The Sun*.

Kavanagh, T. (1999a, February 20). We're diving into cauldron of discontent. *The Sun*.

Kavanagh, T. (1999b, February 24). Our rights are not Blair's to give away. *The Sun*.

Kavanagh, T. (1999c, February 25). You say no to euro by 15-1. *The Sun*.

Kavanagh, D. (2001). The cabinet and prime minister. In B. Jones, D. Kavanagh, M. Moran, & P. Norton (Eds.), *Politics UK* (4th ed., pp. 409–436). Harlow: Longman.

Kavanagh, D. (2005). The Blair premiership. In A. Seldon & D. Kavanagh (Eds.), *The Blair effect 2001–5* (pp. 3–19). Cambridge: Cambridge University Press.

Kavanagh, T., & Black, E. (1991, December 10). 'F' off. *The Sun*.

Kavanagh, D., & Butler, D. (Eds.). (2005). *The British general election of 2005*. Basingstoke: Palgrave Macmillan.

Kavanagh, D., & Seldon, A. (Eds.). (1994). *The Major effect*. London: Macmillan.

Kavanagh, D., & Seldon, A. (2000). *The powers behind the prime minister: The hidden influence of Number Ten* (2nd ed.). London: HarperCollins.

Kay, J. (1989, June 28). So what the 'eck does an ECU mean? *The Sun*.

Keegan, W., & Stephens, R. (1978, December 10). L'Entente de Giscard et Jim. *The Guardian*.

Kelly, R., & Elliott, L. (1991, December 9). Germany calls the monetary tune. *The Guardian*.

Kelly, R., & Maer, L. (2016, February 25). *The Parliament Acts,* House of Commons Library Briefing Paper No. 00675.

Kelly, R., & White, I. (2016, June 24). *Fixed-term Parliaments Act 2011*. House of Commons Library Briefing Paper No. 6111.

Kemp, D. (1989a, June 27). Just listen! I'm fighting for Britain. *The Sun*.

Kemp, D. (1989b, June 28). Maggie wins time to save the pound. *The Sun*.

Kennedy, E. (1978, December 16). Euro-cash fear for 'odd man out' Britain. *Daily Mail*.

Kerr, J. (2004, January 6). *British Diplomatic Oral History Programme (BDOHP) interview*. Cambridge: Churchill Archives Centre, Churchill College.

King, A. (Ed.). (2001). *British political opinion 1937–2000: The Gallup polls*. London: Politico's.

Knewstub, N. (1989, June 30). PM 'bought time on Delors report'. *The Guardian*.

Knipping, F. (2004). *Rom, 25. März 1957: Die Einigung Europas*. Munich: Deutscher Taschenbuch Verlag.

Lamont, N. (1999). *In office*. London: Little, Brown.

Lawson, D. (1990, July 14). Saying the unsayable about the Germans. *The Spectator*.

Lawson, N. (1992). *A view from No. 11: Memoirs of a Tory radical*. London: Bantam.

Lee, J. M., Jones, G. W., & Burnham, J. (1998). *At the centre of Whitehall*. Basingstoke: Macmillan.

Levy, D. A. L., Aslan, B., & Bironzo, D. (2016). *UK press coverage of the EU referendum*. Oxford: Reuters Institute for the Study of Journalism. http://reutersinstitute.politics.ox.ac.uk/sites/default/files/UK%20Press%20Coverage%20of%20the%20EU%20Referendum_0.pdf. Accessed October 11, 2016.

Liddle, R. (2014). *The Europe dilemma: Britain and the drama of EU integration*. London: I.B. Tauris.

Lijphart, A. (2012). *Patterns of democracy: Government forms and performance in thirty-six countries* (2nd ed.). New Haven: Yale University Press.

Littlejohn, R. (1991, December 12). Dud match. *The Sun*.

Littlejohn, R. (1999, March 9). Warning: Pro euro demo, no traffic delays expected. *The Sun*.

Ludlam, S. (1998). The Cauldron: Conservative parliamentarians and European integration. In D. Baker & D. Seawright (Eds.), *Britain for and against Europe: British politics and the question of European integration* (pp. 31–56). Oxford: Clarendon.

Ludlow, P. (1982). *The making of the European Monetary System*. London: Butterworth.

MacIntyre, D. (1991, December 8). Playing for high stakes at Maastricht. *The Independent*.

Major, J. (2000). *The autobiography* (2nd ed.). London: HarperCollins.

Mance, H., & Neville, S. (2016, July 15). Strategic intends drives reform of ministries. *Financial Times*.

Mandelson, P. (2010). *The third man: Life at the heart of New Labour*. London: Harper Press.

Marsh, D. (1978, November 23). Britain and Italy find common ground on EMS. *Financial Times*.

Marsh, I. (1990). Liberal priorities, the Lib-Lab-Pact and the requirements for policy influence. *Parliamentary Affairs, 43*(3), 292–321.

Marsh, D., Richards, D., & Smith, M. J. (2001). *Changing patterns of governance in the United Kingdom: Reinventing Whitehall?* Basingstoke: Palgrave.

Marsh, D., Richards, D., & Smith, M. J. (2003). Unequal plurality: Towards an asymmetric model of British politics. *Government and Opposition, 38*(3), 306–332.

Marshall, A. (1991, December 10). Single currency comes a step closer. *The Independent*.

Marshall, A., & Usborne, D. (1991, December 10). ECU likely to take over by 1999. *The Independent*.

Massie, A. (1999, March 3). We're all doomed but not inevitably. *Daily Mail*.

Mauthner, R. (1991, December 4). The persistent odd man out. *Financial Times*.

Mayntz, R., & Scharpf, F. W. (1995). Der Ansatz des akteurszentrierten Institutionalismus. In R. Mayntz & F. W. Scharpf (Eds.), *Gesellschaftliche Selbstregulierung und politische Steuerung*. Campus: Frankfurt.

Mayring, P. (2000). Qualitative content analysis. *Forum Qualitative Sozialforschung/Forum: Qualitative Social Research, 1*(2), Art. 20.

Mayring, P. (2010). *Qualitative Inhaltsanalyse* (11th ed.). Weinheim: Beltz Verlag.

McElvoy, A. (1999, February 24). Mr Blair remains a cautious soul—And not without good reason. *The Independent*.

McNair, B. (1999). *An introduction to political communication* (2nd ed.). London: Routledge.

Miller, V. (2005, December 2). *The UK parliament and European business*, House of Commons Library Research Paper No. 05/85.

Miller, V. (2008, January 22). *EU treaty bills: The whip and referendum clauses*. House of Commons Library Standard Note No. SN/IA/4650.

Milner, M. (1989, June 24). Bite the sugar-coated bullet, Mrs Thatcher. *The Guardian*.

Moore, C. (2015). *Margaret Thatcher: The authorized biography, Volume two: Everything she wants*. London: Allen Lane.

Morgan, D. (2003). Media coverage of the European Union. In M. Bond (Ed.), *Europe, parliament and the media* (pp. 35–54). London: The Federal Trust.

Morgan, K. (2007, July 5). *Leadership and change: Prime ministers in the post-war-world: James Callaghan*. Lecture at Gresham College. http://www.gresham.ac.uk/lectures-and-events/leadership-and-change-prime-ministers-in-the-post-war-world-james-callaghan. Accessed May 19, 2016.

Mughan, A. (2000). *Media and the presidentialization of parliamentary elections*. Basingstoke: Palgrave.

Neil, A. (1999, March 9). To the north, separatists seek to dismember the country. To the south, federalists conspire to turn us into a province of Euroland. We must win this Battle for Britain… and to do it we must, above all, have faith in ourselves. *Daily Mail*.

Newman, C. (2000, January 17). Blair acknowledges British are opposed to euro. *Financial Times*.

Norton, P. (1980). *Dissension in the House of Commons 1974–1979*. Oxford: Clarendon.

Norton, P. (1985). Behavioural changes, backbench independence in the 1980s. In P. Norton (Ed.), *Parliament in the 1980s* (pp. 22–47). Oxford: Basil Blackwell.

Norton, P. (1993). *Does parliament matter?* Hemel Hempstead: Harvester Wheatsheaf.

Norton, P. (1994). *The British polity* (3rd ed.). New York: Longman.

Norton, P. (1996). The United Kingdom: Political conflict, parliamentary scrutiny. In P. Norton (Ed.), *National parliaments and the European Union* (pp. 92–109). London: Frank Cass.

Norton, P. (2002). The Conservative party: Is there anyone out there? In A. King (Ed.), *Britain at the polls, 2001* (pp. 68–94). New York: Chatham House.

Norton, P. (2003). National parliaments and the European Union. *Managerial Law, 45*(5/6), 5–25.

Norton, P. (2011). Divided loyalties: The European Communities Act 1972. *Parliamentary History, 30*(1), 53–64.

Nugent, N. (1992). British public opinion and the European Community. In S. George (Ed.), *Britain and the European Community: The politics of semi-detachment* (pp. 172–201). Oxford: Clarendon.

Nugent, N. (2000). The European Union and UK governance. In R. Pyper & L. Robins (Eds.), *United Kingdom governance* (pp. 194–218). Basingstoke: Macmillan.

Owen, D. (2009). *Time to declare: Second innings*. London: Politico's.

Palmer, J. (1978, November 23). Premier seeks halfway house deal on EMS. *The Guardian*.

Palmer, J. (1989, June 28). Coming home weaker but not wiser. *The Guardian*.

Palmer, J. (1991, December 11). EC unites on historic treaty with Britain in the slow lane. *The Guardian*.

Palmer, J., & Hooper, J. (1989, June 27). Thatcher sets out terms for entry into EMS. *The Guardian*.

Parkinson, C. (1992). *Right at the centre: An autobiography*. London: Weidenfeld and Nicolson.

Peston, R. (1999a, February 11). Pressure over the euro may force Blair off the fence. *Financial Times*.

Peston, R. (1999b, February 23). Blair will unveil UK route to EMU entry. *Financial Times*.

Peston, R. (1999c, February 24). Government comes of age with euro pledge. *Financial Times*.

Peston, R. (1999d, February 25). Sterling will not shadow euro, says PM. *Financial Times*.

Peston, R., & Brown, K. (1999, February 24). Blair lays groundwork for euro changeover. *Financial Times*.

Peters, B. G., Rhodes, R. A. W., & Wright, V. (2000). Staffing the summit – the administration of the core executive: Convergent trends and national specificities. In B. G. Peters, R. A.

W. Rhodes, & V. Wright (Eds.), *Administering the summit: Administration of the core executive in developed countries* (pp. 3–22). Basingstoke: Macmillan.
Pickering, C. (2002). 'Sir Douglas in Euroland': Treasury officials and the European Union, 1977–2001. *Public Administration, 80*(3), 583–599.
Poguntke, T., & Webb, P. (Eds.). (2005). *The presidentialization of politics: A comparative study of modern democracies*. Oxford: Oxford University Press.
Powell, C. (2000, July 18). *British Diplomatic Oral History Programme (BDOHP) interview*. Cambridge: Churchill Archives Centre, Churchill College.
Powell, J. (2010). *The new Machiavelli: How to wield power in the modern world*. London: The Bodley Head.
Prescott, J. (with Davies, H.) (2008). *Prezza: My story: Pulling no punches*. London: Headline Review.
Presse- und Informationsamt der Bundesregierung. (2016). *Dienstsitze des Bundeskanzleramts*. http://www.bundesregierung.de/ContentArchiv/DE/Archiv17/Artikel/2009/10/2009-09-22-bk-dienstsitze.html?nn=391346. Accessed May 17, 2016.
Price, L. (2011). *Where power lies: prime ministers v. the media* (2nd ed.). London: Simon & Schuster.
Putnam, R. D. (1988). Diplomacy and domestic politics: The logic of two-level games. *International Organization, 42*(3), 427–460.
Quinn, B. (2016, January 14). EU membership terms 'disastrous' for UK, says cabinet minister Chris Grayling. *The Guardian*.
Rachman, G. (2016, October 4). May walks into a Brexit trap. *Financial Times*.
Rasmussen, J. (1997). 'What kind of vision is that?' British public attitudes towards the European community during the Thatcher era. *British Journal of Political Sciences, 27*(1), 111–118.
Rawnsley, A. (1989, June 30). Thatcher finds herself mistress of a new lingo. *The Guardian*.
Rawnsley, A. (2001). *Servants of the people: The inside story of New Labour* (2nd ed.). London: Penguin.
Rawnsley, A. (2010). *The end of the party* (2nd ed.). London: Penguin.
Rawstorne, P. (1978a, December 5). New moves to boost left-wing influence. *Financial Times*.
Rawstorne, P. (1978b, November 30). Britain not to join EMS without changes—Healey. *Financial Times*.
Rees-Mogg, W. (1989, June 27). Listen to the young to steer clear of the political rocks. *The Independent*.
Rees-Mogg, W. (1991, December 16). The Euro-dodo that was too stupid and fat to fly. *The Independent*.
Reid, J. (1989, June 27). Euro-money is our best bet. *The Sun*.
Rentoul, J. (2001). *Tony Blair: Prime minister*. London: Warner Books.
Rhodes, R. A. W. (1995). From prime ministerial power to core executive. In R. A. W. Rhodes & P. Dunleavy (Eds.), *Prime minister, cabinet and core executive* (pp. 11–37). Basingstoke: Macmillan.
Rhys, D. (1978, December 9). Lever gives strong support for new monetary system. *Financial Times*.
Riddell, P. (1978a, December 1). Getting deeply involved with the technicalities. *Financial Times*.
Riddell, P. (1978b, November 23). Treasury attacked for failing to reveal EMS impact. *Financial Times*.
Riddell, P. (1994). Major and parliament. In D. Kavanagh & A. Seldon (Eds.), *The Major effect* (pp. 46–63). London: Macmillan.
Riddell, P. (2000). *Parliament under Blair* (2nd ed.). London: Politico's.
Riddell, P. (2004). Prime ministers and parliament. *Parliamentary Affairs, 57*(4), 814–829.
Riddell, P. (2005). Europe. In A. Seldon & D. Kavanagh (Eds.), *The Blair effect 2001–5* (pp. 362–383). Cambridge: Cambridge University Press.
Rifkind, M. (2016). *Power and pragmatism: The memoirs of Malcolm Rifkind*. London: Biteback.
Rose, R. (2001). *The prime minister in a shrinking world*. Cambridge: Polity Press.

Roth, A. (1999, November 4). Edmund Dell. *The Guardian*.

Rutherford, M. (1978, December 8). A time of uncertainty. *Financial Times*.

Scammell, M., & Harrop, M. (1997). The press. In D. Butler & D. Kavanagh (Eds.), *The British general election of 1997* (pp. 156–185). Basingstoke: Macmillan.

Scharpf, F. W. (2000). *Interaktionsformen: Akteurszentrierter Institutionalismus in der Politikforschung*. Opladen: Leske + Budrich.

Schmidt, H. (1990). *Die Deutschen und ihre Nachbarn: Menschen und Mächte II* (2nd ed.). Berlin: Siedler.

Scott, D. (2004). *Off Whitehall: A view from Downing Street by Tony Blair's adviser*. London: I. B. Tauris.

Seldon, A. (1990). The Cabinet Office and coordination 1979–87. *Public Administration, 68*(1), 103–121.

Seldon, A. (1994). Policy making and cabinet. In D. Kavanagh & A. Seldon (Eds.), *The Major effect* (pp. 154–166). London: Macmillan.

Seldon, A. (with Baston, L.) (1998), *Major: A political life* (2nd ed.). London: Phoenix.

Seldon, A. (with Ballinger, C., Collings, D., & Snowdon, P.) (2005). *Blair* (2nd ed.). London: Free Press.

Seldon, A. (with Snowdon, P., & Collings, D.) (2008). *Blair unbound* (2nd ed.). London: Pocket Books.

Seymour-Ure, C. (1994). Mass media. In D. Kavanagh & A. Seldon (Eds.), *The Major effect* (pp. 399–417). London: Macmillan.

Seymour-Ure, C. (1995). Prime minister and the public: Managing media relations. In D. Shell & R. Hodder-Williams (Eds.), *Churchill to Major: The British prime ministership since 1945* (pp. 169–199). Armonk: M. E. Sharpe.

Seymour-Ure, C. (2002). New Labour and the media. In A. King (Ed.), *Britain at the polls, 2001* (pp. 117–142). New York: Chatham House.

Seymour-Ure, C. (2003). *Prime ministers and the media: Issues of power and control*. Oxford: Blackwell.

Shaw, E. (2004). The control freaks? New Labour and the party. In S. Ludlam & M. J. Smith (Eds.), *Governing as New Labour: Policy and politics under Blair* (pp. 52–69). Basingstoke: Palgrave Macmillan.

Shell, D. (1995). The office of prime minister. In D. Shell & R. Hodder-Williams (Eds.), *Churchill to Major: The British prime ministership since 1945* (pp. 1–29). Armonk: M. E. Sharpe.

Shell, D., & Hodder-Williams, R. (Eds.). (1995). *Churchill to Major: The British prime ministership since 1945*. Armonk: M.E. Sharpe.

Shrimsley, A. (1978a, December 1). Britain misses the money train. *The Sun*.

Shrimsley, A. (1978b, December 8). How Britain won last place. *The Sun*.

Smith, M. J. (1994). The core executive and the resignation of Mrs Thatcher. *Public Administration, 72*(3), 341–363.

Smith, M. J. (1995). Interpreting the rise and fall of Margaret Thatcher: Power dependence and the core executive. In R. A. W. Rhodes & P. Dunleavy (Eds.), *Prime minister, cabinet and core executive* (pp. 108–124). Basingstoke: Macmillan.

Smith, M. J. (1998). Reconceptualizing the British state: Theoretical and empirical challenges to central government. *Public Administration, 76*(1), 45–72.

Smith, M. J. (1999). *The core executive in Britain*. Basingstoke: Macmillan.

Smith, J. (2012). The European dividing line in party politics. *International Affairs, 88*(6), 1277–1295.

Stack, F. (1983). The imperatives of coordination. In F. E. C. Gregory (Ed.), *Dilemmas of government: Britain and the European Community* (pp. 124–152). Oxford: Martin Robertson.

Stephens, P. (1989a, December 12). Thatcher says Britain may join ERM ahead of general election. *Financial Times*.

Stephens, P. (1989b, June 27). Thatcher ceases to thump the table over monetary union. *Financial Times*.

Stephens, P. (1989c, June 30). Thatcher pledges to counter Delors plan. *Financial Times.*

Stephens, P. (1991a, December 9). Spokesman who wields unsung influence. *Financial Times.*

Stephens, P. (1991b, November 29). Major's charm offensive promises summit dividend. *Financial Times.*

Stephens, P. (1994, May 4). Backbench dismay over in-fighting on EMU. *Financial Times.*

Stephens, P. (1997). *Politics and the pound: The Tories, the economy and Europe* (2nd ed.). London: Papermac.

Stephens, P. (1999, February 26). Liberated by Europe. *Financial Times.*

Stephens, P., & Holberton, S. (1989, June 15). Thatcher rejects calls to dismiss economic advisor. *Financial Times.*

Straw, J. (2011, December 6). *Britain and Europe.* Speech at the European Institute, University College London. https://www.ucl.ac.uk/european-institute/analysis-publications/analysis/straw/Jack_Straw_061211.pdf. Accessed October 19, 2016.

Straw, J. (2012). *Last man standing: Memoirs of a political survivor.* London: Macmillan.

Stuart, M. (2009). The role of parliament under Blair. In T. Casey (Ed.), *The Blair legacy: Politics, policy, governance and foreign affairs* (pp. 178–189). Basingstoke: Palgrave Macmillan.

Sutcliffe, T. (1999, February 24). On a momentous day for our island race, Blair turns up. *The Independent.*

Sylvester, R. (1999, February 28). Can they save the pound? *The Independent on Sunday.*

Temple, M. (2008). *The British press.* Maidenhead: Open University Press.

Terry, W. (1978a, December 4). Lone-wolf Jim in big euro crunch. *The Sun.*

Terry, W. (1978b, December 5). Britain gets the bird at Euro talks. *The Sun.*

Terry, W. (1978c, December 6). Big Jim comes up all smiles! *The Sun.*

Thatcher, M. (1988, September 20). *Speech to the College of Europe ("The Bruges Speech").* http://www.margaretthatcher.org/document/107332. Accessed August 31, 2016.

Thatcher, M. (2011). *The Downing Street years.* London: Harper Press.

The Guardian. (1978, November 29). Half-way to a better Europe.

The Guardian. (1989a, June 20). Spain's conquest.

The Guardian. (1989b, June 26). Bulldog tantrums not in order.

The Guardian. (1989c, June 28). A defeat with the seeds of victory.

The Guardian. (1989d, July 11). Inflation may threaten EC monetary union.

The Guardian. (1999a, February 24). Going for the euro.

The Guardian. (1999b, February 24). Introducing Euro-Blair.

The Independent. (1989a, June 17). Outsider at the heart of Thatcherism: Sir Alan Walters, No. 10's economic adviser.

The Independent. (1989b, June 26). Crossing rubicons at Madrid.

The Independent. (1989c, June 28). Spanish rhetoric.

The Independent. (1991a, November 28). Lonely future on the margin.

The Independent. (1991b, November 29). Nothing to fear but fear itself.

The Independent. (1991c, December 11). A classic British error.

The Independent. (1991d, December 12). Maastricht summit.

The Independent. (1991e, December 12). A triumph, despite the legacy.

The Independent. (1999a, February 24). Fine words, but a change of tone does not a policy make.

The Independent. (1999b, March 1). Come on, Mr Blair: Call a referendum on the euro now.

The Sun. (1978a, December 7). Relegation.

The Sun. (1978b, December 13). Blow to Britain over Euro money.

The Sun. (1989a, June 26). Keep up the fight, Mrs T!

The Sun. (1989b, June 29). Still champ.

The Sun. (1991a, November 30). PM 'won't be bullied'.

The Sun. (1991b, December 12). Come the hour, come the man!

The Sun. (1991c, December 12). How Britain succeeded at Maastricht.

The Sun. (1999a, February 20). Is Blair taking us for granted?

The Sun. (1999b, February 24). This thing is bigger than both of us...

The Sun. (1999c, February 25). People power.

The Sun. (1999d, March 6). This is our finest hour.

Thomas, G. P. (1998). *The prime minister and cabinet today.* Manchester: Manchester University Press.

Thomas, G. P. (2004). United Kingdom: The prime minister and parliament. *The Journal of Legislative Studies, 10*(2/3), 4–37.

Thompson, H. (1996). *The British Conservative government and the European Exchange Rate Mechanism, 1979–1994.* London: Pinter.

Thompson-Noel, M. (1991, December 14). A turning point—Or maybe not. *Financial Times.*

TNA. (1976, May 6). *CAB 128/59*, CM (76) 3rd conclusions.

TNA. (1976, May 25). *CAB 128/59*, CM (76) 7th conclusions.

TNA. (1977, February 25). *CAB 128/61*, CM (77) 8th Conclusions.

TNA. (1977, July 1). *Records of the Prime Minister's Office [hereafter PREM] 16/1492*, Kenneth Stowe to the prime minister.

TNA. (1978, January 26). *CAB 128/63*, CM (78) 2nd conclusions.

TNA. (1978, June 8). *CAB 128/64*, CM (78) 21st Conclusions.

TNA. (1978, July 3). *PREM 16/1634*, Note of a meeting held at 10 Downing Street at 0930 on 3 July 1978.

TNA. (1978, July 6). *CAB 128/64*, CM (78) 25th conclusions.

TNA. (1978, July 13). *CAB 128/64*, CM (78) 26th conclusions.

TNA. (1978, September 28). *CAB 193/212/3,* Kenneth Berrill to John Hunt. The United Kingdom and the European Monetary System.

TNA. (1978, September 29). *PREM 16/1635,* Kenneth Berrill to the prime minister. European Monetary System.

TNA. (1978, October 12). *CAB 128/64*, CM (78) 34th conclusions.

TNA. (1978, October 26). *CAB 128/64*, CM (78) 36th conclusions.

TNA. (1978, November 2). *CAB 128/64*, CM (78) 37th conclusions.

TNA. (1978, November 16). *CAB 128/64*, CM (78) 39th conclusions.

TNA. (1978, November 23). *CAB 128/64*, CM (78) 40th conclusions.

TNA. (1978, November 29). *PREM 16/1638*, Tom McCaffrey to the prime minister. E.M.S. Decision: Presentation.

TNA. (1978, November 30). *CAB 128/64*, CM (78) 41st conclusions.

TNA. (1978, December 7). *CAB 128/64*, CM (78) 42nd conclusions.

TNA. (1978, December 14). *CAB 128/64*, CM (78) 43rd conclusions.

TNA. (1978, December 19). *CAB 128/64*, CM (78) 44th Conclusions.

TNA. (1980, March 20). *CAB 128/67*, CC (80) 12th conclusions.

TNA. (1981, February 24). *CAB 128/70*, CC (81) 8th conclusions.

TNA. (1982, February 18). *CAB 128/73*, CC (82) 6th conclusions.

TNA. (1982, February 25). *CAB 128/73*, CC (82) 7th conclusions.

TNA. (1982, June 17). *CAB 128/74*, CC (82) 34th conclusions.

TNA. (1983, March 24). *CAB 128/76*, CC (83) 11th conclusions.

Trewin, I. (Ed.). (2009). *The Hugo Young papers: A journalist's notes from the heart of politics* (2nd ed.). London: Penguin Books.

UK Parliament. (2016a). Allocation of time motions. http://www.parliament.uk/site-information/glossary/allocation-of-time-motion/. Accessed September 28, 2016.

UK Parliament. (2016b). Programme motion. http://www.parliament.uk/site-information/glossary/programme-motion/. Accessed September 28, 2016.

UK Parliament. (2016c). Whips. http://www.parliament.uk/about/mps-and-lords/principal/whips/. Accessed August 28, 2016.

Usborne, D., & Cottrell, R. (1989, June 22). The loser at the summit. *The Independent.*

Usborne, D., Bevins, A., & Lambert, S. (1991a, December 2). UK isolated on right to opt out of one currency. *The Independent.*

Usborne, D., Lambert, S., Helm, S., Bevins, A., Torday, P., & Marshall, A. (1991b, December 6). Economic Union: How EMU works. *The Independent.*

Usherwood, S. (2002). Opposition to the European Union in the UK: The dilemma of public opinion and party management. *Government and Opposition, 37*(2), 211–230.

Wall, S. (2008). *A stranger in Europe: Britain and the EU from Thatcher to Blair*. Oxford: Oxford University Press.

Wallace, W. (1994). Foreign policy. In D. Kavanagh & A. Seldon (Eds.), *The Major effect* (pp. 283–300). London: Macmillan.

Walters, A. (1988, April 6). Britain does best outside the EMS. *Financial Times*.

Ward, A. J. (1994). Margaret Thatcher and foreign policy. In J. S. Thompson & W. C. Thompson (Eds.), *Prime minister indomitable* (pp. 73–98). Boulder: Westview.

Waterhouse, K. (1999, February 25). A hundred yard start in the euro race. *Daily Mail*.

Watkins, A. (1999, February 28). Blair wants a fait accompli, not a poll. *The Independent on Sunday*.

Watt, D. (1976, April 6). 'Steady as we go' – at least for now. *Financial Times*.

Wessels, W. (2016). *The European Council*. London: Palgrave.

Wessels, W., & Schäfer, M. (2014). Europäischer Rat. In W. Weidenfeld & W. Wessels (Eds.), *Europa von A bis Z: Taschenbuch der Europäischen Integration* (pp. 233–240). Bonn: Bundeszentrale für Politische Bildung.

White, M. (1978, December 2). Whitehall reassures EEC on Euro-cash. *The Guardian*.

White, M. (1989, June 30). Thatcher alert against 'Paris-Bonn domination'. *The Guardian*.

White, M. (1991, December 12). Tories hail Major triumph. *The Guardian*.

White, M., & Elliott, L. (1999, February 24). Blair 'crosses the rubicon' towards Euroland. *The Guardian*.

White, M., & Pick, H. (1991, November 28). Mr Nice Guy and his chums. *The Guardian*.

White, M., Ward, L., & MacAskill, E. (1999, February 20). Euro timetable to be shortened. *The Guardian*.

Wilkes, G., & Wring, D. (1998). The British press and European integration: 1948 to 1996. In D. Baker & D. Seawright (Eds.), *Britain for and against Europe: British politics and the question of European integration* (pp. 185–205). Oxford: Clarendon.

Willetts, D. (1987). The role of the prime minister's Policy Unit. *Public Administration, 65*(4), 443–454.

Wilson-Smith, P. (1989, June 27). Currency system which challenges nations to curb inflation. *The Independent*.

Woosey, B. (1978, December 16). Jim's left in the lurch. *The Sun*.

Wright, P. (2000, October 16). *British Diplomatic Oral History Programme (BDOHP) interview*. Cambridge: Churchill Archives Centre, Churchill College.

Young, H. (1989a). *One of us: A biography of Margaret Thatcher* (2nd ed.). London: Macmillan.

Young, H. (1989b, June 29). The devil's advocate bows to reality. *The Guardian*.

Young, H. (1991, December 12). Sub plot of the social chapter. *The Guardian*.

Young, H. (1994). The prime minister. In D. Kavanagh & A. Seldon (Eds.), *The Major effect* (pp. 18–28). London: Macmillan.

Young, H. (1999a). *This blessed plot: Britain and Europe from Churchill to Blair* (2nd ed.). London: Papermac.

Young, H. (1999b, February 24). Caesar Blair casts the die and there's no going back. *The Guardian*.

The manufacturer's authorised representative in the EU is Springer
Nature Customer Service Centre GmbH, Europaplatz 3, 69115 Heidelberg,
Germany. If you have any concerns regarding our products, please
contact ProductSafety@springernature.com

Printed and bound by CPI Group (UK) Ltd, Croydon, CR0 4YY
30/09/2026
02225601-0011